GEOMETRIC KEYS OF VEDIC WISDOM

LORI TOMPKINS

360Lotus Press
www.360lotus.com
San Rafael, CA

First U.S. Edition
ISBN 978-0-9996149-0-7

Acknowledgements

I would like to express my eternal gratitude to Sri Aurobindo, the Mother and Patrizia Norelli-Bachelet (Thea) for the progress they made towards the restoration of Vedic Wisdom and hence their uplifting of the *Sanatana Dharma* or Eternal Truth of the ancient Rishis. Without their collective and individual maha yoga this book would never have been born, and the keys of Vedic Gnosis herein would likely remain hidden. Special thanks to my colleagues at Aeon Centre of Cosmology and Aeon Trust in Southern India and Aeon Group in the USA who have been helpful to me in various ways over the years. I am grateful to these groups for their work towards preserving Thea's legacy and for permissions granted to use quotes and images from Thea's writings. I am also grateful to my fantastic friends and family for their love and support throughout the unusual course of my life's adventure and throughout the course of birthing this book.

I need to acknowledge from the start that I do not read Sanskrit and that I have relied on English translations of the Rig Veda and other Sanskrit texts, mainly translations by Sri Aurobindo, R.T.H. Griffith and Raimundo Panikkar. I am eternally grateful for these translations even if in some cases the Rishis' intent may be somewhat lost in translation. Sri Aurobindo has acknowledged that the Rishis deliberately veiled the true meaning of their words and symbols, and that this meaning has been lost in India and hence, throughout the rest of the world, for at least 2,000 years. I am grateful that the symbols and words of the Rishis have been preserved and conveyed well enough in these English translations, so that the underlying geometric keys of these symbols can now come forward.

Contents

PART ONE

For [the Supramental] being, the very basis of his existence is different; instead of being based on division, it is based on union. Man talks a lot about union, but he doesn't have the least idea what it is.

The Mother, January 3, 1970, *The Mother's Agenda, Volume 11*, p. 26

To rise into the new consciousness, the first condition is to have enough modesty of mind to be convinced that all that you think you know is nothing in comparison to what yet remains to be learnt.

The Mother, December 16, 1969, *CMA, Volume 12*, p. 114

*Men as soon as they begin to receive something of [the] solar illumination, strive to yoke their whole mentality and its thought-contents to the conscious existence of the divine Surya [Sun] within them. That is to say, they apply, as it were, all their obscure mental state and all their erring thoughts to this Light manifested in them so that it may turn the obscurity of the mind into clearness and convert the errors of thought into those truths which they distortedly represent. This yoking (*yuñjate*) becomes their Yoga. "They yoke the mind, and they yoke their thoughts... of (i.e. to, or so that they may be part of or belong to) the Enlightened, the Large, the Clear-perceptioned."*

Then the Lord of Truth orders all the human energies offered up to him in the terms of the Truth; for he becomes in man a sole and sovereign Power governing all knowledge and action.

Sri Aurobindo, *The Secret of the Veda, CWSA, Volume 15*, p. 289

CHAPTER ONE

432,000

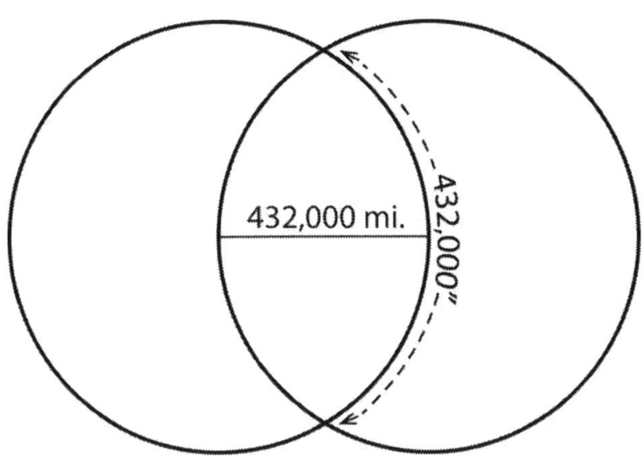

In the early hours of February 7, 2016, I woke up with the above image of the vesica piscis in my head, measures included. Seeing the image, I understood it to be a demonstration of how the 432,000-mile measure of the Sun's radius and the 432,000″ (seconds) of arc of the circle function *together* to establish the 432,000 measure of the Kali Yuga which is widely misunderstood in our day and age. As I got up to draw what I had seen, the clock read 4:32 a.m.

The radius of any circle cuts out a full 432,000″ arc into the circumference of that circle. This arc is exactly one-third of the 360° circle (120° x 60′ x 60″ = 432,000″). This geometry is eternal. The length or unit of measure of the radius may change, but regardless, it carves or measures out the same 432,000″ (120°) arc in the circle. I knew as I woke up that the equivalence between the Sun's 432,000-mile radius and the 432,000″ arc of the radius was established long ago and that it was a key of recovering the lost Sun or Son of the Vedic Rishis' *sanatana dharma.*[1] The next day I remembered that the Rig Veda itself is said to contain 432,000 syllables.

The feeling that came with the 4:32 a.m. vesica piscis vision, was a feeling of victory. It seemed that in and of itself the ancient equivalence between the measure of the vesica piscis and the measure of the Sun was going to help reestablish the singular context of the entirety of India's deities, myths, rituals, symbols and measures, which have become disconnected and taken out of context in India and across the world via different languages, religious sects, and our fragmented mental consciousness like a widely scattered jigsaw puzzle or a long-drawn-out game of "Telephone".[2] I felt that the realization of the vesica piscis would shed light not only on the *trayi vidya* (triadic gnosis) of the ancient Vedic Rishis, but also on the *trayi vidya* of modern-era Rishis Sri Aurobindo, the Mother and Thea who have recovered the triadic Soul of Vedic Wisdom in our day and age, over the course of the past 144 years.[3]

I also had the impression that coming to know and appreciate the vesica piscis as a key of Vedic Gnosis will demand a shift in consciousness, because it is a key that has come forth entirely via supramental means. The process by which this key has revealed itself has demonstrated a certain mathematical precision and supramental control over the unified field of Time and Space. This supramental or divine control is experienced as the orderly, coherent, cohesive and multi-dimensional unfolding of a divine singularity which extends itself into the multitude of details, circumstances and geometry of life. It is experienced as a profound convergence wherein ALL is known to be coinciding. All that was, is and will be is simultaneously experienced as one superconscious or all-conscious field of Being and Becoming. All is experienced

---

[1] *Sanatana dharma* means "eternal law", "eternal truth" or "eternal order".

[2] In this game (a.k.a. "Chinese Whispers"), a message is whispered from ear to ear in a group, and the last to hear it reveals how the badly message has been distorted.

[3] August 15, 2016 marked Sri Aurobindo's 144th birth anniversary.

as Divine Synchronicity organized by the Soul's truth, force and consciousness. From the mind's fragmented point of view, this kind of divine control over the whole of creation does not exist, or it exists only in terms of belief or faith, not as how we see and experience our mundane environment. The supramental yoga of Sri Aurobindo, the Mother and Thea has been a combined effort to open the doors of this higher seeing and experience of our Self. Their triadic yoga has been one extended maha yoga, or great yoga, fulfilling the Vedic mission of restoring the lost Sun or truth-consciousness of the Rishis' *sanatana dharma* by which our fragmented consciousness is re-yoked and made whole. Central to this mission has been the reestablishment of the Oneness of Spirit and Matter (the Divine Masculine and the Divine Feminine) in human consciousness.

> *In the superconscient truth of the Self-Existence these two [Ishwara-Shakti, the Divine Self and Creator and the Divine Mother and Creatrix of the universe] are fused and implied in each other, one and indistinguishable, but in the spiritual-pragmatic truth of the dynamism of the universe, they emerge and become active; the Divine Mother – Energy as the universal creatrix, Maya, Para-Prakriti, Chit-Shakti, manifests the cosmic Self and Ishwara and her own self-power as a dual principle; it is through her that the Being, the Self, the Ishwara, acts and he does nothing except by her; though his Will is implicit in her, it is she who works out all as the supreme Consciousness-Force who holds all souls and beings within her and as executive Nature; all exists and acts according to Nature, all is the Consciousness-Force manifesting and playing with the Being in millions of forms and movements into which she casts his existence.... If we would realise a higher formation or status of being, then it is still through her, through the Divine Shakti, the Consciousness-Force of the Spirit that it has to be done; our surrender must be to the Divine Being through the Divine Mother: for it is towards or into the supreme Nature that our ascension has to take place and it can only be done by the supramental Shakti taking up our mentality and transforming it into her supramentality.*
>
> *A certain difficulty arises for our mind in reconciling these different faces or fronts of the One Self and Spirit, because we are obliged to use abstract conceptions and defining words and ideas for*

something that is not abstract, something that is spiritually living and intensely real.

Sri Aurobindo, *The Life Divine, CWSA, Volumes 21-22*, pp. 371-72

[D]harma, the law is that which holds things together and to which we hold....

Sri Aurobindo, *The Secret of the Veda, CWSA, Volume 15*, p. 512

There is a mighty law of life, a great principle of human evolution, a body of spiritual knowledge and experience of which India has always been destined to be guardian, exemplar and missionary. This is the sanatana dharma, the eternal religion. Under the stress of alien impacts she has largely lost hold not of the structure of that dharma, but of its living reality. For the religion of India is nothing if it is not lived. It has to be applied not only to life, but to the whole of life.... We believe that it is to make the yoga the ideal of human life that India rises today; by the yoga she will get the strength to realise her freedom, unity and greatness, by the yoga she will keep the strength to preserve it.

Sri Aurobindo, *Karmayogin, CWSA, Volume 8*, p. 24

This book unfolded as a journey of discovery. I followed the trail of the vesica piscis as it revealed more and more of its hidden and eternal truth to me. The first chapters are an attempt to establish the singular Vedic context, lens or field in which the vesica piscis emerges as a master key. This is the lens or field of the Circle. For the Rishi or Seer, the Circle is the Divine Eye and Kshetra (field) of the One Deva – the God of all Gods. It is the unified field of the Soul's journey or *yajna* in Time and Space. After laying down this layer, I then followed the thread of the triple law of the radius, vesica piscis and circle discussing how it applies to the measure of the Kali Yuga and the Maha Yuga cycle. This thread subsequently led to the discovery of how the lore of Vishnu's ten avatars arise out of the geometry of the vesica piscis. After discussing the lore of Vishnu's avatars in the light of this discovery, came the full descent of the vesica piscis's role in the recovery of Vedic Gnosis, which forms Part Two of this book.

CHAPTER TWO

The Recovery of the Lost Sun

[By] the coming of the Dawn the Truths are won out of the Nights. This is the rising of the Sun which was lost in the obscurity—the familiar figure of the lost sun recovered by the Gods and the Angiras Rishis—the sun of Truth, and it now shoots out its tongue of fire towards the golden Light:—for hiraṇya, gold is the concrete symbol of the higher light, the gold of the Truth....

Sri Aurobindo, *The Secret of the Veda, CWSA, Volume 15*, p. 130

[T]he Night of the Veda is the obscured consciousness of the mortal being in which the Truth is subconscient, hidden in the cave of the hill;... the recovery of the lost sun lying in this darkness of Night is the recovery of the sun of Truth out of the darkened subconscient condition....

Sri Aurobindo, *The Secret of the Veda, CWSA, Volume 15*, p. 202

It is in the revolution of the year that the recovery of the lost Sun and the lost cows is effected....

Sri Aurobindo, *The Secret of the Veda, CWSA, Volume 15*, p. 177

Let us meditate on the most auspicious form of Savitr [the Sun], on the Light of the Supreme which shall illumine us with the Truth.

Gayatri Mantra (revised), Sri Aurobindo, March 19, 1933,
Letters on Himself and the Ashram, CWSA, Volume 35, p. 831

The "legend of the lost Sun and its recovery by sacrifice" is the central theme of the Rig Veda. It is the recovery of the all-unifying Soul from the veils of the egoic-mental consciousness. The sacrifice or *yajna* of the Rishis had nothing to do with murdering animals, or humans for that matter. The Vedic *yajna* is the Earth's twelve-month year. *Yajna*, also spelled *yaga*, is the ancient basis of yoga. In the West, the word "yoga" is typically understood as the physical practice of performing asanas (poses) and pranayama (breathing exercises) to improve health and wellbeing. Whereas hatha yoga is a valuable branch of yoga, in the West it is typically far-removed or even severed off from the seed, core, heart or full (*purna*) expression of yoga, often falling more in the category of physical exercise rather than spiritual *sādhana* or practice. The deeper and fuller scope of yoga was well-illuminated by Sri Aurobindo.

> *By Yoga we can rise out of falsehood into truth, out of weakness into force, out of pain and grief into bliss, out of bondage into freedom, out of death into immortality, out of darkness into light, out of confusion into purity, out of imperfection into perfection, out of self-division into unity, out of Maya into God. All other utilisation of Yoga is for special and fragmentary advantages not always worth pursuing. Only that which aims at possessing the fullness of God is purna Yoga; the sadhaka of the Divine Perfection is the purna Yogin....*
>
> *All Yoga which takes you entirely away from the world, is a high but narrow specialisation of divine tapasya. God in His perfection embraces everything; you also must become all-embracing.*
>
> *God in His ultimate existence beyond all manifestation and all knowledge, is the Absolute Parabrahman; in relation to the world He is that which transcends all universal existence while regarding it or in turning away from it; He is that which contains and upholds the universe, He is that which becomes the universe and He is the universe & everything which it contains.*
>
> *...God descending into world in various forms has consummated on this earth the mental and bodily form which we call humanity.*

> *...In brief, we have to replace dualities by unity, egoism by divine consciousness, ignorance by divine wisdom, thought by divine knowledge, weakness, struggle and effort by self-contented divine force, pain and false pleasure by divine bliss. This is called in the language of Christ bringing down the kingdom of heaven on earth, or in modern language, realising and effectuating God in the world.*
>
> *...To rise into divine existence, force, light and bliss and recast in that mould all mundane existence is the supreme aspiration of religion and the complete practical aim of Yoga. The aim is to realise God in the universe, but it cannot be done without realising God transcendent of the Universe.*
>
> Sri Aurobindo (circa 1913), "The Entire Purpose of Yoga", *Essays Divine and Human, CWSA, Volume 12*, pp. 98-99

The true base, field and journey of yoga is the Vedic yajna (*yaga*). Yajna is the field and progressive journey in Time and Space within which we come to discover, recover or rebirth the hidden divine flame or inner Sun of our being and of our world which yokes Spirit and Matter and ALL together. It yokes together what is unmanifest as well as what is manifest. It yokes together past, present and future. The Earth's 12-month year, and its 24-hour day are microcosms of the whole field or yajna of Time and Space. The Rishis' primary name for the hidden unifying flame, Sun, Son or Soul of this unified field of Time and Space was Agni, the priest of the sacrifice. We will see, however, that there are many names of this Hero-Soul of creation. In Rig Veda 3.4.10, Agni is described as "the carrier of the [sacrificial] offerings who was hidden in the Secrecy."[1] He is also described as "the King of the immortal world"[2] and as "the King of all who live."[3] In Rig Veda 3.9.4 Agni "wanders at his own free will...hidden from our view." The Rishi of Rig Veda 1.23.14 sings of the recovery of this Divine Son, coinciding with the recovery of the lost cows or herd.

---

[1] Tr. R.T.H. Griffith.

[2] I.e., the King of Swar, the Rishis' realm of Truth-Consciousness.

[3] Rig Veda 5.28.2; 5.2.6, tr. R.T.H. Griffith.

> *O shining Pushan, bring to us, as if our lost herd, the God of the varied fullness of flame who upholds our heavens. Pushan finds the shining King who was hidden from us and concealed in the cave.*
>
> Rig Veda 1.23.14, tr. Sri Aurobindo, *The Secret of the Veda, CWSA, Volume 15*, p. 487

Pushan here is equivalent to the thunder god Indra who breaks open the cave in which the Sun, the cows and the holy waters or sacred rivers of truth are enclosed. Like Indra, Agni is described as freeing the rivers "that were bound in fetters"[1] or restraints. Pushan and Indra are both names of Agni – the One God with many names and forms. The varied language of the Vedic victory and the many names of the one Hero or God of the Rig Veda will become clearer in further chapters. For now, it is important to flush out the field of the Vedic yajna – the true field and origin of Yoga in which the recovery of eternal law or *sanatana dharma* takes place. There is not one word, symbol or name in the Rig Veda that is not a figure or character of this singular field, which the Rishis knew as the unified field of Time and Space.

> *The whole of karma yoga, or any yoga for the matter of that, is centred round this principle governing all life and existence – the principle of yajna, sacrifice.*
>
> Swami Krishnananda, *The Teachings of the Bhagavadgita (1982)*, p. 33

> *The sacrifice is also a journey; indeed the sacrifice itself is described as travelling, as journeying to a divine goal; and the journey and the sacrifice are both continually spoken of as a battle against the dark powers....*
>
> *...[T]his journey, if principally of the nature of a quest, the quest of the hidden light, becomes also by the opposition of the powers of darkness an expedition and a battle.*
>
> Sri Aurobindo, *The Secret of the Veda, CWSA, Volume 15*, p.183

[1] Rig Veda 1.93.5, tr. R.T.H. Griffith.

> *This victory [the recovery of the lost Sun] is won in twelve periods of the upward journey, represented by the revolution of the twelve months of the sacrificial year, the periods corresponding to the successive dawns of a wider and wider truth, until the tenth secures the victory.* ***What may be the precise significance of the nine rays and the ten, is a more difficult question which we are not yet in a position to solve****; but the light we already have is sufficient to illuminate all the main imagery of the Rig Veda.*
>
> Sri Aurobindo, *The Secret of the Veda, CWSA, Volume 15*, pp. 181-82 [bold emphasis added]

The "nine rays and the ten" are figures of the ninth and tenth months of the twelve-month year. These rays are personified as the "Navagwas who sacrificed for nine months, the other Dashagwas whose sessions of sacrifice endured for ten".[1] In the following verse, *Navagwas* (or *Navagvas*) refers to a hero who is nine-rayed. This nine-rayed hero is a symbolic figure of the 9th sign of the zodiac, Sagittarius.

> *Navagvas, with heroes, on his knees he sought the cattle. There, verily with ten Daśagvas Indra found the Sun lying hidden in the darkness.*
>
> Rig Veda 3.39.5, tr. R.T.H. Griffith

> *This great evolution [from darkened consciousness to "the divine brilliance"] is effected in Time gradually....*
>
> Sri Aurobindo, *The Secret of the Veda, CWSA, Volume 15*, p. 274

> *The great Light of lights, the Sun of Truth, the illumination of the Truth-consciousness is rising up out of the movement of life to create the illumined Mind, Swar, which completes the evolution of the lower triple world.*
>
> Sri Aurobindo, *The Secret of the Veda, CWSA, Volume 15*, p. 329

---

[1] Sri Aurobindo, *The Secret of the Veda, CWSA, Volume 15*, p. 175.

[It] is indicated that it is only by the confirming of the thought which conquers Swar, the solar world, that the Rishis are able to get through the ten months.... This Swar-conquering thought is certainly the same as [the] thought which was born from the Truth and discovered by Ayasya[1]*... for by it, we are told, Ayasya becoming universal, embracing the births in all the worlds, brought into being a fourth world or fourfold world, which must be the supramental beyond the three lower.... This fourth world must be therefore Swar.*

Sri Aurobindo, *The Secret of the Veda, CWSA, Volume 15*, p. 176

[We] find that it is with the help of the Navagwas that Indra pursues the trace of the lost kine, but it is only with the aid of the ten Dashagwas that he is able to bring the pursuit to a successful issue and find that Truth, satyaṃ tat, *namely, the Sun that was lying in the darkness. In other words, it is when the nine-months' sacrifice is prolonged through the tenth, it is when the Navagwas become the ten Dashagwas by the seven-headed thought of Ayasya, the tenth Rishi, that the Sun is found and the luminous world of Swar in which we possess the truth of the one universal Deva, is disclosed and conquered. This conquest of Swar is the aim of the sacrifice and the great work accomplished by the Angiras Rishis. But what is meant by the figure of the months? [F]or it now becomes clear that it is a figure, a parable; the year is symbolic, the months are symbolic.*[2] *It is in the revolution of the year that the recovery of the lost Sun and the lost cows is effected, for we have the explicit statement in X.62.2,* ṛtenābhindan parivatsare valam, *"by the truth, in the revolution of the year, they broke Vala,"*[3] *or, as Sayana interprets it, "by sacrifice lasting for a year."*

Sri Aurobindo, *The Secret of the Veda, CWSA, Volume 15*, p.177

---

[1] Ayasya is an epitaph of the Vedic hero.

[2] Sri Aurobindo's note: "Observe that in the Puranas the Yugas, moments, months, etc. are all symbolic and it is stated that the body of man is the year."

[3] Vala is defined in the *Cologne Digital Sanskrit Lexicon* as "enclosure", "a cave", cavern" as well as "cloud". It is likely the origin of the English word "veil".

In *The Secret of the Veda*, written circa 1914-1916, Sri Aurobindo shed much light on both the form and the spiritual significance of the Vedic sacrifice. He identified the form of the yajna as equivalent to the twelve-month year, and indicated that this year's journey is symbolic of the collective evolutionary process by which the hidden "Sun of Truth-consciousness" is found and the fourth (Supramental) world of Swar is born out of the three lower worlds (Physical, Vital and Mental). He noted that, according to the Rishis, finding the hidden Sun (and along with it the lost cows and rivers) corresponds somehow to the movement through the 9th and 10th months of the year. He acknowledged that he did not know or was "not yet in a position to solve" the real significance of the Rishis' emphasis on these two months.[1] Throughout his teachings he did, however, make it abundantly clear that a higher understanding and consciousness of Time is part and parcel of our passage into the higher strata of our collective yajna or evolutionary journey.

> *Certain eternal worlds (states of existence) are these which have to come into being, their doors are shut to you (or, opened) by the months and the years; without effort one (world) moves in the other, and it is these that Brahmanaspati[2] has made manifest to knowledge.*
>
> Sri Aurobindo, *The Secret of the Veda, CWSA, Volume 15*, p. 179

> *Time is the remaining aid needed for the effectivity of the process. Time presents itself to human effort as an enemy or a friend, as a resistance, a medium or an instrument. But always it is really the instrument of the soul.*
>
> Sri Aurobindo, *The Synthesis of Yoga, CWSA, Volumes 23-24*, p. 68

> *The timeless Infinite holds in itself, in its eternal truth of being, beyond this manifestation, all that it manifests in Time. Its time consciousness too is itself infinite and maintains in itself at once*

---

[1] *The Secret of the Veda, CWSA, Volume 15*, p. 182.

[2] Brahmanaspati (meaning Lord of the Word) is another name of the Vedic Hero.

in a vision of totalities and of particularities, of mobile succession or moment sight and of total stabilising vision or abiding whole sight what appears to us as the past of things, their present and their future.

Sri Aurobindo, *The Synthesis of Yoga, CWSA, Volumes 23-24*, p. 885

It is here [in the transition from mind to supermind] that a change begins to take place in the time-consciousness and time-knowledge which finds its base and complete reality and significance only on the supramental levels.

Sri Aurobindo, *The Synthesis of Yoga, CWSA, Volumes 23-24*, p. 904

All time is one body, Space a single book.

Sri Aurobindo, *Savitri, Book 10, Canto 4, SABCL, Volume 29*, p. 660

[The Supramental being's] time consciousness...will be different from that of the mental being, not swept helplessly on the stream of the moments and clutching at each moment as a stay and a swiftly disappearing standpoint, but founded first on its eternal identity beyond the changes of time, secondly on a simultaneous eternity of Time in which past, present and future exist together for ever in the self-knowledge and self-power of the Eternal, thirdly, in a total view of the three times as one movement singly and indivisibly seen even in their succession of stages, periods, cycles, last – and that only in the instrumental consciousness – in the step by step evolution of the moments. It will therefore have the knowledge of the three times, trikāladṛṣṭi *– held of old to be a supreme sign of the seer and the Rishi, – not as an abnormal power, but as its normal way of time knowledge.*

Sri Aurobindo, *The Synthesis of Yoga, CWSA, Volumes 23-24*, pp. 886-87

Sri Aurobindo's yogic mission of recovering the true sense of Vedic Gnosis was impressed upon him by the spiritual presence of Vivekananda and Krishna during his imprisonment in Alipore Jail (1908-09), under charge of conspiracy against the British Raj. It is clear in his writings that Sri Aurobindo believed India had a long way to go to recover the deepest sense of its own spiritual heritage.

When spirituality is lost all is lost. This is the fate from which we have narrowly escaped by the resurgence of the soul of India in Nationalism. But that resurgence is not yet complete. There is the sentiment of Indianism, there is not yet the knowledge. There is a vague idea, there is no definite conception or deep insight. We have yet to know ourselves, what we were, are and may be; what we did in the past and what we are capable of doing in the future; our history and our mission.

Sri Aurobindo, 19 June 1909, *Karmayogin, CWSA, Volume 8*, p. 20

I believe [the] Veda to be the foundation of the Sanatan Dharma; I believe it to be the concealed divinity within Hinduism, — but a veil has to be drawn aside, a curtain has to be lifted. I believe it to be knowable and discoverable. I believe the future of India and the world to depend on its discovery and on its application, not to the renunciation of life, but to life in the world and among men.

Sri Aurobindo, *India's Rebirth* (written circa 1910-1914), pp. 256-57

Religious movements and revolutions have come and gone or left their mark but after all and through all the Veda remains to us our Rock of the Ages, our eternal foundation.... Yet for some two thousand years at least no Indian has really understood the Vedas.

Sri Aurobindo, *India's Rebirth*, pp. 265-66

As the Veda had passed from the sage to the priest, so now it began to pass from the hands of the priest into the hands of the scholar. And in that keeping it suffered the last mutilation of its sense and the last diminution of its true dignity and sanctity. Not that the dealings of Indian scholarship with the hymns, beginning from the pre-Christian centuries, have been altogether a record of loss. Rather it is to the scrupulous diligence and conservative tradition of the Pandits that we owe the preservation of Veda at all after its secret had been lost and the hymns themselves had ceased in practice to be a living Scripture. And even for the recovery of the lost secret the two millenniums of scholastic orthodoxy have left us some invaluable aids.

Sri Aurobindo, *The Secret of the Veda, CWSA, Volume 15*, pp. 16-17

[In] the later ages the very device used by the Rishis turned against the preservation of the knowledge. For language changed its character, rejected its earlier pliability, shed off old familiar senses; the word contracted and shrank into its outer and concrete significance.... The letter lived on when the spirit was forgotten; the symbol, the body of the doctrine, remained, but the soul of knowledge had fled from its coverings.

Sri Aurobindo, *The Secret of the Veda, CWSA, Volume 15*, pp. 56-57

Much of India and the Indian diaspora throughout the world struggles to preserve the integrity of India's spiritual heritage against constant degradation, looking forward to the day when India will reclaim Her power and role as *Vishwa Guru* or Bringer of Light into the world. Sri Aurobindo, the Mother and Thea considered India's uprising, based on the recovery of its *sanatana dharma*, to be essential for the establishment of Unity and Truth-Consciousness in the world. On this subject, the Mother wrote:

There must be a group forming a strong body of cohesive will with the spiritual knowledge to save India and the world. It is India that can bring Truth in the world. By manifestation of the Divine Will and Power alone, India can preach her message to the world and not by imitating the materialism of the West. By following the Divine Will India shall shine at the top of the spiritual mountain and show the way of Truth and organise world unity.

The Mother, February 1954
Words of the Mother I, CWM, Volume 13, p. 353

Given their collective accomplishments in the arena of recovering the secrets and true context of Vedic Gnosis, Sri Aurobindo, the Mother and Thea must be counted as forerunners of this group, and yet their accomplishments go largely unnoticed and consequently remain largely unutilized towards India's uprising. Together, they recovered the singular context of the Rishis' *sanatana dharma*, which is the Earth's twelve-month solar year or yajna. Without this context, the symbols of the Rig Veda would remain for the most part veiled, undecipherable, and thus unusable for raising consciousness in the world.

> *[The body of esoteric meaning in the Veda] is only discoverable if we give a constant and straightforward meaning to the words and formulas employed by the Rishis, especially to the key-words which bear as keystones the whole structure of their doctrine.... [The inner significance of the Vedic symbols] is there deliberately hidden by a veil, but the veil is not so thick as we first imagine; we have only to use our eyes and the veil vanishes; the body of the Word, the Truth stands out before us.*
>
> Sri Aurobindo, *Hymns to the Mystic Fire, CWSA, Volume 16*, pp. 11-12

> *Once the sense of the Vedic symbols is known, the spiritual intention of these legends becomes apparent and inevitable. Every element of the Veda is inextricably bound up with every other and the very nature of these compositions compels us, once we have adopted a principle of interpretation, to carry it to its farthest rational limits. Their materials have been skilfully welded together by firm hands and any inconsistency in our handling of them shatters the whole fabric of their sense and their coherent thinking.*
>
> Sri Aurobindo, *The Secret of the Veda*, *CWSA, Volume 15*, pp. 46-47

Hopefully by the end of this book, readers will have a better feeling for the singular context and the extraordinary coherency of the Rishis' *sanatana dharma*, which has become splintered and scrambled via our fragmented mental-egoic consciousness in the course of Time.

CHAPTER THREE

The Eye of the Sun

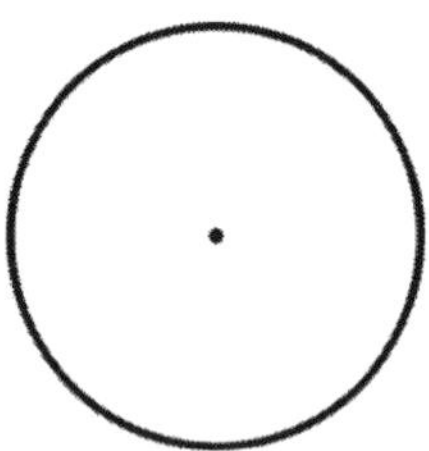

Footless at first was he produced, footless he brought celestial light.... Him too they call eternal; he may become new again today.

Atharva Veda 10.8.21-23, tr. R.T.H. Griffith

[The Sun, Surya is] a symbol of the divine illumining Power, Swar the world of the divine Truth and the conquest of divine Truth the real aim of the Vedic Rishis and the subject of their hymns.

Sri Aurobindo, *The Secret of the Veda, CWSA, Volume 15,* p. 150

[The] rising of the Sun which was lost in the obscurity — the familiar figure of the lost sun recovered by the Gods and the Angiras Rishis — the sun of Truth...the higher light, the gold of the Truth, ...this [is the] treasure...for which the Vedic Rishis pray to the Gods.

Sri Aurobindo, *The Secret of the Veda, CWSA, Volume 15*, p. 130

The "footless" Sun Symbol, unassuming as it is, is a primary key of the recovery of the Rishis' astoundingly cohesive and integral gnosis. This symbol may be vaguely recognized as a symbol of unity in our world, but the full realization and significance of this fixed basis of the eternal gnosis, vision and yajna of the ancient Rishis has yet to dawn on most. In the Vedas we find frequent mention of the singular eye of the Sun, also called the eye of light and the eye of the gods (*devānāṃ cakṣuh*), which is the basis of divine vision or gnosis. This singular eye or *cakṣuh* is commonly associated with the physical Sun, but it must also be seen as the Sun's symbol – the circle with its bindu or point. *Cakṣuh* (eye) is closely related to the Sanskrit word *cakra* meaning circle or wheel. In the Rig Veda *cakra* is the wheel of the Sun's chariot or in other words, the wheel of the Solar Year. *Cakṣuh* is related to *akṣa*, also meaning "eye", and *ákṣa* indicating a wheel, axle, axis, measure or snake.[1] An essential step in the process of the recovery of the lost Sun and lost *sanatana dharma* of the Rishis is to remember how the Sun symbol or solar wheel (*cakra*) functions as the singular lens, eye (*cakṣuh*) and context of the Rishis' divine vision.

> *That One Thing [tadekaṃ], breathless, breathed by its own nature: apart from it was nothing whatsoever. ...[By] the great power of Warmth was born that Unit. ...Sages who searched with their heart's thought discovered the existent's kinship in the non-existent. He, the first origin of this creation, whether he formed it all or did not form it, whose eye [akṣa] controls this world in highest heaven, he verily knows it, or perhaps he knows not.*
>
> Rig Veda 10.129.2-7, tr. R.T.H. Griffith

From the dimensionless point • arises the two-dimensional Sun symbol ⊙, which is a symbol and key of the coherency and harmony of all dimensions of Time and Space. This symbol shows the eternal relationship between source and creation,

[1] All definitions are from *Cologne Digital Sanskrit Lexicon.*

between the non-existent and the existent. Its geometry is the foundation of our existence in Time and Space.

The eternal law and measure of this symbol or circle is the foundation of the Rishis' eternal gnosis. Outside this one circle, knowledge or *jjana* of the whole is lost and we are left to our tangents and fragmented ideas, void of the true center and context of our common existence and journey. The loss of the Sun symbol or circle as a key of gnosis is an ongoing source of our modern civilization's disharmony which itself amounts to ignorance of the One Being (*ekam sat*) that we are.

> *Ekam sat vipra bahudha vadanti – that which exists is One: sages call it by various names.*
>
> Rig Veda 1.164.46, tr. Swami Vivekananda

Priest King, Mohenjodaro, 2200-1900 BC (National Museum, Karachi).

The solar eye or symbol of this One Being is found on the forehead of the 4,000-year-old Priest King sculpture of the Indus Valley civilization. Via this ancient sculpture we can see that the Sun symbol is the origin of modern-day conceptions of the third eye of the awakened-seer. This third eye is often thought of as a *spiritual* eye, but in full truth it is the eye that sees the unity of Spirit *and* Matter (Heaven *and* Earth). It is the eye of the heroes of the Rig Veda, including Indra the Bull. From this Vedic eye comes the image and term "Bull's-Eye" indicating the center of an archer's target. The circular band around the Priest King's head also gives us an indication of the Vedic origin and significance of the halo of light that is often depicted around the heads of gods, goddesses, avatars, angels and illumined sages. The triple-petal pattern of the Priest King's shawl is likely an expression of the Rishis' triadic gnosis established by the radius – the "priest" of the circle.

Related to the Priest King's circular third eye is the mythology of Shiva's third eye which is often depicted as a vertical eye on his forehead. The shape of the human eye is akin to a vesica piscis within which the pupil and the body of the iris form the Sun

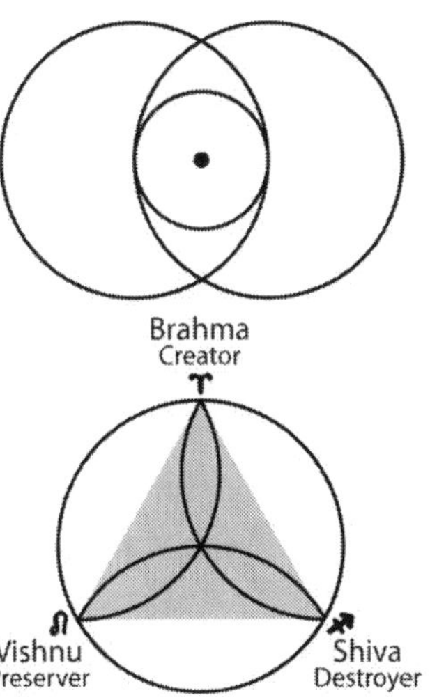

symbol. The three eyes of Shiva, who is one of the three principle gods (Trimurti) of the Rishis' circle of gnosis, could well be a reference to the three vesicae piscis that are nested within and define the central trinity of the circle and fire trine of the zodiac.[1] In viewing the symbolism of the eye in the Rig Veda, it appears that in some cases the eye refers to the Sun symbol and in other cases it refers to the vesica piscis. The Rishi of Rig Veda 1.72 sung of "both eyes of heaven".[2] These two eyes are thought of as the Sun and the Moon, but they also appear to be the eye of the Sun symbol and the eye of the vesica piscis which is moon-like in its arc and in its partial appearance within the whole circle. In Rig Veda 9.9.4 the Rishi sung of "the Single Eye"[3] which is likely the Sun symbol.[4]

I will conclude this chapter with a variety of quotes which convey the importance of the Sun's Eye or Sun symbol in Vedic Gnosis. It is the primary lens through which the Vedic Seer sees. The Rishis knew it to be the basis of recovering the Light of our eternal Truth and the basis of uplifting mankind from its darkened or fragmented consciousness. Given that the 360° circle was the primary field, lens and basis of Vedic Gnosis, the Sun symbol is necessarily a primary key for anyone called to the task and journey of recovering unity consciousness in their own being. It is the Eye of the Seer of eternal truth and there can be no real vision or comprehension of the Rishis' unified field of Time and Space apart from this Eye of Unity.

---

[1] Thea illuminated the connection between the Trimurti, the fire trine and the three energy flows or gunas of the zodiac in *The Gnostic Circle*, pp. 54-56.

[2] Rig Veda 1.72.10, tr. R.T.H. Griffith.

[3] Tr. R.T.H. Griffith.

[4] The eye as a symbol of the vesica piscis is further discussed in Part Two.

He who dwells in the sun, he is One. The man who knows this, he verily attains the Oneness of the One.

Maitri Upanishad 6.17, tr. Raimundo Panikkar, *The Vedic Experience*, p. 667

He who dwells in the eye, yet is other than the eye, whom the eye does not know, whose body is the eye, who controls the eye from within — he is the ātman within you, the Inner Controller, the immortal.

Brihadaranyaka Upanishad, 3.7.18, Ibid., p. 707

He who knows that Person[1] whose support are the forms, whose world is the eye, whose light is the mind, the ultimate resort of the self of all — he is truly a knower, Yājñavalkya[2].

Brihadaranyaka Upanishad, 3.9.12, Ibid., p. 731

The Sun, dispeller of darkness, whose eye contemplates all things.... He guards heaven's vault, the sky's pillar.

Rig Veda 4.13.3, Ibid., p. 324

The Seers by the power of truth in their thoughts discover this Sun lying in the darkness, they liberate this knowledge, this power of undivided and all-embracing vision, this eye of the gods concealed in our subconscient being; they release his radiances, they create the divine Dawn.

Sri Aurobindo, *The Secret of the Veda, CWSA, Volume 15*, p. 478

*[The light of knowledge] is called also the eye of the gods and the divine dawn that makes manifest the whole of existence. The result of this birth of divine vision is that man's path manifests itself to him and those journeyings of the gods or to the gods (*devayānāḥ*) which lead to the infinite wideness of the divine existence.*

Sri Aurobindo, *The Secret of the Veda, CWSA, Volume 15*, 196-97

---

[1] "Person" was likely translated from "Purusha" – the Cosmic Man, *maha-atman*, great soul or inner Sun of the universe and its forms.

[2] Yājñavalkya is a knower or sage of the yajna (sacrificial year) and its laws.

...[T]he Sun, the eye of the whole world, is not touched by external blemishes seen by the eye....

Katha Upanishad 5.11, tr. Raimundo Panikkar, *The Vedic Experience*, p. 666

The light of Surya is the form, the body of that divine vision. He is described as the pure and visioned force of the Truth which shines out in his rising like the gold of Heaven. He is the great godhead who is the vision of Mitra and Varuna; he is the large and invincible eye of that Wideness and that Harmony; the eye of Mitra and Varuna is the great ocean of vision of Surya. His is that large truth-vision which makes us give to its possessors the name of seer. Himself the "wide-seeing", "the Sun, the Seer who knows the triple knowledge of these gods and their more eternal births".... It is by this eye of light that Indra [the Bull], who has made [Surya] arise in heaven for far vision, distinguishes ... the children of light from the children of darkness so that he may destroy these but raise those to their perfection. ...The victory of that vision, the arising of this Light to "its own home of the truth", the outflooding of this great ocean of vision of Surya which is the eye of the infinite Wideness and the infinite Harmony, is in fact nothing else than the [divine creation]....[T]his new-seeing of all things, this new-moulding of thought, act, feeling, will, consciousness in the terms of the Truth, the Bliss, the Right, the Infinity is a new creation. ...To prepare that new birth and new creation for man by his illumination and upward voyaging is the function of Surya, the divine Light and Seer.

Sri Aurobindo, *The Secret of the Veda, CWSA, Volume 15*, pp. 479-80

Ignorance, this matrix of sin, has in its substantial effect the appearance of a triple cord of limited mind, inefficient life, obscure physical animality.... The whole result is a struggling or inert poverty of being; it is the meagreness of a mortal undelight and the insufficiency of a being that collapses at every moment towards death. When Varuna the Mighty comes and sunders this threefold restraint, we are freed towards riches and immortality. Uplifted, the real man arises to his true kingship in the undivided being. ...As ignorance or falsehood in the being...is the cause of wrong and suffering, so Knowledge or Truth is the agent which purifies and liberates. It is because of the eye with which he sees,

> *– the luminous symbolic Sun, – that Varuna is the purifier. ...[He] abolishes by his royal power our debts of the Ignorance.*
>
> Sri Aurobindo, *The Secret of the Veda, CWSA, Volume 15*, p. 505

> *Savitar*[1] *God of all men hath sent upward his light, designed for all mankind, immortal. Through the Gods' power that Eye was first created.*
>
> Rig Veda 7.76.1, tr. R.T.H. Griffith

Sri Aurobindo translated this last verse as:

> *Savitri, the god, the universal Male, has ascended into the Light that is immortal and of all the births...by the work (of sacrifice) the eye of the gods has been born (or, by the will-power of the gods vision has been born).*
>
> *The Secret of the Veda, CWSA, Volume 15*, p. 196

---

[1] Savitar (or Savitri) in the Rig Veda is a name of the Solar God, Soul or Purusha.

CHAPTER FOUR

Trayi Vidya – The Triple Knowledge

[D]esiring the Treasure, [we] call by our words Fire, the universal godhead, discerning him by the mind, as the follower of the truth, who finds the world of the sun, the great giver, the divine and rapturous charioteer.

We call to guard us that brilliant Fire, the universal godhead, who grows in the mother, the master of the word, the speaker and the hearer, for the human being's forming of the godhead, the illumined Seer, the guest, the swift Traveller....

I am the Fire, I am from my birth the knower of all things born; light is my eye, in my mouth is immortality; ***I am the triple Ray, I am the measurer of the mid-world****, I am the unceasing illumination, I am the offering.*

He has purifed through the three filters the Ray, following the thought with the heart he has reached knowledge of the light; he has created by the self-laws of his nature the supreme ecstasy and his sight has embraced earth and heaven.

He is a fountain with a hundred streams that is never exhausted, with his illumined consciousness he is the father and accorder of all that must be spoken; he takes his rapture in the lap of the Father and Mother and earth and heaven fill him full, the speaker of truth.

Rig Veda 3.26.1-9, tr. Sri Aurobindo,
Hymns to the Mystic Fire, *CWSA*, *Volume 16*, pp. 203-05

The subject and sometimes speaker in this sukta or hymn is Agni. He is the triple-fire, the "triple Ray",[1] chief god, hero, leader and hidden Son of the Vedic sacrifice. The eternal wisdom, science, lore or light of the Vedas is referred to as the *trayi vidya. Trayi* means "triad" or "triple" and *vidya* and *veda* both hail from the root *vid* meaning "knowledge". *Vid* is specifically knowledge in the sense vision.[2] Seeing and knowing were equivalent in the Rishis' conception. In the highest sense, *vidya* and *veda* refer to vision and knowledge of the One, knowledge of the unified field of the Soul which extends itself into Time and Space.

It is clear throughout the Rig Veda, as well as throughout post-Vedic literature and Sri Aurobindo's writings that the unity-vision or luminous knowledge of the Rishis is triply-constructed, triply-born, triply-one, and triply-won or recovered in the course of the yajna.

> *Yaska himself [an ancient sage] declares that there is a triple knowledge and therefore a triple meaning of the Vedic hymns, a sacrificial or ritualistic knowledge, a knowledge of the gods and finally a spiritual knowledge; but the last is the true sense and when one gets it the others drop or are cut away. It is this spiritual sense that saves and the rest is outward and subordinate. He says further that "the Rishis saw the truth, the true law of things, directly by an inner vision"; afterwards the knowledge and the inner sense of the Veda were almost lost and the Rishis who still knew had to save it by handing it down through initiation to disciples and at a last stage outward and mental means had to be used for finding the sense....*

Sri Aurobindo, *Hymns to the Mystic Fire, CWSA, Volume 16*, p. 9

---

[1] "Triple Ray" is Sri Aurobindo's translation of *arkastridhatu*. *Arka* in the *Cologne Digital Sanskrit Lexicon* is defined as "ray", "Sun", "lightning" and "fire" and is associated with the number 12. *Arkastridhatu* is translated by R.T.H. Griffith as "light threefold". In *Satapatha Brahmana 10.3.4*, *Arka* is also a name of Agni.

[2] From *vid* comes our modern English word "video".

Come hither unto us, O Aśvins,[1] *with those aids wherewith in fight ye speed the war-cry to the spoil.... Wherewith the sapient one acquired his triple lore.... Wherewith Triśoka*[2] *drove forth his recovered cows [light]....*

Rig Veda 1.112.1, 4, 12, tr. R.T.H. Griffith

He hath filled full the regions of the heaven and earth.... Lighting all living creatures, ne'er to be deceived, Savitar, God, protects each holy ordinance....Savitar thrice surrounding with his mightiness mid-air, three regions, and the triple sphere of light, [sets] the three heavens in motion and the threefold earth, and willingly protects us with his triple law.

Rig Veda 4.53.3-6, tr. R.T.H. Griffith

We know your threefold triads, Agni; we know your domains dispersed in many places. We know your highest name, which is hidden; we know the wellspring whence you have come here.

Rig Veda 10.45.2, tr. by Stephanie W. Jamison and Joel P. Brereton[3]

Three are thy powers, O Agni, three thy stations, three are thy tongues, yea, many, Child of Order! Three bodies hast thou which the Gods delight in: with these protect our hymns with care unceasing.

Rig Veda 3.20.2, tr. R.T.H. Griffith

[Trita Aptya][4] *on the third plane of existence consummates our triple being....*

Sri Aurobindo, *Hymns to the Mystic Fire, CWSA, Volume 16*, p. 28

---

[1] In *The Secret of the Veda* (*CWSA, Volume 15*, p. 82), Sri Aurobindo describes the Aśvins as twin "powers of Light" who "move in the paths of Light". They are twin horsemen, or twin riders of the Horse.

[2] Griffith translated *Triśoka* (an epitaph of Agni) as "triple splendor" (RV 10.29.2).

[3] *The Rig Veda: The Earliest Religious Poetry of India*, Oxford University Press (2014), p. 1450.

[4] Trita Aptya is a reference to Agni who is hidden and born in the waters (*aptya*).

> *By his will Trita*[1] *in the secret cave desiring by his movements the thinking of the supreme Father, cherished in the lap of the Father and Mother, speaking the companion-word, seeks his weapons.*
>
> *Trita Aptya discovered the weapons of the Father and missioned by Indra went to the battle; he smote the Three-headed, the seven-rayed [foe or dragon] and let loose the ray-cows of the son of Twashtri the form-maker.*
>
> Rig Veda.10.8.7-8, tr. Sri Aurobindo,
> *Hymns to the Mystic Fire, CWSA, Volume 16*, p. 401

> *Trita Aptya takes this high-flaming force and forges it into a weapon of sharpness that shall destroy all evil and ignorance.*
>
> Sri Aurobindo, *The Secret of the Veda, CWSA, Volume 15*, p. 390

The basis for this triple essence and form of Vedic knowledge, and the triple flame that recovers the Rishis' *trayi vidya* is the eternal and universal fact that the arc of the radius and vesica piscis of any circle marks out one third of that circle's circumference. Three such arcs form the triple division of the circle, which can be seen as three petals or three flames within the Sun symbol. This triadic vision (and division) of the One forms the basis of the Rishis' entire system of eternal gnosis which is the basis and origin of our 0/9 (3 x 3) number system, our 360° (3 x 120°) measure of the circle, as well as our 1,296,000″ (3 x 432,000″) measure of the circle. We may widely utilize these ancient numbers and measures of the circle across the world, but most remain entirely ignorant of the gnosis the ancient Rishis conveyed therein. I have drawn out the following figure to demonstrate how these numbers and measures are based on the triadic geometry of the circle, informed by the radius and vesica piscis.

---

[1] Sri Aurobindo defines Trita (a name of Agni) as "the triple born from the All-pervading Substance" (*CWSA, Volume 15*, p. 413).

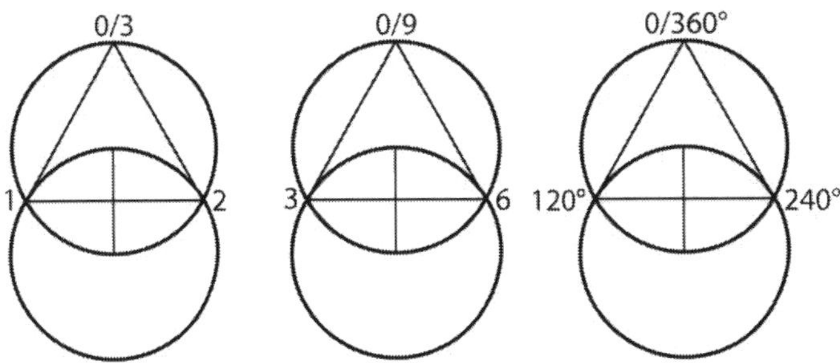

The 360° measure of the circle can be further broken down into seconds of degrees of arc wherein 120° of the circle is equivalent to 432,000″ as shown on the following page. The sacred numbers 3, 9 and 360 and 432,000 are clearly born of the Law of Three – the law of the circle and its radius – well known to the Rishis.

> *Men versed in sacred knowledge know that living Being [in creation's center] that abides in the nine-portalled Lotus Flower, enclosed with triple bands and bonds.*
>
> *Desireless, firm, immortal, self-existent, contented with the essence, lacking nothing, Free from the fear of Death is he who knoweth that Soul courageous, youthful, undecaying.*
>
> Atharva Veda 10.8.43-44, tr. R.T.H. Griffith

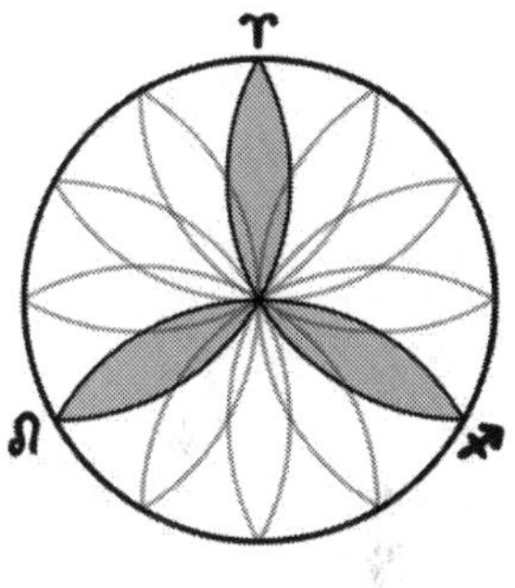

In Thea's writings the upright triangle of the circle is equivalent to the fire trine of the zodiac, made up of the three fire signs Aries ♈, Leo ♌ and Sagittarius ♐. This is the true sense of the triple fire, triple ray or triple flame of Agni – the Hero-Son of the Rig Veda. Agni is depicted as triple-headed (*trimūrdhānam*)[1] as well as the third or triple one (Trita). He is the central protagonist, Purusha (Soul), priest and leader of the Rishis' twelve-month sacred year or yajna. The first of Agni's three

[1] Rig Veda 1.146.1.

births is the zero point of the 360° sacred year – 0° Aries, the apex of the fire trine. From this first point or birth in the field of Time and Space, Agni leads the march toward the Soul's victory or full manifestation. Thea understood the equilateral triangle of the circle to be the geometric basis of the Vedic Rishis' *trikala drishti*. In *The Gnostic Circle* she wrote of *trikala drishti* as "the perception of simultaneous time" and as "the simultaneous experience of the 'three times', past-present-future".[1] In this view, Time or *Kala* is triply-one, whole and indivisible. All dimensions of Time and Space are united and harmonized by the Soul's triadic law.

Kala is commonly known as the masculine form of the goddess Kali. Both are figures of the triple-force and body of Time. In the early 1970s, Thea saw that the 432,000 figure of the Kali Yuga is meant to be understood as one-third (432,000″) of the circle. We can clearly see in the image to the right how together the radius and vesica piscis firmly establish the Kali Yuga measure. We can also see that the 432,000-mile solar radius sets and supports the 432,000″ measure of the vesica piscis and the Kali Yuga.

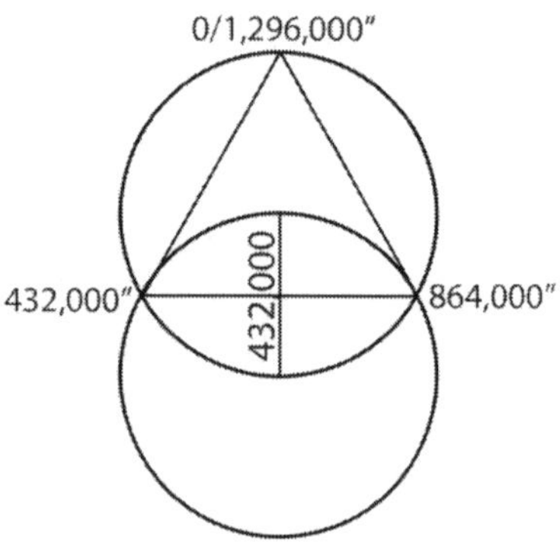

This triadic geometry as applied to Time and Space is the real core and essence of the ancient and eternal dharma which India is responsible for helping restore in our current day and age. This *sanatana dharma*, it must be understood, is not some nebulous idea of eternal truth, law and order. It is the eternal truth, law and order laid down by the radius or the ray of the Soul/Sun in the unified field of Time and Space. The word *dharma* is formed via the roots *dhar* and *ma* indicating that which supports, holds or bears forth the sacred measure (*ma*). In this light we can see that the word *dharma* itself is a name or descriptor of the radius. This true sense of *dharma* has been long forgotten.

---

[1] *The Gnostic Circle*, pp. 12-13, 46.

Once the 432,000-measure of the Kali Yuga is established as one-third (432,000″) of the 360° circle, it becomes clear that the 864,000-measure of Dwarpara Yuga (two yugas) is equivalent to two-thirds of the circle, and that the 1,296,000-measure of the Treta Yuga (three yugas) is equivalent to the full 360° circle. These three measures of the circle (432,000″, 864,000″ and 1,296,000″), as drawn out on the previous page, are firmly based on the triadic law or dharma of the radius. Satya Yuga (four yugas) is in turn four-thirds of the circle. Via this simple math, long-held misinterpretations of the Kali Yuga measure can finally be put to rest. These long-held misinterpretations are purely based upon the loss of the Rishis' triadic gnosis (*trayi vidya*) along with its sacred, solar or golden reed of measure, and are naturally dismantled as the Rishis' triadic gnosis and vision of Time is restored. I will discuss the triadic geometry of the yugas more fully in a later chapter.

The hero of the Triple Veda, Agni, is sometimes called *Trita* – "the third" or "triple one". This name is an indication of Agni's three births in the fire sign of the zodiac, the third of which is Sagittarius. The task of this hero, equivalent to both Agni and Indra in the Rig Veda, is to slay the serpent or dragon Vritra whose name means "coverer" or "restrainer". He blocks the flow of the rivers of truth and is thus associated with drought, darkness and ignorance. By their victory over this dragon, the Vedic heroes reclaim or reopen the doors to the Rishis' unified vision and experience of Time and Space for the world. The root *vri* of Vritra means "to cover", the root *tra* means "three" and the Vedic dragon is at times depicted as three-headed. This triple demon or guardian can be thought of both in terms of the geometry of the circle and in terms of our fragmented consciousness of Time, wherein Time occurs as a mortal-enemy to be escaped or transcended. With the defeat of this "coverer", the Hero-Purusha wins back the *trikala drishti* wherein all three phases of time – past, present and future – are seen and known as a cohesive Whole, and Time releases its torrents of treasures. The unseen value and perfection of the seemingly mundane details of one's past and present becomes apparent. In a sense, all experiences are redeemed or known as valuable no matter how negative the experience. With this revelation comes the experience of the eternal and divine continuity and coherency of the individual and collective Soul. Upon this victory in one's consciousness, the world – which under the cover of ignorance seems to be a random and meaningless march towards death, void of a real or absolute cohesive point – becomes filled by the all-unifying light of the Immortal Soul or Purusha. In *The Life Divine* Sri Aurobindo referred to the Purusha as the Spirit, the All-Being and the Conscious Being as well as "the Self as originator, witness, support and lord and enjoyer of the forms and works of Nature".[1] In *The Synthesis of Yoga* he wrote, "[E]xistence in its relations with and its experience of the becoming is what we call soul or Purusha, individual soul in the individual, universal soul in the cosmos; the principle and the powers of the becoming are what we call Nature or Prakriti."[2]

> *[T]here is a transformation which replaces the separative ego by the Purusha, a conscious face and figure of the universal being and a self and power of the transcendent Divine in cosmic Nature.*
>
> *In the same movement, by the very awakening into the spirit, there is a dissolution of the cosmic ignorance; for we have the knowledge of ourselves as our timeless immutable self possessing itself in cosmos and beyond cosmos: this knowledge becomes the basis of the Divine Play in time, reconciles the one and the many, the eternal unity and the eternal multiplicity, reunites the soul with God and discovers the Divine in the universe. It is by this realisation that we can approach the Absolute as the source of all circumstances and relations, possess the world in ourselves in an utmost wideness and in a conscient dependence on its source, and by so taking it up raise it and realise through it the absolute values that converge into the Absolute.*
>
> Sri Aurobindo, *The Life Divine, CWSA, Volumes 21-22*, p. 769

---

[1] *CWSA, Volumes 21-22*, pp. 363, 368.

[2] *CWSA, Volumes 23-24*, pp. 448-49.

Sri Aurobindo discussed the hero's journey (*yajna*) by which the Purusha or Soul emerges victorious over the forces of ignorance and death in great depth in *The Secret of the Veda*.

> *[The] journey, that victory [of the Light and the secret worlds of the luminous Bliss] is the ancient, primal achievement set... by the luminous Ancestors for the mortality that was to come after them. It was the conquest of the powers of the circumscribing Night* (rātrī paritakmyā), *Vritras, Sambaras and Valas, the Titans, Giants, Pythons, subconscient Powers who hold the light and the force in themselves, in their cities of darkness and illusion, but can neither use it aright nor will give it up to man, the mental being. Their ignorance, evil and limitation have not merely to be cut away from us, but broken up and into and made to yield up the secret of light and good and infinity. Out of this death that immortality has to be conquered. Pent up behind this ignorance is a secret knowledge and a great light of truth; prisoned by this evil is an infinite content of good; in this limiting death is the seed of a boundless immortality. Vala, for example, is Vala of the radiances,* valaṃ gomantam, *his body is made of the light,* govapuśaṃ valam, *his hole or cave is a city full of treasures; that body has to be broken up, that city rent open, those treasures seized. This is the work set for humanity and the Ancestors have done it for the race that the way may be known and the goal reached by the same means and through the same companionship with the gods of Light. "Let there be that ancient friendship between your gods and us as when with the Angirases who spoke aright the word, thou didst make to fall that which was fixed and slewest Vala as he rushed against thee, O achiever of works, and thou didst make to swing open all the doors of his city" (VI.18.5). At the beginning of all human traditions there is this ancient memory. It is Indra and the serpent Vritra, it is Apollo and the Python, it is Thor and the Giants, Sigurd and Fafner, it is the mutually opposing gods of the Celtic mythology; but only in the Veda do we find the key to this imagery which conceals the hope or the wisdom of a prehistoric humanity.*
>
> Sri Aurobindo, *The Secret of the Veda, CWSA, Volume 15*, pp. 190-91

Triple-headed dragon, The Tomb of the Infernal Chariot, 4th cent. BCE, Sarteano (Siena), Italy.

Vritra shows up in St. John's *Revelation* as the dragon who swipes precisely *one third* of the stars out of the sky with its tail. In my mind this destructive act reflects the eclipsed or veiled truth of the radius and the vesica piscis, which swipes through one-third of the circumference of the circle. This dragon can be understood equally as a guardian and an obstructer of the passage into the higher gnosis and higher world of the last 120° or four signs of the zodiac where the lost Sun or Soul is found. The dragon symbolizes the difficulty the hero faces in winning or opening the passageway into the higher realms of the Self. The slaying of the serpent-dragon does not indicate Time itself to be a force of evil or an illusion. Rather, it represents the victory of the illuminating Sun or Soul of our field of Time and Space. Via this victory we evolve beyond our experience of Time as a mortal enemy or as an illusion to be escaped, and attain the immortal, vast and all-integrating consciousness of the Rishis, wherein all of life is experienced as a divine treasure.

Before further delving into the significance of the radius and vesica piscis in relation to this Vedic victory, I would like to give readers more history and context regarding the yoga of Sri Aurobindo, the Mother and Thea via which this gnosis has been recovered. I hope to convey the progressive and supramental nature of this recovery.

CHAPTER FIVE

The Progressive Recovery of Gnosis

On November 24, 1926, some 18 years after his yogic mission or *adesh* was impressed upon him in Alipore Jail, Sri Aurobindo had a pivotal experience which he later described as "the descent of Krishna into the physical".[1] That day was henceforth known as Sri Aurobindo's Siddhi Day, when at the age of 54 he retired from the public "to work things out"[2] as he put it. Given what has been discussed regarding the three-headed dragon of the Vedas, it is notable that three dragons figure into the lore of Sri Aurobindo's Siddhi Day.

> *In the verandah on the wall near Sri Aurobindo's door, just behind his chair a black silk curtain with gold lace work representing three Chinese dragons was hung. The three dragons were so represented that the tail of one reached up to the mouth of the other and the three of them covered the curtain from end to end. We came to know afterwards that there is a prophecy in China that the Truth will manifest itself on earth when the three dragons (the dragons of the earth, the mind region and of the sky) meet.[3] On 24 November the Truth was descending and the hanging of the curtain was significant.*
>
> Udhaya Kumar, *Mira to Mother*, Sura Books (2004), p. 72

In 1935 Sri Aurobindo clarified that his November 24 experience was a preparation, "not itself actually bringing, the descent of

---

[1] Udhaya Kumar, *Mira to Mother*, Sura Books (2004), p. 74.

[2] Sri Aurobindo, *Letters on Himself and the Ashram, CWSA, Volume 35*, p. 271.

[3] Thea wrote of these dragons in terms of the interwoven Lunar Nodes of Sri Aurobindo's lineage. In my mind, these dragons also symbolize the three vesicae piscis whose heads and tails meet at the fire trine of the zodiac.

Supermind and Ananda."[1] These 1935 clarifications came via the questions of a student who wanted answers about what was accomplished on that day. The student commented, "You have unnerved a lot of people by that statement that you haven't achieved the supermind"; to which Sri Aurobindo responded:

> *Good Lord! And what do these people think I meant when I was saying persistently that I was trying to get the supermind down into the material? If I had achieved it on Nov. 24. 1926, it would have been there already for the last nine years.... If all that was achieved on the 24th [of November] 1926, what on earth remained to work out, and if the Supramental was there, for what blazing purpose did I need to retire? Besides are these things achieved in a single day?*
>
> Sri Aurobindo, *Letters on Himself and the Ashram, CWSA, Volume 35*, p. 271

According to K. D. Sethna, on November 26, 1926, two days after this descent of Krishna consciousness, the Mother "declared that a most important and fundamental event had occurred but it was both very sacred and secret....According to her, the divine principle of Immortality had been brought down on that day".[2] The Mother and all at the Sri Aurobindo Ashram thus came to refer to November 26, 1926 as Immortality Day. As Thea would later note, this date turned out to fall exactly at the midpoint of the day and month of Sri Aurobindo and the Mother's departures, respectively in 1950 and 1973. Sri Aurobindo passed on December 5 and the Mother passed on November 17. November 26 falls in the middle of this 18-day span.

In 1962, 36 years after Immortality Day and 12 years after Sri Aurobindo's passing, the Mother discussed the progressive and collective nature of Sri Aurobindo's work toward the restoration of divine gnosis in our world. Via her own words, we can understand that the yogic mission or intended yogic victory of Sri Aurobindo and the Mother was far from complete in 1962.

---

[1] Sri Aurobindo, *Letters on Himself and the Ashram, CWSA, Volume 35*, p. 272.

[2] K. D. Sethna, "Immortality Day", www.searchforlight.org (accessed May 2016).

I feel a very strong need for someone who knows. ...Who knows something. That's what I was expecting from Sri Aurobindo. But he himself was searching. Had he continued, he probably would have found it.... But obviously it wasn't possible. For he never said he didn't know. ...He always told me, "Each thing in its own time."...But truly, if someone (I don't know who or what this "Someone" is) ... if I am given the time, I will know – I am convinced of it. For despite all the growing difficulties, there is also a growing knowledge, a constant progress. So from that standpoint, I CANNOT *be mistaken; it is impossible. This Presence is becoming so concrete and so (what shall I say?) ... so helpful, so concrete in its help. But it obviously takes a long time.*

The Mother, *The Mother's Agenda, Volume 3*, February 13, 1962, pp. 82-84

On January 1, 1969, the Mother experienced what she called the "descent of the Superman consciousness" which Sri Aurobindo had been very clear was not what he experienced or achieved in 1926.

It's the descent of the superman consciousness. I had the assurance of it afterwards. It was on the 1st of January after midnight. I woke up at 2 in the morning, surrounded by a consciousness, but so concrete, and NEW, in the sense that I had never experienced that. It lasted, quite concrete and present, for two or three hours, and then it spread out and went to find all those who could receive it. And at the same time I knew it was the consciousness of the superman, that is, the intermediary between man and the supramental being.

The Mother, *The Mother's Agenda, Volume 10*, January 8, 1969, p. 26

On the last day of 1969, the Mother had a vision of the interior of a temple. In the first weeks of January 1970 she described her vision to her entourage. She saw a 12-sided inner chamber with a 24-meter diameter,[1] featuring 12 pillars (each 9-meters tall). In the core of this temple, the Mother saw a singular ray of light

[1] This diameter (i.e., sacred measure) was not adhered to in the subsequent building of the Mother's Temple (Matrimandir) in Auroville.

descending upon and illuminating a translucent globe resting on a four-sided marble pedestal, which in turn rested on the Mother's three-tiered twelve-petal symbol. Sri Aurobindo's "Lotus of the Avatar" symbol was to be carved into each of the four sides of the pedestal, so that the ascending and descending triangles holding the lotus in its center would meet at the four corners. In these first weeks of 1970, the Mother encountered immediate resistance to building the temple as she saw it. This resistance inevitably resulted in the mismeasure and misconstruction of the Mother's Temple in Auroville.

The Inner Chamber of the Matrimandir (Thea, The New Way, Volumes 1&2, inserted between pp. 202-03).

> *I told R. [Auroville's architect] about it, I asked him to see Paolo, and I also told him that I had seen what should be done. Naturally, he didn't say no, he said yes to everything, but I felt he wasn't too keen.... But here is what happened. I clearly saw – very, very distinctly saw, which means it was like that, and it still IS like that, it's there (gesture showing an eternal plane) – the inside of that place [the Matrimandir].*

The Mother, *The Mother's Agenda, Volume 11*, January 3, 1970, pp. 15-16

> *As for me, you know, I don't believe in external decisions. Simply, I believe in only one thing: the force of Consciousness exerting a PRESSURE like this (crushing gesture). And the Pressure keeps increasing.... Which means it's going to sift people.*
>
> *Otherwise, there would be no solution, because, you see, in the past (just some ten years ago) I used to go about and see things.... But that's over. It wasn't a decision I made, I didn't at all think it was over, it's not that at all: it was something that COMPELLED me. You understand? So I said all right. It's not incapacity: this body is extremely docile, it does everything it's asked to do; if it were asked to go out, it would manage to go out. It's extremely docile. But that's how it is, there is a Command: NO. And I know why....*

So, you know, I only believe in this: the pressure of the Consciousness. All the rest is all the things people do; they do them well or not so well, it all lives and dies and changes and gets distorted and... – all the things they've done. It's not worth it. The power of execution has to come from above, like this, imperative (gesture of descent). And for that, this (Mother points to her forehead) has to keep still. It shouldn't say, "Oh, we don't want this, oh, we want that, oh, we must do this..." – Peace, peace, peace, He knows better than you what needs to be done. There.

And as not many can understand, I don't say anything: I look and wait.

I LOOK.... For instance, I am given a piece of paper as you just did when you gave me that drawing, I look like that, and I very clearly see the part in the paper that's the result from above, the part that has got mixed, the part... Like that. But you don't go and say all that! – Moreover they wouldn't believe me.

The Mother, *The Mother's Agenda, Volume 11*, January 17, 1970, pp. 54-55

Three months later in March of 1970, while living in Rome, Thea experienced a vision of the twelve-month year (related to the Mother's vision of the twelve-pillared temple), which became her first book *The Magical Carousel – a zodiacal odyssey*. Thea told her students that this book, which illuminates the true nature of the zodiac as a cohesive journey towards higher worlds of consciousness, was projected upon her third eye as if she were watching a movie.

On February 21, 1971 ground was broken for the Mother's Temple in Auroville. Five months later Thea was called by the Mother to the Sri Aurobindo Ashram. Thea tells the story of this occult and inner call to Pondicherry in the first volume of her autobiographical series, *The Tenth Day of Victory*.

The 'Divine Mother' had said the 27th of September was the day ....[We left] on the last 9 day of the 9th month of that 9 year; with the 'Divine Mother' assuring me that all was arranged....

Thea, *The Tenth Day of Victory, Volume 1*, p. 103

Thea's flight from Rome to Bombay, India was by way of Cairo, with a layover that afforded her and her son enough time to visit the Great Pyramid and Sphinx of Giza.

> *I stood before the Sphinx and her 9 companions silently spaced behind her on those bare and placid Egyptian sands. Within me I knew, at some very deep level, that an intrinsic part of the process I was living was in some inscrutable way connected to this visit to the Sphinx and the Great Pyramid. The knowledge I was receiving was somehow linked to those sacred, ancient and mystifying monuments.*
>
> Thea, *The Tenth Day of Victory, Volume 1*, p. 105

Thea's arrival in India on September 28, 1971 and in Pondicherry the next day was timed in such a way, without her knowledge, to correspond with the 9th and 10th day of the Durga Puja festival. The 9th day and night of this festival symbolizes the final battle and difficulties faced in the 9th month of the Vedic sacrifice; and the 10th day, *Vijaya Dashami*, signifies the victory of the Divine Mother over the forces of ignorance, corresponding to successful passage through the 10th month of the Vedic sacrifice. In addition to this coincidence, September 27th, the date of Thea's departure from Rome, falls exactly 270 days into the calendar year (from January 1st). Two hundred and seventy days is equivalent to 270° of the zodiac which marks the passage from the 9th into the 10th month of the sacred year. In other words, September 27 sits at the same point in the Gregorian year that December 21 sits at in the Tropical Year.

Thus, it came to be that, nine years after the Mother's discussion of the need for "someone who knows" and her quest of "a third point…where the two paths [of science and spirituality] merge into a third that would be the TRUE thing", Thea arrived in Pondicherry in the 8th month of her 33rd year and began to progressively uncover and reveal the secrets of this third position. These secrets included shedding light on the circle and its equilateral triangle as keys of eternal gnosis, and on the true role the twelve-month Vedic Year plays in the restoration of eternal gnosis in India and in the world. She shed light upon the true significance of the passage from the 9th month into the 10th month of Capricorn (Makar). She also shed light on the forgotten fact that the true and fixed measure of the sacred year (*yajna*) of the Rishis is Earth's Solar Year – the Tropical (*Sayana*) Zodiac – anchored by the Earth's equinoxes and solstices, not by uneven and imaginary (or man-conjoined) constellations of stars out beyond the Earth's ecliptic plane. She taught that what goes by the name of Vedic astrology in India and throughout much of the world is not in fact Vedic, but rather a post-Vedic divergence from the true measure of the Rishis' sacred year.[1]

> *In the Rig Veda the tenth month of the natural order is Makar, and it is held as the month of Victory for the initiate who has undertaken the Journey, as it is called in the Veda. ...[T]he Year is understandably the central figure of the Veda, around which the Sacrifice is conducted. The victory of the tenth month is when Time becomes the Ally and ceases being the Destroyer. Therefore Makar Sankranti is the portal to Immortality, the entry to the realm of the Immortal Ones....*
>
> *...[T]here is an eternal Dharma which Capricorn, better than any other sign/month, describes. Disconnecting it from the [December] Solstice as our latter-day pundits have done, hides that Dharma from view: it can be anything to all men. There is nothing absolute and eternal, constant and unshakable to uphold motion (the journey through Time) as the natural Year does. To succeed in cementing this aberration only one thing was required: to separate the inseparable. Then all is relative, nothing is permanent and eternal, above all not the Dharma.*
>
> *How was this accomplished?...The sacred duty of time reckoning for the Hindu Samaj was handed over not to astrologers but to astronomers who are not versed in the Veda. More appropriately, not just 'versed' because that accomplishment does not imply a Vedic Realisation, which alone grants keys to the higher knowledge contained in the Veda.*

---

[1] Thea's many articles on the Earth-based measure of Makar Sankranti (the entrance into the sign of Capricorn) and the Vedic Year, are featured on Aeon Centre of Cosmology's website: www.aeoncentre.com.

These astronomers made the fatal mistake of eliminating the natural year – Vedic to the core – and replacing it with another circle, the wrong one for temple purposes and horoscopy. They established their time reckoning in the constellations rather than in the ecliptic pathway of the tropical zodiac as in the Vedic Age. And because it is nearly impossible to establish an absolute and not 'relative' ayanamsha[1] *in that outermost sphere of the constellations – erroneously also called zodiac by astronomers – the true measure of the Earth was lost. Different theories were then proffered to the point where today Makar has been distanced from her true position and this most important of all Sankrantis is alleged to occur 23 days after the Solstice, an aberration known only in India and bearing no sanction in the Veda.*

Thea, "The Importance of Makar Sankranti in Hindu Calendar Reform", Part 2, *Puranic Cosmology Updated* (blog), Dec. 30, 2010

[The] calculations [of the sacred year in India] are wrong. They are based on an irrelevant measure, – irrelevant with respect to the immediate destiny and its fulfilment.... The Dharma cannot be saved on the basis of a corrupt measure.... [T]he zodiac, as a path of yoga, can be understood and experienced only with the Divine Measure intact.

Thea, "The Capricorn Factor", Part II, *The Vishaal Newsletter*, Volume 2.5, September 1987, pp. 2-6

The Vedic system must be balanced on the unchanging four Cardinal pillars of the Tropical Zodiac, which do not hold any prominence in the Nirayana system advocated by Al Biruni.... There was no VEDIC basis involved in the introduction of the current Nirayana system of calendar observances for Hindus, – a tragic state of affairs.

Thea, "The Dawn of a New Era", *The New Way (blog)*, July 2007

---

[1] *Ayanamsha* is the number of degrees of celestial longitude between the Tropical (*Sayana*) Zodiac and the Sidereal (*Nirayana*) measurement of the Zodiac. There are varying opinions in India about where to place the correct zero point (0° Aries) of the Sidereal year in the constellations, which amounts to varying opinions about the correct measure of the *ayanamsha* (as well as of holy days and festivals).

I found [the culprit] was the scholar, Al Biruni, in the 12th century, who came into India and criticised Hindu pundits because they were not following the Nirayana (constellation) system. In critiquing Varahamihira's famous work, Brhad Samhita, he wrote, 'The solstice has kept its place, but the constellations have migrated, just the opposite of what Varaha has fancied' (India, II, p.7). This means that as late as the 12th century the correct Vedic method connecting Capricorn to the Solstice, as well it must be, was still in vogue. Scholars came into the country, with invading armies, and were in a position to undermine the pundits. By then, the cosmological foundation was already lost; so it was easy to undermine their understanding of what had to be measured and impose this other irrelevant system. Today this mis-measure has resulted in the discrepancy of 23 days, and it will go on increasing until somewhere down the line the Makar Sankranti, or Pongal, will be celebrated in the middle of summer! No one asks, how can this be? This is how science stepped into the sacred and brought in a disturbing, disruptive element where it had no business interfering. This is what you are faced with in India today: No one says this is wrong, you must go back to the Vedic practice.

Thea, "India's True History is in its Myths" – II,
Bhavan's Journal, Volume 54.2, August 31, 2007

[T]he Tropical Zodiac...never varies in time and [its] 12-month segments of the year are inseparable from the solstices and equinoxes. This is the true VEDIC astrology. It was still in force when Al-Biruni came to India in the 11th century....By the 11th century all that was needed were a few well pointed 'poison arrows' to bring about a 'vast decay, confusion and inertia', the inevitable result when Knowledge by initiatic Realisation, the very method minutely detailed in the ancient Veda, no longer exists. It would await the next Age of Vishnu, or the passage of another millennium, to be resuscitated. This Age is now upon us.

...Presently the mis-measure [of the Vedic Year/Zodiac] is 23 days, or a shift from the Solstice on 21-22 December to the current arbitrary 15 January. But with each passing day and month and year the distance goes on increasing through these wandering phantom ayanamshas....

Hinduism is still paying for this calculated undermining. It lies at the very heart of its decline. Therefore this is the area we must

> *focus on if we wish to bring back the soul of Vedic Wisdom to the culture....*
>
> Thea, *The Origins and Nature of Hindu Decline, Part 2* (2006)

In addition to illuminating the importance of reestablishing the solar measure of the Rishis' twelve-month sacrificial year, Thea also illuminated the importance of the equivalence between the 432,000″ arc of the circle and the measures of the solar radius, the Kali Yuga and the Rig Veda.

> *[It] is necessary to understand that the figures of the Yugas (Ages) are not in actual fact years, but refer rather to seconds of degrees of celestial longitude....432,000 would be four zodiac signs converted into seconds of degrees. The seconds of one sign are 108,000, and 4 times that is 432,000....*
>
> *It can be understood how this figure [of the Kali Yuga] would be the key to the measure of Time since it is also the radius of the Sun. The Sun's radius is the key of Truth in that it unites the outer circle of the disk (the Multiple) with the inner central core (the One). We could call this: 'The Measure of Unity.' It is precisely the Sun's symbol, the point within the circle, that contains the Knowledge...showing the harmony between space and time and the evolutionary cycles of man on Earth which are determined by the unfolding and perfectioning of consciousness.*
>
> *The Rig-veda also appears to contain the same key to the measurement of Time based on the Sun of Truth because it is said to have 432,000 syllables.*
>
> Thea, *The Gnostic Circle*, pp. 61-62

Thea wrote in *The Gnostic Circle* that the Kali Yuga measure is specifically to be understood as one-third of the 25,920-year Precession of the Earth's Equinoxes. The ancient division of this Precession or "Great Year" into twelve "months" is the origin of the Earth's astrological ages, spanning 2,160 years each.[1] One-

[1] It is notable that one sign/month of the 12-month year is 108,000″ (30°) of the circle and the measure of the Moon's radius is 1080 miles. The 2160-mile diameter of the Moon is equivalent to the 2160-year measure of one age of the Great Year.

third or 120° of this Great Year is equivalent to four zodiacal ages or 8,640 years. In this clear accounting, the Treta Yuga or triad of three Kali Yugas spans the full 360° degrees and 12 Ages of the Earth's Great Year. Thea also indicated in the same book that the ten avatars of Vishnu *the Preserver* are evolutionary catalysts who manifest in the *Preservation* ages of the Great Year: Taurus, Leo, Scorpio and Aquarius. She wrote that Sri Aurobindo, not Gautama Buddha, is the 9th of this line of avatars. This revision of the line is entirely justifiable considering that the Buddha's teachings represented a clear departure from the eternal dharma and sacred yajna of the Vedic Rishis, and Sri Aurobindo's yogic mission or *adesh* was to fully recover and preserve this eternal dharma in our current age, the Age of Aquarius, the beginning of which Thea places at 1926.

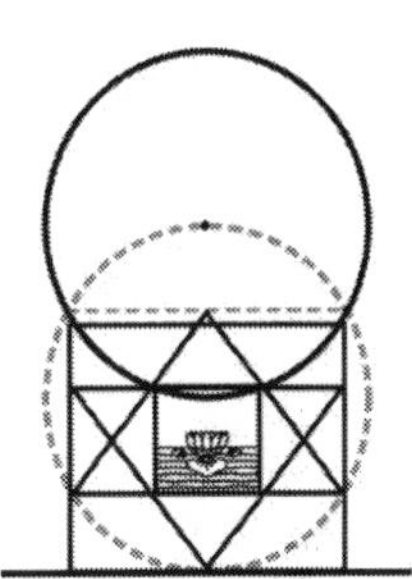

Globe and Pedestal (Thea, The New Way, Vols. 1&2, p. 238).

In 1976 the vesica piscis presented itself to Thea as a key of the sacred geometry of the Mother's Temple. It also served as the key by which she became aware of Sri Aurobindo's rebirth in 1963. Perhaps a week after being awakened by the vesica piscis in February of 2016, I remembered Thea's account of her son coming into her room early one morning circa the age of six announcing that a footless being had come into his room, and that the being "came from the Sun!" … "How could he come into my room without feet!" he asked. He proceeded to draw what looked like a figure 8 on her wall.[1] Some seven years later, on March 12, 1976, Thea had the intuition that the vesica piscis was the key to understanding the measure and significance of the solar ray and core (or soul) of the Mother's Temple as recorded in *The New Way, Volumes 1&2*. This intuition came to Thea as the diameter of the Mother's Temple was about to be wrongly and irrevocably set in concrete Auroville in November of 1976.[2]

---

[1] *The Tenth Day of Victory, Volume 2, Part 1*, p. 340. Thea did not record or remember the exact date of her son's vision.

[2] See *Chronicles of the Inner Chamber*, Matrimandir Action Committee (2003).

The intuition was simple and straightforward, unassuming, we could say: What if the Globe of 70cm is the basis for a vesica piscis construction – vertical, upright – and the lower circle holds the Pedestal?...That was all I needed to know.... It was the key to unlock the secrets of the Mother's chamber....

Thea, *The Tenth Day of Victory, Volume 2, Part 1*, p. 317

This intuition led to nine days of luminous realizations about the sacred measure of the Mother's Temple, culminating on March 21 (the March Equinox) with the realization that the measure of the descending solar ray and the measure of the luminous globe and pedestal upon which this ray fell, contained the year of Sri Aurobindo's death in 1950 as well as his rebirth in 1963. Thea recounted:

What [my son] drew according to his ability at the time was simply two circles, one above the other, which I must have concluded was an 8 because that was what he himself assumed....

...What was placed on my wall, a clear message given to me, was actually a Vesica Piscis, one circle above the other .... It was this simple design that held the secret of who he was and who he came to be in this life. It was the magical geometric figure that subtly enveloped the Core of the Mother's chamber, meticulously designed by her, containing therein all the details of the 'the future realisation', and with it all the pertinent details of Sri Aurobindo's rebirth.[1]

Thea, *The Tenth Day of Victory, Volume 2, Part 1*, pp. 341-42

On [March 21st, 1976] the most astonishing 'secret' [the Mother's] plan contained was revealed. It proved to be the culmination – or rather the key to the future not only of Sri Aurobindo's mission but the future of planet Earth herself. It made sense of the prophecies found scattered throughout the world, cross-cultural, cosmic and terrestrial: the birth of the Male Child.

[1] For more on this subject see *The New Way, Vols. 1&2*, pp. 191, 207-08, 418-22.

> *This was Sri Aurobindo himself in the form of the Son. This was the fourth missing or hidden power I had intuited was lacking. This was the secret laid bare of the transmutation of Transcendence to Immanence. Or, as he has described this power in* Savitri, *the 'masked Transcendent mounting his throne'. Such was the immensity of the unveiled 'secret'. It was Sri Aurobindo's rebirth.*
>
> Thea, *The Tenth Day of Victory, Volume 2, Part 1*, pp. 318-20

> *Sri Aurobindo's return...was revealed through the vesica piscis."*
>
> Ibid., p. 343

Remembering this account, I knew my 4:32 a.m. vision of the 432,000 measure of the vesica piscis and the solar radius was connected to Thea's son's early morning vision of a footless solar being, circa 1969-1970. I also knew that his vision of the solar being with "no feet" was connected to the hero of the Vedic sacrifice, described as footless in Atharva Veda 10.8 (quoted at the beginning of this book). This theme of the footless hero is repeated in Rig Veda 8.2.

> *[T]he Mighty One, Lord of the Brave.... Strong Friend, who, with no trace of feet, restores the [rays of Divine Light] to the men, who rest their wish and hope on him.*
>
> Rig Veda, 8.2.38-39, tr. R.T.H. Griffith

The reason I am certain these events are connected, and the reason I trust Thea's realizations regarding the supramental yoga of Sri Aurobindo and the Mother should become clear in the following section wherein I briefly recount how I was called into this yoga. The reason boils down to the yogic experience of convergence and coherency wherein only one thing (one victory) is being played out or borne out through all circumstances. Via this experience, certain truths and connections have become entirely self-evident.

CHAPTER SIX

Remembering the Plot

I was born on February 12, 1969 in West Virginia and grew up in Virginia where I received a thoroughly Western, private school education. My parents were not religious, though my mother took my siblings and I to church on occasion to give us the church experience, which made little sense to me. My father committed suicide in the summer between my first and second year at the University of Virginia, after which I had no interest in mirroring my life based on what I had seen and what I had been taught thus far. At that point, my spiritual adventure began. I felt the presence of God in my life and went through a Christian phase because that was the spiritual community available to me at the time; but in truth, other than the acknowledgment of a Divine power at play in the world, the basic tenants of Christianity never made real sense to me.

My first encounter with yoga was the book *Remember, Be Here Now* by Ram Dass given to me by a friend a week or two after graduating from UVA in 1991. This book, described on *Wikipedia* as "one of the first guides for those not born Hindu to becoming a yogi", was the beginning of my explorations into Eastern spiritual philosophy. Mostly I found myself reading the writings of Buddhist, Sufi and Taoist teachers. At some point my self-guided spiritual study included *Autobiography of a Yogi* by Paramahansa Yogananda, which reads like fiction and documents Yogananda's encounters with yogis possessing hard-to-believe yogic powers (*siddhis*) such as levitation. A few years later, circa the age of 24, I was introduced to Sri Aurobindo's writings and yogic philosophy. I felt a strong familiarity with his writing, so much so that it often felt like I was remembering his words as I was reading them. I frequently intuited what he would write in chapters I had not read yet. I felt that I was born to remember his yoga and that his yoga was mine as well. His illuminations on the unity of Spirit and Matter and his teachings on the supramental rhyme and reason underlying all circumstance occurred as better spiritual food than anything I had read and studied up to that point in my life. His proposal that our evolutionary goal is to fully manifest our divine soul in the material world rang utterly true to me, and I entirely lost interest in spiritual teachings propagating the idea that the material world is an illusion, or the idea that the goal of life is to transcend material existence.

Around that time my dream life became increasingly vivid and fascinating, consistently pointing towards some truth, beauty or form that was hidden from our normal human view. In one dream this hidden beauty was a dazzling city hidden in a valley, whose substance was akin to liquid diamonds. In other dreams, I came upon exquisite animals that no one else knew existed. I also dreamt of being the goddess Kali complete with four arms and a bloody knife, before knowing anything at all of who she was or how many arms she had or what she represented in terms of the power of Time (Kala). In one seemingly eternal dream which felt more real than real life, I was taken on a tour of millions of years of past, present and future evolution on Earth. Lucid in the dream, I thought I would be writing about the Earthly and evolutionary changes I had been shown for the rest of my life; but as I began to be expelled from that vast vision of Time into my normal waking consciousness, my guide told me, "You won't remember any details of this experience. *You will remember WHAT you need to remember, WHEN you need to remember it.*" Devastated by this news, I struggled futilely to set the details of what I had learned in my head. As I let go and woke up, the guide said, *"You are the Keeper of the Passageway"*. I had absolutely no idea what this meant at the time (age 25). I knew I would just have to live into the answer as my second favorite author at the time recommended.

Be patient toward all that is unsolved in your heart and try to love the questions themselves, like locked rooms and like books that are

> *now written in a very foreign tongue. Do not now seek the answers, which cannot be given you because you would not be able to live them. And the point is, to live everything. Live the questions now. Perhaps you will then gradually, without noticing it, live along some distant day into the answer.*
>
> Rainer Maria Rilke, July 1903, *Letters to a Young Poet*

That same year (1994), while helping my mother empty out our family home for its new buyer, I found a hand-written card from my father congratulating me for graduating from high school:

> *Dear Lori, Time is constant as the speed of light, we cannot change it. It is mathematically impossible for Life to be chance or accidental. It has purpose though we don't understand. Basic truths have evolved and are evolving. Someday we will know and understand. You are more than well equipped to probe these frontiers — to be a seeker, a doer, a changer, and to bring light to the dark corners. Go for it! Love, Dad*

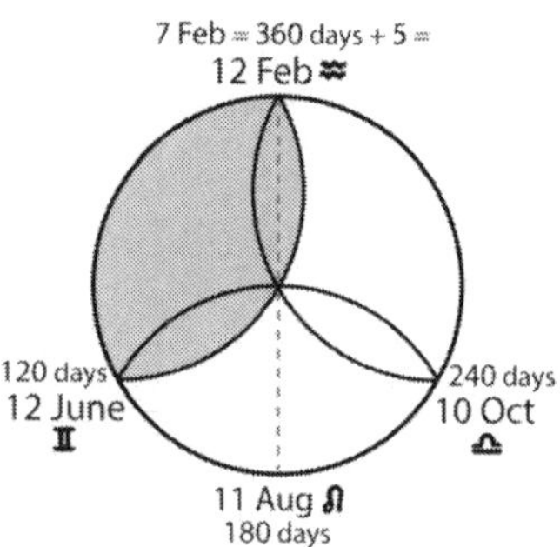

This card, dated June 12, 1987, shocked me when I read it seven years after my father's death. I did not at all remember the card or its message. I was most shocked that, in a way, my father had previsioned the path before me, and then a year later set me on this path via his own departure. The card occurs now as even more stunning, considering that it was written *exactly* 120 days after my 18th birthday, and that the importance of the 120° (432,000″) arc of the 360° Vedic Year is what I am now tasked with helping to bring to light. To add to this play of Time and revelation, February 7, the date of my 4:32 a.m. vesica piscis vision, falls exactly 360 days after my birthday.

This geometry did not occur to me in 1994, though that was the year I began to develop an interest in astrology and in the geometry of Time. I became increasingly curious about the Leo-Aquarius axis of the zodiac which seemed to prominently emphasize itself in my natal chart, in my mother's natal chart, in my personal life and via births and deaths in my family. For starters I was born in the Sun sign of Aquarius and in the rising sign of Leo. On the following day (February 13, 1969) my paternal grandmother left the planet. One of my brothers was born on August 14 (my "half birthday") in the Sun sign of Leo, and my maternal grandfather was born on August 13. In 1994 I saw that I was born at the specific degree of 24° Aquarius and that my mother's North and South Lunar Nodes fell at 24° Leo and 24° Aquarius. Seeing this Leo-Aquarius axis in my mother's natal chart, along which two of her children and her father were born, and my father's mother passed, gave me the sense for the first time that astrology was worth studying.[1] That same year I found out that Sri Aurobindo was born on August 15 (22° Leo), along or conjunct this same axis, opposite my birthday.

The fact that Sri Aurobindo's birthday fell opposite mine in the year felt important to me, though I did not fully know why at the time. It simply seemed to reflect the deep connection I felt with his yoga. Later, perhaps in 2002, I came to find that the Mother's North and South Lunar Nodes fell at 22° Aquarius and 22° Leo. In other words, her natal North Node – an indicator of one's karmic destiny – conjuncts my birthday; and her South Node conjuncts Sri Aurobindo's birthday. While writing this book I came to find that the year Sri Aurobindo was born (1872) the Sun's position was 22° Aquarius on February 12, my future birthday, directly opposite his natal Sun position.

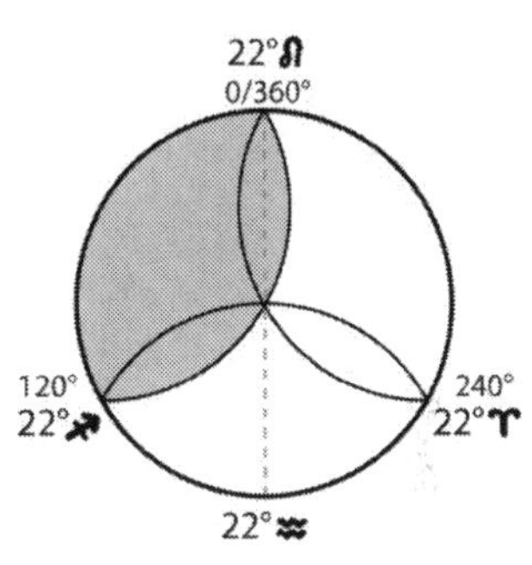

In 1996, at the age of 27, while on a Thanksgiving camping trip with friends, the Sun broke over the eastern horizon to start the day and conveyed (planted in my head) an unexpected forewarning that my life was about to completely change. I returned from that trip to find out that my 9-month-old cat Tuna

[1] In 2000 my first niece was born with her natal Sun at 24° Aquarius.

was missing,[1] and then I became very ill with what I thought was a bad flu. I abandoned my job of substitute teaching in Boulder, Colorado and went to convalesce in my mother's unused condo in Aspen where I got sicker and sicker. For whatever reason, my doctor failed to diagnose a simple case of giardia and over the course of a month I became dangerously dehydrated, underweight and eventually delirious.

Once properly diagnosed, I had the feeling that I needed to learn how to better take care of myself if I really wanted to stick around on planet Earth. Too weak to engage in any of my usual physical activities, I felt compelled to take my first hatha yoga class wherein I remembered that I was a yogi and a writer and stopped trying to be anything else. I thereupon got a job working as an editorial assistant and writer for a newspaper in the Roaring Fork Valley. Via this job, I came to meet and work part-time for author Hunter S. Thompson at his home in Woody Creek. I also developed a daily hatha yoga practice and dove deep into my studies of Sri Aurobindo's supramental yoga. His yogic mission, which I still didn't fully understand at the time, felt increasingly inseparable from my own soul and its work in the world.

After beginning my hatha yoga practice, I began to have a series of painful experiences which I dubbed "brain fry". The pain often arose from the base of my spine before lodging in my head, amounting to what felt like my brain on fire. Given my yogic path I decided to chalk this pain up to a re-awakening of Kundalini energy rather than considering it a medical emergency. These experiences gradually became less painful as I surrendered to however the energy wanted to move and to whatever it wanted to accomplish in my body.

In April of 1999 I became a certified hatha yoga instructor, and later that year, on September 9 (9.9), 1999, while on a hike with a friend with whom I was about to open a yoga studio, I had a vision of Sri Aurobindo standing in front of the Front Range of the Rocky Mountains and in front of thousands of other ethereal beings. Sri Aurobindo told me that I was going to India with the

[1] Weeks later he was found frozen in a snow bank, presumably hit by a car.

friend standing beside me at the time. That was all that was conveyed, and it instantly occurred to me as a fact. I thereupon said to my friend, "Let's go to India", and he immediately agreed. We abandoned our business plan and an offer we had made on a commercial-residential property, sold most of our worldly possessions, and flew to India three months later. That trip, spanning from December of 1999 to March of 2000, served as the doorway into an entirely new understanding of Sri Aurobindo's yoga, and hence an entirely new understanding of my own yoga.

I knew that Sri Aurobindo had a yogic partner, but like most people concerned with Sri Aurobindo and the Mother's work, I assumed that after these two maha yogis left the planet, students were on their own to cultivate some knowledge and experience of the supramental consciousness. In short, I was not at all aware of Thea's existence or of her teachings. After a month in northern India, my friend and I arrived in Pondicherry on January 11, 2000 and we immediately headed to the Sri Aurobindo Ashram visitor center to orient ourselves. The receptionist invited us to peruse the photographic timeline of the lives of Sri Aurobindo and the Mother mounted along the walls of the center. We walked and read our way through the whole exhibition which ended with the last pictures ever taken of Sri Aurobindo and the Mother while alive. While standing face to face with the end of the road of their great storyline, news of a third stage of the supramental descent was simply impressed upon me out of thin air with the same kind of force and certainty as when Sri Aurobindo had told me I was going to India. I saw that a third portrait, a third person was missing in this story. The daunting impression that came with this news was the feeling of standing next to and looking up at an impenetrable and unscalable sky-high wall representing the old and obstructive consciousness that this third level of Sri Aurobindo's yoga (the third level of the Supramental Descent) would have to face and somehow dismantle.

The following week, upon my companion's suggestion, I visited the mountain town of Kodaikanal where I felt blissfully at home and enjoyed illuminating glimpses of the continuity and rhyme and reason of my life thus far. Neither my travel companion nor I were aware at the time that Thea existed or that she lived just outside Kodaikanal where she carried on the third stage of the Supramental Descent that I had been informed of in the ashram visitor center. The next month, while studying yoga at Vivekananda Yoga Kendra on the outskirts of Bangalore, I had my last painful kundalini incident. In the pre-dawn hours of my 31st birthday I was jolted out of sleep and jumped out of bed onto hands and knees. My brain felt like it was on fire as per previous episodes, but this time I felt as if I were amidst a high-voltage field of energy which could incinerate me just as the Sun would incinerate anyone who found themselves in it. I crawled back into bed and surrendered to the excruciating pain and let go of the fear of dying via brain hemorrhage or spontaneous combustion and thereupon the pain soon disappeared. The pain was replaced by the feeling of being immersed in an infinite field or ocean of high-voltage bliss. After this experience I had the thought, "If this is the energy field of the solar or supramental world about which Sri Aurobindo wrote, it is GOOD that it is not descending or emerging all at once in our world." I also had the thought that it is impossible to imagine the potential or future of Life on Earth once that indwelling energy and bliss comes forward in our world, in our consciousness and in our bodies, making way for something *entirely* new. I continued to feel blissful through that morning and as I walked towards breakfast had the thought, *I feel like I'm ten years old.* Perhaps a half minute later an Indian man passing in the opposite direction commented, "You look like you're 10 years old." I just smiled, nodded and told him that that was how I felt.

I experienced this field of energy-bliss again a couple weeks later on February 28 in an astoundingly vivid dream wherein I was trekking in the Himalayas with a group of family and friends. The dream began with our arrival at a verdant and paradisiacal high-altitude plateau surrounded by seven mountain peaks. The snow pack of each of the mountains was slowly melting in the warm weather. The descending water formed rivulets down the mountains which in turn formed beautiful ice sculptures in the caves situated where the base of the seven mountains met the plateau. As I gazed up in reverence at the highest peak, which I knew to be Sri Aurobindo's peak, a shard of ice broke off from the top. It flew down and hit me like a bolt of lightning, knocking me out. When I woke (still in the dream), I saw that the bolt of ice had pierced through a sliver of skin on my left shoulder and had transformed into two magnificent long-stem red roses, still dripping with melting ice. The stems of these roses were firmly embedded into the Earth. Upon waking up (in the dream) and seeing these roses, my body was once again immersed in the same field or ocean of energy-bliss as experienced two weeks earlier, on February 12, 2000.

At the time, I had not read *The Secret of the Veda* and was still entirely ignorant of the importance of the number 7 in the Vedas and in Indian mythology. I was entirely ignorant that the Rig Veda celebrates the Hero's journey up a mountain wherein he slays the obstructer of truth with a lightning bolt, thereby setting seven rivers of truth free from the mountain summit to flow out upon the world. I equally had no idea at the time that there actually is a cave in the Himalayas where dripping water forms an ice stalagmite, revered as a Shiva Lingam.

A few days after that experience my companion treated me to a session with an Indian palm leaf reader who read my past (from the Akashic record) with great accuracy and then told me, among other intriguing things, that in my last life I was a master/teacher of Kundalini Yoga (Tantra) in India and that in this life I would solve a great problem for the world and achieve God-realization. He also told me that I had lost my yogic partner. Stunned by that reading and by my experiences in India, I returned to the USA without any concrete plans of how to proceed. I had no idea what I was supposed to do with what I had seen, what I had experienced and what I had been told, nor did I even know where in the USA I wanted to call home. My worldly possessions at the time included a backpack and a couple boxes full of some clothes as well as a pair of Shiva statues and a pair of bronze elephants ridden by Lakshmi that I had claimed from my maternal grandparents' house after they passed.

Upon my return, I visited my brother and sister in San Francisco where I immediately found Thea's book *The Gnostic Circle* in my sister's book collection. As I read the book, which was published in 1975, I understood that the author was laying out the third-stage of the yoga I had been informed of in the Sri Aurobindo Ashram visitor center. After finishing the book, I discovered the author was still alive and living in Kodaikanal. This news of her abode made my hair stand on end as I realized how controlled my entire trip, and my entire life had been up to that point in time. I became fully and irrevocably aware that my mental consciousness was not at all in the driver's seat. My soul apparently had set plans and designs that I didn't really know much about. I had reached a point of no return in the sense that I could not return to how I had previously thought about reality. I also could not unsee or ignore the things that had been revealed to me indicating I had some serious work to grow into.

After reading *The Gnostic Circle* I dreamt of a small flame alight in a bowl which I stumbled across deep in the midst of a vast, ancient, uncharted and untouched forest whilst the rest of the world was deep in the throes of World War III and mass destruction. This flame, I understood, had the power to end the world war. It had the power to unify *everything*. The challenge, it was clear in the dream, was how to lead others back to this flame, because I knew people had to see it and experience its power and truth for themselves. Just telling people about it would be futile. It had to be experienced. This dream imagery entirely preceded my knowledge of Agni as the sacred hidden flame, leader and hero of the Vedic yajna.

Circumstances then unfolded over the next three years so that eight months into my 33rd year, I would meet Thea for the first time at high noon on the 9th day of the 2002 Durga Puja festival (October 14) at Skambha, Thea's home and yoga center near Kodaikanal, also known as Aeon Centre of Cosmology. I had no idea of the dates of the 2002 Durga Puja until arriving in India and seeing news of the celebration in the airport. Thea's first words to me as we met and hugged in the middle of her horse pasture were, "Like family." On the next day – the victorious 10th

day of the Durga Puja (*Vijaya Dashami*) – Thea told me I had arrived 9 months and 9 days after her birthday.

I would never have guessed growing up in Virginia that I would be concerned with the restoration of the *sanatana dharma* (the universal and eternal truth of Being and Becoming) which has been widely distorted and largely forgotten on Earth. Yet this is where my path has led. This path has unfolded in such a precise and seemingly preplanned way, like an elaborate treasure hunt Sri Aurobindo left for me to follow, continuing to validate its own authenticity and continuing to draw me forward via illuminations or treasures of higher perspective. Each progressive illumination occurs as a step upward into a wider consciousness or wider view wherein I remember something I need to remember or see something I needed to see that then becomes the basis for the next higher illumination whereupon even more of the hidden design is revealed and recovered or brought into the proverbial light of day.

What I want to get across with this short autobiographical account which is in parts stranger than fiction but nonetheless true, is that the vesica piscis vision was not some isolated insight I just happened to have one night. Rather, it is a treasure acquired or won via the real steps and stages of the Vedic journey as reestablished by Sri Aurobindo, the Mother and Thea. This treasure, it seems to me, is also a weapon akin to Indra's lightning bolt (*vajra*), instrumental in dismantling the Ignorance and Falsehood in our world that masquerades as truth and thrives on fragmentation, distortion and mismeasure.

Now I will get on with sharing what the vesica piscis has taught or revealed to me about the *sanatana dharma*. What I have learned has not only greatly deepened my understanding and appreciation of the yoga of Sri Aurobindo, the Mother and Thea, but has also given me an even greater sense of the supramental coordination, cohesion and perfection that lies waiting to be noticed in the smallest details of life. Readers should keep in mind that the revelations and research I present throughout Part One of this book only set the stage for the subsequent full revelation or descent of the vesica piscis's key role in the Vedic victory as presented in Part Two.

CHAPTER SEVEN

Vishnu and the Vesica Piscis

The vast high vault of heaven hast [Vishnu] supported, and fixed earth's eastern pinnacle securely.... Both these worlds [Heaven and Earth], Viṣṇu, hast thou stayed asunder, and firmly fixed the earth with pegs around it.

Rig Veda 7.99.2-3 tr. R.T.H. Griffith

Through all this world strode Viṣṇu; thrice his foot he planted, and the whole Was gathered in his footstep's dust. Viṣṇu, the Guardian, he whom none deceiveth, made three steps; thenceforth Establishing his high decrees.

Rig Veda 1.22.17-18, tr. R.T.H. Griffith

A week or so after my 4:32 a.m. vision of the vesica piscis I began looking for the Sanskrit word for the vesica piscis. I figured that given its central role in the Rishis' gnosis, it had to have a central role and name in the Rig Veda. I found that the word *vesica* is likely related to the Sanskrit root *viṣk* or *vishk,* meaning "to see, perceive". This root, which is clearly related to the English word "vision", is the prefix of *viṣkambha*, meaning among other things, the radius or diameter of a circle. *Viṣkambha* and its close relative *skambha* are equally regarded as a pillar, support, post, fulcrum or axis. Found within the words *skambha* and *viṣkambha* is *ambha*, closely related to the Sanskrit words *ambu* and *ambhas* which refer to water in the Rig Veda. In my mind, just as *skambha* and *viṣkambha* are intimately tied to the radius of the circle, the words *ambu* and *ambhas*, and thus *ambha* of *skambha*, are intimately tied to the waters of the vesica piscis. In the following verse the pillar of the radius is referred to as a peg (*viṣkabdhe*) holding two leaves, wheels or worlds apart. The two leaves, wheels and worlds can easily be seen as the two arcs or circles which form the vesica piscis.

> *As two leaves might be propped apart by means of a peg [viṣkabdhe], or two wheels by means of an axle, so these [two] worlds are propped apart by means of this [viṣkabdhau]*[1].
>
> Jaiminıya-Upanishad-Brahmana, 1.20.3, tr. H. Oertel
> *Journal of the American Oriental Society, Volume 16*, 1896

In the Samudra Manthan mythology this peg or pillar is portrayed as Mount Meru, the axis of the world (axis-mundi) which is saved from sinking in the waters of the ocean by Vishnu in the form of a Turtle. According to this myth, the gods and demons play tug of war with a snake or cord wrapped around Mount Meru causing the "Churning of the Milky Ocean" by which the nectar of immortality (*amrita*) is produced for the gods. *Samudra* is defined as "ocean" and *manthan* as "churning". Another name for Mount Meru is Mount Mandara, which is likely an ancestor of *mandorla* – the Italian word for the vesica piscis, also meaning "almond". The Sanskrit roots of *mandara* seem to suggest a door (*dar*, *dur*) of perception (*man*) or a door of the Soul/Purusha (*Manu*). While researching this etymology and mythology, I found that Mount Meru is sometimes said to be surrounded by four supporting mountains (*viṣkambha-parvata*). I thereupon saw that these four mountains surrounding and supporting Mount Meru are the four arcs of the radius or vesica piscis drawn out from the four cardinal points of the Earth's Solar Year, which give us the full twelve-fold (3 x 4) division of the zodiac.

---

[1] Oertel translated *viṣkabdhau* as "atmosphere" though it seems to be another indicator of the peg/radius or *viṣkambha*/*skambha* of the circle and zodiac.

I saw these four mountains as four conjoined arcs of the radius forming four flower petals extending from the center of the circle. These four petals mark out and encompass the four preservation signs of the zodiac: Taurus ♉, Leo ♌, Scorpio ♏ and Aquarius ♒. Vishnu's flower petals join to establish the four intercardinal points of the zodiac which, together with the cardinal points, mark out the eight-fold division of the circle. These intercardinal points fall 15° into each preservation sign of the zodiac. The eight-fold division of the Earth's year is found in Rig Veda 1.35.8 wherein the solar Purusha Savitar is said to have illumined "the earth's eight points" with his "brightness" (tr. R.T.H. Griffith). It is important to note that whereas the Earth's relationship with the Sun does determine the four cardinal points of the zodiac, it is the ray or radius of the circle that subsequently establishes the four intercardinal points, not the physical Sun. I constructed this four-petalled zodiacal flower for the first time in 2009 for an article I wrote entitled "Vishnu, Sri Aurobindo and the Force of a Secret Unity". I later came to call this design "Vishnu's Flower". At the time of constructing the image, I wasn't at all aware of the four mountains (*viṣkambha parvata*) of the Churning Ocean myth.

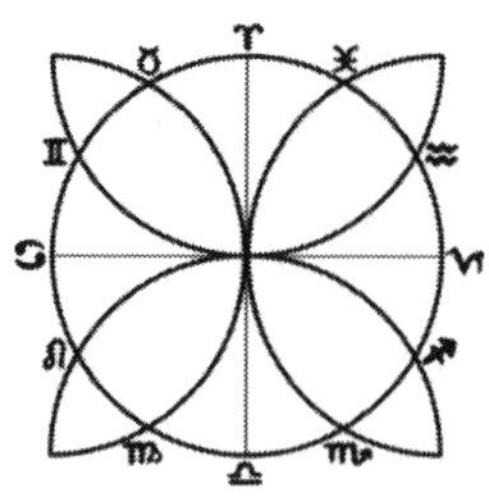

I was using the image solely to highlight how the four spokes of the second tier of the Mother's three-tiered symbol extend out to Vishnu's preservation signs. I had written about this emphasis of Vishnu's preservation signs in the Mother's Symbol in an addendum to an article entitled "Waving the Flag of Cosmic Ignorance in the Face of Sri Aurobindo and the Vedic Tradition of Avatars" which I published on August 15, 2009, the 137th anniversary of Sri Aurobindo's birth. The article was a response to Barindranath Chaki's 2008 assessment that Sri Aurobindo "need not be included" in the series of Vishnu's ten

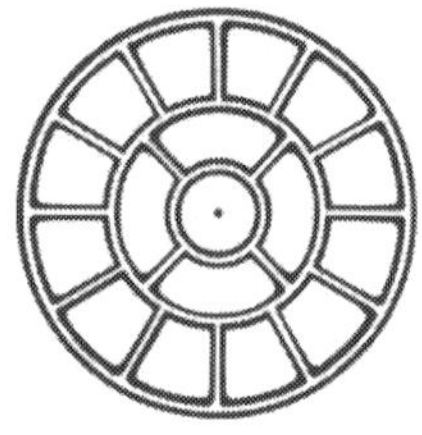

avatars,[1] countering Thea's teachings regarding Sri Aurobindo's place in this avataric lineage. While writing that article I took a late afternoon walk in a neighborhood I didn't usually walk in and came upon a garage sale. As the home owner was putting unsold items back into his garage, I found and purchased a large multi-metal sculpture of Vishnu and his two female consorts, Sridevi and Bhudevi, resting on the serpent Shesha. I later found that this sculpture was made in Tamil Nadu, the seat of Sri Aurobindo's, the Mother's and Thea's yoga. For whatever reason, no one else who scoured through the garage sale that day had any sense of the sculpture's value. I took this Indian treasure as a good omen and as a sign that I was on the right track in my yoga and writing.

Kurma – Vishnu's Second Avatar

Kurma Avatar, below Mount Mandara, with the serpent Vasuki, during Samudra Manthan, ca. 1890 (unknown artist, V&A Museum).

According to the Samudra Manthan mythology, as the Gods and Demons pulled on opposite ends of a cord (or serpent) wrapped around Mt. Meru, this mountain axis began to sink into the ocean. Thereupon the great preserver Vishnu came to the rescue in the form of Kurma (the Turtle) supporting and preserving Mt. Meru

[1] Barindranath Chaki, "Sri Aurobindo need not be in the series of the Ten Avatars", *All Choice* (blog), June 27, 2008.

on his back. As I was writing about the vesica piscis in the context of this mythology, I came to realize through a confluence of events that this fanciful myth of a sacred mountain or axis-mundi being saved by Vishnu in the form of a Turtle only makes real sense in terms of the geometry of the circle and in terms of the zodiac. The confluence of events transpired as follows.

On the day before the 2016 March Equinox I took a picture of a family of wild peacocks that come and go as they please on my family's property. While viewing the picture on the March Equinox I noticed that in addition to three young peacocks, the photograph also featured a square cement tile in the shape of Vishnu's Flower built into our driveway wall by previous owners, as well as two rusty metal rings that my mom (a Pisces) had propped up against the wall, forming a misaligned vesica piscis. It had somehow never registered to me that Vishnu's Flower was embedded in our property in this way before my mother had bought it.

Ten days later, while studying the Samudra Manthan myth, I realized that Vishnu's Flower was the geometric basis of Vishnu's Turtle. I saw that the Turtle's four legs are equivalent to the four petals sticking out of the "shell" of the circle. These four "legs" are formed by four vesicae piscis arced from the four cardinal (creation) points of the zodiac, and they establish the zero points of the remaining eight signs. Thus, it can be seen that in addition to clearly defining the four preservation signs, Kurma's four "legs" are connected to all twelve signs of the zodiac. With this discovery, it became immediately apparent why the Turtle of all animals is an ancient symbol of gnosis, found in Indian, Asian and pre-Colombian Mesoamerican mythology and iconography. It also became apparent why, in Indian mythology, Vishnu chooses the form of a Turtle (Kurma) to fulfill the epic task of preserving the eternal gnosis or *sanatana dharma* from submerging in the dark waters of humanity's unconsciousness.

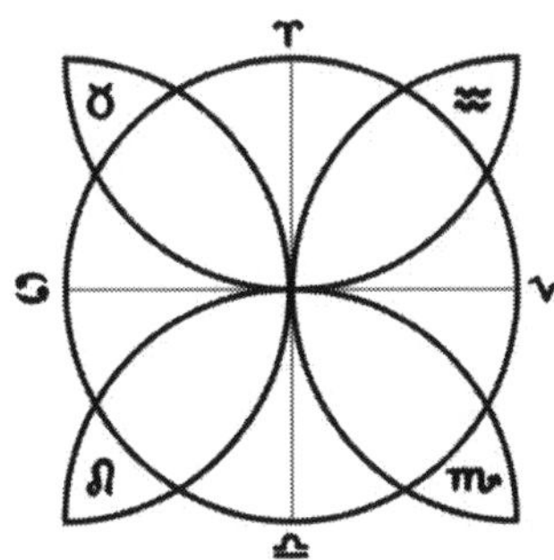

I was impressed by the sequence of events that had staged the recovery of the true sense and context of this ancient myth which has apparently not been understood for ages. I was also impressed that it occurred in conjunction with the March Equinox and that it involved three young peacocks, one of whom was just learning how to show off his beautiful plumage. In India, the peacock symbolizes the supreme victory of the divine Hero-Son.

The connection between Vishnu's dharma-saving Turtle, the vesica piscis and the preservation signs of the zodiac proves that the mythology arising from the eternal dharma or law of the Vedic Rishis is inseparable from the basic laws of geometry, and is furthermore inseparable from the twelve-month zodiac. Via this connection, we can begin to see that the basis of MYTH is MATH. While working on this chapter in March of 2017, I found an old email from a colleague at Skambha:

> *[Thea] says there is so much churning going on in the Earth, and this is necessary; but there is NO AXIS... no churning stick.* ***Vishnu the avatar (kurma) is lost.*** *It's everyone spewing out their thoughts and ideas, etc. etc. ...but nothing to hold it in place.* ***One gets a sinking feeling because the turtle/kurma is not holding it up, supporting the discussion.*** *That is what [Skambha/Aeon Centre of Cosmology] is about....There has to be a reinstatment of the Dharma....*

Patricia Heidt, Director, Aeon Centre of Cosmology
December 14, 2015 [bold emphasis added]

Finding this, I revisited Thea's 1993 article "Churning of the Milky Ocean at the Dawn of Time" which discusses the Turtle (Vishnu) of the Samudra Manthan as a stable or constant base of evolution.

Kurma Avatar (unknown artist, 1849, Wikimedia Commons).

> *[The human structure] is a structure which does not repose upon the Tortoise, which has no stable constant or base to uphold its 'churning', and that therefore begins to age at a certain critical turning point in its evolution and begins to consume itself or feed upon an energy supply which has not made contact with an ever-replenishing source. Expansion is overtaken by contraction in such a situation. They are not Simultaneous directions or mutually supportive....*
>
> *There is no further replenishing source insofar as the Tortoise is missing. More appropriately, we do not possess an axial alignment based on centrality (Mt. Meru). Ours is a binary system by consequence of which the two directions are not mutually supportive but at odds with each other....*
>
> *[No order or] no harmony of elements can come into being without that central Mt. Meru; and for Mt. Meru to serve in this noble act of creating order there must, above all else, come into being the stable constant, the base, the Evolutionary Avatar in the mythic form of the Tortoise.*
>
> Thea, www.aeongroup.com, 1993

The discovery of the underlying geometry of Kurma avatar constitutes clear progress in the progressive recovery of the *sanatana dharma* in our world. It entirely supports Thea's seeing that Vishnu's avatars must be understood in the context of the zodiac. It also demonstrates that it is possible and necessary to see through age-old veils of Ignorance and become conscious of the deeper truth of our world's ancient symbols and lore.

Matsya, Vishnu's First Avatar

Matsya Avatar (unknown artist, 1816, Wikimedia Commons).

Once I saw the geometric basis of Vishnu's second avatar Kurma, it became entirely clear that Vishnu's first avatar Matysa the Fish or Fish-Man is a symbol of the vesica piscis. The Fish is the natural and now-obvious geometric precursor or basis of his subsequent form as the four-legged Turtle. Vishnu as Matsya is said to warn the first Man (Manu) of a great flood, instructing him to preserve seeds and creatures in an ark. *Arka* in Sanskrit means "ray" or "Sun" and is associated with the number 12 (as in the 12 months of the Solar Year). Via Matsya's connection to the vesica piscis and to the zodiac, we can begin to see the geometric, zodiacal and Vedic basis of the lore of Noah's Ark. We can see that this mythological ark, with all its animals, is the zodiac, and its builder is the solar ray or radius. The following image demonstrates the geometry of the two fish and hieroglyph of Pisces.

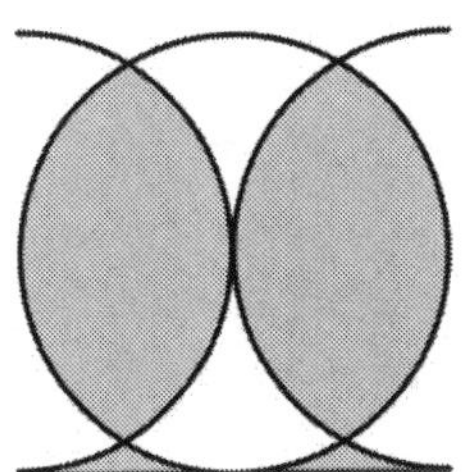

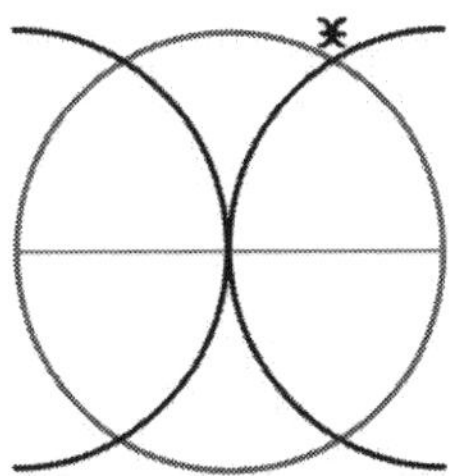

It needs to be pointed out here that *vish* (or *viś*), meaning "all-pervasiveness" or "moving in all directions", is not only the root of *Vishnu* and *vishwa*, it is also found in the word *viśkambha* (*vishkambha*). It also appears to be the root of the English words "fish" as well as "vision".

Vishnu, the Great Pyramid and the Sphinx

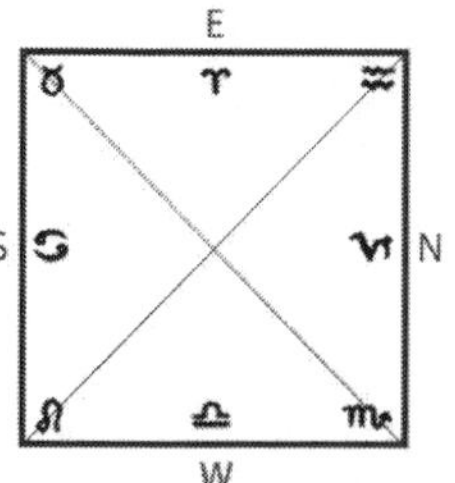

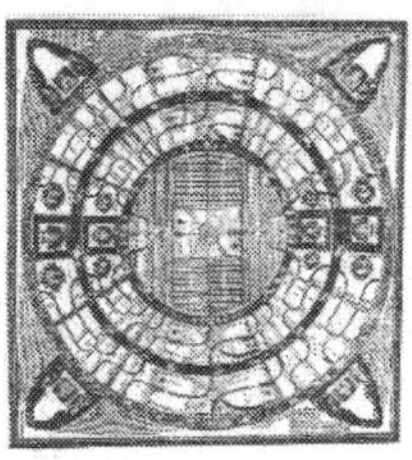

Via the math-born myth of Vishnu's Matsya and Kurma avatars we can come to better appreciate the shape and significance of the world's pyramids. Pyramids serve the same sacred and occult function of Vishnu's dharma-preserving Turtle. Given that the four faces of ancient pyramids are oriented to the Earth's four cardinal directions, their four corners can be seen as equivalent to Vishnu's fixed signs. This eternal connection between the corners of the pyramid and Vishnu's signs became clear to me the moment I saw Vishnu's Flower in the square cement tile in my driveway. I later found an 18th century Rajasthani painting of Mount Meru and its four supporting mountains (as shown right) which mirrors the four-petal design or form of Vishnu's Flower. This painting is a top-down view of Mount Meru. It helps to flush out the connection between Mount Meru and the world's mountain-like pyramids.

The world's pyramids were built like mountains to survive great spans of time as well as great floods. In the course of time some pyramids have been submerged deep under the Earth's waters paralleling the mythology of the sinking of Mount Meru. The triadic face and quadrilateral-base of pyramids are a symbol of the 3 x 4 measure of the Earth's solar year. Thus, pyramids are preservers of the ancient gnosis of the unified field of Time and Space. Regarding the Great Pyramid of Giza, Thea wrote:

> *[C]ertainly the Great Pyramid and the Sphinx were constructed with a mind to preserve the Knowledge for our times.... [They convey] the measure of the year, and the cardinal point alignment that forms a part of this sacred measure.*

Thea, "The Third Way", www.aeongroup.com, June 30, 2004

The Great Pyramid and the Sphinx were monuments of the Age of Leo – both figures forming the colossus at Giza; the Mother's temple-vision is a monument of our Age of Aquarius. Thus, the Sphinx holds the secret of a Time Axis. She stands as a marker, as hands on a cosmic clock indicating a connected process....

...Therefore the Sphinx and the Great Pyramid, together with their other companions on the Egyptian sands, preserve the Eternal Script...to preserve the key to the time factor, to the great moment when the Earth and her evolving species cross a determined and very special threshold of the Precession of the Equinoxes and move into the Age of Aquarius as the Sphinx prophesied many thousands of years ago, that 'highest stride' of Vishnu Trivikrama.

Thea, *Chronicles of the Inner Chamber – Part XI-2*, Feb 2004

The Sphinx is equivalent to Narasimha, Vishnu's fourth avatar the Lion-Man, demonstrating the ancient connection between Vishnu and the pyramid. The Lion-Man is a chimera of the Leo-Aquarius axis of the zodiac. Narasimha, like all avatars of Vishnu, is a preserver of eternal dharma and a destroyer of falsehood. This eternal dharma, truth or law is lost as soon as it is disconnected from the sacred and solar year of the Rishis.

(Left) Sphinx with Pyramid (Daniel Mayer, 2008, Wikimedia Commons; (center) Lord Narasimha, Simhachalam Temple (N. Madhav, 2010, via Wikimedia Commons); (right) Lion-man of the Hohlenstein-Stadel (Ulmer Museum, c. 36,000 BCE).

The antiquity of the Giza Sphinx (or Giza Narasimha) is debated, some positing, including Thea, that the monument was built in our last Age of Leo, which ended approximately 10,000 years ago. Considering the zodiacal ages are measures within a 25,920-year cycle, we must wonder how ancient the gnosis of the zodiac truly is. The 38,000-year-old Lion-Man statue found in a German cave in 1939 (the third image on the previous page) suggests that the zodiac is much more ancient than our modern conception of history has allowed. Thea wrote of the Sphinx as a symbol of the Leo-Aquarius axis in *The Gnostic Circle*, noting that in ancient times the Aquarian half of the Lion-Man chimera was most frequently portrayed as a woman.

Sekhmet (the Lion Goddess), Kom Ombo, Egypt, c. 100 BCE (Wikimedia Commons).

> *[T]he Sphinx of Giza represents the same axis of Leo and Aquarius, or August and February, the birth months of Sri Aurobindo and the Mother*[1] *.... August is naturally the Lion and February the Man, but in fact in ancient times the Sphinx was most often portrayed in its human part as a Woman....*
>
> *The Age of Leo, when the pyramid was built or conceived, was a time of kingly, élite rule. The Age of Aquarius, our present era on the scale of Time, stands directly opposite to the former and it is the time of universal transformation; the movement descends into the masses and there is a general uplifting.*

Thea, *The Gnostic Circle*, p. 278

[1] The Mother was however born in the sign of Pisces, on February 21, 1878. Accordingly, she does not fulfill the Aquarian component of this fixed cosmological axis.

CHAPTER EIGHT

Indus Valley Iconography

Vishnu's Flower design is featured on an ancient Indus Valley jar found in Chanhudaro, Pakistan, as shown in the image to the right. This pattern, together with the triple-petal shawl design and Sun symbol of the Priest King of Mohenjodaro and certain shapes of the ancient Indus Valley script, indicates knowledge of the vesica piscis and of the basic geometry of the circle.

Indus Valley Jar, 2700-2000 BCE (National Museum, New Delhi).

While researching this design I found an article entitled "The Flower of Life Vesica Pisces (Vessel of Fish)" by Dr. Arputharani Sengupta, an Associate Professor of the History of Art at the National Museum Institute in New Delhi. Her article featured the same Indus Valley jar and she wrote, "The Indus Valley painted pottery are literally 'Vessel of the fish' that convey [an] amazing grasp of geometry and alchemy aimed to bring forth renewed life." She also wrote, "The earliest sacred architecture and art is distinguished by the monumental phallic pillar and the Vessel of Fullness called Amrit Kalash[1], the vessel containing the ambrosia of immortality."[2]

One of the symbols found on ancient Harappan seals is a six-spoked wheel: ⊛, which can be seen as a symbol of the measure of the radius, dividing the circle into six even parts. Another

---

[1] *Kalash* means pitcher, jar or pot, equivalent to *kumbha*.

[2] As found in, *Mani-Sushma: Archaeology and Heritage*. A Felicitation Volume in the Honour of Dr. Buddharashmi Mani. (eds.) Vinay Kumar, Brijesh Rawat, New Delhi: B R Publishing Corporation, 2015: Volume 1 pp.103-118.

figure of Indus Valley script looks like a six-spoked vesica piscis: [symbol]. Another figure is a vertical fish-like symbol [symbol] which has many variations. Many Indus Valley symbols seem to speak of or utilize the form of the vesica piscis, including but not limited to [symbol], [symbol], [symbol] and [symbol].

Fish seem to be common symbols on Indus Valley pottery. In the bowl to the right, fish swim around an inner circle containing the Sun symbol. The second circle contains two fish, and the third circle contains three fish. The circle of three fish is especially notable due to the fact that three vesicae piscis measure out the full circumference of the circle. The fish and the Sun symbol show up in other instances of Indus Valley pottery as well.

Indus Valley Bowl (Heritage.gov.pk).

In at least one instance the symbol of the fish or a fish-man is shown in conjunction with a crocodile. This image is intriguing considering the Crocodile is a symbol and name of Capricorn (*Makar* in Sanskrit), the Man is a symbol of Aquarius and the Fish is the name and symbol of Pisces. All these signs comprise the fourth quadrant of the zodiac which is the fourth world (Swar) of the Rishis.

Mohenjodaro Tablet, Crocodile and Fish, New Delhi, ASI.

In my research, I found that others have recognized symbols of the zodiac in Indus Valley script as well. Especially notable in this regard is an article by S. Srinivasan, J. V. M. Joseph and P. Harikumar entitled "Indus script deciphered: the method of semblance at work". The article includes a compelling table of possible equivalences between Indus Valley symbols and symbols of the zodiac. As far as I understand, many Indologists and historians do not yet recognize the connection between the Indus Valley civilization and the Vedic civilization or the connection between the twelve-month zodiac and the twelve-month yajna of the Rig Veda. Thea fully revealed this second connection in her writings. She brought to light the manner by which the circle of the zodiac functions as an all-unifying "eye" of seers, ancient or new. It functions as a lens by which the oneness of creation becomes increasingly apparent despite all appearances. The undivided body of the zodiac is the Sun symbol. It functions as a unit of whole time such as the Earth's day or year, and as a symbol of the whole macrocosmic body of Time.

The Bull in Indus Valley Iconography

The Bull figures prominently in Indus Valley iconography as well as in the Rig Veda and in later Mithraic iconography. Once the connection is seen between this iconic Bull and the Bull of the Vedas (Agni/Indra/Vishnu), then the connection between the Indus Valley civilization and Vedic civilization becomes all the more clear. Symbols of the zodiac (the Vedic yajna) bind the two civilizations together.

Indus Valley Bull Seal (www.ancientindia.co.uk).

In the zodiac, the Bull of Taurus is also known as the Ox, and the symbol of Taurus ♉ is recognized as the Bull's head and horns. These horns can also be seen in terms of the arc of the vesica piscis, wherein the arc is shifted above the circle. It is worth noting that the combined letters of "OX" give us the figure ⊗, in which the indwelling "X" points to the four fixed signs of the zodiac. The Bull's horns can also been seen, like the Turtle's legs, as being formed via conjoining arcs of the radius. In the following image we can see that the two upward reaching horns (the upward petals of Vishnu's Flower) encompass the signs of

Taurus and Aquarius. This same image also demonstrates the geometry of the ram-horn heiroglyph of Aries ♈ and the more bowl-like horns of the Taurus heiroglyph ♉.

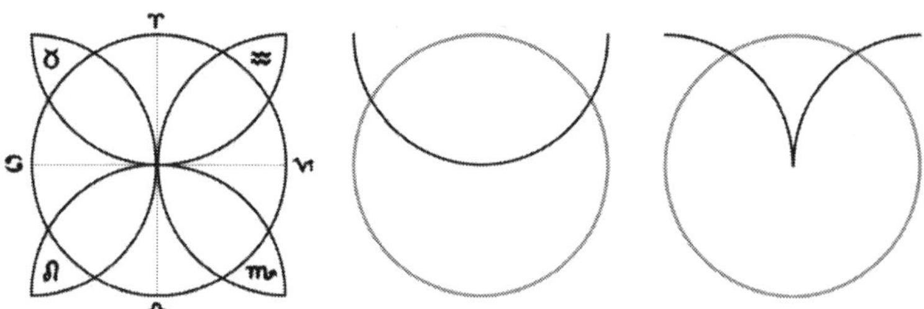

These horns of Aries and Taurus seem to be equally represented in the unusual hat found on the triadic head of the central figure of a seal found in Mohenjodaro dated to circa 2,000-2,300 BCE. This seal is called the Pashupati seal because the horned figure is thought to be Pashupati – the Lord of animals.[1] His chest bears what looks like four descending triangles which can be taken as a symbol of the 3 x 4 structure of the yajna. In the Rig Veda, the lord of animals or king of all creation is Indra the Bull, equivalent to the solar god Pushan – the guardian or herdsman (*paśupā*) of cattle. Pashupati and Pushan are equally figures of the Purusha – the primordial hero or divine male who fertilizes and upholds creation, also known as Agni and as Vishnu.

Pashupati Seal (Wikimedia Commons).

> *Pushan also is especially the knower and thinker and guardian of the shining thoughts of the seer — the keeper of the herds delighting in the thought who is immanent in the whole world and all-pervading fosters all the forms of creative knowledge.*
>
> Sri Aurobindo, *The Secret of the Veda, CWSA, Volume 15*, p. 487

[1] "Lord of animals" is a fit name for the radius of the Zodiac – the circle of life.

For, Agni, like a herdsman [paśupā], thou by thine own might rulest o'er all that is in heaven and on the earth....

Rig Veda 1.144.7, tr. R.T.H. Griffith

He, Pusan Viṣṇu, poured forth three great vessels to him, the juice that cheers, that slaughters Vṛtra.

Rig Veda 6.17.11, tr. R.T.H. Griffith

The connection between Pushan and Vishnu and the vesica piscis is clear in this last verse wherein the three great vessels are no doubt the three vesicae piscis that divide the circle into three. In *The Secret of the Veda*, Sri Aurobindo wrote that the Purusha is the divine soul in creation, described in Rig Veda 4.58 as a four-horned man-bull.[1] In Rig Veda 10.90, he is the Lord of Immortality.

From [Purusha – the Lord of Immortality] Virāj was born; again Puruṣa from Virāj was born. As soon as he was born he spread eastward and westward o'er the earth.

Rig Veda 10.90.5, tr. R.T.H. Griffith

In Griffith's translation of this verse, Virāj appears to be a figure of the Purusha (masculine), akin to the Hero-Son of the sacrificial year. Panikkar translated Virāj in this same verse as the "Shining One". Elsewhere Virāj appears as the universal or Cosmic Mother (Cow). In Yajur Veda 5.6.7, Virāj is the twelve-month year. In Atharva Veda 8.10, Virāj appears to be a figure of the vesica piscis, from which the radius – the "lord" and herder of all the creatures of the zodiac – is born. Indra the Bull is said to mark "all living creatures",[2] indicative of the radius which marks out the twelve signs of the zodiac. Lauding this same pillar of gnosis, the Rishis reported that "all creatures in existence rest" upon

[1] Sri Aurobindo, *The Secret of the Veda, CWSA, Volume 15*, pp. 307-08.

[2] Rig Veda 10.89.3, tr. R.T.H. Griffith.

Agni's head[1] and that Agni knows "by [his] birth, all creatures".[2] One Indus Valley seal features a triple-headed bull which can be seen as a depiction of Agni, the triple-headed hero of the Rig Veda. His triadic nature we now know is a reflection of the law of the radius and its triadic division of the circle and year. This Bull or herdsman is also Vishnu, the preserver of the zodiac whose three steps (*trivikrama*) through the zodiac are recorded in Rig Veda 1.154.

> *Let our strength and our thought go forward to Vishnu the all-pervading, the wide-moving Bull whose dwelling-place is on the mountain, he who being One has measured all this long and far-extending seat of our self-accomplishing by only three of his strides.*
>
> *[His] three steps are full of the honey-wine and they perish not but have ecstasy by the self-harmony of their nature; yea, he being One holds the triple principle and earth and heaven also, even all the worlds.*
>
> Rig Veda 1.154.3-4, tr. Sri Aurobindo,
> *The Secret of the Veda, CWSA, Volume 15*, pp. 343-44

Regarding these three steps, Thea wrote:

> *A simple perusal of the praises to Vishnu (RV, I, 154) will prove that the so-called Western Zodiac was not only fully known in Vedic times but that it was a fundamental part of the culture (PNB, 1981). Vishnu's famous* ***three*** *strides (to measure the universe) cannot be more revealing. The first 'step' is* ***like a lion*** *(Leo), according to the Veda; the second is* ***a bull*** *(Taurus); the third, and most revealing of all, is* ***the Friend****. This is the same Aquarius of Agastya's birth, which is also known as the sign of the Friend. More conclusively, they are given in their correct backward moving order,[3] and are Vishnu's own zodiacal domains because*

---

[1] Rig Veda 6.7.6, tr. R.T.H. Griffith.

[2] Rig Veda 3.26.7, tr. R.T.H. Griffith.

[3] Regarding this backward order Thea wrote: "[A]lways it is the 'one circle' that provides the framework for all computation....[T]he Rishi has Vishnu 'measuring

> *of their quality of PRESERVATION ('Fixed' in zodiacal terminology, stable, balancing). This is just one among many explicit references in the Rigveda to the tropical zodiac with the same symbols still in use throughout the world, except in India.*
>
> Thea, "Cosmology in Rigveda – the third premise", *The Hindu*, July 9, 2002

A noteable display of the connection between the Bull and the fixed signs of the zodiac is found in the Indus Valley Bison Seal. On the front side of this seal is a bison bull which can be seen as a symbol-figure of Vishnu, and on the backside is Vishnu's swastika, moving in a counter-clockwise direction, the direction the Sun moves through the zodiac or Solar Year.

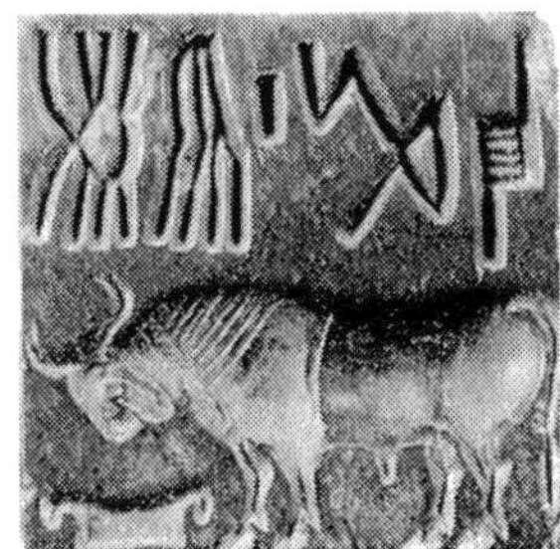

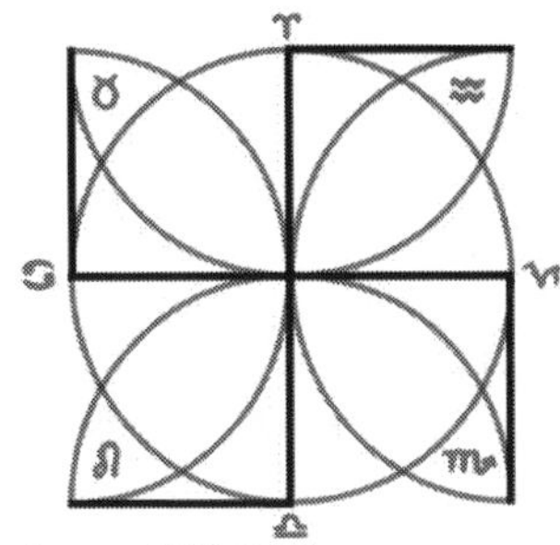

(Left) Bison Seal (Mohenjodaro, c. 2500 BCE); (right) Swastika on Vishnu's Flower.

The Indus Valley civilization is commonly considered to have spanned from 3000 to 1500 BCE. According to Thea, the Age of Taurus the Bull (4554-2394 BCE) was the central age of the last quarter (6714-234 BCE) of the Earth's last precessional cycle.[1] This Age of the Bull encompassed the time span of the Indus Valley civilization and it is fitting that the Bull would be a prominent symbol therein.

---

the universe' in a BACKWARD, or clockwise motion through the zodiac, unlike the annual rotation which is counter-clockwise. The verses are more than specific: each 'step' touches one of the Vishnu signs of Preservation in the correct order: first Lion (Leo), next Bull (Taurus), then Friend (Aquarius) in the 'highest reaches'" (*Secrets of the Earth*, 2009, p. 34).

[1] Thea's seeing of the correct timing of the precessional Ages will be further discussed in Part One, Chapter 13.

Both the Bull and the swastika are well-known symbols of Vishnu in India. The swastika is said to signify good luck and auspiciousness. It is also known as a solar symbol. In truth it is a symbol of the Earth's Solar or Tropical (Sayana) Year. The good-luck and auspiciousness of this symbol remains in the realm of wishful thinking and superstition as long as it is seperated from its Vedic or gnostic context, wherein the central cross is the cardinal axis of the Earth's Solar Year and the outer arms stretch to the corners of Vishnu's preservation signs.[1] The Sanskrit roots of *swastika* are *sva* meaning "one's own" and *stika* from *stigha*, meaning "to step". The words "stigma" and "stigmata" come from this same root. *Ma* and *mata* mean "measure", "matter" and "mother". Properly understood these are the steps, marks or measures of the radius as applied to the Solar Year.

Christianity has thoroughly lost and distorted the true meaning of Vishnu's cross, which is through and through a mathematical, zodiacal and Vedic symbol. It is a symbol of the hero-priest of the Rishis' sacrificial year, a symbol of the Divine Son who, via his birth or revelation in the course of Time, establishes the Divine Law (and with it the Life Divine) for humanity – a victory that the historical figure of Christ did not accomplish via his life or his death.

The swastika is known in India as a symbol of Vishnu's wheel or Sudarshana Chakra. It is a symbol of eternal truth and immortality. It is a symbol of the Divine Maya or measure of the Rishis' unified field of Time and Space. This sacred cross symbolizes the crucifiction of God incarnate only so long as its true meaning and context is "crucified", buried, distorted or taken out of context as it has been for millennia throughout the world. Hitler's use of this symbol represents the extreme degree to which

---

[1] The swastika is depicted both with the arms "spinning" in clockwise and counter-clockwise directions. Thea wrote that the counter-clockwise direction of the swastika symbolizes evolution and clockwise symbolizes involution (*The New Way, Volumes 1&2, p. 470*). The counter-clockwise direction of the zodiac is the normal flow of months in the Solar Year. As mentioned on the previous page, the Precession of the Equinoxes moves clockwise (backward) through the zodiac.

the true luck or light of this symbol has been veiled and usurped by forces of Ignorance on our planet.

One notable Indus Valley seal that I came across depicts a chimera of perhaps five different animals.[1] It has the head of a man, the horns, midsection and perhaps neck of a bull, the hind quarters of a lion or tiger, the trunk of an elephant, and the tail of a snake. This chimera includes three of Vishnu's creatures – the Man, the Bull and the Lion, as well as other animals associated with Agni in the Rig Veda, including the elephant and the snake. This iconography seems to be a clear portrayal of the multi-faceted hero of the Rig Veda. In my mind, all ancient animal-chimeras are figures of the zodiac (i.e. of the Rishis' sacrificial year) but the Bull-Man-Lion combination in particular is a symbol of the fixed signs of the zodiac.

As the geometric keys of the Sun symbol, radius and the vesica piscis prove Vishnu's inseparability from the zodiac, it should become increasingly difficult for anyone to hold on to the idea that the script and iconography of the Indus Valley civilization are disconnected from the Rig Veda. It should also become increasingly difficult to hold onto the false notion held across the world that the zodiac was imported into India via Babylonia.

[1] See "Harappan Chimaeras as 'Symbolic Hypertexts'. Some Thoughts on Plato, Chimaera and the Indus Civilization", by Dennys Frenez & Massimo Vidale, *South Asian Studies, 28:2*, 2012, pp. 111, 115.

CHAPTER NINE

The Many Names of the One Purusha

The Rig Veda itself, indeed, asserts that the gods are only different names and expressions of one universal Being who in His own reality transcends the universe; but from the language of the hymns we are compelled to perceive in the gods not only different names, but also different forms, powers and personalities of the one Deva.

Sri Aurobindo, *The Secret of the Veda, CWSA, Volume 15*, p. 32

[The one Deva] can be realised through any of his names and aspects….

Sri Aurobindo, *The Secret of the Veda, CWSA, Volume 15*, p. 353

[H]ow keep it in the mind of the hearer that all these gods are personalities of the one universal Deva? The names of the gods in their very meaning recall that they are only epithets, significant names, descriptions, not personal appellations. Mitra is the Deva as the Lord of love and harmony, Bhaga as the Lord of enjoyment, Surya as the Lord of illumination, Varuna as the all-pervading Vastness and purity of the Divine supporting and perfecting the world. "The Existent is One," says the Rishi Dirghatamas, "but the sages express It variously; they say Indra, Varuna, Mitra, Agni; they call It Agni, Yama, Matarishwan."

Sri Aurobindo, *The Secret of the Veda, CWSA, Volume 15*, p. 56

In *The Secret of the Veda* Sri Aurobindo laid out many of the names the Rishis used to speak of the divine Purusha. He also wrote that we come to "possess the truth of the one universal Deva" with the conquest or entry into the fourth world of Swar which he identified as "the aim of the sacrifice and the great work accomplished by the Angiras Rishis". The following excerpts help to flush out Sri Aurobindo's conception of this One Deva.

> *The Deva or Godhead is both the original cause and the final result. Divine Existent, builder of the worlds, lord and begetter of all things, Male and Female, Being and Consciousness, Father and Mother of the Worlds and their inhabitants, he is also their Son and ours: for he is the Divine Child born into the Worlds who manifests himself in the growth of the creature. He is Rudra and Vishnu, Prajapati and Hiranyagarbha, Surya, Agni, Indra, Vayu, Soma, Brihaspati, — Varuna and Mitra and Bhaga and Aryaman, all the gods. He is the wise, mighty and liberating Son born from our works and our sacrifice, the Hero in our warfare and Seer of our knowledge, the White Steed in the front of our days who gallops towards the upper Ocean. The soul of man soars as the Bird, the Hansa, past the shining firmaments of physical and mental consciousness, climbs as the traveller and fighter beyond earth of body and heaven of mind by the ascending path of the Truth to find this Godhead waiting for us, leaning down to us from the secrecy of the highest supreme where it is seated in the triple divine Principle and the source of the Beatitude. The Deva is indeed, whether attracting and exalted there or here helpful to us in the person of the greater Gods, always the Friend and Lover of man, the pastoral Master of the Herds who gives us the sweet milk and the clarified butter from the udder of the shining Cow of the infinitude. He is the source and outpourer of the ambrosial Wine of divine delight and we drink it drawn from the sevenfold waters of existence or pressed out from the luminous plant on the hill of being and uplifted by its raptures we become immortal. Such are some of the images of this ancient mystic adoration.*
>
> Sri Aurobindo, *The Secret of the Veda, CWSA, Volume 15*, p. 371

> *[The foundation of Sama Ananda] is the Atmajnana or Brahmajnana by which we perceive the whole universe as a perception of*

> *one Being that manifests itself in multitudinous forms and activities. This One is therefore the one Self of all beings, my Self as well as the self of all others, friend and enemy, saint and sinner, man, bird and beast, tree & stone, and all things in the manifestation are the forms and activities of my Self. Moreover, this Self is again the Lord of the Cosmos, the Purushottama, the divine Vishnu, Shiva or Krishna, of whom every individual soul is a conscious centre, aware of its unity with Him in being and also of its difference in the universe; and the manifestation is a Lila or play of the Lord who is in His being all delight; the play, too, therefore, is not only a play of Existence and Consciousness, but also a play of delight. It is the dualities born of ego-sense in the heart, mind & body which creates grief and pain. We have to unite ourselves with this Self, Lord & One & with all things in Him, viewing them as our self, in order to get rid of pain & enjoy the divine Ananda.... The soul accepts all things as the play of the all-Blissful Lord, the Will of the supreme self and Ishwara. It accepts action also & the results of action, without being attached to them. But, though not attached, it must learn to take delight in all things even as the Lord takes delight in them.*
>
> Sri Aurobindo, *Record of Yoga, CWSA, Volume 10-11*, pp. 28-29

Another name of the one Deva or Purusha in the Rig Veda is Manu, the primordial man. The English words "man", "manifest" and "manifestation" have descended from this figure who is depticted as the "representative man and father of the human race…regarded in the [Rig Veda] as the first to have instituted sacrifices and religious ceremonies…associated with the Rishis".[1] The name Manu can be broken down into the Sanskrit roots *ma* "to measure" or "mark out", and *nu* meaning "time" and "ship" or "vessel".[2] It must be understood that the ship or vessel of Time that Manu measures and marks out is the 360° zodiac or yajna. Manu's ages are referred to as *Manu-vantara* or *Manvantara*. In the *Brahma-Vaivarta Purana, Prakriti Khanda*

---

[1] *Cologne Digital Sanskrit Lexicon.*

[2] Ibid.

an Age of Indra is said to be equivalent to one Manvantara.[1] In my mind, this period is entirely equivalent to what Thea calls Vishnu's "Manifestations" which will be discussed in Chapter 13. In the following verses of the Rig Veda, Manu is equivalent to the Sun, the Father, the Sage, the Rishi and to Indra who demolishes the villain's forts or caves of Ignorance. The son of Manu is the Divine Purusha born victorious in the world, equivalent to Vishnu's final avatar, the victorious hero Kalki.

> *I was aforetime Manu, I was Sūrya: I am the sage Kakṣīvān, holy singer....I am the sapient Uśanā behold me. I have bestowed the earth upon the Ārya, and rain upon the man who brings oblation. I guided forth the loudly-roaring waters, and the Gods moved according to my pleasure. In the wild joy of Soma I demolished Śambara's forts, ninety-and-nine, together....*
>
> Rig Veda 4.26.1-3, R.T.H. Griffith

> *Ye raised the Sun to heaven by everlasting Law, and spread broad earth, the Mother, out on every side.... Welcome the son of Manu, ye who are most wise.*
>
> Rig Veda 10.62.3, R.T.H. Griffith

> *Over this earth with mighty step strode Vishnu, ready to give it for a home to Manu.*
>
> Rig Veda 10.62.3, R.T.H. Griffith

> *In the conscious individual Prakriti turns back to perceive Purusha, World seeks after Self; God having entirely become Nature, Nature seeks to become progressively God....[M]an cannot rest permanently until he reaches some highest good. He is the greatest of living beings because he is the most discontented, because he feels most the pressure of limitations....To the Life-Spirit, therefore, the individual in whom its potentialities centre is pre-eminently Man, the Purusha. It is the Son of Man who is supremely capable of incarnating God. This Man is the Manu, the*

[1] *Brahma-Vaivarta Purana, Prakriti Khanda*, 7.72-75.

thinker, the Manomaya Purusha, mental person or soul in mind of the ancient sages.

Sri Aurobindo, *The Life Divine, CWSA, Volume 21-22*, pp. 50-51

Another name for this incarnating Purusha is *Janusha Purohit*, an epitaph of Agni indicating that he is the priest or lord of the sacrifice from birth. The Sanskrit root *ja* simultaneously means "father", "victorious" and "birth", and *janus* means "birth", "creation" and "descent",[1] from which are derived the English words "gene", "genus" and "generate", and the names "Jan" and "John", as well as the name of the month "January". One of many Indian myths which encode the victory of the Purusha features the Rishi Jahnu releasing the river Ganges from his ear,[2] and with it the souls of the ancestors of Bhagiratha. Bhagiratha is etymologically related to *Bhaga*, an epitaph of the Hero-Purusha which Sri Aurobindo has called the "Lord of enjoyment". *Ratha* in the Rig Veda is the chariot or vehicle of the hero. In later Indian sacred texts, *ratha* seems to indicate the hero or warrior himself. Bhaga is another name of the divine male, skambha, lingam or radius which fills, delights and fertilizes creation. His *ratha* or vehicle of victory is the vesica piscis or circle. In the verse below this hero or ray of God (ray-*deus*) is Agni.

Up springs the imperishable flame, the flame of the Refulgent One Most bright, with glowing jaws[3]*.... [Agni's] fair form [is kind] as a friend to men who keep the holy Law. Him, true to Law, who perfecteth the sacrifice....*

Rig Veda 8.23.4,8-9, tr. R.T.H. Griffith

Vishnu is another name of this hero of the sacrificial year (zodiac) and in turn he himself is known to have a thousand epitaphs as put forth in the *Vishnu Sahasranama*.

---

[1] All definitions are from *Cologne Digital Sanskrit Lexicon*.

[2] It appears to me that Jahnu's ear in this myth is a symbol of the vesica piscis.

[3] Agni's "glowing jaws" are also a symbol of the vesica piscis.

> *Vishnu maintains [his three strides] unfailingly, preserves them imperishably. He is the One, he alone is, the sole-existing Godhead, and he holds in his being the triple divine principle to which we attain in the world of bliss....*
>
> Sri Aurobindo, *The Secret of the Veda, CWSA, Volume 15*, p. 349

Four of the names of Vishnu the Preserver – and thus of the One Deva – are the figures of the preservation signs of the zodiac: the Bull, Lion, Eagle and Friend. All except the Eagle are characters of Rig Veda 1.154 as translated by Sri Aurobindo. The fourth figure of the Eagle (of Scorpio) shows up in Rig Veda 1.164 as Garutman, mentioned as one of the many names of the Purusha followed by measurements of the twelve-month year.[1]

> *They call him Indra, Mitra, Varuṇa, Agni, and he is heavenly nobly-winged Garutmān. To what is One, sages give many a title they call it Agni, Yama, Mātariśvan. Dark the descent: the birds are golden-coloured; up to the heaven they fly robed in the waters. Again descend they from the seat of Order, and all the earth is moistened with their fatness. Twelve are the fellies, and the wheel is single; three are the naves. What man hath understood it? Therein are set together spokes three hundred and sixty, which in nowise can be loosened.*
>
> Rig Veda 1.164.46-48, tr. R.T.H. Griffith

Garutman eventually came to be known as Vishnu's vehicle Garuda (the Eagle), also called *Suparna*, meaning "golden-winged". *Suparna* is one of Vishnu's thousand names listed in the *Vishnu Sahasranama*. This golden or celestial bird or bird-man is refered to in Rig Veda 7.15 as the guardian "Hawk of Heaven"

[1] The name of the Aztec Sun Stone (Calendar) is *Cuauhxicalli*, the Eagle's Bowl (or vessel).

who "flames in front of the sacrifice".[1] This celestial bird is another symbol of the Divine Purusha and radius whose golden wings are equivalent to the arcs of the vesica piscis.

The Purusha, His Wife, His Mothers and His Virgin Birth

> *I know that Primordial Man, golden as the sun, beyond darkness. Knowing him a man even now becomes immortal. This is the way to attain him; there is no other.*
>
> Yajur Veda 31.18, tr. Raimundo Panikkar, *The Vedic Experience*, p. 759

R.T.H. Griffith translates this same verse and the one after it as:

> *I know this mighty Purusha whose colour is like the Sun, beyond the reach of darkness. He only who knows him leaves Death behind him. There is no path save this alone to travel.*
>
> *In the womb moves Prajâpati: he, never becoming born, is born in sundry figures. The wise discern the womb from which he springeth.*

The author of this hymn conveys that there is no other way, path or means to attain the Immortal Purusha (Soul) other than via his own womb of Time and Space – the sacred yajna. The Divine Purusha is immanent within and born out of this sacred womb. The Rishis understood that there is no full gnosis or experience of this Divine Soul as separate from his Matrix. In this hymn Purusha and Prajapati are two names of the same One Deva, equivalent to the radius whose womb is the circle. Just as the radius marks out, upholds and preserves the eternal law of this womb of creation, so does the Divine Purusha of the Rig Veda mark out, uphold, preserve, protect and guard its own field and womb of creation. In this sense, the radius and circumference of the circle are equivalent to the pairing of Purusha and Prakriti, the archetypal Father and Mother or Husband and Wife. This pair

---

[1] Rig Veda 7.15, tr. Sri Aurobindo, *Hymns to the Mystic Fire, CWSA, Volume 16*, pp. 323-25.

represents the unity of Spirit and Matter, sometimes in the Veda referered to as the divine parents Heaven and Earth. Often the Rishis expanded this divine pair to a divine trinity, wherein the Purusha is described as having two wives or mothers.[1] Sri Aurobindo discussed this briefly in *The Secret of the Veda*.

> *The One was recognized as the basis and continent; in this One there were the two principles divine and human, mortal and immortal. The dual number is also otherwise applied in the two principles, Heaven and Earth, Mind and Body, Soul and Nature, who are regarded as the father and mother of all beings. It is significant, however, that Heaven and Earth, when they symbolise two forms of natural energy, the mental and the physical consciousness, are no longer the father and mother, but the two mothers.*
>
> Sri Aurobindo, *The Secret of the Veda, CWSA, Volume 15*, p. 98

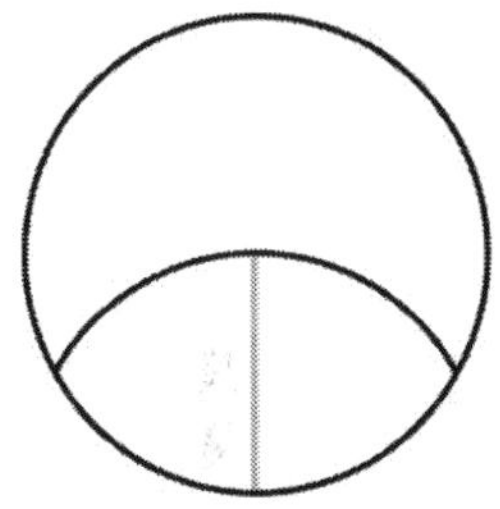

These dual mothers of the Soul are the dual matrices of the Cosmos and the Earth. They are the macrocosm and the microcosm. They are also known as the Divine Mother and Daughter. These two mothers, referred to in the Rig Veda as the *Rodasi,* are the vessels by which the Father or Transcendent Divine Purusha, is born Immanent in material creation. In terms of geometry these two mothers or vessels are the circle and the vesica piscis.

> *[Agni] cleaves to the teat in the lap of the two secret ones in…the hidden seat of the being.…*
>
> *The two mothers in whom is the Truth, in whom is the mage-wisdom, formed him and brought to birth like an infant child, they have put him firm in his place and make him grow. Men found in*

[1] In the lore of Vishnu these two wives or mothers are Sridevi and Bhudevi.

him the navel-centre of all that is moving and stable and they weave by the mind the weft of the seer.

Him well-born the routes of the Truth[1] *and its ancient impulsions close companion for the plenitude. Heaven and earth [the Rodasi] give lodging to him [who is their inhabitant]*[2]*, they make him grow by the lights and foods of their sweetnesses.*

Rig Veda 10.5.1, 3-4, tr. Sri Aurobindo,
Hymns to Mystic Fire, CWSA, Volume 16, p. 395

[In] the Cow's home was born the Great Eternal....Child of two Mothers, he wanders unrestrained, the single youngling.... Where the two Cows, the Mother and the Daughter, meet and give suck yielding their lordly nectar, I praise them at the seat of law eternal. Great is the Gods' supreme and sole dominion.

Rig Veda 3.55.1, 6, 12, tr. R.T.H. Griffith

He bore the child of the Father and of him that begot him.... In this pure Male both these powers... (Earth and Heaven) have their common lord and lover; do thou guard them both.

Rig Veda 3.1.10, tr. Sri Aurobindo,
The Secret of the Veda, CWSA, Volume 15, p. 116

So mid these tribes [Agni] rests, the friendly envoy, borne on two paths, refulgent Lord of fuel. When, ***like a line, the Babe springs up erectly****, his Mother straight hath borne him strong to bless us.*

Rig Veda 10.61.15, tr. R.T.H. Griffith [bold emphasis added]

Which of you has awakened to the knowledge of this secret thing, that it is the Child who gives birth to his own mothers by the right workings of the law of his nature? Born in the womb of many

---

[1] I believe this implies that Agni (i.e. the radius) bears forth "the routes of the Truth"; or possibly that Agni is well-born *within* his own "routes of Truth" (i.e. within the vesica piscis).

[2] Sri Aurobindo wrote here, "to him whose dwelling is above them", with the note, "Or, as their inhabitant".

> *waters, he comes forth from their lap a vast Seer, possessed of the law of his being.*
>
> Rig Veda 1.95.4, tr. Sri Aurobindo, *Hymns to the Mystic Fire, CWSA, Volume 16*, p. 146

Sometimes this Hero-Child is also said to have three, seven or ten mothers. The three mothers are likely a reference to the three vesicae piscis which create Agni's fire trine in the circle; and the ten mothers correspond to the ten months of the zodiac which bear Agni forth in the sacred year.

> *[N]ew-born [Agni] stands up high like an arrow-shaft well-planted and firm and shows by his light the herds....*
>
> *The twice five sisters who dwell together have given birth to the Fire in the human peoples, the waker in the dawn, like a tusk of flame, brilliant and fair of face, like a sharp axe.*
>
> Rig Veda 4.6.3,8, tr. Sri Aurobindo, *Hymns to the Mystic Fire, CWSA, Volume 16*, pp. 235-36

> *The husband enters the wife.*
> *Becoming an embryo he enters the mother.*
> *In her become a new man again,*
> *He is born in the tenth month.*
> *A wife is called wife,*
> *Because in her he is born again....*
>
> *Aitareya Brahmana* 7.13, tr. Patrick Olivelle, *The Saṃnyāsa Upaniṣads*, Oxford Press (1992), pp. 26, 50

Agni's seven mothers will be discussed later on, but what I would like to convey here is that, in a sense, Agni has infinite Mothers. He is the hidden law of all individual form (all microcosms), as well as the hidden law of the macrocosmic Whole. Thus Agni is described as "One who has spread wide within the infinite [Mother]".[1] As already indicated, the Purusha does not stay

[1] Rig Veda 4.1.7, tr. Sri Aurobindo, *Hymns to the Mystic Fire*, Lotus Light Publications, 1996, p. 163. Sri Aurobindo's translation of the same verse in *CWSA,*

transcendent, hidden, unborn in material creation. It is born forth, though not via the usual methods of human procreation. The Purusha inherently dwells and gestates or "increases" in the womb of material creation in the course of evolution, and is said to be self-born. Along these same lines, in Rig Veda 4.7 we find the origin of the Virgin Birth mythology of the Divine Child:

> *[Agni, the] swift messenger of the illumining Sun who comes to all the seeing people; men hold him as the ray of intuition and he shines as the Bhrigu-flame-seer for each being....*
>
> *Him in the many mothers linked together, wide-spread and unapproached in the forest, abiding in the secret Cave and rich with many lights, full of knowledge or moving to some unknown goal....*
>
> *He journeys knowing the embassies of the pilgrim-sacrifice between both the firmaments [Heaven and Earth], utterly awakened to knowledge. A messenger, the Ancient of days, ever widening, ever greater in knowledge, thou travellest the mounting slopes of heaven....*
>
> *Black is the path of thy shining, thy light goes in front, a journeying ray, the one supreme of all thy bodies;* ***when one unimpregnated bears thee as the child of her womb****, in the sudden moment of thy birth thou art already the messenger.*

Rig Veda 4.7.4, 6, 8-9, tr. Sri Aurobindo, *Hymns to the Mystic Fire, CWSA, Volume 16*, pp. 238-39 [bold emphasis added]

The Victorious Purusha

The Stallion or male Horse is a recurring symbol of the victorious Divine Purusha in the Rig Veda.

> *From [Agni] is born the steed of swiftness that carries the plenitude, that has the force of Truth, that makes the great approach, that has the vastness; from thee is the treasure sent by*

Volume 16 is: "within in the infinite he is spread wide everywhere and has come to us pure and brilliant and noble, shining in his beauty" (p. 215).

the gods that creates the bliss, from thee the rapid speeding war-horse, O Fire.

Rig Veda 4.11.4, tr. Sri Aurobindo,
Hymns to the Mystic Fire, CWSA, Volume 16, p. 245

He who grasps the head of the father and mother they set within in the pilgrim-sacrifice, a sea from the Sun-world; in his path are the shining rays that are the foundations of the Horse of Power and they accept embodiment in the native seat of the Truth.

Rig Veda 10.8.3, tr. Sri Aurobindo,
Hymns to the Mystic Fire, CWSA, Volume 16, p. 400

Six-headed Murugan and his consorts, by Ravi Varma (Wikimedia Commons).

One the grandest symbols of the Purusha is the Peacock, whose colorful feathers fan out like radii in an extraordinary circular array. In India the Peacock is a symbol of spiritual victory though this glorious bird does not seem to be mentioned in the Rig Veda. We do however find mention of 21 or "thrice-seven" (9 + 12) peahens who along with the Sun and the Hero-Rishi of Rig Veda 1.191, defeat the lowly Scorpion, neutralizing or purifying his deadly poison. These thrice-seven peahens are entirely equivalent to the 21 seats of the Divine Mother whose victorious Son is the Hero of the Sacrifice. In Indian iconography this Hero-Son or Hero-Purusha by whatever name (Agni, Kartikeya, Skanda, Murugan, Kumara, Subrahmanya, etc.) is commonly depicted riding a peacock, poised as the conqueror of a poisonous serpent (akin to the poisonous Scorpion). The Horse-Hero of the Rig Veda, and of subsequent Indian mythology, is equally considerd a conqueror or slayer of the serpent.

The symbols of the Peacock and the victorious War-Horse equally convey the victory of the Divine Purusha or Soul in material creation. It is the point in the evolutionary journey or *yajna* wherein the One or Universal Deva is borne forth, emmerging from its hidden status within the womb of creation. The Divine Purusha or Soul is thereupon victorious over the poisonous, toxic, divisive or all-diminishing mental-egoic consciousness. It is a victory for all of creation. In terms of the myth of the *Dasavatara* or Ten Avatars of Vishnu, this victory is the completed 9-fold descent culminating in the birth of Vishnu's final avatar, the 10th who is the Immortal One. It is the victory of the Transcendent Father born Immanent in creation. However different religions portray this divine victory, it all boils down to the same evolutionary shift, wherein the Immortal Purusha and its eternal law and divine measure are reestablished on Earth.

Without the reemergence of this law and measure, humans would long remain under the dark cloud of age-old distortions and gross misunderstandings regarding the immortal hero of the Rig Veda. Just as these distortions and misunderstandings of the Divine Purusha have inevitably generated and continue to bear forth disastrous fragmentation, antipathy and violence in our world, reestablishing this Sun or Son of eternal truth will inevitably generate and bear forth unity and harmony.

CHAPTER TEN

The Golden Reed and Golden Lion

Who out of many, tell me, is that Skambha. To whom the Deities with hands, with feet, and voice, and ear, and eye. Present unmeasured tribute in the measured hall of sacrifice?

Darkness is chased away from him: he is exempt from all distress. In him are all the lights, the three abiding in Prajāpati.

He verily who knows the Reed of Gold that stands amid the flood, is the mysterious Lord of Life....

Atharva Veda 10.7.39-41, tr. R.T.H. Griffith

Skambha set fast these two, the earth and heaven, Skambha maintained the ample air between them. Skambha established the six spacious regions: this whole world Skambha entered and pervaded.

Atharva Veda 10.7.35, tr. R.T.H. Griffith

The churning stick or Viṣkambha of Mt. Meru is more commonly called Skambha, referred to in the Atharva Veda as a Golden Reed (*hiraṇyáyo vetasó*) as well as the Lord of Life. This Golden Reed is also a figure of Rig Veda 4.58, mentioned in conjunction with the "triple shape the Gods discovered laid down within the Cow, concealed by Paṇis" (tr. R.T.H. Griffith). Skambha, like Viṣkambha, is considered a world axis (*axis mundi*), simultaneously described as upholding Heaven and Earth *and* keeping them apart in the mid-space, air or sky. Heaven, Earth and this mid-space are referred to as "three

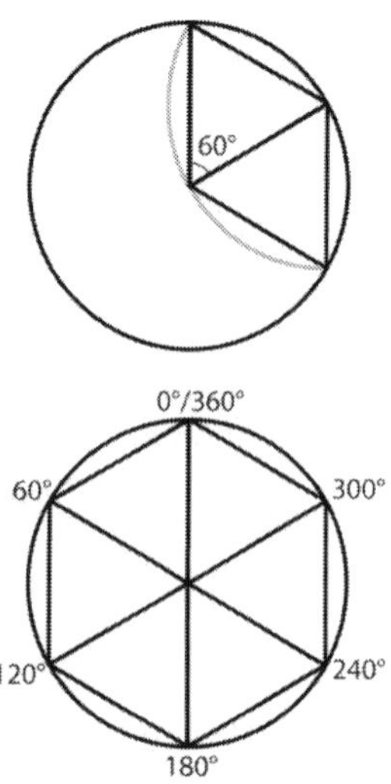

worlds". These three worlds are lauded at the beginning of the 24-syllable Gayatri Mantra: *Om, Bhur, Bhuva Svaha.*

In terms of sacred geometry, Heaven (*Svaha*) is the circumference of the circle, Earth (*Bhur*) is the vesica piscis (the Daughter of the Heavens), and Skambha is the radius, ray or Golden Reed that simultaneously holds the two apart *and* together via the atmosphere or mid-space of the circle (*Bhuva*). Skambha's role in establishing "the six spacious regions" in Atharva Veda 10.7 is entirely attributable to the fact that in addition to dividing the circumference into three 120° (432,000″) sections, the radius also divides the circumference into six 60° (216,000″) sections. The golden pillar of Skambha is said to eternally pervade the whole world, which is the essence of the word *Vishwa (Vishva)*, as well as *Vishnu* and *Vishwakarma (Visvakarman)* – the Divine Architect of creation, also known as *Tvashtri (Twashtri)*. It seems clear enough now that the golden or sacred pillar, reed or measure which "fashions" and "weldeth" Heaven and Earth together is the radius of the circle – the divine ray, flame and Son of the Rig Veda.

> *He who sate down as Hotar-priest, the Ṛṣi, our Father, offering up all things existing,—He, seeking through his wish a great possession, came among men on earth as archetypal.*
>
> *What was the place whereon he took his station? What was it that supported him? How was it? Whence Visvakarman, seeing all, producing the earth, with mighty power disclosed the heavens.*
>
> *He who hath eyes on all sides round about him, a mouth on all sides, arms and feet on all sides, He, the Sole God, producing earth and heaven, weldeth them, with his arms as wings, together.*
>
> *What was the tree, what wood in sooth produced it, from which they fashioned out the earth and heaven? Ye thoughtful men*

inquire within your spirit whereon he stood when he established all things.

Rig Veda 10.81.1-4, tr. R.T.H. Griffith

[Twashtri] the Lord hath made all forms....

Rig Veda 1.188.9, tr. R.T.H. Griffith

May Viṣṇu form and mould the womb, may [Twashtri] duly shape the forms....

Rig Veda 10.184.1, tr. R.T.H. Griffith

Men know Hiranyagarbha [the golden egg] as supreme and inexpressible: In the beginning, in the midst of the world, Skambha poured that gold. On Skambha Fervour rests, the worlds and Holy Law repose on him.

Atharva Veda 10.7.28-30, tr. R.T.H. Griffith

Who out of many, tell me, is that Skambha to whom with longing go the turning pathways? Whitheward go the half-months, and, accordant with the full year, the months in their procession? Who out of many, tell me, is that Skambha to whom go seasons and the groups of seasons?

Atharva Veda 10.7.4-5, tr. R.T.H. Griffith

One, the Supporter, takes the heaven and bears it: some keeping watch guard all the quarters safely. The man who knows the drawn-out string on which these creatures all are strung, [the] man who knows the thread's thread, he may know the mighty Brahmana. I know the drawn-out string, the thread whereon these creatures all are strung.

Atharva Veda 10.8.36-38, tr. R.T.H. Griffith

Who out of many, tell me, is that Skambha...[in] whom the future and the past and all the worlds are firmly set....

Atharva Veda 10.7.22, tr. R.T.H. Griffith

Skambha figures prominently in St. John's *Revelation* as the golden reed or rod which measures out God's Temple.

> *I was given a reed like a measuring rod and was told, "Go and measure the temple of God and the altar, with its worshipers.... Then God's temple in heaven was opened, and within his temple was seen the ark of his covenant.*
>
> Revelation 11:1, 19, NIV

> *I saw the Holy City, the new Jerusalem.... He who was seated on the throne [said to me]: ... "Come, I will show you the bride, the wife of the Lamb." And he carried me away in the Spirit to a mountain great and high, and showed me the Holy City, Jerusalem.... It had a great, high wall with twelve gates, and with twelve angels at the gates. On the gates were written the names of the twelve tribes of Israel. There were three gates on the east, three on the north, three on the south and three on the west. The wall of the city had twelve foundations, and on them were the names of the twelve apostles of the Lamb. The angel who talked with me had a measuring rod of gold to measure the city, its gates and its walls.*
>
> Revelation 21:2-15, NIV

Simply by coming to understand St. John's *Revelation* as a derivative rendition of the lore, characters and geometry of the Rishis' sacrificial or sacred year, the world can quickly shed many of its tragic misunderstandings and distortions of ancient gnosis. The temple and the holy city in the verses above are clearly symbols of the zodiac and the "ark of [God's] covenant" is, in all probability, the arc of the vesica piscis measured out by the Golden Reed, ray or radius.

The Golden Lion of Revelation

In Thea's 1976 book *The Hidden Manna*, she discussed St. John's *Revelation* as a purely zodiacal prophecy foretelling the work of Sri Aurobindo – the Avatar of Age of Aquarius – who born in the sign of Leo, fulfilled the avataric role of St. John's Lion by opening the sealed "Book of Life", equivalent to the Mandala of the Earth's twelve-month year. This opening was accomplished via his work towards recovering the "Secret of the Veda", and hence the secret or keys of the Vedic Year. Sri Aurobindo instigated and made great progress in this arena, opening the door for the further recovery of Vedic Gnosis by the Mother and Thea. Via this collective yoga, many crucial keys of the Rishis' Yoga or Yajna have been recovered. Without these keys, the Rishis' "Book of Life" would remain well-sealed.

> *Then one of the elders said to me, "Do not weep! See, the Lion of the tribe of Judah, the Root of David, has triumphed. He is able to open the scroll and its seven seals. Then I saw a Lamb, looking as if it had been slain, standing at the center of the throne, encircled by the four living creatures and the [24] elders.*
>
> Revelation 5:4-6, NIV

> *[It] is one born in the sign of the Lion who will commence the loosening of the seals, one who bears the symbol which at times has been called 'the star of David'.... John reveals that this is the one who will give forth the knowledge that is hidden, and must remain [hidden] for those who cannot see....*
>
> *...In the Indian tradition the Lamb is Agni, a figure who plays a fundamental part in the Return.... The avatar, who is the Lamb because he is the soul of the Earth, embodies in his life the process of transformation and redemption. Therefore being so much at one with the Earth he, or she, will naturally reveal in life the cycles of time-harmony of the Earth to the most perfect degree possible at that point of evolution. In the soul these harmonies are written, therefore it is only the Lamb who can loosen the seals and reveal the contents of the sacred scroll.*
>
> Thea, *The Hidden Manna*, pp. 63-65

The 24 "elders" encircling the Lion-turned-Lamb signify the 24 hours of the day, and the four creatures signify the four fixed signs of the zodiac. In *Revelation 6*, this immortal Lamb proceeds to open six of the seven scrolls of the Book of Life. In *Revelation*

8, he opens the seventh scroll, an act which initiates wide-scale destruction as well as the establishment of Heaven on Earth. Both the Lion and the Lamb are symbols of Agni the divine priest, Hero-Son, golden flame, skambha and measurer of the Vedic sacrifice. In *Revelation 21* we find that the wife (Prakriti) of the Lamb (Purusha) is the sacred city with its twelve gates divided into four sections of three, entirely equivalent to the 12-month Vedic year or yajna, measured out by the golden reed or rod. Below are some of Thea reflections on the Lamb's city and bride.

> *[The Lamb's bride, the] feminine principle is the body of the Spirit, thus the symbol of the new consciousness...the city is a womb, as it were, a house for the descending Spirit....[Its] descent upon Earth, as the prophet foresees, is the confirmation of the victory of the avatar. Thus, the city [the zodiac] is the bride of the Lamb".*

Thea, *The Hidden Manna*, pp. 304-05

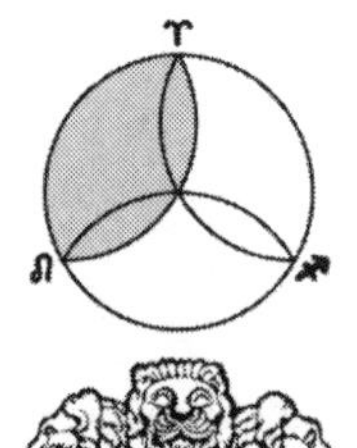

It has become apparent that in addition to being a figure-symbol of Vishnu's avatar in the Age of Aquarius, the Lion of *Revelation* is equally a symbol of the radius. He is the golden Purusha marking out his territory. His seat at 0° Leo in the zodiac is precisely 432,000″ of the full circle, marking off the first 432,000-measure of the solar radius or golden reed. This gives us a better sense as to why, in astrological tradition, Leo's "ruler" is the Sun, as well as why the Lion has long been associated with rulership and royalty, as well as law and order. India's state and supreme court emblems both feature the Lion Capitol of Ashoka (shown right) accompanied by the slogans "Truth always triumphs" and "Whence law (dharma), thence victory".

> *[The Lord Immortal] standing in the firmament hath meted the earth out with the Sun as with a measure.*

Rig Veda 5.85.5, tr. R.T.H. Griffith

Christ in Mandorla & the four Beasts, 13th c. Musée de Cluny (Wikimedia Commons).

The Lion represents the key measure of the radius without which the ancient book of the Rig Veda and hence the book of *Revelation* cannot be opened or read. The seal itself is a symbol of the vesica piscis which will be discussed in Part Two. With this geometric key in mind, we can better appreciate the fact that the number of syllables of the Rig Veda is said to be 432,000, mirroring the measure of the solar radius (the Golden Reed and Golden Lion) and the measure of the vesica piscis. The importance of comprehending Leo's central role in laying down the eternal law of the yajna will be further discussed in subsequent chapters.

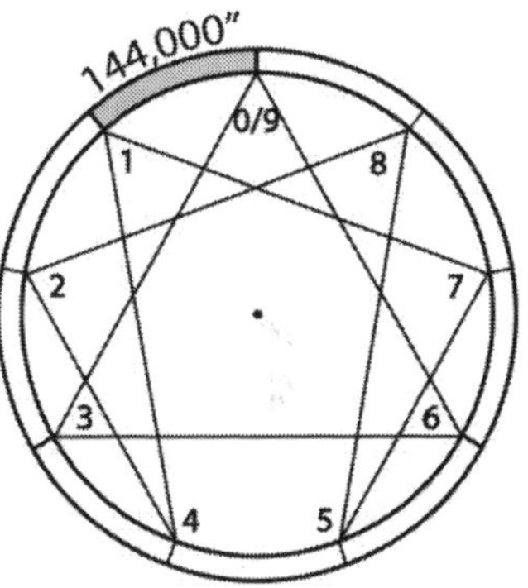

Though the Lion is itself an occult symbol of the 432,000 measure of the solar radius and vesica piscis, the number 432,000 does not show up explicitly in St. John's *Revelation.* However, the number 144,000 does, referring to those who can sing the new song of the Lamb or Son of God. 144,000 is one-third of 432,000, and 144,000″ is one-ninth or 40° of the 360° circle (40° x 60′ x 60″ =144,000″). Thus, the song of the Lamb is mathematically linked to the base unit or the One of the circle of 9. This unit of our number system is central to the Rishis' gnosis of unity. In other words, the number 144,000 in *Revelation* does not, in truth, indicate God's chosen people, but rather represents the geometry and gnosis of the One, in which the number One stands for both $1/9^{th}$ of the circle and the totality ($9/9^{ths}$) of the circle itself.

The Root of David, Satkona and the Radius

Thea wrote in *The Hidden Manna* that the "Root of David", associated with the Lion of *Revelation*, is the Star of David.[1] In India this "star" is called Satkona, indicating six (*sat*) corners or angles (*kona*). As we have seen, the six angles of this geometric symbol are marked out by the radius and vesica piscis of the circle. The name David appears to descend from the Sanskrit word *deva* or *devata* meaning "divine" or "godhead". In the Rig Veda the divine son Agni is considered to be the "root" (and first) of all devas or gods. I suspect that the word "root" is etymologically connected to radius, rod and reed, and that the "Root of David" is the radius, rod, reed or skambha which measures out the six angles of Satkona. In India, Satkona is considered Agni and Vishnu's abode and his sacrificial wheel (Sudarshana Chakra).

> *O great Cakra, remove the life of all our enemies. I meditate upon You, residing in the middle of the Sat-kona holding conch, cakra, bow, axe, sword, trident, noose, goad, missile, thunderbolt, plough, pestle and mace. You have terrible fangs, fiery hair, three eyes and you have the intensity of a raging inferno and You are adorned with ornaments and necklaces.*

Sri Vaisnava pancaratrika texts, as found in "Sudarśana Chakra – The Wheel of the Lord" by A.C. Bhaktivedanta Swami Prabhupāda[2]

> *O Sudarśana wheel, you are religion, you are truth, you are encouraging statements, you are sacrifice, and you are the enjoyer of the fruits of sacrifice. You are the maintainer of the entire universe, and you are the supreme transcendental prowess in the*

---

[1] *The Hidden Manna*, p. 63.

[2] This quote and image are from www.harekrsna.de (accessed, June 2016).

hands of the Supreme Personality of Godhead. You are the original vision of the Lord, and therefore you are known as Sudarśana. Everything has been created by your activities, and therefore you are all-pervading.

Srimad Bhagavatam 9.5.5, Ibid.

Satkona and the Seal of Solomon

Satkona is also known as the Seal of Solomon. "Solomon" likely originates from the Sanskrit word *zala*, indicating a length of measure, a house or a door of a house. *Zala* is the root of shalagrama, a stone or spiral-shaped fossil, known throughout India as a sacred symbol of Vishnu. According to Jewish lore, Solomon's Seal was a ring engraved by God and given to King Solomon. The ring was stolen by a demon who threw it into the sea, whereupon it was swallowed by a fish. The fish was caught by a fisherman and subsequently served to Solomon who found the ring in the fish. It is not difficult to see that this myth of a fish who saves the sacred seal of Solomon from sinking in the sea is a derivation of Vishnu's avatar Matsya the world-saving Fish whose form and mythology is born of the vesica piscis.

Similar imagery is found in the Mahabharata, wherein King Dushyanta finds and weds Shakuntala in a forest, then leaves her with a royal ring by which he will recognize her when he comes back to fetch her. Sadly, via a curse, the king forgets Shakuntala; and on her way to find him, she loses the ring in a river. The ring is then ingested by a fish and later found by a fisherman who gives it back to the king, restoring his memory of his bride.[1] When the king finally finds his wife, he also finds they have a strong young son (Bharata) who is busy counting the teeth of a lion whose mouth he has propped open. The lore of this royal ring (or seal) and the fish who recovers it, depicts the loss and recovery of the geometric keys of Vedic gnosis in the course of Time.

[1] Interestingly, according to Nolini Gupta, the Mother sent the Seal of Solomon to Sri Aurobindo circa 1911 to determine if he was the Great Soul guiding her, which of course he was. This "seal" was instrumental in their recognition of each other.

CHAPTER ELEVEN

The Divine Ruler

It is not a random coincidence that the word "ruler" means both a measuring stick and a king or leader. This dual meaning can be traced back to the Rig Veda wherein Agni, the chief or ruler of the Vedic sacrifice is, as we have seen, equivalent to the radius of the circle, the golden rod or ruler which measures out and harmonizes the unified field of Time and Space.

> *Heaven and Earth, bestow prosperity on all, sustainers of the region, Holy Ones and wise, Two Bowls of noble kind: between these Goddesses the God, the fulgent Sun, travels by fixed decree.*[1] *...Son of these Parents, [Agni] the Priest with power to cleanse, Sage, sanctifies the worlds with his surpassing power. ...Among the skilful Gods most skilled is he...who with great wisdom measured both the regions out, and stablished them with pillars that shall ne'er decay.*
>
> Rig Veda 1.160.1-4, tr. R.T.H. Griffith

> *Agni the Immortal...never breaks their everlasting laws. He, wondrous envoy, goes between the earth and heaven, firm seated as the Herald, great High Priest of men. He compasseth with rays the lofty dwelling-place, Agni, sent forward by the Gods....* ***Agni, the measure and the symbol of the priests****, hath entered heaven and earth that show in varied form.... Agni sprang into being, magnifying both his Parents, Heaven and Earth....*
>
> Rig Veda 3.3.1-11, tr. R.T.H. Griffith [bold emphasis added]

---

[1] These two bowls, equivalent to the two Goddesses Heaven and Earth, are the circle and the vesica piscis, whose immortal or never decaying "Son" is the radius.

Him, messenger of earth and head of heaven, Agni Vaisvanara, born in holy Order, Agni Vaisvanara, no one hath ever resisted these thy mighty ordinances, when thou, arising from thy Parents' bosom, foundest the light for days' appointed courses.... [Agni] Vaisvanara, who measured out the realms of air, Sage very wise who made the lucid spheres of heaven, the Undeceivable who spread out all the worlds, keeper is he and guard of immortality.

Rig Veda 6.7.1-7, tr. R.T.H. Griffith

May [Agni] the Priest come circling the measured stations, and with him bring the earth's autumnal fruitage.

Rig Veda 1.173.3, tr. R.T.H. Griffith

Agni am I who know, by birth, all creatures.... ***I am light threefold, measurer of the region*** *exhaustless heat am I, named burnt-oblation. Bearing in mind a thought with light accordant, he purified the Sun with three refinings; by his own nature gained the highest treasure, and looked abroad over the earth and heaven. The Spring that fails not with a hundred streamlets...joyous in his Parents' [Earth and Heaven's] bosom...him, the Truth-speaker....*

Rig Veda 3.26.7-9, tr. R.T.H. Griffith [bold emphasis added]

In this last hymn, we see that it is "by his own nature" that Agni gains "the highest treasure", which in the Rig Veda is the liberation of the light and the waters of truth from the caves and forces of Ignorance. Agni's triumphant nature in this verse is firmly linked to the radius and its three-fold measure of the circle. One of Agni's epitaphs is *Hiranyagarbha* meaning "Golden Germ". *Hiranya* in Sanskrit indicates gold, a metal whose brilliance does not diminish with time, just as the eternal law and light of the radius of the circle does not diminish with time. *Hira* in Sanskrit is said to mean "thunderbolt" and "lion", as well as "diamond"[1] and is likely the root of the English word "hero".

---

[1] *Cologne Digital Sanskrit Lexicon.*

> *In the beginning rose Hiranyagarbha, born Only Lord of all created beings. He fixed and holdeth up this earth and heaven. What God shall we adore with our oblation?...Who by his grandeur hath become Sole Ruler of all the moving world that breathes and slumbers...? His arms are these [heavenly regions]....By him the heavens are strong and earth is stedfast, by him light's realm and sky-vault are supported. By him the regions in mid-air were measured....He is the God of gods, and none beside him. What God shall we adore with our oblation? Neer may he harm us who is earth's Begetter, nor he whose laws are sure, the heavens' Creator....*
>
> Rig Veda 10.121.1-9, tr. R.T.H. Griffith

Other epitaphs and examples of the divine hero and his sacred rule or measure in the Rig Veda are found in the following verses.

> *I will declare the great and the mysterious power of the renowned and the powerful god Varuna, who standing in the firmament, has measured the Earth with the sun as if with a measuring rod.*
>
> Rig Veda 5.85.5, tr. R.T.H. Griffith

> *[Indra the Bull] fixed fast and firm the earth that staggered, and set at rest the agitated mountains, who measured out the air's wide middle region and gave the heaven support....Who slew the Dragon, freed the Seven Rivers, and drove the kine forth from the cave of Vala*[1] *....*
>
> Rig Veda 2.12.2-3, tr. R.T.H. Griffith

> *[Indra] ruled and measured; pierced with his bolt [vajra] the fountains of the rivers, and made them flow at ease by paths far-reaching....*
>
> Rig Veda 2.15.3, tr. R.T.H. Griffith

> *The Ṛbhus, with a rod measured, as 'twere a field, the single sacrificial chalice, wide of mouth....Heroes, with surpassing skill*

[1] Vala here is a demon, a power of darkness, a concealer of Light/Truth.

ye made your aged Parents [Heaven and Earth] youthful as before.

Rig Veda 1.110.5, 8, tr. R.T.H. Griffith

The Ribhus of the Rig Veda are a triad of heroes. They are a triadic extension of the one hero. They are builders or "Artisans of Immortality" who accomplish "the great work of upward human evolution which is the summit of the world-sacrifice."[1] Via their measuring rod they "restore [the soul] to constant companionship with its infinite mother."[2] Thea understood the three immortal Ribhus as the triple energy flow of the zodiac – creation, preservation and destruction (or dissolution), equivalent to the three gunas (*trigunas*): *rajas*, *sattva* and *tamas.*[3]

[The three Ribhus] are the energy flows that in the zodiac are repeated four times....

Thea, *The New Way, Volumes 1&2*, p. 401

The image to the right shows the three gunas of the fire trine. Each of the four elemental trines of the zodiac (fire, earth, air and water) similarly mark out all three gunas. We can see that three arcs of the radius or three vesicae piscis create this triadic flow. Via this simple geometry, it seems clear that the measuring rod of the triple and immortal Ribhus who are said to dwell in the solar sphere and to measure the sacrificial chalice, is the radius which establishes the central trinity and all trines of the circle.

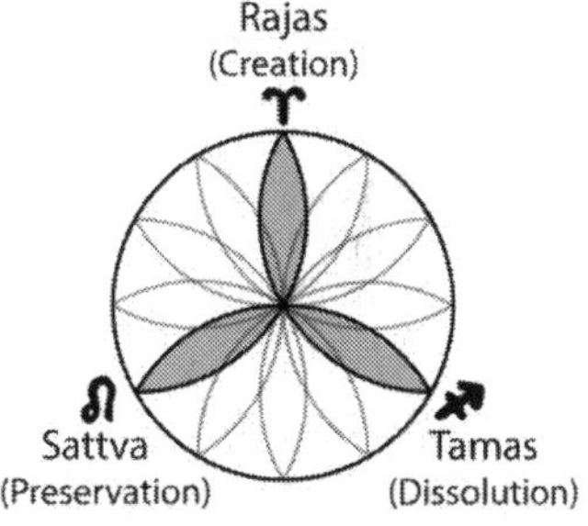

It is quite possible that the English word "rib", referring both to the ribs of the chest and the ribs of a boat or ark, hails from the

[1] Sri Aurobindo, *The Secret of the Veda, CWSA, Volume 15*, p. 340.

[2] Ibid., p. 340.

[3] Thea, *The Gnostic Circle*, pp. 54-56.

Vedic Ribhus. In this light, it appears to me that the Old Testament mythology of Eve being constructed out of one of Adam's ribs is an occult and misunderstood reference to the geometry of the Vedic Year which, as we have seen, is the eternal wife of the Sun.

God creating Eve out of Adam. Line engraving (Wellcome Library, London, Wellcome Images).

CHAPTER TWELVE

Trayi Vidya and Kali

In "Trayi Vidya – The Triple Knowledge" I wrote:

> *[T]he 432,000 measure of Kali's yuga is solely meant to be understood in the terms of...triadic geometry and gnosis. ...[T]ogether the radius and the vesica piscis establish the yuga measure....Via this simple math, long-held misinterpretations of the 432,000 Kali Yuga measure should be finally put to rest. These misinterpretations are purely based upon the loss of the Rishis' triadic gnosis along with its sacred, solar or golden reed of measure, and must be duely corrected....*

In this chapter, we will begin to explore this matter more deeply. In the Rig Veda Kali is a Sage,[1] which I take to be both a figure of the Purusha and a figure of Time, akin to Father Time or the Soul of Time. At some point, the name Kali came to indicate the Goddess of Time. It is possible that the sage Kali became the goddess Kali due to the lost understanding of how the radius (equivalent to the Sage) and its arc or vesica piscis (a figure of the divine feminine) together measure out the Rishis' field of Time and Space.

> *[Kali] is derived from the Sanskrit root kāla, to measure, the stem of our English word calculate. It is connected to the Goddess Kali in that she is the power of the Time-Spirit, Kāla.*
>
> Thea, *The Gnostic Circle*, p. 61

Kala and Kali both personify the triadic body of Time (past, present and future) as well as the triple gunas of creation,

---

[1] Rig Veda 1.112.15 and 10.39.08, tr. R.T.H. Griffith.

preservation and destruction. By the dim light of our fragmented, mortal and mental consciousness, however, the destructive aspect of Time and respectively of Kali and Kala, has overshadowed their full triadic nature or essence. Without gnosis of the triple vision and measure of Time, Kala and Kali are experienced and portrayed as killers or devourers of man. In gnosis, all of Time is an extension of the indwelling Soul or Sage; and the destructive aspect of Time is experienced as the dissolution of that which needs to be left behind in the course of the Soul's progressive journey. In order for higher expressions and experiences of the Soul to manifest, lower forms and structures naturally need to be broken up and dissolved.

The triadic essence of the goddess Kali is conveyed via the inverted triangle of her yantra (the top image to the right). This inverted triangle is also a feature of the symbol of the Anja or "Third Eye" chakra (middle right). It is also featured on the chest of Pashupati on the ancient Pashupati seal of Mohenjodaro. The triangle is a fitting symbol of the Third Eye, especially given that the three overlapping vesicae piscis which divide the circle into three can be seen as equivalent to three almond-shaped eyes. In this same vein, the arc and dot of the *chandra-bindu* symbol ँ found within both the Third Eye symbol and the OM symbol can easily be seen as a symbol of the center point and 120° arc of the circle. In this light the *chandra-bindu* reveals itself as a powerful symbol of the divine measure and triple Veda (or vision) of the ancient Rishis.

The *Nirvana Tantra* indicates that the Trimurti of Indian tradition – Brahman, Vishnu and Shiva – arises from the goddess Kali like "bubbles" in water. This odd imagery makes complete sense in terms of the geometry of the circle. The Trimurti is the

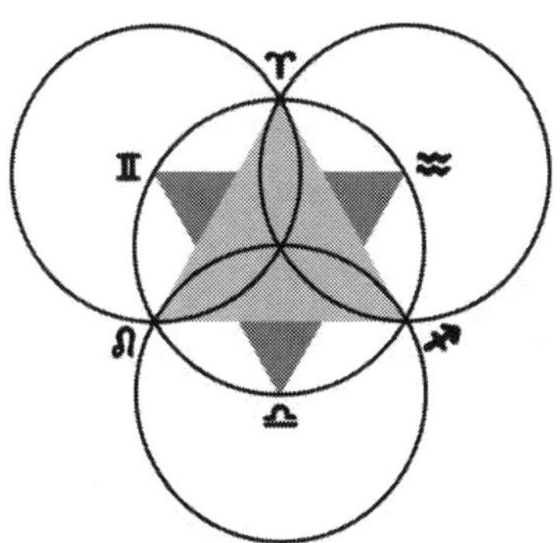

ascending (masculine) trinity of the circle, an extension of Agni's triple nature. The descending (feminine) trinity of the circle is the Tridevi – Saraswati, Lakshmi, and Parvati or Durga – the goddess-companions of the Trimurti. In the image to the right, we can see that the three "bubbles" or circles which mark off the three angles of the Trimurti arise from the three points of Kali's inverted triangle. Via this origin story of the Trimurti and this drawing, we can better appreciate Kali's triple nature and the importance of her association with the descending triangle.

As shown in the figure above, the upward triangle is equivalent to the fire trine of the zodiac (Aries, Leo and Sagittarius), and the downward-facing triangle is the air trine (Gemini, Libra and Aquarius). Each of these trines naturally contain all three trigunas or energy flows of the zodiac – creation, preservation and destruction. Once taken outside this context of the Rishis' sacrificial or sacred year, which is the Body of Time (the Body of Kala), the idea of the Trimurti and the Tridevi became increasingly distanced from the truth-consciousness of the Rishis and thus increasingly misunderstood. Our modern understanding of Kali has suffered this same fate. Her triple nature must be reconnected to the twelve-month sacrificial year or yajna of the Rishis.

Kali's four-sided, eight-petal yantra with its triangular core subtly contains the division of the twelve-month sacred year, emphasizing Vishnu's four preservation signs as well as the four cardinal points. In the image to the right, I have drawn Vishnu's Flower over Kali's yantra to demonstrate that her yantra preserves Vedic gnosis in a similar manner as the four triangular walls of the pyramid. Kali's yantra can be seen as a two-dimensional pyramid, symbolizing the 3x4 structure of the Earth's Year.

What has been presented or illuminated thus far should help readers understand that the Kali Yuga cannot be seen or measured apart from the geometry of the Sun symbol and the twelve-month solar year which is the singular context and wellspring of the Rishis' eternal dharma. As long as this context is lost, our "Third Eye" (or eye of unity consciousness) is essentially blinded and the Kali Yuga occurs as a time of darkness, wherein gnosis or the Light of the Soul is eclipsed. On this subject, Thea wrote:

> *In truth, mankind is in the 'dark' simply by not realizing that there is no such thing as a Kaliyuga, and that in effect the Age of Darkness is only determined by an ignorance of Truth, which can come about in any Age. Man has believed himself to be in an age of darkness, which is only the illusion of Time, and consequently Time is illusion only in so far as vision is fragmentary. When one breaks through to a full vision of Truth, Time then is the key and savior, not the bondage.*
>
> *The Kali Yuga exists whenever man has lost the Knowledge, then he becomes lost within the measure of Time, Kali, and cannot see beyond. He has divided time – past, present and future – and lost the vision of Unity whereby he is able to follow the real movement of the ages. The man of ignorance is always bound by Kali to the wheel of life and death, and never realise himself within the Age of Truth, while the gnostic being has the key of knowledge, the light of Immortality.*
>
> Thea, *The Gnostic Circle*, p. 63

Kali's Weapons

The goddess Kali is often depicted with an out-stretched red tongue, which is considered one of her weapons.[1]

---

[1] The same imagery is found in the center of the Aztec Sun Stone, wherein the solar deity Tonatiuh is depicted with an out-stretched tongue. Considering the Aztec Sun Stone or Eagle's Bowl (*Cuauhxicalli*) is a calendar, the connection between the tongue of the Sun God and the tongue of Kali is self-evident.

> *[Kali] spreads her tongue across the battlefield, and swallows in one gulp, the swarm of blood-born demons and sucks the blood from the original Rakta-bija until he falls lifeless. Kali's tongue here is a weapon, to be feared, a reminder that nature ultimately consumes all life.*
>
> Devdutt Pattanaik, "Kali and her tongue", *The Times of India,* Dec. 12, 2011

Kali, c. 1855, West Bengal (Wikimedia Commons).

Other weapons of Kali include the sword, scimitar and the trident. It seems apparent that in the Rig Veda and in post-Vedic Indian lore, the weapons of the gods and goddesses are *always* symbols or keys of gnosis (*jjana*) of the sacred year. For example, the trident is a symbol of the sacred measure and the *trayi vidya* of the Rishis by which the forces of ignorance are conquered. Forces of ignorance in the Vedic sense are those who mismeasure, misconstrue, distort and eclipse the true form, body and context of *sanatana dharma*. Both Kali's tongue and sword are symbols of the radius which measures out the field of Time and Space. The scimitar is a curved blade and could be a symbol of the vesica piscis. Once Kali and her weapons are understood in terms of the Rishis' *trayi vidya*, this goddess is no longer a figure of the consuming power of nature or of our mortality, but of our eternal Self and its eternal field of Being and Becoming.

CHAPTER THIRTEEN

The Triadic Structure of the Yugas

O Fire, we know the triple three of thee, we know thy seats borne widely in many planes, we know thy supreme Name which is in the secrecy, we know that fount of things whence thou camest.... The ray of intuition of the universe, the child in the womb of the world, in his coming to birth he filled earth and heaven.

Rig Veda 10.45.2,6, tr. Sri Aurobindo,
Hymns to the Mystic Fire, CWSA, Volume 16, pp. 410-11

O Fire, O universal godhead, earth and heaven and the mid-realm clove to the triple law of thy workings....

Rig Veda 7.5.4, tr. Sri Aurobindo,
Hymns to the Mystic Fire, CWSA, Volume 16, p. 309

Three are the jars, the triple offering is prepared. Three are the worlds, and moving on above the sky ye guard the firm-set vault of heaven through days and nights. Where are the three wheels of [the Ashwins] triple chariot, where are the three seats thereto firmly fastened?

Rig Veda 1.34.8-9, tr. R. T. H. Griffith

These verses are a few of many depictions in the Rig Veda of the triadic measure and law of the Rishis' yajna or yoga. The Ashwins or twin horsemen of the Vedic year assist in the manifestation and victory of the Purusha. They are agents of Time and, in my mind, are related to the twin Equinoxes and their

Precessional movement. They help to bring forth the White Horse (or equine) of victory in the sacrificial journey. Their car or vehicle "circles heaven with never-injured fellies" and is described as having three wheels and three seats.

For quite some time our world has been entirely in the dark regarding this triadic law and yajna or field of the Immortal Hero-Soul. Naturally, this ignorance resulted in the widespread and long-standing misunderstanding and mismeasure of the Kali Yuga and of the larger yugas based upon it. By one account, the Kali Yuga is 432,000 years, measuring out one-tenth of the Maha Yuga spanning 4,320,000 years (below left).

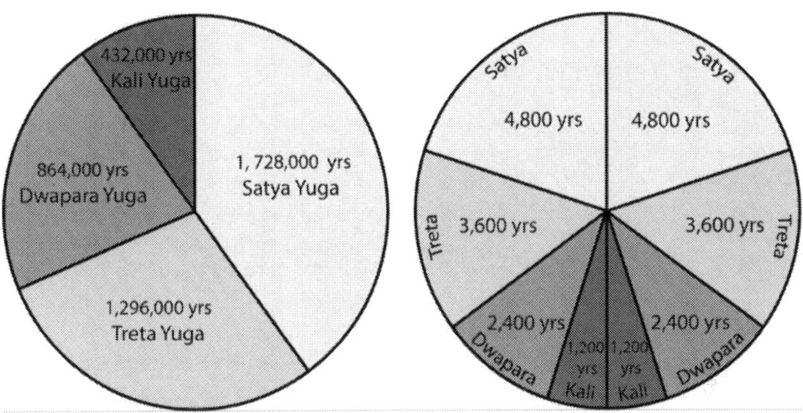

By the second account, the Kali Yuga is 1,200 years, measuring out one-tenth of the Maha Yuga cycle spanning 12,000 years.[1] In this second account, the Maha Yuga is thought to approximate one half of a full Precessional cycle, though this approximation amounts to the mismeasure of the Precession of the Equinoxes by almost a full Age. The idea that the Maha Yuga cycle would measure out *half* of a full cycle or field of Time (and *mismeasure* it at that) is an anathema to the gnosis of the Vedic Rishis. In both of these accounts of the Maha Yuga, the triple law and measure of the Divine Purusha has been entirely lost.

---

[1] Sri Yukteswar, *The Holy Science*, 8th Edition, Yogoda Satsanga Society of India, p. 9 (Originally published in 1894).

Thea restored the triadic essence of the Kali Yuga and the Maha Yuga in *The Gnostic Circle*, wherein she presented the Kali Yuga measure as one-third or 432,000 seconds of degrees of arc (120°) of the 25,950-year Precession of the Equinoxes, and the Maha Yuga as comprised of three Precessional cycles which together span 77,760 years (3 x 25,920 years). By this account the Maha Yuga consists of 9 (3 x 3) Kali Yugas and 36 (3 x 12) Astrological Ages. The following table demonstrates Thea's seeing of the triple (and triple-three) cycle of the Maha Yuga as found in *The Gnostic Circle*.

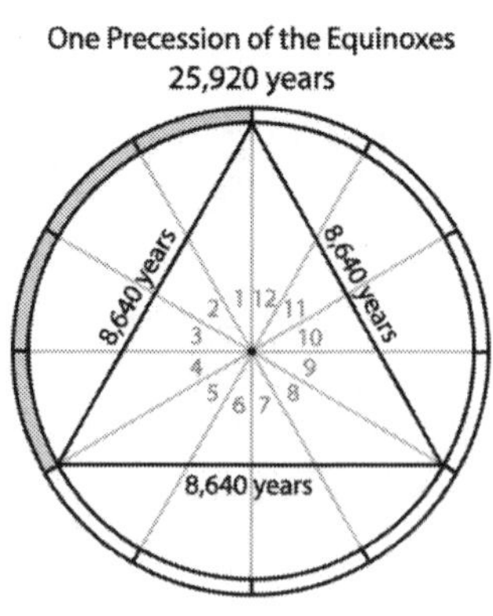

Dwapara (2) Yuga	= 864,000″	= 240°	= 8 signs	= 17,280 yrs.
Treta (3) Yuga	= 1,296,000″	= 360°	= 12 signs	= 25,920 yrs.
Satya (4) Yuga	= 1,728,000″	= 480°	= 16 signs	= 34,560 yrs.
Maha (9) Yuga	= 3,888,000″	= 1080°	= 36 signs	= 77,760 yrs.

In her discussion of these circle-based measures, Thea made it clear that the Kali Yuga does not *add* to the span of the Maha Yuga count because it functions as the *unit of measure*. As one-ninth of the Maha Yuga (8,640 years), the Kali Yuga is equivalent to one unit of our 0/9 number system. Thea believed our world's ignorance of the true measure and zodiacal context of the Kali Yuga extends back some 5,000 years.

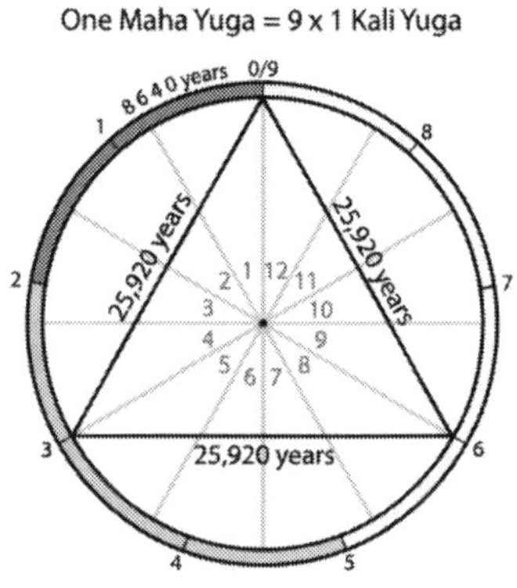

> *[T]he Dark Age began with the death of Sri Krishna, because it was just at that time that the knowledge of the zodiac was lost and man could not insert himself into the pattern of evolution in the correct manner.…It was man's illusion regarding time, loss of the*

> *key of Truth. Kaliyuga has since then become synonymous with darkness, ignorance and illusion, and the difficult part in the matter is that we are forever in a Kaliyuga, because we are forever in the measurement of Time.*
>
> Thea, *The Gnostic Circle*, p. 66

In other words, considering that every Precessional cycle consists of three Kali Yuga, the Earth is *always* in one of them. Those who come to understand the real geometry and light of the Kali Yuga will not able to continue associating this sacred measure with an Age of Ignorance or Darkness.

The number 432,000 is itself a key to how the Yugas must be understood. The base number power of 432,000 is 9. If we write out the equation by which 432,000 is reduced to its 9 base, 4 + 3 + 2 + 0 + 0 + 0 = 9, we can see that the number 1 is not included in the equation. The number 1 necessarily remains hidden from the 4 + 3 + 2 structure of the yugas, because it is the unit of measure of the 0/9 circle or cycle. Below I have drawn out the triply-three (3 x 3) Maha Yuga cycle as three circles or cycles.

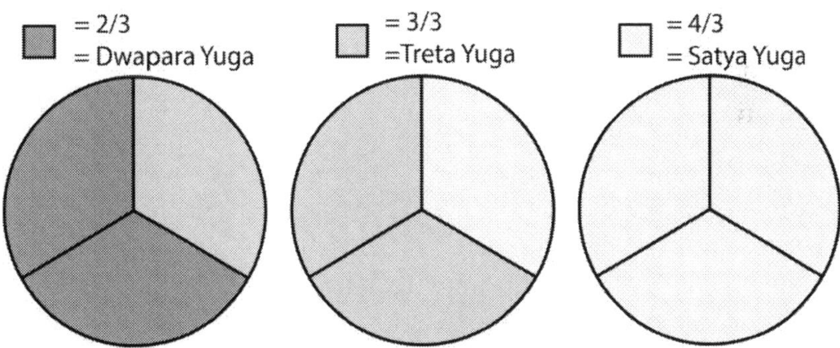

3 Precessional Cycles = 9 Kali Yugas

Thea understood that the three Precessional cycles of the full Maha Yuga are to be seen as *three concentric cycles*, similar to the three-tier structure of the Mother's symbol.

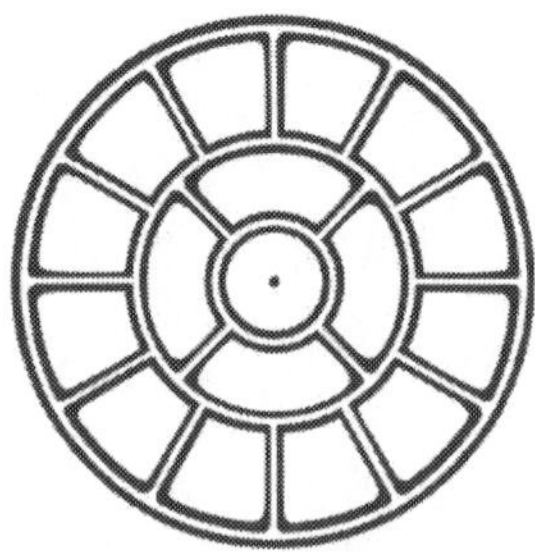

As Thea often noted, the Rishi of Rig Veda 1.164 portrayed this triple structure as one wheel with twelve "fellies", three navels and 360 spokes.[1] Rig Veda 4.6 also supports this view of three concentric cycles in which Agni measures out the course of his own manifestation or evolution.

> *Fire, the priest of the call, like a guardian of the herds thrice moves round them, the Ancient of days, ever widening his circle.... He goes round in his self-motion with measured run....*
>
> Rig Veda 4.6.4-5, tr. Sri Aurobindo, *Hymns to the Mystic Fire, CWSA, Volume 16*, pp. 235-36

Upon this Vedic foundation, Thea constructed her Map of the 12 Manifestations in which three spirals of the Earth's Precessional Year span the full Maha Yuga cycle of 9 Kali Yuga. Each Manifestation of the Map of 12 Manifestations contains in itself three ages or one quarter of one Precessional cycle, equivalent to a season of the year. Thus, in total 36 ages (3 x 12) are contained in this triple cycle. According to Thea, we entered the third Precessional cycle and the 9th Manifestation of our current Maha Yuga cycle in 234 BCE. This point marked the beginning of the Age of Pisces spanning from 234 BCE to the zero point of our current Age of Aquarius, 1926 CE.[2] In her map and throughout *The Gnostic Circle*, Thea emphasized Vishnu's preservation signs or Ages as the center or heart of each Manifestation.

---

[1] Rig Veda.1.164.48 R.T.H. Griffith (fully quoted in Part One, Chapter 9).

[2] 234 BCE + 2160 years = 1926 CE.

[It] seems to have been forgotten that [Vishnu's avatars]...can only come during the Ages which pertain to Vishnu, the force of Preservation, the four faces of the Sphinx, or the four fixed signs of the zodiac.

Thea, *The Gnostic Circle*, p. 4

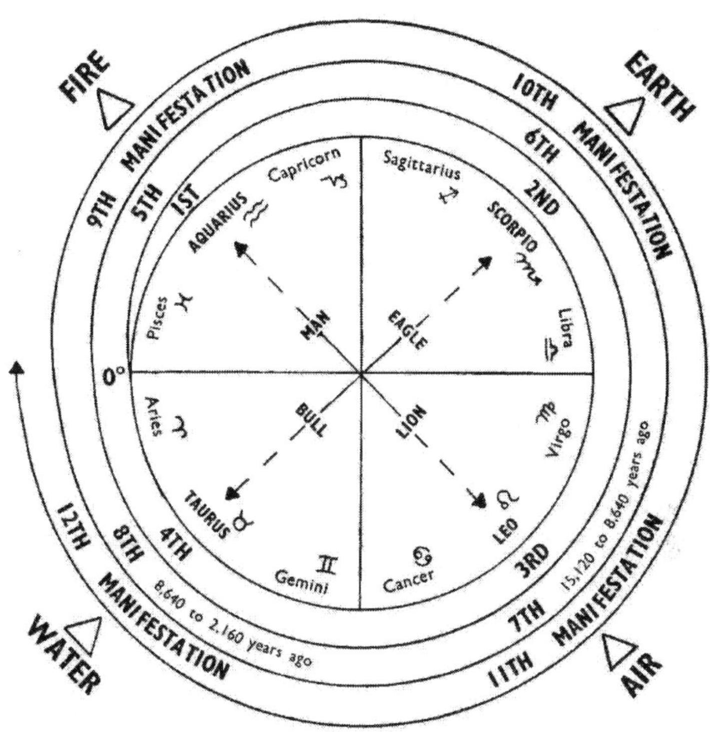

THE 12 MANIFESTATIONS

Map of the Evolutionary Ages

(Dynamic)

1 Age (1 sign)	=	2,160 years
1 Manifestation (3 signs)	=	6,480 years
1 Complete Round (12 signs)	=	25,920 years
1 Great Circle (12 Manifestations or 36 signs)	=	77,760 years

Map of the Manifestations, The Gnostic Circle, Thea (1975), p. 19.

To the right is another view of the same triple cycle which I have drawn out (with 0° Aries at the apex) so readers can see not only the 12 months of each Precessional cycle, but also the three Kali Yugas of each Precessional cycle, totaling 9 via both 3 + 3 + 3 and 4 + 3 + 2. Thus, it can be appreciated that, properly measured, the structure of the Maha Yuga is a harmony of the Rishis' circle of 9 (3 x 3) and their circle of 12 (3 x 4). This harmony, synthesis and structure of the 9 and 12 divisions of the One circle is the basis of Thea's Gnostic Circle.

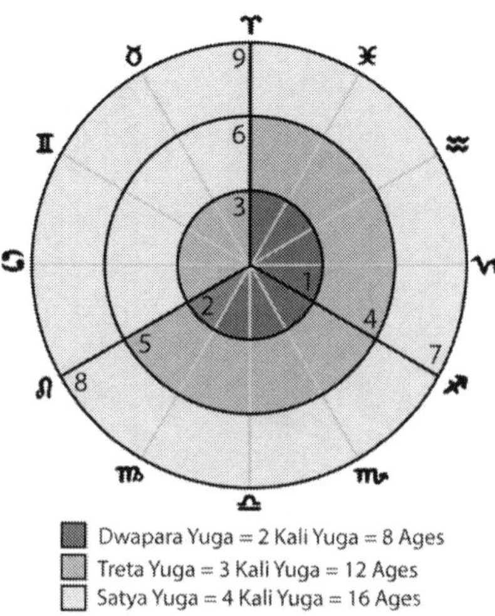

The Gnostic Circle

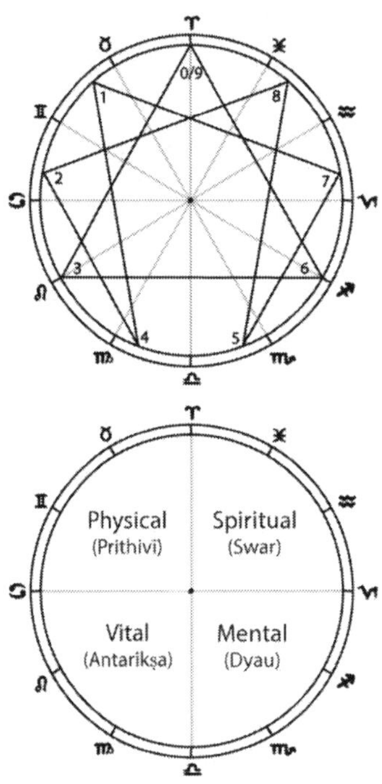

The top image to the left is my own rendition of the Gnostic Circle. Thea's full depiction of this circle features other divisions including the 360 degrees as well as the 36 decanates of the zodiac. She understood this circle to be a central key of restoring the Rishis' gnosis of the One Self of all selves as it unfolds or evolves in Time and Space. She saw each quadrant of the circle as the four sheaths or layers of Being and Becoming (as shown bottom left). The first quadrant of the zodiac is the Physical sheath, which consists of Aries, Taurus and Gemini. The second quadrant is the Vital sheath: Cancer, Leo and Virgo. The third quadrant is the Mental sheath: Libra, Scorpio and

Sagittarius; and lastly, the fourth quadrant is the Spiritual sheath: Capricorn, Aquarius and Pisces. Thea considered these four quadrants to be respectively equivalent to the three lower worlds of *Prithivī*, *Antarikṣa*, *Dyau* and the higher world of *Swar* in the Vedas.[1]

> *The Gnostic Circle is mearely the combination of the zodiac—the occult circle which contains the knowledge of evolution—and the structural pattern of the solar system. The Circle of 12 is the zodiac, and the Circle of 9 is our actual solar system, each orbit representing one year of earth life. The joint harmony of these two, superimposed or synthesized in one circle, is what constitutes our key to the evolution and flowering of the seed of the Spirit.... [W]e can say that the Gnostic Circle is mainly for this purpose: it shows mankind the ultimate and ideal perfection that can be attained during this particular phase of the evolution, during this great transition point from the animal-mental to the more divine mankind.*
>
> Thea, *The Gnostic Circle*, p. 159

> *[The Circle of 12 and the Circle of 9] together, superimposed, offer the most formidable key of higher knowledge of all times. I have called it the Gnostic Circle. Without it there could be no updating.*[2]
>
> Thea, *Puranic Cosmology Updated (blog)*, March 22, 2010

Thea found that the Rishis portrayed this one circle or year divided by 9 and 12 as the "thrice-seven ecstasies", planes or seats of the Divine Mother. Thrice-seven (3 x 7) amounts to 21, the sum of 9 + 12. Each third of the circle consists of 3 out of 9 number units, and 4 out of 12 astrological signs which together give us the occult basis of the "thrice-seven ecstasies" or seats of the Divine Mother.

[1] *The New Way, Volumes 1&2*, p. 413.

[2] I understand Thea's use of the word "updating" here and elsewhere in her work to mean the restoration of the orignal sense of the Rishis' gnosis in a way that makes it comprehendable and applicable in our modern world.

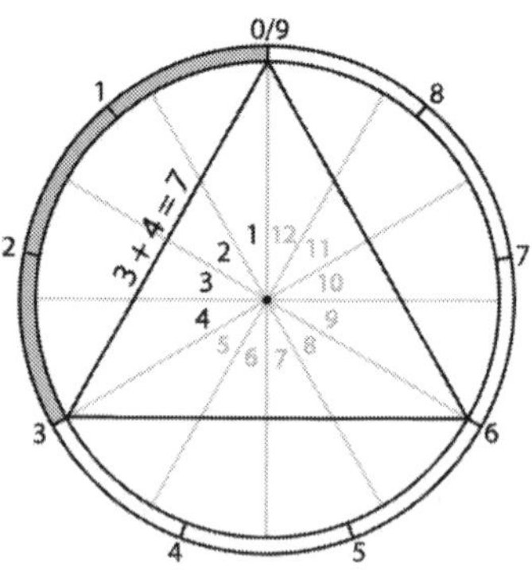

'[T]his bowl of Twashtri new and perfected you made again into four. So establish for us ***the thrice seven ecstasies****, each separately by perfect expressing of them.' (I.20-6.7). These three synonyms of movement are the energy flows that in the zodiac are repeated four times; hence it is said 'this bowl of Twashtri...you again made into four.'* ***The thrice-seven, or twenty-one, ecstasies are the combined scales of 9 and 12****, based on the multiples of three times three and three times four that the Ribhus, artisans of Immortality, personify.... 'For such perfect division', writes Sri Aurobindo, 'is the whole condition of the effective sacrifice, the perfect work.'*[1]

Thea, *The New Way, Volumes 1&2*, pp. 401-02 [bold emphasis added]

When the masters of sacrifice have found hidden in thee the thrice seven secret planes, by them they guard with one mind of acceptance Immortality.

Rig Veda 1.72.6, tr. Sri Aurobindo
Hymns to the Mystic Fire, CWSA, Volume 16, p. 104

The first name of the Mother with her thrice seven supreme seats, that which the dawns or mental illuminations know and move towards, must be the name or deity of the supreme Deva, who is infinite being and infinite consciousness and infinite bliss, and ***the seats are the three divine worlds, called earlier in the hymn the three supreme births of Agni*** *... which correspond to these three infinities of the Deva and each fulfils in its own way the sevenfold principle of our existence: thus we get the series of thrice seven seats of Aditi manifested in all her glory by the opening out of the Dawn of Truth.*[2] *Thus we see that the achievement of the Light and*

---

[1] Sri Aurobindo, *The Secret of the Veda, CWSA, Volume 15*, p. 342.

[2] Sri Aurobindo's foot note: "The same idea is expressed by Medhatithi Kanwa (I.20.7) as the thrice seven ecstasies of the Beatitude, *ratnani triḥ sāptāni*, or more

*Truth by the human fathers is also an ascent to the Immortality of the supreme and divine status, to the first name of the all-creating infinite Mother, to her thrice seven supreme degrees of this ascending existence, to the highest levels of the eternal hill (*sānu, adri*). This immortality is the beatitude enjoyed by the gods of which Vamadeva has already spoken as the thing which Agni has to accomplish by the sacrifice, the supreme bliss with its thrice seven ecstasies (I.20.7).*

Sri Aurobindo, *The Secret of the Veda, CWSA, Volume 16*, p. 205 [bold emphasis added]

The Manifestation of the Divine

Thea used the word "Manifestation" for the twelve stages of the Maha Yuga cycle purposefully. Manifestation means something that is brought forward or born into material creation. Thea understood, as the Rishis did, that the twelve-month year is the evolutionary blueprint of the manifestation of the indwelling Purusha or Soul of creation, by whatever name – Agni, Vishnu, Indra, Manu, etc.[1] The Purusha can be thought of as THAT ONE (*tad ekam*) which is self-born within its own field of Time and Space. Sri Aurobindo describes the manifesting Purusha in the following terms:

Brahman the Reality is Atman, Purusha, Ishwara.... [He is the] Lord of Beings...that which is conscious in the conscious being, but he is also the Conscious in inconscient things, the One who is master and in control of the many that are passive in the hands of Force-Nature. He is the Timeless and Time; He is Space and all that is in Space.... All realities and all aspects and all semblances are the Brahman; Brahman is the Absolute, the Transcendent and incommunicable, the Supracosmic Existence that sustains the cosmos, the Cosmic Self that upholds all beings, but It is too the self of each individual: the soul or psychic entity is an eternal

---

literally, the ecstasies in their three series of seven, each of which the Ribhus bring out in their separate and complete expression, *ekam ekaṃ suśastibhiḥ*."

[1] It is worth repeating here that the English word "manifestation" is an etymological descendent of the Sanskrit name *Manu*.

> *portion of the Ishwara; it is his supreme Nature or Consciousness-Force that has become the living being in a world of living beings. The Brahman alone is, and because of It all are, for all are the Brahman; this Reality is the reality of everything that we see in Self and Nature. Brahman, the Ishwara, is all this by his Yoga-Maya, by the power of his Consciousness-Force put out in self-manifestation: he is the Conscious Being, Soul, Spirit, Purusha, and it is by his Nature, the force of his conscious self-existence that he is all things; he is the Ishwara, the omniscient and omnipotent All-ruler, and it is by his Shakti, his conscious Power, that he manifests himself in Time and governs the universe.*
>
> Sri Aurobindo, *The Life Divine, CWSA, Volume 21- 22*, pp. 338-39

Sri Aurobindo recognized that the descent or manifestation of the Purusha corresponds entirely to the ascent of the human being to the Truth of the Divine Self.

> *An existence, wholly self-aware and therefore entirely master of itself, possesses the phenomenal being in which it is involved, realises itself in form, unfolds itself in the individual.*
>
> *That luminous Emergence is the dawn which the Aryan forefathers worshipped. Its fulfilled perfection is that highest step of the world-pervading Vishnu which they beheld as if an eye of vision extended in the purest heavens of the Mind. For it exists already as an all-revealing and all-guiding Truth of things which watches over the world and attracts mortal man, first without the knowledge of his conscious mind, by the general march of Nature, but at last consciously by a progressive awakening and self-enlargement, to his divine ascension. The ascent to the divine Life is the human journey, the Work of works, the acceptable Sacrifice. This alone is man's real business in the world and the justification of his existence....*
>
> Sri Aurobindo, *The Life Divine, CWSA, Volume 21- 22*, p. 48

One of the ways the descent and manifestation of the divine Purusha is portrayed in Indian lore is the *Dasavataras* or Ten Avatars of Vishnu. The word *avatar* means "descent", indicating the descent of the Transcendent Divine into the material cosmos and world. Thea understood that Vishnu's descent is inseparable from the Vedic yajna and from the Maha Yuga cycle. She demonstrated in her Map of the 12 Manifestations that the central Age of each Manifestation (or quarter of the Precessional Year) is an Age of Vishnu the Preserver. In other words, she saw that the preservation ages of the Precession of the Equinoxes correspond to the manifestation (or incarnation) of Vishnu's avatars. By the light of this Map of the 12 Manifestations, it becomes apparent that Vishnu's 9th avatar is the avatar of the preservation Age of Aquarius. Thea saw that Vishnu's 9th avatar completes the full descent and incarnation of the Hidden One – the Divine Purusha, Son or Soul of the unified field of Time and Space. In terms of Vishnu's avatars, this 9 who is the embodiment of the One is Kalki. In terms of the geometry of the 0/9 circle this is simply the 9 which is equivalent to the totality and fullness of the One circle. In this light, Kalki avatar can be understood as the 9-fold One – the Soul fully manifested in its womb of Time and Space.

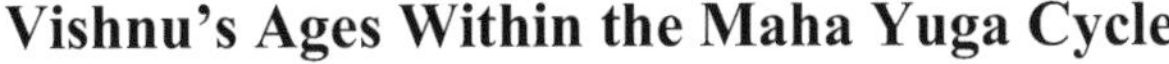

Vishnu's Ages Within the Maha Yuga Cycle

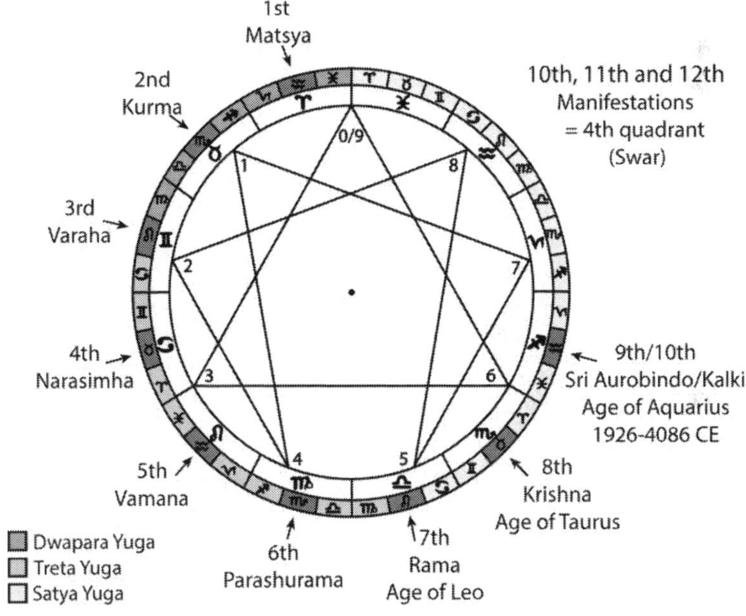

I constructed the image on the previous page to demonstrate the progression of Vishnu's ages and avatars within the Maha Yuga cycle, leading humanity to its completed gestation and birth or awakening into the higher ranges of our evolutionary journey. In case it needs clarifying, the Dwapara Yuga spans two Kali Yugas, ending at the 2 Point of the circle of 9 Kali Yugas; the Treta Yuga spans three Kali Yugas, ending at the 5 Point of the circle; and the Satya Yuga spans four Kali Yugas, ending at the 0/9 Point of the circle, completing the Maha Yuga cycle.

I have placed the 9th and 10th avatar together in the same Age of Aquarius because, according to Thea, there is no waiting for the 10th avatar, he is the 9th avatar reborn after completing his full descent as the tri-fold and nine-fold Oneness. This tri-fold and nine-fold One, by whatever name, is the victorious Purusha or Hero-Son of the Rishis' unified field.[1] He is considered victorious from birth over the world's falsehood and ignorance, or in other words, victorious over mankind's fragmented egoic, mental and mortal consciousness. Vishnu's 10th avatar Kalki is commonly portrayed as a Horse-Man or as a hero riding a White Horse. The association of Kalki with the Horse gives us the important clue that the mythology of his birth can only be understood in the context of the Vedic Year which in the *Brihadaranyaka Upanishad* is described as the body of a horse. More specifically this symbolism of the horse provides the key that the hero Kalki is specifically a figure of the 9th month of the 12-month year – the 9th month of Sagittarius, the Horse or Horse-Man (centaur) of the zodiac. This equally provides the key that Kalki is the avatar of the 9th Manifestation of Sagittarius. He is equivalent to the conquering War Horse of Rig Veda 4.15.4 who is said to be like a shining babe of heaven. The bringing forth of this Hidden One, Hero-Son,

[1] In the Buddhist tradition his name is Maitreya, derivative of the Vedic God Mitra "the Friend". Thea recovered the forgotten truth that the real origin and context of the Buddhist prophecy of Maitreya's coming is the Vedic Yajna, the Maha Yuga cycle and Vishnu's manifestation in the Age of Aquarius. Aquarius is known as the Friend (Mitra) of the zodiac.

Hero-Horse or "son of force"[1] is the fulfillment of the movement of the Ashwins' (the twin horsemen's) triple chariot.

Humans have cultivated many divergent and fanciful ideas about what this fulfillment would mean, despite having no real understanding of the ancient gnosis and context of this victory. From Sri Aurobindo's, the Mother's and Thea's teachings on the matter, we can now understand that this victory is the victory of the indwelling, hidden or Transcendent Purusha or Soul which is borne out or fully manifested in our field or womb of Time and Space. From this birth onward, the higher and supramental ranges and potentials of our Being and of our consciousness become progressively realized and progressively manifest in the world.

Regarding my diagram of the 77,760-year Maha Yuga cycle at the beginning of this section, the inner ring of the circle marks off the 12 Manifestations and the outer ring marks off the 36 Ages. The 9 Ages of Vishnu of the first three "trimesters" of this cycle correspond to the 9 stages of Vishnu's descent, equivalent to the 9-month gestation of a human being. In this view, we can clearly see the rhythm of Vishnu's incarnations. In keeping with the backward movement of the Precession of the Equinoxes, the 36 ages of the Maha Yuga unfold counter-clockwise through the 12 months of the sacred year. Thus, from the zero point (apex) of the circle moving counter-clockwise, we begin the 36-Age cycle with an Age of Pisces, and then move into an Age of Aquarius.

According to Thea's seeing, the year 2016 put us 90 years into the Age of Aquarius within the 9th Manifestation of Sagittarius. It is also worth noting that in this view, we have unknowingly been in the Satya Yuga stretch of this Maha Yuga cycle since the culmination of the last Age of Leo some 10,800 years ago, which falls at the 5 Point of the whole cycle. Given the backwards movement of the Precession of the Equinoxes through the zodiac, the Age of Leo *ended* at 0° Leo.

---

1 "Son of force" is Sri Aurobindo's translation of *sahasaḥ sūno*, a common description of Agni in the Rig Veda.

> *This point [0° Leo], ruled by the Sun, is then captured in the essence of the 9th Manifestation, for which reason* the knowledge of the Satya Yuga is revealed during that time, *because the essence of the Satya Yuga is Truth, which is the Sun. In the number scale the Sun is Zero, the Nought that contains the All.... [T]he Sun is the seed of the 9th Manifestation....*
>
> Thea, *The Gnostic Circle*, p. 84

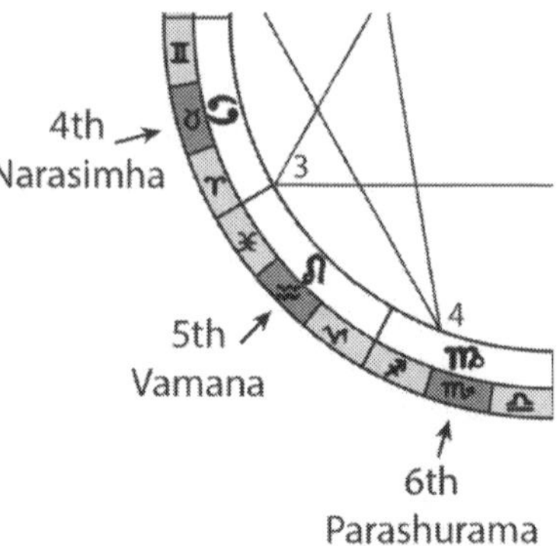

In my diagram of the Maha Yuga cycle we can see that the preservation age corresponding to the 5th Manifestation (ruled by Leo) is an Age of Aquarius. Given that Narasimha (the Lion-Man) is a chimera of Leo ♌ and Aquarius ♒ which fall opposite each other in the twelve-month zodiac, it is quite possible that Narasimha should be positioned as the 5th avatar of Vishnu instead of as the 4th. In the 9th Manifestation of Sagittarius, the corresponding preservation age is Aquarius "the Man". Thus, it is entirely fitting that the chimera of the 9th Manifestation of Vishnu is the Horse-Man Kalki. Before further discussing Kalki it is necessary to continue to flush out the clear connection between the mythology of Vishnu's avatars and the geometry of the circle. It is important to make it abundantly clear that, in truth, mythology has a mathematical basis and is inseparable from the geometry of the Rishis' twelve-month yajna.

CHAPTER FOURTEEN

The Lore and Geometry of Vishnu's Avatars

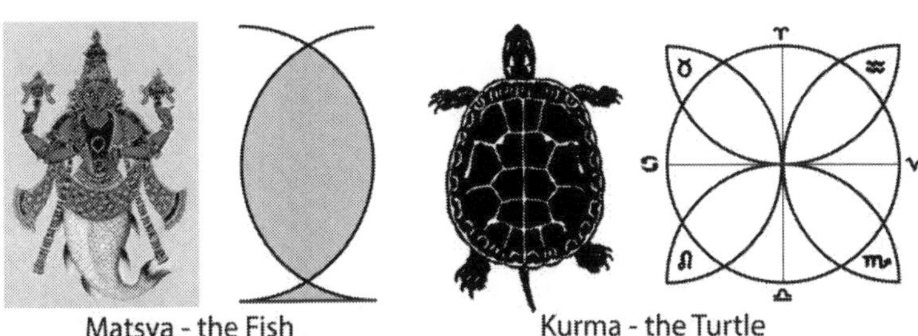

Matsya - the Fish

Kurma - the Turtle

After seeing the connection between the geometry of the vesica piscis and Vishnu's first and second avatars Matsya and Kurma, I began to review the lore of Vishnu's other avatars via this same lens and key. This connection between Vishnu's avatars and the vesica piscis only makes full sense in conjunction with Thea's finding that Vishnu and his avatars and yugas are meant to be understood in the context of the Rishis' 12-month year.

Varaha – Vishnu's 3rd Avatar

Varaha, c. 1740, (Wikimedia Commons).

Vishnu's third avatar Varaha the boar, saves the Earth from sinking into the waters with his curved tusks, resetting her "original position". This original position can be understood in terms of the set or fixed cardinal points of the Earth's year. The boar's upholding tusks are likely symbols of the vesica piscis. *Vara*, the root of *Varaha,* means "circumference" among other things. The word "boar" hails from the Sanskrit words *bha* meaning "sun", and *bhara* meaning "to bear or carry". Varaha's body is said to be the size of the space between Heaven and Earth. We have already seen in previous chapters that that the space between Heaven and Earth is upheld by skambha,[1] the sacred pillar, golden reed or radius of the circle. We have also seen that Agni and other epitaphs of the Purusha likewise uphold, fill or measure out this space.[2]

> *[Up Indra] sprang himself, assumed his vesture, and filled, as soon as born, the earth and heaven.*
>
> Rig Veda 4.18.5, tr. R.T.H. Griffith

Narasimha – Vishnu's 4th Avatar

It has already been made clear that Narasimha is a chimera of the Leo-Aquarius (Lion-Man) axis of the zodiac. But what is most interesting about the lore of Narasimha in terms of math and myth is that this incarnation of Vishnu is found hiding in a pillar which is a symbol of the radius or skambha of the Veda. In the myth of Narasimha, a demon taunts his own Vishnu-loving son regarding the whereabouts of the all-pervading god Vishnu. The demon asks, "Why is He not present before me in this pillar?"[3] The son responds saying that Vishnu IS in the pillar. Furious, the demon smashes the pillar from which Vishnu emerges as the Lion-Man, thereupon killing the demon. The demon in this story and throughout Vishnu's

Narasimha, Venkateswara Temple (Wikimedia Commons).

[1] Atharva Veda 10.7.35.

[2] Instances of this can be found in Rig Veda 1.160.3-4, 4.53.3-6, 6.8.3, 6.72.2, 8.6.5, and 10.5.3-4.

[3] Bhagavata-Purana 7.8.13, as found in David N. Lorenzen's book *Praises to a Formless God: Nirguni* Texts from North India, SUNY Press, 1996, p. 24.

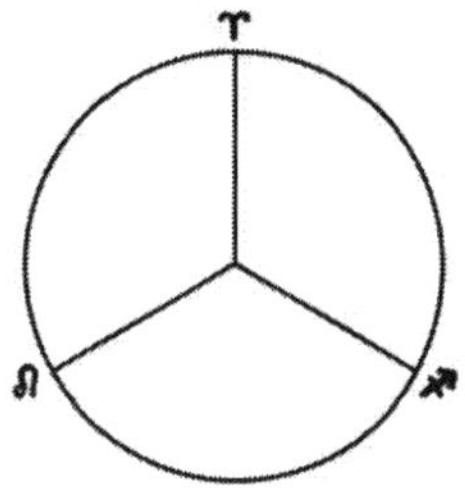

mythology is a representative of Ignorance regarding the twelve-month yajna and its divine measure. It is very telling that Vishnu emerges from a pillar to destroy the demon, who represents not only ignorance of the Rishis' measure of Time and Space, but the distortion of it as well. 0° Leo, it is important to recall, falls 120° (432,000″) into the circle. Thus, the Lion is a symbol of the triadic law of the radius. Why the Lion was chosen as the animal to symbolize the triadic law of the circle can be discovered simply by looking at the Lion's face. The structure of its mouth looks like the three rays or radii of the fire trine of the zodiac and the Lion's nose looks like the Aries symbol. Also, the Lion's fur is golden making the Lion an apt symbol of the golden ray, measure, pillar or skambha of the Solar Year.

Vishnu's 5th Avatar – Vamana

Vamana, unknown author, c. 1825 (Wikimedia Commons).

Vishnu's fifth avatar is the dwarf Vamana, also known as Trivikrama. He is often depicted carrying a parasol, a water pot (*kumbha*)[1] and sometimes a staff. The staff and parasol appear to be symbols of the radius and its arc or circle. According to myth, Vamana interrupted a demon's sacrifice and tricked the demon into giving him as much land as he could cover in three steps. The demon agreed and Vamana then assumed his divine form and took three steps (*trivikrama*) across Earth and Heaven and all the worlds. By this ruse Vishnu reestablished the law and truth of the Rishis' sacrifice. The

[1] This water pot (*kumbha*) is a symbol of the vesica piscis which will be discussed in greater depth in Part Two of this book.

demons' sacrifice signifies the point in the circle and the stage of consciousness wherein mental distortion (mismeasure) of the Rishis' sacrificial year is bound to occur, which is in the 8th sign of Scorpio ♏, also known as *Martanda* meaning "dead egg" or "undeveloped egg". With this in mind, readers can perhaps better appreciate Thea's conclusion that Vamana takes his three steps from the sign of Scorpio.

> *If the Eagle, the fourth sign, was left out of Vishnu's measuring[1] it is because this Eagle is Garuda, his own carrier. He begins his measuring from that point in the wheel, also known as Scorpio, and takes 'three steps'. Scorpio, otherwise known as the zodiacal Eagle.*
>
> Thea, "Cosmology in Rigveda – the third premise", *The Hindu*, July 9, 2002

In light of the geometric keys underlying the lore of Vishnu's avatars, it became clear that the dwarf Vamana is equivalent to the radius of the circle. His three steps are equivalent to three arcs of the radius or vesica piscis, three of which cover the entire circle, and three of which touch all four corners of Vishnu's flower and all four of Vishnu's preservation signs.

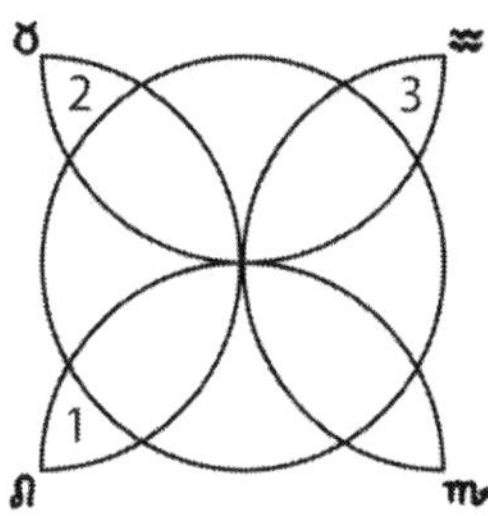

After seeing this, I looked for depictions of Trivikrama as having a 120° upward leg or step and found that the toe of Trivikrama in the Badami caves of Karnataka comes quite close to marking out a full 120° arc from the base of his standing foot. His upward leg,

[1] Thea is referring to Rig Veda 1.154 (tr. Sri Aurobindo) wherein Vishnu's steps are described as "like terrible a lion", "a wide-ranging Bull", and "the Friend of Man", mirroring the backwards order of the Precession through the fixed ages.

measured from the hip, does appear to be equivalent to the radius of the circle whose vertical axis or diameter stretches from Trivikrama's crown to toe. This radius also equals the length of the sword in Trivikrama's right hand. I added the Aquarius hieroglyph to the upward "step" of this vesica piscis because, as already discussed, Trivikrama's (Vishnu's) third step in the Rig Veda is connected with the sign of Aquarius the Friend. In this circle, Trivikrama's standing big toe is 0° Libra and his upward toe points to 0° Aquarius.

Trivikrama, Badami Caves, Karnataka, c. 6th century (Wikimedia Commons) [Circle, arc and hieroglyph added].

After coming to see the truth of the Vamana (Trivikrama) mythology, I recalled a perplexing dream I had after reading of Sri Aurobindo's rebirth in Thea's book *The New Way, Volumes 1&2*. In the dream, I was sitting with my eyes closed in a beautiful meadow. Sri Aurobindo sat down behind me so that we were back to back, spine to spine. Even with my eyes closed I knew who he was. I waited for him to speak, but he did not say a word. After sitting in silence for some time, I turned around to see what he looked like in his new incarnation. I was thereupon surprised to see that he appeared as a dwarf at which point I woke up and recorded the dream.

At the time of the dream and up until writing this chapter and section, I did not at all understand why he chose this form of all forms in which to greet me. At the time, I was not familiar enough with Vishnu's ten avatars or the full scope of Sri Aurobindo's yoga to make the connection between meeting him as a dwarf and the mythology of Vamana the Dwarf. At the time, I felt it was perhaps some kind of test to see if I could recognize him in whatever form he chose. Now it is clear that his dwarf-form was simply a symbol, a precursor of what I would come to learn about the radius, which underlies the mythology and form of Vishnu's avatars, including learning that the radius perpetually establishes, preserves and restores the eternal measure and hence the eternal law of its own field of Time and Space.

Parashurama – Vishnu's 6th Avatar

Parashurama (Unknown artist, c. 1820, Wikimedia Commons).

Vishnu's sixth avatar is Parashurama, translated as "Rama with the Axe". *Parashu* is commonly translated as "axe", but from what I can tell *Parashu* also indicates a quick movement or a quick crossing, as in the swinging of the axe or radius. Parashurama is described as a martial arts expert who wielded supernatural weapons, including *Vijaya* – the bow of victory Indra used to destroy demons, as well as arrows, a lightning-like spear, and *Naranayastra* – the weapon Narasimha used to destroy the demon Hiranya-kashipu. *Naranayastra* is said to call forth all twelve Rudras in the sky to defeat the forces of ignorance. Rudra is an epitaph of the Purusha, thus the twelve Rudras are likely the twelve radii of the twelve-month year.

In one account[1] Parashurama comes back from collecting sticks to perform his sacrifice with the priest-sage Jamadagni and

[1] From "Parashurama – The 6th Avatar of Lord Vishnu", www.IndiaDivine.org.

finds the divine cow Kamadhenu has been stolen by a warrior *(Kshatriya)* king. Parashurama kills the king and his allies and returns the sacred cow to Jamadagni. The king's sons in turn kill the priest-sage of the sacrifice and Parashurama retaliates by killing the sons of the warrior king twenty-one times with arrows shot from his divine and ever-victorious bow (*Vijaya Dhanush*). From this tale, we can see that Parashurama is a protector of the Vedic sacrifice. The sacred cow Kamadhenu is a symbol of the Divine Mother Aditi and of the sacrificial year whose supreme seats are twenty-one ("thrice-seven" or 9 + 12). Parashurama's divine bow and arrow appear to be symbols of the vesica piscis and radius. His axe also appears to a symbol of the radius which swings through the circle, quickly reestablishing the law and measure of the sacrifice and destroying those who distort, mismeasure or otherwise abuse the sacrifice in ignorance.

Rama – Vishnu's 7th Avatar

Rama (Unknown artist, c. 1820, Wikimedia Commons).

Vishnu's seventh avatar is Rama, the hero or Purusha of the Ramayana epic. Rama in Sanskrit is said to mean "charming", though its roots *ra* and *ma* are clues to the deeper significance of this charm. *Ra* (the root of the English word "ray" and "radius") means "fire" and "gold" as well as "speed"; and *ma* means "measure".[1] From this etymology we can see that Rama's name connotes a golden measure or ray. As we have seen, in Vedic gnosis this golden measure is the radius of the circle which upholds and holds apart Heaven and Earth. In the *Ramayana*, Rama's wife Sita is kidnapped by the demon Ravana, and Rama then initiates the building of a bridge across the ocean to recover her. This bridge crossing the ocean is either a symbol of the radius aligned straight across the waters of

[1] The definitions of *ra* and *ma* are from *Cologne Digital Sanskrit Lexicon*.

the vesica piscis, or of the vesica piscis built by the radius, arcing across the ocean of the circle.

Rama's wife Sita is equivalent to Vishnu's wife Lakshmi, and to Indra's wife Kamadhenu – the cow of plenty who is stolen and recovered by Vishnu's 6th avatar Parashurama. Sita, like the sacred cow, is equivalent to the twelve-month sacrifice which in *Revelation 21:2* is called the Holy City and the bride of the Lamb. The Sanskrit word *sita* means "bound", "tied" or "joined with" which is the essence of the Vedic *yajna* and yoga, bound by the pillar, priest or Soul of the sacrificial year. Given the connection between the city and the bride, it is entirely possible that the English word "city" is a cognate of "Sita" the bride of Rama. In the *Kurma Purana*, it comes to light that the demon Ravana only stole an *illusory* version of Sita. This illusory Sita is entirely symbolic of the mismeasured 12-month Vedic year which is not the *real* wife, cow, yajna, holy city or domain of the Purusha.

The circumstances of Sita's marriage to Rama further help to shine light upon the connection between Vishnu and the zodiac. According to the *Ramayana*, young Sita lifted a table that no one in her father's kingdom had been able to lift. Under this table was the bow of the divine architect, Vishwakarma. Subsequently, her father declared that the man who could lift and shoot the divine bow would have Sita's hand in marriage, knowing that no mortal man could lift or string the bow. Vishnu, as Rama, was able to lift and string the bow but broke it in half while testing its tautness. Regardless, he won Sita for his bride.

Knowing that the bow of the divine architect is a symbol of the vesica piscis, I was at first confused by the symbolism of the breaking of this sacred bow which is, in essence, eternal and unbreakable. Then I saw that the hieroglyph of Aries ♈ can be seen as a broken bow, or an arc of the vesica piscis "broken" in two. So now, in my mind, the breaking of Vishwakarma's bow in the *Ramayana* is symbolic of Rama as an emanation of Agni, the immortal priest of the twelve-month sacred year who is first born as the Ram (*Mesha*) of Aries. I realized the geometric basis of Rama's broken bow while looking at an image I had constructed for an earlier chapter.

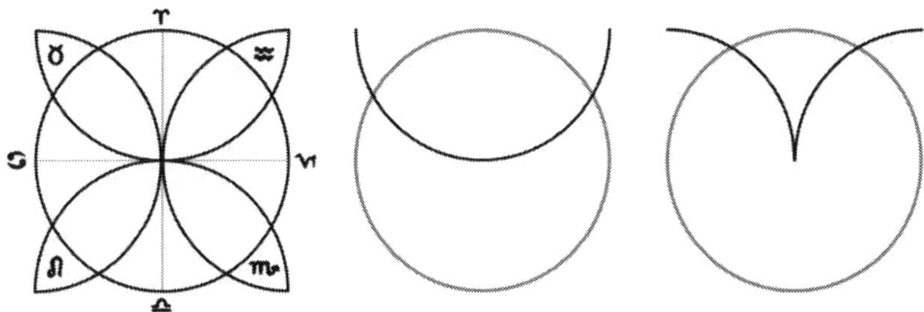

Regarding the time frame of Rama's incarnation, Thea wrote:

> *Rama's period corresponds to Libra, the sign of union and marriage, where Saturn is known to be in exaltation, hence the high tone of morality that his incarnation captured. The appearance of Rama hinges in great part on his union with Sita; this marriage is one of the Principle factors in the advent, in a quasi-moralistic way, in accordance with the work of the Age.*
>
> *...[Rama's] coming would have occurred during the Age of Leo, approximately 12,000 years ago, whose opposite sign is Aquarius, the Man, showing the accuracy of Sri Aurobindo's reference to Rama as 'the Man', and the avatar of the sattvic Human.*

Thea, *The Gnostic Circle*, p. 36

This placement of Rama in the Age of Leo within the 7th Manifestaion of Libra is shown in the figure to the right featuring the third quadrant of the Maha Yuga cycle.

> *We are aware that his incarnation is usually not placed so far in the past, but it must be pointed out that there are no precise records as to the actual time Rama was incarnated. The only accurate information is that he preceded Krishna.*

Thea, *The Gnostic Circle*, p. 34

Krishna – Vishnu's 8th Avatar

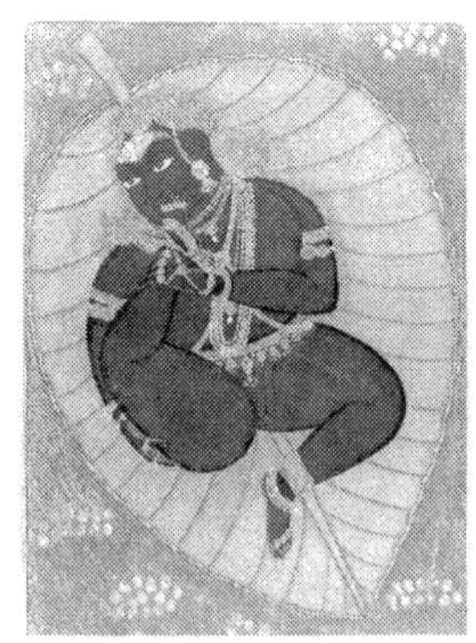

The Infant Krishna Floating on the Cosmic Ocean (Author unknown, c. 1840, Harvard Art Museums/Arthur M. Sackler Museum).

Vishnu's 8th Avatar is Krishna. The lore surrounding this figure is vast, but I will just focus on a few key elements which demonstrate the underlying geometric and zodiacal context of the mythology. As a baby, Krishna protects creation from a flood by inhaling it all into his belly, wherein the entire universe is contained. A sage finds the baby Krishna (Bala Krishna) floating happily on a Banyan leaf, unscathed by the all-consuming deluge. The impervious baby reveals to the sage that he is the Divine Purusha, Vishnu. The leaf that holds Bala Krishna and creation up from the waters of dissolution, like Vishnu's Fish and Turtle avatars, can be understood as a geometric figure. In this case, the leaf is a symbol of the vesica piscis and the child Krishna is a symbol of the radius. Like Bala Krishna and his leaf, the radius and the vesica piscis are impervious to harm and together they perpetually establish and reestablish the Earth's sacred mandala of life (the zodiac).

Krishna's names include *Govinda* "finder of the cows" and *Gopala* "protector of the cows". As we have seen, the cow is a symbol of the Vedic year which Vishnu eternally protects and preserves. Multiple cows (*gau* or *go* in Sanskrit) represent forms or divisions of the one circle, such as the months. Krishna is often depicted in a triadic stance *(tribhanga)* playing a reed flute and dancing with his gopis (female cow-herders) who are sometimes said to number 108 (9 x 12). Krishna's flute can be understood as a symbol of the measuring reed, rod or radius which establishes the cosmic harmonies of the Rishis' sacred year.

The name Krishna is translated as "black" or "dark", but the root of Krishna appears to be *krs* connected in the Rig Veda to the act of plowing by which furrows are drawn or dug out in a field. Such plowing, often accomplished via the help of a Bull, can be taken as a symbol of the radius's function of drawing (or digging) out multiple vesicae piscis in the field of the circle.[1]

> *[T]hese steeds of thine [Agni] are yoked, impatient, lightly running, ploughing blackened lines...gliding with easy speed, urged onward by the wind and rapid in their course. Dispelling on their way the horror of black gloom, making a glorious show these flames of his fly forth.... O Agni, shine resplendent with our wealthy chiefs, like a loud-snorting bull, accustomed to the house. Thou casting off thine infant wrappings blazest forth as though thou hadst put on a coat of mail for war.*
>
> Rig Veda, 4-5, 10, tr. R.T.H. Griffith

Krishna's main consort is Radha, whose name suggests she is the bearer or holder (*dha*) of the golden ray (*ra*). In terms of geometry, she is either a symbol of the circle or the vesica piscis. Krishna is said to be the eighth son of his parents, and to eventually take eight wives. When this lore is understood in the context of the twelve-month year, the eight sons and wives point to the 8th month of Scorpio. Regarding Krishna's association with this 8th month of the zodiac, Thea wrote:

> *The sign upholding the 8th Manifestation is Scorpio...thus Mars is the predominant planet of the Manifestation.... The most important document of Krishna's teachings, the Bhagavad Gita, which was revealed supposedly during the Battle of Kurukshetra, is our firmest support. The teachings are centred around the factor of War, which belongs to the domain of Mars.*
>
> Thea, *The Gnostic Circle*, p. 38

Krishna's field is not only a field of battle, it is also a field of cows and gopis, within which he is the master herder equivalent to Indra, the Bull. According to Thea, this symbolism is

---

[1] In addition to being the basis of Krishna, the Sanskrit root, *krs* is likely the origin of "cross" and "Christ".

attributable to the fact that the Vishnu's Age within the 8th Manifestation is the Age of Taurus the Bull.

Krishna's birth is placed around 3100 B.C., which is certainly more accurate than the time given for the birth of Rama....In this case Krishna's birth would have in fact fallen within the age of Taurus, but it may be that it was somewhat closer to the beginning of the Age than is generally believed.

Thea, *The Gnostic Circle*, p. 39

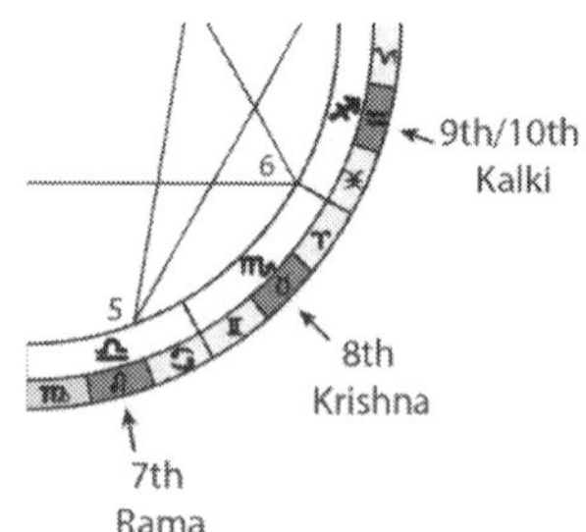

Krishna himself is very much characterized by Taurus, especially in his early years, the pastoral period of Brindavan when he was [a] cowherd and played his flute for the Gopis. If there is a symbol that can most honestly and accurately be associated with Krishna it is the Bull, or the Cow.

Thea, *The Gnostic Circle*, p. 38

Another bit of Krishna mythology worth mentioning is his uplifting of Govardhan Hill.[1] In the *Bhagavat Purana*, Krishna advised people to worship the hill of Govardhana from which their water came, instead of worshipping Indra the storm god. Upset by this situation, Indra sent a seven-day rain storm. Krishna thereupon lifted the hill and used it as an umbrella to shield the people from the storm. Duly humbled, Indra asked for forgiveness whereupon the cow of plenty Kamadhenu named him the divine protector of the cows. This mythology is reminiscent of the instances wherein

Krishna Holding Mount Govardhan (Mola Ram, c. 1790, Wikimedia Commons).

[1] The roots of Govardhan are *go* and *vardhana*, translated as "cow" and "nourishment".

Vishnu's first three avatars lift or otherwise save the world from flood waters. This hill, it seems clear enough now, is the vesica piscis. It is the "hill" of the zodiac upheld by the Purusha.

Lastly Krishna is said to have a virgin birth or, in other words, to have been conceived by divine means rather than by the sex act. This mythology, which is also attributed to Jesus Christ, hails from the Vedic sacrifice, wherein the Hero-Son's mother or mothers are characterized as virgins. The Virgin (*Virgo*) is a sign and symbol of the zodiac. It also appears to be a symbol of the vesica piscis – one of the two occult and virgin wombs of the Divine Son (i.e., of the radius). The other womb is the circle itself. With this geometry and symbolism in mind, it is worth revisiting the following verse from Rig Veda 4.7 regarding the virgin birth of Agni, whose path, like Krishna himself, is depicted as black (*krs*). This black path can be understood as the hidden path of Agni, the "Hidden One" of the Vedas.

> *Black is the path of thy shining, thy light goes in front, a journeying ray, the one supreme of all thy bodies; when one unimpregnated bears thee as the child of her womb, in the sudden moment of thy birth thou art already the messenger.*

Rig Veda 4.7.9, tr. Sri Aurobindo,
Hymns to the Mystic Fire, CWSA, Volume 16, pp. 239

Kalki – the 9th Avatar of Vishnu

Kalki (V&A Museum, Wikimedia Commons).

As previously discussed, Vishnu's 9th and last avatar is Kalki, the nine-fold One. He is commonly characterized as riding a white horse and brandishing the sword of supreme truth. In Indian lore, Kalki's role is to end to the reign and era of falsehood on Earth and to reestablish the *sanatana dharma* or eternal law and order on Earth. In our day and age Kalki is widely considered to be the 10th avatar of Vishnu, after Gautama Buddha. Thea recognized that this is an error resulting from the long-standing loss of the correct time-frame, the Vedic sense, and the zodiacal basis of the mythology. She saw that positing Gautama Buddha as the 9th avatar of Vishnu was not only premature in terms of the Age of his incarnation, but it was also entirely antithetical to the mission, sense and true context of Vishnu's lineage.

> *The Buddha was not the 9th Avatar; he was a shadow, as it were, of that Coming. But he has served a great and noble purpose. This was to carry the evolving spirit of humankind in the opposite direction from the goal (apparently), in order that the fullest depths be reached and the greatest distance from God be experienced by the collective soul* of the negation itself: *so that this darkest night would permit the rise of the new Dawn as the Time-Spirit indicates for this, our Age [of Aquarius]. It is this dawn that the 9th Avatar ushers in. Indeed, 9 is his number-power,*[1] *and 9 is the number of Birth and the New.*
>
> Thea, *Time and Imperishability*, pp. 47-48

Thea has written much on this subject in her books which I will not try to expand upon here. The gist of the error of considering Gautama Buddha an avatar of Vishnu can be explained in terms of the mythology we have already encountered. Whereas Vishnu is responsible for protecting and saving material creation and its eternal law, Gautama Buddha's teachings encouraged the transcendence of material creation and thus the rejection of the Divine Maya and sacred yajna of the Rishis. Sri Aurobindo described this rejection as a "trend of revolt against an ancient and universal religious practice…which destroyed in India the sacrificial system of the Vedic religion".[2] This revolt or rejection, based on the loss of the Divine Maya (the Divine Feminine principle) throughout the world, is akin to the mythology of Parashurama and Rama wherein the avatar must reclaim the stolen sacrificial cow or his kidnapped wife. In

[1] Thea was referring here to Sri Aurobindo, born in a 9-power year (1872).

[2] Sri Aurobindo, *Essays in Philosophy and Yoga, CWSA, Volume 13,* p. 246.

Buddhism's case however, the cow, wife or Divine Mother is deemed *unreal* and discarded as an illusion. Vishnu's perpetual role is to redeem and reclaim the Divine Feminine from such degradation, perpetually establishing and reestablishing the eternal union of Spirit and Matter, or Purusha and Prakriti.

We have seen that Vishnu is the *Preserver* of the Vedic year, and we have also seen that the key to Vishnu's preservation of eternal law is undeniably connected to the radius of the circle. Kalki's war horse and sword of truth can both be understood as symbols of the radius which establishes the eternal law (*sanatana dharma*) of the Soul within its field of Time and Space. The "galloping" of the horse is equivalent to the movement of the radius in its course or arc.

> *[The Horse of the Worlds bears all beings] up on His infinite strength and speed and motion. He bears all of them without respect of differences, sambhāvena, with the divine impartiality and equality of soul – samaṁ hi brahma. To the type of each individual being this Universal Might adapts himself.... It is He who bears them on in the courses of Time that are marked out for Him by His hidden Self; He is free and exults in the swiftness of His galloping.*

Brihadaranyaka Upanishad, 1.1, commentary by Sri Aurobindo,
Kena and Other Upanishads, CWSA, Volume 18, p. 283

> *The Aswamedha or Horse-Sacrifice is, as we shall see, taken as the symbol of a great spiritual advance, an evolutionary movement, almost, out of the dominion of apparently material forces into a higher spiritual freedom.* ***The Horse of the Aswamedha is, to the author, a physical figure representing, like some algebraical symbol, an unknown quantity of force & speed. From the imagery it is evident that this force, this speed, is something worldwide, something universal; it fills the regions with its body, it occupies Time, it gallops through Space,*** *it bears on in its speed men and gods and the Titans. It is the Horse of the Worlds, — and yet the Horse sacrificial.*

Sri Aurobindo, *Kena and Other Upanishads,*
CWSA, Volume 18, p. 276 [bold emphasis added]

In this light, it appears that Kalki (pronounced "Kal-key") is the personification or deification of the radius of the circle which emerges as the hidden KEY of the *sanatana dharma* of the Vedic yajna. Via the emergence of this essential key of gnosis, the world's ignorance concerning the Divine Son is naturally conquered. With this key, the Hidden One of the Rishis is no longer hidden, and the falsehood and mismeasure that is built up upon millennia of compounded misunderstandings of the veiled symbols of the Rishis becomes increasingly apparent to anyone interested in pursuing truth rather than protecting and perpetuating long-held misinterpretations of ancient gnosis.

The name *Kalki* does not appear in the Rig Veda, though it is clear enough that he is an incarnation of Agni – the immortal Hero-Son, priest and victor of the Vedic sacrifice. The root of Kalki, is *kal*, which is also the root of *Kali*, *Kala*, and *calendar* indicating that his victory is related to the victory of Time itself – the victory of the Sage. He is equivalent to Aeon, the Son of Time.

> *Time is the self of the horse sacrificial. [[Time is that which upholds existence in material space & is the soul of it.*[1]*]]*

Brihadaranyaka Upanishad, 1.1, tr. Sri Aurobindo,
Kena and Other Upanishads, CWSA, Volume 18, p. 268

> *He who is one and without hue, but has ordained manifoldly many hues by the Yoga of his Force and holds within himself all objects.... May He yoke us with a good and bright understanding....*
>
> *There is One, unborn...who is ever bringing forth many creatures with forms and her one unborn loves and cleaves to and lies with her....*
>
> *He in Time is the guardian of the world of existence and the master of the universe secret in all existences, — in whom have union of*

[1]This double-bracketed text is Sri Aurobindo's footnote for *Brihadaranyaka Upanishad 1.1.*

Yoga the holy sages and the gods; thus knowing him one cuts asunder the snares of Death.

Knowing him...the Benign secret in all existences, knowing the God who being one encompasses all, one is released from every bondage.

This is the God, the mighty Soul, the Architect of all, seated for ever in the hearts of creatures and he is realised by the heart and the intellect and the mind; who know this, they become immortal.

Svetasvatara Upanishad, 4.1, 5, 15-17, tr. Sri Aurobindo,
Kena and Other Upanishads, CWSA, Volume 18, p. 238

O Fire, from thee is born the Seer, the Horse and of thee are the Heroes whose might overcomes the adversary. O King, O universal Power, found in us the desirable treasures.

O Immortal, all the Gods come together to thee in thy birth as to a new-born child. O universal Power, they travelled to immortality by the works of thy will when thou leapedst alight from the Father and Mother.

Rig Veda 2.7.3-4, tr. Sri Aurobindo,
Hymns to the Mystic Fire, CWSA, Volume 16, p. 66

The Son of the sacrifice is a constant image in the Veda. Here it is the godhead himself, Agni who gives himself as a son to man, ***a Son who delivers his father. Agni is also the War-Horse and the steed of the journey, the White Horse, the mystic galloping Dadhikravan who carries us through the battle to the goal of our voyaging.***

Sri Aurobindo, *The Secret of the Veda,*
CWSA, Volume 15, p. 461 [bold emphasis added]

The Deva or Godhead [Agni] is both the original cause and the final result [of the Vedic sacrifice]. Divine Existent, builder of the worlds, lord and begetter of all things, Male and Female, Being and Consciousness, Father and Mother of the Worlds and their inhabitants, he is also their Son and ours: for he is the Divine Child born into the Worlds who manifests himself in the growth of the creature. ...He is the wise, mighty and liberating Son born from our works and our sacrifice, the Hero in our warfare and Seer of our knowledge, the White Steed in the front of our days who gallops towards the upper Ocean.

Sri Aurobindo, *The Secret of the Veda, CWSA, Volume 15*, p. 371

[Agni] great priest of the call has been born; the knower of the heavens.....Him greatly desiring Trita, son of the master of wide riches, found on the head of the light unslayable; he is born the youth who increases the felicity in our mansions and becomes the navel-centre of the luminous world.... [T]he rapturous priest of the call, the sacrificer ever-moving forward, the leader of the pilgrim-sacrifices, the traveller, the carrier of the offering, the purifying Flame...has come into being and leading him like a golden-maned war-horse, the great, the victorious, the founder of the Light...one who is free from ignorance, the render of the cities, the child of the forests, whose wealth is the illumined word....

Rig Veda 10.46.1-5, tr. Sri Aurobindo,
Hymns to the Mystic Fire, CWSA, Volume 16, p. 413

Ye [Ashwins] gave again the vigour of his youthful life to the sage Kali when old age was coming nigh....

[Ye] bestowed...a courser white, mighty with nine-and-ninety varied gifts of strength, a horse to be renowned, who bore his friend at speed, joy-giving, Bhaga-like to be invoked of men....

We have prepared this laud for you, O Aśvins, and...[have] decked it as a maid to meet the bridegroom, and brought it as a son, our [support] for ever.

Rig Veda 10.39.8, 10, 14, tr. R.T.H. Griffith

True, guardian of the Law....Fierce is [Agni's] gait and vast his wondrous body: he champeth like a horse with bit and bridle...darting forth his tongue, as 'twere a hatchet.... Archer-like, fain to shoot, he sets his arrow, and whets his splendour like the edge of iron....

Rig Veda 6.3.1-5, tr. R.T.H. Griffith

CHAPTER FIFTEEN

Kalki and the 9th Manifestation

> *The Gods kindle, most strong to slay the... adversary, the supreme Fire, the Horse of swiftness by whom the Riches are brought and pierced the demon keepers.*
>
> Rig Veda 6.16.48, tr. Sri Aurobindo, *Hymns to the Mystic Fire*, *CWSA, Volume 15*, p. 283

Once Vishnu's avataric lineage is rightfully reconnected to the geometry and gnosis of the twelve-month zodiac, it becomes clear that the horse-riding or horse-headed conqueror Kalki is a symbol-figure of Sagittarius, the 9th sign of the zodiac and the third of Agni's three fire signs. Much prophecy and speculation has been put forth regarding the time and place of Kalki's birth or coming. The most telling indication of his coming turns out to be his Horse-Man form, also known as Hayagriva. This zodiacal chimera of Sagittarius the Horse (♐) and Aquarius the Man (♒) tells us the *exact* Age in which Vishnu incarnates as Kalki within the Maha Yuga cycle. The *only time* in this great 77,760-year cycle wherein the Horse-Man chimera (the Centaur) appears is in Vishnu's Age of Aquarius within the 9th or Sagittarian Manifestation. According to Thea, we have been in this special Age of Vishnu in since 1926.

Hayagriva restoring Vedas to Brahma, by Ramanarayanadatta Astri (Wikimedia Commons).

Kalki's victory, which is the victory of the Divine Soul, necessarily involves the recovery and reclamation of his unified field of Being and Becoming – the field of the Vedic year. This is the essential task of Vishnu's lineage, by which the Soul of Time and its eternal law is reborn and reestablished on Earth, opening the gates of higher realms or stages of manifestation on Earth.

Thea on the 9th Manifestation and its Avatar

The 9th Manifestation is the period of Kalki, the unmasking of the illusion in which man has been living since the death of Sri Krishna, the 8th Avatar, the Incarnation of the 8th Manifestation which was the reign of Scorpio, the sign of Death.... Kalki comes to re-establish [order], to awaken man from his slumber in illusion to the reality of the Satyayuga.

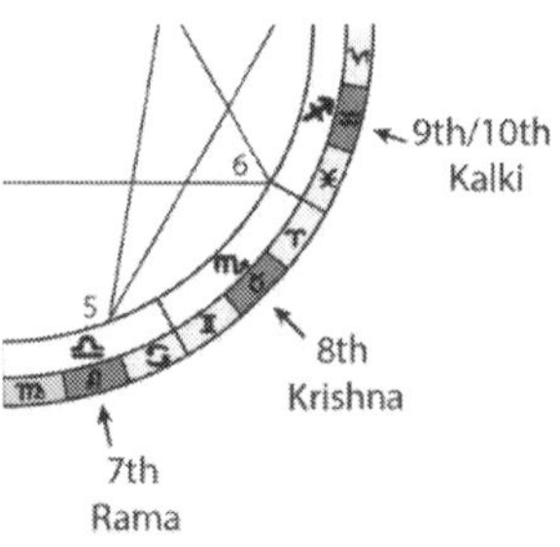

...[The illusion] was man's illusion regarding Time, the loss of the key of Truth.

Thea, *The Gnostic Circle*, p. 66

...The next step in the evolution of the species cannot fail to introduce a very different experience of death.

The 9th Avatar has demonstrated what that next step must be. His own 'death' has opened the door with the right Key. This is done with the allegiance of Time, and not otherwise. Indeed, the breakthrough is precisely a new experience of time whereby at death the flow is not severed, resulting in an unconscious rebirth. The second coming, if we dare use the phrase, implies an unbroken line in time – in this case between the 9th appearance [of the Avatar] and the 10th. They are thus one and the same because the line is not broken. 'Death' is not unconscious, not a sojourn 'on the other side' disconnected from this plane.

This can be achieved when Supermind is fully manifested and established here, the mission of the 9th and his collaborators.

Through his conscious 'death' the victory is cemented in the evolutionary matrix when the 9th Avatar himself becomes the 10th in an unbroken line of time between two. This is in a nutshell the definitive purpose of his coming

Thea, *Secrets of the Earth*, p. 86

In order...to move into the sphere of total vision and all-embracing time, man must move out of the sphere of Mind. This is the plane of Supermind that Sri Aurobindo has revealed. The 9th Manifestation is the period of transition in to the realm of Supermind. Therefore we say that Sagittarius is the sign of Supermind. To be more accurate we must say that in relation to our times this sign indicates the state where the evolution moves out of the realm of Mind and into the sphere of the Supermind. And this then preceeds the passage into the final three signs which are Sat-Chit-Ananda, Capricorn, Aquarius, Pisces, precisely the signs that make up the 9th Manifestation. We can easily say, therefore, that of all the periods of evolution, this is one of the most momentous, where man is offered the greatest possibilities and the fullest experience. For our civilization, what we are experiencing at present is preparing the way for the maximum we can aspire to in this Great Circle of 77,760 years, approximately 17,000 of which remain....

Thea, *The Gnostic Circle*, p. 47

Sagittarius is the last sign of the [Mental sheath, the third body or quarter]....[S]howing us that we are pushing through to the realm of Higher Mind and beyond [and] this great birth is nothing more than a preparation for the true spiritual transformation of the species. And through the sign Sagittarius and the birth cycles indicated, it is evident that the number 9 is a predominating factor and through it much can be understood in the harmonies of the spheres.

Thea, *The Gnostic Circle*, pp. 43-44

The time is upon us in this Aquarian Age to bring about a universal transformation of consciousness and to open man up to the consciousness of the universe, to expand in the Sagittarian way beyond the present limits of his mental instrument and prepare for the descent of a power and light that will allow him to live in the consciousness and being of the Whole. This is the Aquarian universality, the vision of Unity, and the Sagittarian impulse to reach the planes of consciousness of Truth.

Thea, *The Gnostic Circle*, p. 74

Kalki comes…to establish the reign of Truth. In order to do this he wields the sword of Fire, the power of Truth, and thus eradicates the falsehood prevailing, first and foremost in the spiritual realm on Earth.

The true Evolutionary Avatars have never formed religions, nor have religions sprung from their teachings.…The Avatar of the 9th Manifestation does not lay the foundations for a new religion, which would defeat the purpose of his advent. It is only the revelation of the next phase of spiritual experience and expression, and the discipline and yogic sadhana that accompanies it, that is his purpose, because each coming must lay before mankind a fuller experience of God. Each Manifestation signifies for humanity a greater possible expression and realisation of the Divine, and it is this that he comes to reveal. The Avatar cannot follow the traditional way, except insofar as he shows how that way prepares for the next step, the next piece in the divine Mosaic. He must explore the past, digest it and assimilate it into his own experience, and then he begins to reveal the actual thrust of the Age. He is the seed of the movement, as we have shown in our diagram of the Manifestation based on the quincunx (inconjunct) aspect.

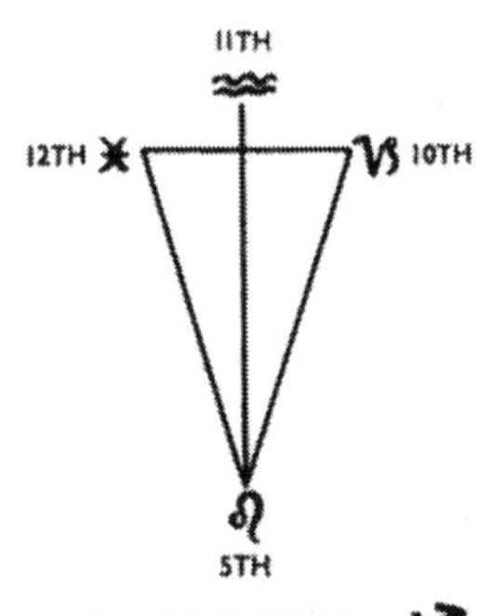

Sri Aurobindo is this seed. He was born with the Sun in Leo, the upholder of the three signs of the 9th Manifestation. However, he does not come alone in this work.… Sri Aurobindo's advent is intimately bound with the Mother's birth, and in the diagram she fills the position of Pisces, being born, in fact with the Sun in that sign. The third

position falls in Capricorn,[1] *and the Age of Aquarius, cupped in between the two, is the entire humanity, the collectivity as a whole, standing directly in opposition to Leo, the seed, the puruṣa. In fact, the meaning of Leo in the zodiac is the Purusha, and the spiritual quarter of the Circle, unlike any other quarters, is upheld by the Sun, which is also the Purusha of the entire system. Here in the Spiritual Quarter, the Sun is a direct influence. What it signifies for the structure of the whole solar system – the central and sustaining Light – shows itself to be true also for the spiritual quarter of the evolution of the divine body. It is the Sun, the Light of Truth, that feeds the trinity of the body of the Spirit in manifestation.*

Thea, *The Gnostic Circle*, pp. 42, 50

In this 9th Manifestation...the way of Mahakala[2] *[emerges], carrying humanity to the threshold of the 9th and highest of the Puranic stages of creation. Central to this process, upholding it, controlling it, securing its inevitable, victorious fulfilment is that Golden Bija,–Hiranyaretas. Our experience of God must thus be in this Immanence; and the Seed contains the totality of that which is extra-cosmic. It is the Transcendent born in the manifest universe, it is the Eternal born in time, and there is no difference between the two. Rather we may say, this manifestation in matter presents an enhanced and more complete experience. The purpose of material creation is thus to express the fullest attributes of the Supreme Consciousness. Multiplicity is the truth of the cosmos, a splendid diversity whose reason for being is that all aspects of God can be given expression, that the Absolute can know Itself, can enjoy Itself. Self-knowledge and self-enjoyment are the propellants for deployment of the Absolute in material creation, in this great Dance of Shiva. The hierarchy that exists in the universe covers the entire range of such a self-knowing and self-enjoyment, resulting in the fact that at any given moment all possibilities of expression, of manifestation, exist simultaneously. For this is the nature of that Golden Seed: simultaneity and wholeness and compactness are its keywords. All is contained within the Seed....*

---

[1] This "third position" is Thea, born on January 5, 1938 in the sign of Capricorn.

[2] Mahakala is the god of Time, from *maha* "great", and *kala* "time".

> *...[T]he first foundation of a new seeing arises: it is that the Transcendent and its immanent Seed, standing at the heart of material creation, are one and indivisible....*
>
> Thea, *Time and Imperishability, Part 1: Transcendence and the Immanence of the One*, pp. 15-16

The Reclamation of the Divine Feminine

In the previous chapter I discussed the mythology of Vishnu's avatars, who figure as preservers, heroes and protectors of the material world, the sacrificial cow, the Vedic sacrifice and the Divine Feminine. Essentially, Vishnu preserves and protects the Divine Maya. In this section, I will share some excerpts from Sri Aurobindo's writings that demonstrate his yoga of correcting what he considered to be Buddha's mistake, and his work towards reestablishing the eternal connection between the Divine Masculine (Spirit) and the Divine Feminine (Material Creation). Sri Aurobindo indicated that, in terms of the mythology or parable of Vishnu's avatars, this mistake is corrected by Kalki.

> *I consider that in trying to overshoot, Buddha like Shankara made a mistake, cutting away the dynamic side of the liberation. Therefore there has to be a correction by Kalki.*
>
> Sri Aurobindo, *Letters on Yoga I, CWSA, Volume 28*, p. 488

> *Purusha and Prakriti, Conscious Soul and executive Force of Nature, are in the supramental harmony a two-aspected single truth, being and dynamis of the Reality; there can be no disequilibrium or predominance of one over the other.*
>
> Sri Aurobindo, *The Life Divine, CWSA, Volumes 21-22*, pp. 293-94

> *The Shankara knowledge is...only one side of the Truth; it is the knowledge of the Supreme as realised by the spiritual Mind through the static silence of the pure Existence. It was because he went by this side only that Shankara was unable to accept or explain the origin of the universe except as illusion, a creation of Maya. Unless one realises the Supreme on the dynamic as well as the static side, one cannot experience the true origin of things and*

the equal reality of the active Brahman. The Shakti or Power of the Eternal becomes then a power of illusion only and the world becomes incomprehensible, a mystery of cosmic madness, an eternal delirium of the Eternal. Whatever verbal or ideative logic one may bring to support it, this way of seeing the universe explains nothing; it only erects a mental formula of the inexplicable. It is only if you approach the Supreme through his double aspect of Sat and Chit-Shakti, double but inseparable, that the total truth of things can become manifest to the inner experience. This other side was developed by the Shakta Tantriks. The two together, the Vedantic and the Tantric truth unified, can arrive at the integral knowledge....

[The] completer truth and a wider knowledge...is already indicated in the Gita's teaching of the Purushottama and the Parashakti (Adya Shakti) who become the Jiva and uphold the universe. It is evident that Purushottama and Parashakti are both eternal and are inseparable and one in being; the Parashakti manifests the universe, manifests too the Divine in the universe as the Ishwara and Herself appears at His side as the Ishwari Shakti. Or, we may say, it is the Supreme Conscious Power of the Supreme that manifests or puts forth itself as Ishwara Ishwari, Atma Atma-shakti, Purusha Prakriti, Jiva Jagat. That is the truth in its completeness as far as the mind can formulate it. In the supermind these questions do not even arise: for it is the mind that creates the problem by creating oppositions between aspects of the Divine which are not really opposed to each other but are one and inseparable....

It is possible to go towards the knowledge by beginning with the experience of dissolution in the One, but on condition that you do not stop there, taking it as the highest Truth, but proceed to realise the same One as the supreme Mother, the Consciousness-Force of the Eternal. If, on the other hand, you approach through the Supreme Mother, she will give you the liberation in the silent One also as well as the realisation of the dynamic One, and from that it is easier to arrive at the Truth in which both are one and inseparable. At the same time, the gulf created by mind between the Supreme and His manifestation is bridged, and there is no longer a fissure in the truth which makes all incomprehensible.

Sri Aurobindo, *Letters on Yoga II, CWSA, Volume 29*, pp. 448-49

The object of our Yoga is self-perfection, not self-annulment.... Buddha and Shankara supposed the world to be radically false and miserable; therefore escape from the world was to them the only wisdom. But this world is Brahman, the world is God, the world is Satyam, the world is Ananda; it is our misreading of the world through mental egoism that is a falsehood and our wrong relation with God in the world that is a misery. There is no other falsity and no other cause of sorrow.

God created the world in Himself through Maya; but the Vedic meaning of Maya is not illusion, it is wisdom, knowledge, capacity, wide extension in consciousness. Prajna prasrita purani. Omnipotent Wisdom created the world, it is not the organised blunder of some Infinite Dreamer; omniscient Power manifests or conceals it in Itself or Its own delight, it is not a bondage imposed by His own ignorance on the free and absolute Brahman.

If the world were Brahman's self-imposed nightmare, to awake from it would be the natural and only goal of our supreme endeavour; or if life in the world were irrevocably bound to misery, a means of escape from this bondage would be the sole secret worth discovering. But perfect truth in world-existence is possible, for God here sees all things with the eye of truth; and perfect bliss in the world is possible, for God enjoys all things with the sense of unalloyed freedom. We also can enjoy this truth and bliss, called by the Veda amritam, Immortality, if by casting away our egoistic existence into perfect unity with His being we consent to receive the divine perception and the divine freedom.

The world is a movement of God in His own being; we are the centres and knots of divine consciousness which sum up and support the processes of His movement. The world is His play with His own self-conscious delight, He who alone exists, infinite, free and perfect; we are the self-multiplications of that conscious delight, thrown out into being to be His playmates. The world is a formula, a rhythm, a symbol-system expressing God to Himself in His own consciousness.... Let us lead forward God's movement, play out His play, work out His formula, execute His harmony, express Him through ourselves in His system. This is our joy and our self-fulfilment; to this end we who transcend and exceed the universe, have entered into universe-existence.

Perfection has to be worked out, harmony has to be accomplished. Imperfection, limitation, death, grief, ignorance, matter, are only the first terms of the formula — unintelligible till we have worked out the wider terms and reinterpreted the formulary; they are the initial discords of the musician's tuning. Out of imperfection we have to construct perfection, out of limitation to discover infinity, out of death to find immortality, out of grief to recover divine bliss, out of ignorance to rescue divine self-knowledge, out of matter to reveal Spirit. To work out this end for ourselves and for humanity is the object of our Yogic practice.

Sri Aurobindo, *The Hour of God*,
"The Object of Our Yoga", *CWSA, Volume 12*, pp. 96-97

The Triadic Victory of Kalki

Thea saw the 9th stage of Vishnu's victory unfold as a triadic descent, reestablishing the seed or Hidden One of the Rishis' *trayi vidya* in our new age. In *The Gnostic Circle* Thea demonstrated the 9-6-3 pattern of this descent, wherein the 9, 6 and 3 correspond to the Sacred Trinity of the Transcendent, Cosmic and Individual Divine.

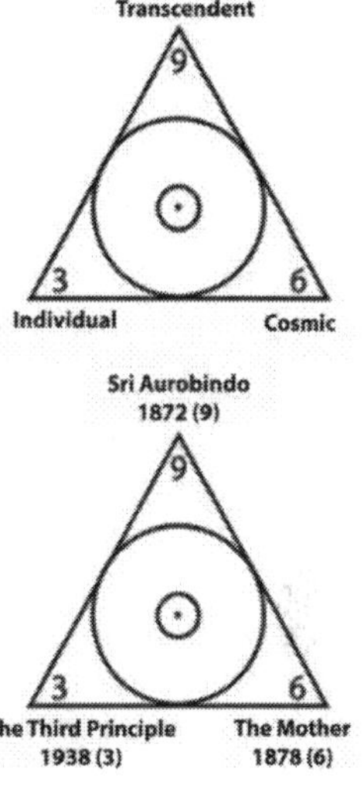

The Sacred Trinity, Thea, The Gnostic Circle, p. 273.

The 0-9 of the Sacred Triangle represents the Transcendent Divine, the 6 is the Cosmic Divine, and the 3 is the Individual Divine. A human being in his development moves from 0 (Transcendent) to 3 (Individual) to 6 (Cosmic) and then back to 9 (Transcendent)....

In terms of the evolution of the Manifest Divine in the Cosmos the process is reversed: the Transcendent descends, moves into the Cosmic, and then touches the Individual in the descent; the Seed appears to become smaller as it plunges, which in fact is the method of Descent.

Thea, *The Gnostic Circle*, p. 220

Thea did not make it explicit in *The Gnostic Circle* (1975) that she was the "Third Principle" of this triadic descent as laid out in her diagram, but her understanding of her own role is implicit in the fact that 1938 is her birth year. In 1976 Thea came to realize that Sri Aurobindo had taken rebirth in 1963, adding the number 1 to this descending pattern. In *The New Way, Volumes 1&2* (1981), Thea presented the following understanding of Vishnu's 9th and 10th avatars and the significance of the descending 9-6-3 pattern which gives rise to the birth of the 9-fold One.

> *[T]he avatars are nine because the tenth is the ninth returned. Moreover, the 9th is accompanied by two others who in terms of numbers are the 6 and 3 that grant it stability; and these three united become the supramental avataric womb that allows for the birth of the 10th or the 1, from this very womb, for the last is the first reborn. The 10 is the same 9 who once having appeared as the Father Transcendent, returns as the Son-Conqueror, the 10th avatar: Kalki.*
>
> Thea, *The New Way, Volumes 1&2*, p. 123

Thea's understanding of this triadic descent of Kalki was based on Sri Aurobindo's own yogic goal of bringing down and embodying the Transcendent Divine.

> *[If my aim is] to realise and also to manifest the Divine in the world, bringing down for the purpose a yet unmanifested Power, – such as the Supermind, – a harmonisation of all three [Transcendent, the Cosmic, the Individual] becomes imperative. I have to bring it down, and from where shall I bring it down – since it is not yet manifested in the cosmic formula – if not from the unmanifest Transcendence, which I must reach and realise? I have to bring it into the cosmic formula and, if so, I must realise the cosmic Divine and become conscious of the cosmic self and the cosmic forces. But I have to embody it here, – otherwise it is left as an influence only and not a thing fixed in the physical world, and it is through the Divine in the Individual alone that this can be done.*
>
> Sri Aurobindo, *Letters on Yoga I, CWSA, Volume 28*, p. 9

The nodus of Life is the relation between three general forms of consciousness, the individual, the universal and the transcendent or supracosmic. In the ordinary distribution of life's activities the individual regards himself as a separate being included in the universe and both as dependent upon that which transcends alike the universe and the individual. It is to this Transcendence that we give currently the name of God, who thus becomes to our conceptions not so much supracosmic as extracosmic. The belittling and degradation of both the individual and the universe is a natural consequence of this division: the cessation of both cosmos and individual by the attainment of the Transcendence would be logically its supreme conclusion.

The integral view of the unity of Brahman avoids these consequences. Just as we need not give up the bodily life to attain to the mental and spiritual, so we can arrive at a point of view where the preservation of the individual activities is no longer inconsistent with our comprehension of the cosmic consciousness or our attainment to the transcendent and supracosmic. For the World-Transcendent embraces the universe, is one with it and does not exclude it, even as the universe embraces the individual, is one with him and does not exclude him. The individual is a centre of the whole universal consciousness; the universe is a form and definition which is occupied by the entire immanence of the Formless and Indefinable.

This is always the true relation, veiled from us by our ignorance or our wrong consciousness of things. When we attain to knowledge or right consciousness, nothing essential in the eternal relation is changed, but only the inview and the outview from the individual centre is profoundly modified and consequently also the spirit and effect of its activity. The individual is still necessary to the action of the Transcendent in the universe and that action in him does not cease to be possible by his illumination. On the contrary, since the conscious manifestation of the Transcendent in the individual is the means by which the collective, the universal is also to become conscious of itself, the continuation of the illumined individual in the action of the world is an imperative need of the world-play. If his inexorable removal through the very act of illumination is the law, then the world is condemned to remain eternally the scene of unredeemed darkness, death and suffering. And such a world can only be a ruthless ordeal or a mechanical illusion.

Sri Aurobindo, *The Life Divine, CWSA, Volume 21-22*, pp. 42-43

The universe and the individual are the two essential appearances into which the Unknowable descends and through which it has to be approached; for other intermediate collectivities are born only of their interaction. This descent of the supreme Reality is in its nature a self-concealing; and in the descent there are successive levels, in the concealing successive veils. Necessarily, the revelation takes the form of an ascent; and necessarily also the ascent and the revelation are both progressive. For each successive level in the descent of the Divine is to man a stage in an ascension; each veil that hides the unknown God becomes for the God-lover and God-seeker an instrument of His unveiling....

...The universe and the individual are necessary to each other in their ascent. Always indeed they exist for each other and profit by each other. Universe is a diffusion of the divine All in infinite Space and Time, the individual its concentration within limits of Space and Time. Universe seeks in infinite extension the divine totality it feels itself to be but cannot entirely realise; for in extension existence drives at a pluralistic sum of itself which can neither be the primal nor the final unit, but only a recurring decimal without end or beginning. Therefore it creates in itself a self-conscious concentration of the All through which it can aspire. In the conscious individual Prakriti turns back to perceive Purusha, World seeks after Self; God having entirely become Nature, Nature seeks to become progressively God.

Sri Aurobindo, *The Life Divine, CWSA, Volume 21-22*, pp. 49-50

One day after his 63rd birthday in 1935, 9 years into the Age of Aquarius, Sri Aurobindo wrote:

Now I have got the hang of the whole hanged thing – like a very Einstein I have got the mathematical formula of the whole affair (unintelligible as in his case to anybody but myself) and am working it out figure by figure.

Letters on Himself and the Ashram, CWSA, Volume 35, p. 344

He did not explain this mathematical formula, it was apparently left for Thea to discover and flush out in conjunction with her discovery of Sri Aurobindo's rebirth in 1963.

The Trinity of Father, Mother and Daughter which brings forward the Divine Son or Immanent Divine in the world is a fully Vedic formula and is found in mythologies throughout the world.

> *The two mothers in whom is the Truth, in whom is the mage-wisdom, formed him and brought to birth like an infant child, they have put him firm in his place and make him grow. Men found in him the navel-centre of all that is moving and stable and they weave by the mind the weft of the seer.*
>
> Rig Veda 10.5.3, tr. Sri Aurobindo, *Hymns to the Mystic Fire, CWSA, Volume 16*, p. 395

> *Earth & heaven, the two mothers of Agni, are liberated from limitation and harmonised with each other....They are the two mothers of Agni, like the rivers, because in them & out of them the force manifests.*
>
> Sri Aurobindo, *Hymns to the Mystic Fire, CWSA, Volume 16*, p. 620

In one Indian myth, this triad and triadic son is the mountain god Himvat, his wife Mena and his daughter Ganga who carries the seed of Himvat in her waters. This is equivalent to the triad of Shiva, his first wife Sati and second wife Parvati (also known as the daughter of the mountains and an incarnation of Sati) whose love play generates the seed of the victorious hero Kartikeya. Another representation is the trio of Vishnu, Sridevi and Bhudevi and the eventual rebirth of Vishnu as Kalki. In Egyptian mythology, Horus is the divine son of Isis and Osiris (whose mother is Nut). In Greco-Roman mythology, this trinity is Zeus, Demeter, Persephone and the son is Iacchus or Bromius also known as Bacchus or Bacche.

The Vedic origin of Bacche, as well as his female entourage the Bacchantes or Bacchae,[1] is *bhaga*, consisting of the roots *bha*

---

[1] *Bacche* appears to be the root of Thea's surname *Bachelet.*

indicating a brilliant ray of light and *ga* meaning "to move quickly". Bhaga is another name of Agni,[1] equivalent to the divine skambha, lingam or radius which fills, delights and fertilizes creation. In the Rig Veda, Bhaga is a "bliss-bestower" and bestower of "the triple wealth and treasure".[2] From this Vedic lore comes the Roman Bacchanalia, which now symbolizes debauchery instead of its original Vedic sense of the victorious or treasure-winning son Agni.

It is a cosmological marvel that this ancient triadic formula has played itself out in the lives of the maha yogis who have accomplished the task of restoring the triadic gnosis (*trayi vidya*) of the Rishis in our current age.

The Lotus of the Avatar

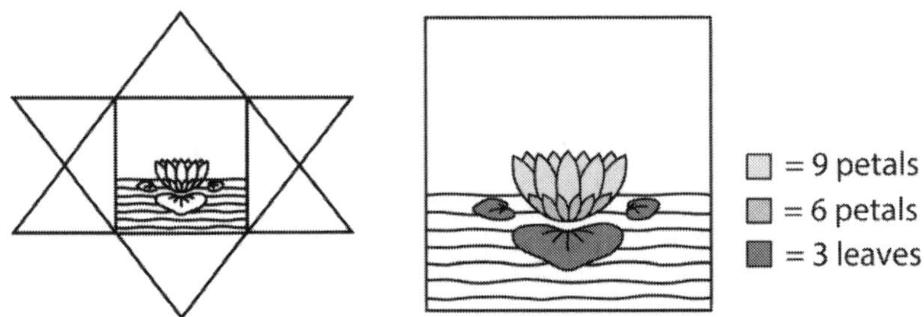

The descending 9-6-3 pattern is not only found in the birth years of Sri Aurobindo, the Mother and Thea, it is also found in Sri Aurobindo's symbol, the center of which is a lotus resting on seven waves.[3] The Mother called this lotus "the Avatar of the Supreme".[4] Sri Aurobindo's lotus fits within the interwoven ascending and descending triangles of his symbol, representing the simultaneous ascent and descent of the Divine on Earth.

---

[1] Rig Veda 6.13.2, tr. R.T.H. Griffith.

[2] Rig Veda 7.41.5, 3.56.6, tr. R.T.H. Griffith.

[3] Thea wrote of this lotus pattern in *The Gnostic Circle*, pp. 271-73.

[4] The Mother, April 4, 1958, *CWM, Volume 13*, pp. 28-29.

The lotus is a central figure in the lore and iconography of Vishnu and his avatars. Whereas Vishnu's Matsya (Fish) and Kurma (Turtle) avatars symbolize the essential and eternal building blocks and keys of the sacred year of which he is the guardian, his lotus symbolizes the fuller geometry and measure of the year. The lotus also symbolizes Vishnu's role as the Lord of the waters of Time and Space, eternally rising out of the waters via his own "stalk" which is a symbol of the radius. Sri Aurobindo's lotus symbolizes both his name,[1] and his avataric role in reestablishing and preserving the eternal law of the Purusha's field of Time and Space.

Thea shed light on the 9-6-3 pattern of the visible petals of Sri Aurobindo's lotus, but if we see this Lotus of the Avatar in three dimensions, rather than two, we can see it has nine top petals, twelve lower petals and rests on four leaves in the water. This geometry symbolizes the 9 + 12 structure of the Rishis' sacred year with its four cardinal points. In this light, Sri Aurobindo's lotus is a symbol of the yajna or yoga that Vishnu is responsible for preserving. In essence, the Lotus is his body, his abode, his Divine Maya, his wife, or his flowering within his own field of manifestation, all of which he protects and recovers from the forces of destruction and ignorance.

The 9:12 ratio of the three-dimensional lotus also reflects the 9 months of the 12-month year which bring forth the divine birth (the return of the Light) of the Vedic year, opening up the higher quadrant of Swar via the gateway of 0° Capricorn (Makar). Sri Aurobindo's lotus rests on seven waves which correspond to the seven rivers and waters of truth in the Rig Veda. These rivers or waves are freed in conjunction with the victory of the Divine Purusha, by whatever name, Agni, Indra, Vishnu, Kalki, etc.

It is worth noting here that the Mother reconfigured the height and width of the triangles of Sri Aurobindo's symbol in May of 1964, six months after Sri Aurobindo's rebirth. The Mother never indicated that this had anything to do with Sri

[1] Aurobindo, an alternate spelling of Aravinda, means Lotus.

Aurobindo's rebirth, and yet twelve years later the modified height of his symbol was one of the keys, together with the vesica piscis, by which Thea came to discover the year of Sri Aurobindo's rebirth in the sacred geometry of the Mother's temple vision, the center of which she saw as a light-filled translucent globe upheld by a marble pedestal featuring Sri Aurobindo's symbol on each of its four faces.[1]

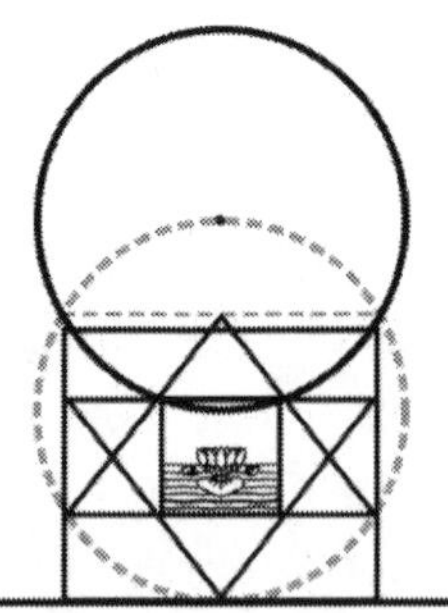

Core and Pedestal, Thea, The New Way, Volumes 1&2, 1981, pp. 238, 241.

> *The pedestal is precisely the support of the globe [of the Mother's Temple]...and bears [Sri Aurobindo's] symbol. Indeed, it is that very symbol – redesigned by the Mother in 1964 – that offers the key to the correct measurements of the pedestal. While serving as a support for the globe/core, at the same time the pedestal gives us all the pertinent details regarding the dissolution of the Father and his return in the form of the Son.*
>
> Thea, *The New Way, Volumes 1&2*, p. 207

Sri Aurobindo's Lion-Horse

In 1967, four years after Sri Aurobindo's rebirth, the Mother had a vision featuring a horse with a lion's head which Thea later recognized as a symbol of Sri Aurobindo's birth as a Leo and his rebirth in the sign of Sagittarius. Given what we have learned about the Horse's role in the completion of Vishnu's descent, this vision is especially poignant.

> *I saw a strange beast who came from there like that [Mother points to her left], made a round around you and went away. It was a horse with a lion's head.*
>
> *Beautiful beast! It was a lion, the head like that, the front form was a lion and behind, it was a horse. And it was the symbol of ... a*

---

[1] For more details on the Mother's original temple vision, see *Chronicles of the Inner Chamber*, www.matacom.com. The figure above is a combination of two images from *The New Way, Volumes 1&2*, pp. 238 and 241.

symbolical animal of something. At the moment I understood perfectly well, I said "Ah!" and ...

Very dignified. Came from there [same gesture to the left], like that, made a round around you and went away. It was for you. Lion is power, and horse...

And like that, it seems silly, but he was very beautiful, and of a beautiful color. And very dignified.

Oh!... (Mother notices she was speaking in English) It was Sri Aurobindo who said all that to you. It's funny, isn't it, it comes like that.

It was something that came to announce something to you. It was a being, but a being... There must be beings like that one. It was all in light, and it was... to announce something to you.

But so real!

The Mother's Agenda, Volume 8, December 16, 1967, pp. 415-16

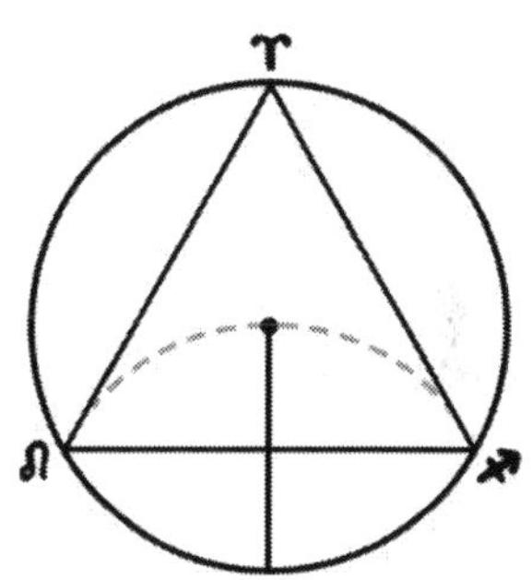

Sri Aurobindo's Lion-Horse chimera can be taken as not only a symbol of his birth and rebirth, but also as a symbol of the base of Agni's fire trine stretching 120° (432,000″) across the circle from 0° Leo to 0° Sagittarius – from the Lion to the Stallion of the zodiac. The 120° arc from Leo to Sagittarius is a step of the Divine Purusha (radius) in the field of Time and Space. Up until Agni's birth as the Horse of the zodiac, he and his law[1] are hidden. This is portrayed in the

[1] The word "law" appears to be etymologically connected to "leo" and "lion". "The Latin word ["leo"] was borrowed throughout Germanic (compare Old Frisian *lawa*; Middle Dutch *leuwe*, Dutch *leeuw*; Old High German *lewo*, German *Löwe*); it is also found in most other European languages, often via Germanic (Old Church Slavonic *livu*, Polish *lew*, Czech *lev*, Old Irish *leon*, Welsh *llew*)" (Douglas Harper, www.etymonline.com, accessed December 2016). In German "loh" indicates a flame. In India *Loh* or *Lava* is Rama's son, and in North India *Lohri* is a bonfire-lit celebration of the Return of the Light upon or the night before the Sun's entrance into the sign of Capricorn/Makar.

following verse as a lion couched (lying in wait) in its lair and as Agni hidden from view.

> *Him who had passed beyond his foes...couched like a lion in his lair. Him wandering at his own free will, Agni here hidden from our view.*
>
> Rig Veda 3.9.4, tr. R.T.H. Griffith

Agni's fire trine within the zodiac is portrayed by the Rishis as his three births and his triple flame.

> *Three are those births, the true, the most exalted, eagerly longed-for, of the God, of Agni.*
>
> Rig Veda 4.1.7, tr. R.T.H. Griffith

> *When threefold flame burns high for thee, to rest on poles of sacrifice, Thou with the living joyest in the self-bright Ship. Thy glory was the speckled cup, thy glory was the flawless scoop. Wherewith thou pourest into thy receptacle.*[1]
>
> Rig Veda 10.105.9-10, tr. R.T.H. Griffith

The ancient mythology and victory of Kalki and his War Horse is equivalent to the reestablishment of the hidden eternal law of the Divine Purusha or Soul in our world. As we have seen, this Purusha and its eternal law cannot be separated from the law or geometry of the radius. The two-dimensional geometries of the radius and circle are eternally linked to the multi-dimensional and dynamic expression of the Purusha in its field of Time and Space. Kalki, the 9th Avatar of Vishnu reestablishes this Vedic truth, in which all dimensions of reality are One. The lived-experience this all-harmonizing Oneness or Wholeness is the newly-opened and uncharted territory of the Supramental consciousness, completely foreign to our fragmented egoic-mental consciousness.

---

[1] The ship (*navam*) in Rig Veda 10.105.10 appears to be a symbol of the circle of nine (*nava*), and the cup, scoop, and receptacle are all symbols of the vesica piscis.

CHAPTER SIXTEEN

On Avatarhood

In order to help readers better understand the subject of avatars and the avataric nature of Sri Aurobindo, the Mother and Thea's supramental yoga, this chapter is entirely comprised of their own commentary on avatarhood.

Sri Aurobindo's Commentary on Avatars and Avatarhood

> *[To] the original being of light on the verge of the descent the one thing unknown was the depths of the abyss, the possibilities of the Divine in the Ignorance and Inconscience. On the other side from the Divine Oneness a vast acquiescence, compassionate, consenting, helpful, a supreme knowledge that this thing must be, that having appeared it must be worked out, that its appearance is in a certain sense part of an incalculable infinite wisdom, that if the plunge into Night was inevitable the emergence into a new unprecedented Day was also a certitude, and that only so could a certain manifestation of the Supreme Truth be effected — by a working out with its phenomenal opposites as the starting-point of the evolution, as the condition laid down for a transforming emergence. In this acquiescence was embraced too the will of the great Sacrifice, the descent of the Divine itself into the Inconscience to take up the burden of the Ignorance and its consequences, to intervene as the Avatar and the Vibhuti walking between the double sign of the Cross and the Victory towards the fulfilment and deliverance. A too imaged rendering of the inexpressible Truth? But without images how to present to the intellect a mystery far beyond it? It is only when one has crossed the barrier of the limited intelligence and shared in the cosmic experience and the knowledge which sees things from identity that the supreme realities which lie behind these images – images*

corresponding to the terrestrial fact — assume their divine forms and are felt as simple, natural, implied in the essence of things. It is by entering into that greater consciousness alone that one can grasp the inevitability of its self-creation and its purpose.

This is indeed only the Truth of the manifestation as it presents itself to the consciousness when it stands on the border line between Eternity and the descent into Time where the relation between the One and the Many in the evolution is self-determined, a zone where all that is to be is implied but not yet in action.

Sri Aurobindo, "The Riddle of this World",
Letters on Yoga I, CWSA, Volume 28, p. 258

Surely for the earth-consciousness the very fact that the Divine manifests himself is the greatest of all splendours. Consider the obscurity here and what it would be if the Divine did not directly intervene and the Light of Lights did not break out of the obscurity – for that is the meaning of the manifestation.

Sri Aurobindo, *Letters on Yoga I, CWSA, Volume 28*, p. 471

The descending Power chooses its own place, body, time for the manifestation....

Ibid., p. 471

An Avatar is supposed to be from birth. Each soul at its birth takes from the cosmic mind, life and matter to shape a new external personality for himself. What prevents the Divine from doing the same? What is continued from birth to birth is the inner being.

Ibid., p. 471

The Avatar is necessary when a special work is to be done and in crises of the evolution. The Avatar is a special manifestation while for the rest of the time it is the Divine working within the ordinary human limits as a Vibhuti.

Ibid., p. 485

Avatarhood would have little meaning if it were not connected with the evolution. The Hindu procession of the ten Avatars is itself, as it were, a parable of evolution. First the Fish Avatar, then the amphibious animal between land and water, then the land animal, then the Man-Lion Avatar, bridging man and animal, then man as dwarf, small and undeveloped and physical but containing in himself the godhead and taking possession of existence, then the rajasic, sattwic, nirguna Avatars, leading the human development from the vital rajasic to the sattwic mental man and again the overmental superman. Krishna, Buddha and Kalki depict the last three stages, the stages of the spiritual development–Krishna opens the possibility of overmind, Buddha tries to shoot beyond to the supreme liberation but that liberation is still negative, not returning upon earth to complete positively the evolution; Kalki is to correct this by bringing the Kingdom of the Divine upon earth, destroying the opposing Asura forces. The progression is striking and unmistakable....

...Buddha tried to shoot from mind to Nirvana in the Supreme, just as Shankara did in another way after him. Both agree in overleaping the other stages and trying to get at a nameless and featureless Absolute. Krishna on the other hand was leading by the normal course of evolution. The next normal step is not a featureless Absolute, but the Supermind. I consider that in trying to overshoot, Buddha like Shankara made a mistake, cutting away the dynamic side of the liberation. Therefore there has to be a correction by Kalki. I was of course dealing with the Ten Avatars as a "parable of the evolution", and only explaining the interpretation we can put on it from that point of view.

Ibid., pp. 487-88

The [divine] teacher is God himself descended into humanity; the disciple is the first, as we might say in modern language, the representative man of his age, closest friend and chosen instrument of the Avatar, his protagonist in an immense work and struggle the secret purpose of which is unknown to the actors in it, known only to the incarnate Godhead who guides it all from behind the veil of his unfathomable mind of knowledge; the occasion is the violent crisis of that work and struggle at the moment when the anguish and moral difficulty and blind violence of its apparent movements forces itself with the shock of a visible revelation on the mind of its representative man and raises the whole question of the meaning of God in the world and the goal and drift and sense of human life and conduct. India has from ancient times held strongly a belief in the reality of the Avatara, the descent into form, the revelation of the Godhead in humanity. In the West this belief has never really stamped itself upon the mind because it has been presented through exoteric Christianity as a theological dogma without any roots in the reason and general consciousness and attitude towards life. But in India it has grown up and persisted as a logical outcome of the Vedantic view of life and taken firm root in the consciousness of the race. All existence is a manifestation of God because He is the only existence and nothing can be except as either a real figuring or else a figment of that one reality. Therefore every conscious being is in part or in some way a descent of the Infinite into the apparent finiteness of name and form. But it is a veiled manifestation and there is a gradation between the supreme being of the Divine and the consciousness shrouded partly or wholly by ignorance of self in the finite. The conscious embodied soul is the spark of the divine Fire and that soul in man opens out to self-knowledge as it develops out of ignorance of self into self-being. The Divine also, pouring itself into the forms of the cosmic existence, is revealed ordinarily in an efflorescence of its powers, in energies and magnitudes of its knowledge, love, joy, developed force of being, in degrees and faces of its divinity. But when the divine Consciousness and Power, taking upon itself the human form and the human mode of action, possesses it not only by powers and magnitudes, by degrees and outward faces of itself but out of its eternal self-knowledge, when the Unborn knows itself and acts in the frame of the mental being and the appearance of birth, that is the height of the conditioned manifestation; it is the full and conscious descent of the Godhead, it is the Avatara.

Sri Aurobindo, "The Divine Teacher",
Essays on the Gita, CWSA, Volume 19, pp. 13-14

The Avatar is not supposed to act in a non-human way — he takes up human action and uses human methods with the human consciousness in front and the Divine behind. If he did not his taking a human body would have no meaning and would be of no use to anybody. He could just as well have stayed above and done things from there.

Sri Aurobindo, *Letters on Yoga I, CWSA, Volume 28*, p. 473

I have said that the Avatar is one who comes to open the Way for humanity to a higher consciousness — if nobody can follow the Way, then either our conception of the thing, which is also that of Christ and Krishna and Buddha, is all wrong or the whole life and action of the Avatar is quite futile. X seems to say that there is no way and no possibility of following, that the struggles and sufferings of the Avatar are unreal and all humbug, — there is no possibility of struggle for one who represents the Divine. Such a conception makes nonsense of the whole idea of Avatarhood — there is then no reason in it, no necessity for it, no meaning in it. The Divine being all-powerful can lift people up without bothering to come down on earth. It is only if it is part of the world-arrangement that he should take upon himself the burden of humanity and open the Way that Avatarhood has any meaning.

Sri Aurobindo, *Letters on Yoga I, CWSA, Volume 28*, p. 476

We are concerned only with the figure of the divine Teacher [Avatar] as it is presented to us in the [Bhagavad] Gita and with the Power for which it there stands in the spiritual illumination of the human being. The Gita accepts the human Avatarhood; for the Lord speaks of the repeated [bahūni me vyatītāni janmāni ...sambhavāmi yuge yuge], the constant manifestation of the Divine in humanity, when He the eternal Unborn assumes by his Maya, by the power of the infinite Consciousness to clothe itself apparently in finite forms, the conditions of becoming which we call birth. But it is not this upon which stress is laid, but on the transcendent, the cosmic and the internal Divine; it is on the Source of all things and the Master of all and on the Godhead secret in man....[Krishna] stands behind the great action of the Mahabharata, not as its hero, but as its secret centre and hidden guide. That action is the action of a whole world of men and nations, some of whom have come as helpers of an effort and result by which they do not personally profit, and to these he is a leader, some as its opponents and to them he also is an opponent, the baffler of their designs and their slayer and he seems even to some of them an instigator of all evil and destroyer of their old order and familiar world.... Where the action pursues its natural course or the doers of the work have to suffer at the hands of its enemies and undergo the ordeals which prepare them for mastery, the

Avatar [Krishna] is unseen or appears only for occasional comfort and aid, but at every crisis his hand is felt, yet in such a way that all imagine themselves to be the protagonists and even Arjuna, his nearest friend and chief instrument, does not perceive that he is an instrument and has to confess at last that all the while he did not really know his divine Friend....

...Arjuna and Krishna, this human and this divine, stand together not as seers in the peaceful hermitage of meditation, but as fighter and holder of the reins in the clamorous field, in the midst of the hurtling shafts, in the chariot of battle. The Teacher of the Gita is therefore not only the God in man who unveils himself in the word of knowledge, but the God in man who moves our whole world of action, by and for whom all our humanity exists and struggles and labours, towards whom all human life travels and progresses. He is the secret Master of works and sacrifice and the Friend of the human peoples.

Sri Aurobindo, *Essays on the Gita, Volume 19*, pp. 17-18

This doctrine [of the Avatar] is...a difficult thing for the human reason to accept; and for an obvious reason, because of the evident humanity of the Avatar. The Avatar is always a dual phenomenon of divinity and humanity; the Divine takes upon himself the human nature with all its outward limitations and makes them the circumstances, means, instruments of the divine consciousness and the divine power, a vessel of the divine birth and the divine works. But so surely it must be, since otherwise the object of the Avatar's descent is not fulfilled; for that object is precisely to show that the human birth with all its limitations can be made such a means and instrument of the divine birth and divine works, precisely to show that the human type of consciousness can be compatible with the divine essence of consciousness made manifest, can be converted into its vessel, drawn into nearer conformity with it by a change of its mould and a heightening of its powers of light and love and strength and purity; and to show also how it can be done. If the Avatar were to act in an entirely supernormal fashion, this object would not be fulfilled. A merely supernormal or miraculous Avatar would be a meaningless absurdity....

...No doubt, the descent of the Avatar, like the divine birth from the other side, is essentially a spiritual phenomenon, as is shown by the Gita's ātmānaṃ sṛjāmi, it is a soul-birth; but still there is here an attendant physical birth. How then were this human mind and body of the Avatar created? If we suppose that the body is always created by the hereditary evolution, by inconscient Nature and its immanent Life-spirit without the intervention of the individual soul, the matter becomes simple. A physical and mental body is prepared fit for the divine incarnation by a pure or great heredity and the descending Godhead takes possession of it. But the Gita...applies the doctrine of reincarnation, boldly enough, to the Avatar himself, and in the usual theory of reincarnation the reincarnating soul by its past spiritual and psychological evolution itself determines and in a way prepares its own mental and physical body. The soul prepares its own body, the body is not prepared for it without any reference to the soul. Are we then to suppose an eternal or continual Avatar himself evolving, we might say, his own fit mental and physical body according to the needs and pace of the human evolution and so appearing from age to age, yuge yuge? In some such spirit some would interpret the ten incarnations of Vishnu, first in animal forms, then in the animal man, then in the dwarf-man soul, Vamana, the violent Asuric man, Rama of the axe, the divinely-natured man, a greater Rama, the awakened spiritual man, Buddha,[1] and, preceding him in time, but final in place, the complete divine manhood, Krishna, — for the last Avatar, Kalki, only accomplishes the work Krishna began, — he fulfils in power the great struggle which the previous Avatars

[1] Here Sri Aurobindo includes Buddha on this list of Vishnu's Avatars as is custom in India, referring to him as the "awakened spiritual man", though elsewhere he refers to the need for correction of the Buddha's far-reaching error of "calling away the dynamic side of the liberation" (*Letters on Yoga I, CWSA, Volume 28*, p. 488). This error, according to Sri Aurobindo, was equivalent to a "revolt of Spirit against Matter that for two thousand years, since Buddhism disturbed the balance of the old Aryan [Vedic] world, has dominated increasingly the Indian mind". For thousands of years India and Eastern spirituality has largely followed and perpetuated the non-Vedic conclusion that "renunciation [is] the sole path of knowledge, acceptation of physical life [is] the act of the ignorant, cessation from birth [is] the right use of human birth, the call of the Spirit, the recoil from Matter" (*The Life Divine, CWSA, Volume 21-22*, pp. 26-27). As Thea later clarified in her writings, Gautama Buddha does not belong on this list of Vishnu's Avatars.

prepared in all its potentialities. It is a difficult assumption to our modern mentality, but the language of the Gita seems to demand it.

Sri Aurobindo, *Essays on the Gita, CWSA, Volume 19*, pp. 164-66

You say that this way[1] *is too difficult for you or the likes of you and it is only "Avatars" like myself or the Mother that can do it. That is a strange misconception; for it is, on the contrary, the easiest and simplest and most direct way and anyone can do it, if he makes his mind and vital quiet, even those who have a tenth of your capacity can do it.... For the Leader of the Way in a work like ours has not only to bring down and represent and embody the Divine, but to represent too the ascending element in humanity and to bear the burden of humanity to the full and experience, not in a mere play or Lila but in grim earnest, all the obstruction, difficulty, opposition, baffled and hampered and only slowly victorious labour which are possible on the Path. But it is not necessary nor tolerable that all that should be repeated over again to the full in the experience of others. It is because we have the complete experience that we can show a straighter and easier road to others — if they will only consent to take it.*

Sri Aurobindo, *The Mother and Letters on the Mother, CWSA, Volume 32*, p. 94

If [the Avatars] are shams, they have no value for others or for any true effect. If they have no value for others or for any true effect, they are perfectly irrational and unreal and meaningless. The Divine does not need to suffer or struggle for himself; if he takes on these things it is in order to bear the world-burden and help the world and men; and if these sufferings and struggles are to be of any help, they must be real. A sham or falsehood cannot help. They must be as real as the struggles and sufferings of men themselves — the Divine bears them and at the same time shows the way out of them. Otherwise his assumption of human nature has no meaning and no utility and no value.... What is the use of admitting Avatarhood if you take all the meaning out of it?...

If the existence of the Divinity is of no practical effect, what is the use of a theoretical admission? The manifestation of the Divinity in the Avatar is of help to man because it helps him to

[1] Or yoga.

discover his own divinity, find the way to realise it. If the difference is so great that the humanity by its very nature prevents all possibility of following the way opened by the Avatar, it merely means that there is no divinity in man that can respond to the divinity in the Avatar.

...You think then that in me (I do not bring in the Mother) there was never any doubt or despair, no attacks of that kind. I have borne every attack which human beings have borne, otherwise I would be unable to assure anybody "This too can be conquered." At least I would have no right to say so. ...I repeat, the Divine when he takes on the burden of terrestrial nature, takes it fully, sincerely and without any conjuring tricks or pretence. If he has something behind him which emerges always out of the coverings, it is the same thing in essence, even if greater in degree, that there is behind others — and it is to awaken that that he is there. The psychic being does the same for all who are intended for the spiritual way — men need not be extraordinary beings to follow Yoga. That is the mistake you are making — to harp on greatness as if only the great can be spiritual....

...I am seeking to manifest something of the Divine that I am conscious of and feel — I care a damn whether that constitutes me an Avatar or something else. That is not a question which concerns me. By manifestation of course I mean the bringing out and spreading of that Consciousness so that others also may feel and enter into it and live in it.

Sri Aurobindo, *Letters on Himself and the Ashram, CWSA, Volume 35*, 7 March 1935, pp. 417-19

The one and only aim we have before us is to bring down the supramental consciousness and the supramental Truth into the world; the Truth and nothing but the Truth is our aim, and if we cannot embody this Truth, a hundred incarnations do not matter. But to bring down the true supramental and nothing but the true supramental, to escape from all mental mixture is not an easy matter.

Sri Aurobindo, *Letters on Yoga II, CWSA, Volume 29*, p. 422

The Mother's Commentary on the Avatar

Sri Aurobindo came on earth from the Supreme to announce the manifestation of a new race and the new world, the Supramental. Let us prepare for it in all sincerity and eagerness.

The Mother, August 15, 1972, *CWM*, *Volume 13*, p. 19

Sri Aurobindo's work is a unique earth-transformation.

The Mother, *CWM*, *Volume 13*, p. 21

Sri Aurobindo incarnated in a human body the supramental consciousness and has not only revealed to us the nature of the path to follow and the method of following it so as to arrive at the goal, but has also by his own personal realisation given us the example; he has provided us with the proof that the thing can be done and the time is now to do it.

Ibid., p. 21

In the eternity of becoming, each Avatar is only the announcer, the forerunner of a more perfect realisation. And yet men have always the tendency to deify the Avatar of the past in opposition to the Avatar of the future. Now again Sri Aurobindo has come announcing to the world the realisation of tomorrow; and again his message meets with the same opposition as of all those who preceded him. But tomorrow will prove the truth of what he revealed and his work will be done.

The Mother, February 21, 1957, Ibid., p. 22

The essential mistake was to have considered Sri Aurobindo's teaching as one among the spiritual teachings — and the work done here now as one among the many aspects of the Divine works. This has falsified your basic position and has been the cause of all the difficulties and confusions. If this mistake is corrected in your mind and in your attitude all other difficulties will disappear easily. You must understand that what Sri Aurobindo represents in the world's history, is not a teaching, not even a revelation; it is a decisive action direct from the Supreme. And I am just trying to fulfil that action.

The Mother, 1961, Ibid., pp. 22-23

In the world's history...[W]hat Sri Aurobindo has come to bring is not a teaching, not even a revelation, but a FORMIDABLE action coming direct from the Supreme.

It is something pouring over the world.

The Mother, *The Mother's Agenda, Volume 2*, February 18, 1961, p. 60

[T]hose who want to flee [physical manifestation] in order to realize the divine Will are in error. What must be done is exactly opposite! The two [the Eternal Truth and the development in manifestation] must be combined in a perfect way....

There are two parallel things that, from the eternal and supreme point of view, are of identical importance, in that both are equally essential for the realization to be a true realization.

On the one hand, there is what Sri Aurobindo – who as the Avatar, represented the supreme Consciousness and Will on earth – declared to me to be, that is, the supreme universal Mother; and on the other hand, there is what I am realizing in my body and through the integral sadhana....Sometimes one predominates, sometimes the other (I don't mean successively in time, but...it depends on the moment), and they are trying to combine in a total and perfect realization: the eternal, ineffable and immutable Consciousness of the Executrice of the Supreme, and the consciousness of the Sadhak of the integral Yoga who strives in an ascending effort towards an ever increasing progression.

To this has been added a growing initiation into the supramental realization which is (I understand it well now) the perfect union of what comes from above and what comes from below, or in other words, the eternal position and the evolutionary realization.

The Mother, *The Mother's Agenda, Volume 2*, October 10, 1958, pp. 209-10

The consciousness is like a ladder: at each great epoch there has been one great being capable of adding one more step to the ladder and reaching a place where the ordinary consciousness had never been. It is possible to attain a high level and get completely out of the material consciousness; but then one does not retain the ladder, whereas the great achievement of the great epochs of the universe has been the capacity to add one more step to the ladder without losing contact with the material, the capacity to reach the Highest and at the same time connect the top with the bottom instead of letting a kind of emptiness cut off all connection between the different planes. To go up and down and join the top to the bottom is the whole secret of realisation, and that is the work of the Avatar. Each time he adds one more step to the ladder there is a new creation upon earth.... The step which is being added now Sri Aurobindo has called the Supramental; as a result of it, the consciousness will be able to enter the supramental world and yet retain its personal form, its individualisation and then come down to establish here a new creation. Certainly this is not the last, for there are farther ranges of being; but now we are at work to bring down the supramental, to effect a reorganisation of the world, to bring the world back to the true divine order. It is essentially a creation of order, a putting of everything in its true place; and the chief spirit or force, the Shakti active at present is Mahasaraswati, the Goddess of perfect organisation.

The Mother, *Questions & Answers, 1929-1931*, *CWM, Volume 3*, pp. 178-79

[M]ore and more these days, I find myself facing the whole problem as if I had never seen it before. Both paths [science and spirituality] may be leading towards a third point, and that third point is what I am at present ... not exactly studying; I am rather in quest of it – the point where the two paths merge into a third that would be the TRUE thing. ...This "something" is what we are seeking. And perhaps not merely seeking – we may be taking part in the MAKING of it.

We are being made use of in the manifestation of this "something."

Something none can yet imagine, for so far it hasn't come into being. It is an expression yet to come.

That is all I can say....

...I don't think any single individual on earth (as it is now) no matter how great he may be, no matter how eternal his consciousness and origin, can all by himself change and realize...

Change the world, change the creation as it is, and realize that higher Truth, the Truth that will be a new world – a truer, if not absolutely true, world. A certain number of individuals (until now they seem to have come in succession, in time, but they might also come as a collectivity, in space) would seem indispensable for this Truth to be concretized and realized.

On a practical level, I am sure of it.

In other words, no matter how great he may be, no matter how conscious, how powerful, ONE avatar all alone cannot realize the supramental life on earth. Either a group in time, a number of individuals staggered over a certain period of time, or a group spread out over a certain space – or maybe both – is indispensable for this Realization. I am convinced of it.

The individual can give the initial impulse, point out the path, WALK the path himself (I mean show the path by realizing it)...but he can't bring the work to fulfillment. The fulfillment of the work depends on certain collective laws that are the expression of a particular aspect of the Eternal and Infinite – naturally, it's all one and the same Being! There aren't different individuals and personalities, it's all one and the same Being. But the same Being expressing itself in a particular way that for us translates as a group or a collectivity.

The Mother, *The Mother's Agenda, Volume 3*, May 24, 1962, pp. 96-97

Thea's Commentary on Vishnu's Avatars

If we have spoken so extensively of the Avatar of the Age and laid such stress on clearly establishing who this is, the student must understand that the reasons which prompt us to do this are not at all connected to aspects of devotion, or faithfulness to a doctrine or school, or any such consideration. It is only for the sake of truth, and mainly for the truth which is contained in the zodiac. The purpose of this work is to show how the zodiac is a map of evolution, and the only way to do this effectively is to pinpoint the Evolutionary Avatars, as we have called them, within this map, and through them to reveal the truth of the zodiac for mankind. There is no other way, because it is only in their lives that the truth is revealed to man. Any sincere student of cosmic harmonies must look at this fact, rid himself of any resistance, and then he can be carried to the essence of astrology, and if this study is to descend from the realm of theory, the concrete facts must be given. It is not our intention to become a mouthpiece for any sect in formation, of any new religion. Our task is to be at the service of Truth, exclusively, and to show some hidden aspects in the studies of the harmonies of the Cosmos.

There is, as well, no intention of setting up comparisons between one spiritual figure and another, seeking to establish the greater. We strive only to show the role they are playing and to bring clarity into the field of knowledge which has been all too much abused and obscured. If, for example, we have spoken of the mistake of placing Gautama, the Buddha, on the list of the Hindu Avatars, it is simply because he does not belong on that list, not that he is unqualified as a spiritual and religious leader. In this study we are dealing with the evolution; which is the essence of astrology; in dealing with the evolution we are dealing with man and his spiritual destiny and experience as well, for none of these can be separated from the other, nor can man extract himself from the evolution of the races of Earth. If he is a part of this Earth life and has taken birth on this planet, there is no way he can escape participating in the destiny of its evolution.... If it seems that we have exalted the two evolutionary Avatars Rama and Krishna and made a definite statement about the third, the Kalki of our times, it is purely to bring to mankind the true understanding of the zodiac, which is the Earth's map of evolution.

Man perhaps does not realize what a sublime revelation the zodiac is, that in effect he can know the destiny of the planet therein. It is time he awakens to this fact.... In order to move ahead in full consciousness with the times, as they demand, man must know and have implicit faith not only in his destiny, but in the destiny of the Earth and its entire evolution.

Thea, *The Gnostic Circle*, pp. 84-85

[It] is necessary to discuss in depth the question of avatarhood, as the Indian tradition calls it. In the world today there is immense confusion as to what this means, and in consequence who these beings may be. It would seem that the Earth is populated by an increasing number of 'incarnations' who see themselves as either

Kalki, or the Christ in his second coming, the Messiah, or even Krishna, Buddha, or Shiva and his Son. There are as well a good number of female incarnations who feel themselves to be representatives on Earth of Durga, or Kali, or the Divine Mother in her full form. How are we to know what is true in this great proliferation?

In the beginning of this work it was stated that our times are characteristic of the manifestation of the Divine Consciousness in a phase of its expression of perfection in detail, – that which the Indian tradition attributes to Mahasaraswati, one of the four aspects of the Divine Shakti. This perfection must therefore be found in the lives of the line of Incarnations who are that Divine Consciousness descended upon Earth. There can be no vagueness in the manifestation of the supramental/solar line; nothing left to speculative deductions of mental knowings. In this study, where all element of speculation is to be eliminated, we are obliged to put forth all the details related to the line of supramental avatars, precisely in order to bring alive the statement that the Divine Consciousness manifests now in its cosmic aspect of perfection in detail. The chamber [of the Mother's Temple] itself is a result of this aspect of the Mother.

As the coming of incarnations who are to bring about the birth of a new Earth is a reality in our times, it is easily understood why many people who are touched by some higher light in any of the many spiritual experiences now begin to see themselves as those Incarnations. This truth is permeating the Earth atmosphere and people who are in some way receptive catch hold of it, but because of an unregenerated nature – usually in the vital – they place themselves at the centre of the new world and believe themselves to be its Messenger. The ego distorts the experience, one opens oneself to the forces of the vital plane that can easily masquerade as higher powers and the seeker often falls under the spell of such forces, from which he can extract himself only with great difficulty. Thus today the world enjoys a proliferation of Christs, Kalkis and Maitreyas, simply because indeed the time has come, only the race has not as yet the new eyes with which to see the truth of the matter.

The Solar Line, or the line of supramental avatars, is known and recognized by the fact that the birth and lives of these Incarnations bear a most unique relationship with Time, as stated off and on throughout [this book]. Because of this, these beings are able to act as the force of unification on Earth. But this is not enough. Such a relationship with the Time-Spirit allows the Solar Line to join the evolution on Earth to the higher laws that govern the entire Cosmic Manifestation. It must be understood that such Incarnations do not develop into what they are <u>*after*</u> *birth. They* <u>*are*</u> *eternally, and their births on Earth at specific moments in Time are, in fact, for the purpose of accelerating the evolution of the involved truth-consciousness seed. Thus they do not develop into avatars but are that from that first moment of entry into Earth-time, and follow it throughout the remainder of their life spans. Likewise it is not merely a personal experience that reveals the destiny, not simply the seeing of some great consciousness whereby one has experienced the oneness with the entire universe and becomes identified with the Divine Mother, depending upon the religious background of the subject.*

These experiences have their worth and on an individual level they are valid and true. Yet in themselves they do not indicate avatarhood. However most people who today proclaim themselves to be avatars, or who are proclaimed as such by their disciples and followers, have no credentials other than these. They have an experience wherein a vital power communicates, in a way that accords with their individual temperament, the apparent destiny of avatarhood and because the nature is impure, the ego still present, the experience is not questioned and the individual immediately accepts his personal interpretation of it as true.

In India there is an even more evident proliferation. But the avatar, or to be more explicit, the 'evolutionary avatar' – as Rama and Krishna were – appears on Earth only at its intervals of approximately 6,000 years. This line of Evolutionary Avatars is the same as the Puranic line of Ten Avatars [of Vishnu], the last of which is Kalki. However, as we have stated in other works, – the avatars are nine because the tenth is the ninth returned. Moreover, the 9th is accompanied by two others who in terms of numbers are the 6 and 3 that grant it stability; and these three united become the supramental avataric womb that allows for the birth of the 10th or the 1, from this very womb, for the last is the first reborn. The 10 is the same 9 who once having appeared as the Father Transcendent, returns as the Son-Conqueror, the 10th avatar: Kalki.

Nine is the number of the Occult Trinity: 3 x 3. It cannot be understood, nor can it serve as the master key to open the doors of higher knowledge, unless it is seen to hold in itself the numbers 6 and 3. The sum of 9, 6, and 3 is 18. In consequence, we can speak of the fourth as either, the One, or the Ten (following the 9), or the Nineteenth (following the 18), all of which do equal 1. Hence we must stress once more in this present study, as we have done in previous ones: only 1 after 9 is unity, and the unity of such a 1 consists in its being in actual fact the Fourth. Therefore the Line of the Sun starts from 9, which is the rhythm of the luminary's own pulse with respect to Earth, passes on to 6 and then down to 3; until finally through the 3, the last of the tri-power original cell, the 9 returns as the One, and this is Kalki or Shiva's son Kartikeya, who is 'Shiva himself'.

9, 6, and 3 is the Occult Trinity inherent in the Zero. These three powers are the essence of the Zero, and their interrelationship eventually gives rise to the number-power 1. A practical example by which the student can come to appreciate the role of the Zero and its tri-fold power structure with respect to the 1 is as follows: If we wish to count we first take a breath and then pronounce the word, which in this case is 'one'. The breath preceding the word is equivalent to the zero/womb; the three phases of the breath, intake, suspension, and output, are the three powers of the occult trinity of Creation, Preservation and Destruction/Dissolution. These are 9, 6, and 3. Finally the Word arises, the One, from the powers of the third in the series, the outgoing breath. The Word, or the Son, cannot be perceived of as separate from the Zero/Breath. In the same manner, there is no unity of the One, unless it is known to be the fourth in the Descent, the product of the Zero Avataric Womb of 9, 6, and 3.

Today India has lost the key to a true understanding of the avataric descent. Thus there are many 'avatars', none of whom have any greater claim to the title than some individual experience that has the power to influence only a limited entourage. Worst of all the Indian is plagued by a fascination with the miraculous, or rather, with the display of miracle-performing. Thus for him the yogi who will perform a greater number of 'miracles' is bound to be the avatar of the new age.

It must be stated here that such miracles are, as it were, sleeping pills. By having a contact with such beings and powers of the vital worlds or planes or by acquiring some siddhis that are the outcome of certain rigorous tapasyas, it is certainly possible to perform such miracles, to materialize objects, to levitate, to appear in different places at one time, to heal the sick, and so forth; but these phenomena in no way alter the human consciousness. This is not a power of transformation. The real Evolutionary Avatar is not distinguished in this way but rather by the Knowledge he brings into the Earth atmosphere from a higher plane, a plane that for our times is the plane of truth-consciousness whose symbol is the Sun. Such Knowledge is the power, the only true power of transformation for it works steadily and surely in the consciousness of the human being and brings about a general uplifting; and it acts as a universal force that affects not just one being or small group, but rather through the Time-Space it is able to work upon the entire collective consciousness. Our age is particularly the Age of the universal transformation, for which purpose the line of supramental avatars alone reveals the most unique affinity with the universal harmonies. Through their very births the Cosmic Truth is unveiled, the cosmos becomes alive and vibrates with a deep, a high and wide Sense, – a meaning that is then brought down to Earth and shown to be the sense not only of the collective evolution but of the individual as well. This only the real Avatar can do. This alone is the real miracle, and this alone can bring salvation to the world. The incarnation who by this very birth accomplishes this, because of the veils that hide the truth, which are cast aside by his coming, is the World Redeemer.

Knowledge is Power. In the past Knowledge was withheld from the masses because it could have been misused by the unenlightened or the spiritually impure. But the Knowledge that has descended today cannot be misused, and therefore it can be revealed. No one can acquire 'control' over another by the use of the Knowledge here put forth because we are simply dealing with the power and harmony of Time. We are revealing the ***sense*** *of Time, and how in the very flow of Time – which no one can arrest or alter or control – the establishment of a life divine upon Earth is certain, for Time is the seed of Destiny. The onward flow of Time is the motor of the evolution that exists in order to unfold the seed of truth-consciousness inherent in all created things. Thus, who can misuse this Knowledge? And for what purpose? He who approaches it is himself transformed, his consciousness is uplifted* *for he is given the means by which to perceive the unity of all things and the great harmony of cosmic existence. Above all he learns of the harmony of his own planet Earth, and with it of the instruments of the Supreme through whom the new Earth is born.*

Nonetheless, though this Knowledge cannot be misused, we are well-aware of the hostility that arises in many who are personally offended when they contact it, either because they believe themselves to be the Avatar or the Messiah, or because they are only aware of a part of the avataric descent. They closet themselves in a partial understanding, for any number of reasons peculiar to human nature, and refuse to accept the full reality because it disturbs their already fixed notions. Others cannot tolerate the decisiveness that accompanies the Descent and the elimination of all speculation – simply because this calls for the silencing of the mind. It is the mental ego that is the scourge that deadens the light in the human consciousness, by means of which one could otherwise perceive reality.

Thus, the true Evolutionary Avatars, and especially the last of the descent that we call the Supramental Avatars, or the Solar Line, can conquer the hold of Mind over the human race by simply being the embodiments of a Truth that they reveal through the details of their own Coming. These details will be found in their lives, then in the community that forms around them, then in the nation that is the home of the descent, India; and from there the truth-consciousness that they bring will be seen at work in the life of the planet itself, and finally in the essence of the entire universal manifestation. The means for an orderly formulation and transmission of this Knowledge is the chamber-core [of the Mother's Temple].

Thea, *The New Way, Volumes 1&2*, pp. 121-25

PART TWO

[It] is by the ray of intuition... that Saraswati
makes us conscious of the great waters....

Sri Aurobindo, *Hymns to the Mystic Fire,*
CWSA, Volume 16, p. 18

[Indra] slew the Dragon, freed the Seven Rivers,
and drove the kine forth from the cave of Vala....
[W]ith seven guiding reins [he] set free
the Seven great Floods to flow....

Rig Veda 2.12.2, 12, tr. R.T.H. Griffith

The seventh angel poured out his bowl into the air,
and out of the temple came a loud voice
from the throne, saying, "It is done!"

Revelation 16:17, NIV

The angel showed me the river of the water of life....

Revelation 22:1, NIV

CHAPTER ONE

An Ending and a New Beginning

On June 30, 2016, as I was trying to finish up what is now Part One of this book, news came that Thea's health was quickly declining. I cleared my teaching schedule and, after recovering from an acute ear infection, I flew to be with her in Mysore where I was immediately gifted with acute bronchitis accompanied by sharp pain in the general area of spleen and pancreas. I soon returned home physically wiped out. I felt clear upon booking my return flight that my highest good was getting back to the task of birthing this book, rather than being part of Thea's end-of-life care team. I also felt clear that my physical illness was simply an unpleasant catalyst to get me back to my desk. I knew these things were true, but was nonetheless deeply sad to leave Thea in her time of need. I was also deeply sad knowing that my days of having her as a living guide and sounding board were quickly coming to an end. Odds were that she would never read my book, which was not even halfway written at the time.

Thus, in early August of 2016, as I was approaching the 4.5 Point (the halfway point) of my 47th year, I felt ill, physically exhausted, emotionally contracted, and painfully on my own. This state of being was an unwelcome contrast to the expansiveness, delight and luminosity of the first third of the year. On August 11,[1] I reread some of what Thea had written about the 4.5 Point of any year or

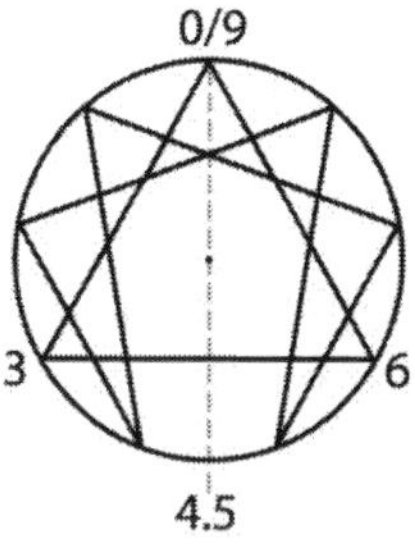

---

[1] In the leap year of 2016, August 11 fell 181 days into my 47th year from February 12. Considering the full 366 days of 2016, the exact 4.5 point was August 13th.

cycle, reminding me that I just needed to let go of how I wanted things to be, and move forward with the work I was given to do.

> *[The 4.5 Orbit is] the abyss of the Asteroid Belt, the disintegrating force or that which brings a profound change in the being, a change at the very depths. It corresponds to the sign of Libra. This is the beginning of passage through the higher half of the wheel, the progression back to the Origin and progress through the sphere of light commences.…[A]ll things and beings must [continue on and]…pass out of the influence of this sphere and touch the Saturn point which would then open the gates to the even fuller experience. This [6] point would be the real birth of the soul. …When the 6th [point] is reached,… the greater the matter that is crystallised and serves as an obstruction in the passage, the greater will the suffering and the destruction be in order to bring about the opening to a new life and a new future.* [1]
>
> Thea, *The Gnostic Circle*, p. 177

On August 13, I had a vivid and beautiful dream of a small ray or quantity of light dancing amidst an otherwise pitch-black cave. The quality of the light was unusual. It was golden and slightly iridescent. It moved quickly and gracefully, as if alive. The delightful light conveyed a sense of bliss and seemed to represent the beginning of the end of the darkness in the cave.[2] Two days later, upon the 144th anniversary of Sri Aurobindo's birth, I finally got back to my desk hoping the illuminating force and flow of the book would return. Then on the night of August 18th I had a remarkable dream reminding me that I was on the right track and all was as it needed to be.

In the dream, I was on a trek in a mountain valley guarded by mountain lions and other large predatory cats as well as huge

---

[1] Two months after reading these illuminations regarding the 4.5 and 6 Point, Thea's passed precisely at the 6 Point of my 47th year.

[2] A year later, in August of 2017 while swimming in a mostly shaded pool I realized that the light in the August 13 cave dream looked and behaved like sunlight refracting through water. I had assumed that the medium the light was moving through in the cave was *air*, but could see in retrospect that it was *water*.

wolf-like dogs. After narrowly surviving being killed by two dogs, my companions and I were allowed passage and taken upward through the valley on a railroad cart. The landscape was extraordinarily vast and beautiful, illuminated by light that seemed brighter and denser than ordinary light. The hillsides were adorned with large translucent jewel outcrops, many of them emitting light. As we approached the final summit of the mountain, it became apparent that water was emerging from within and pouring out through the surface of the mountain. The whole mountain top was a fountain, creating extraordinary lusciousness on the mountain side and in the valleys and plateaus. The water behaved unusually at times, taking on the appearance of liquid jewels as it descended down the luscious peak. With the water came what seemed to be the height of abundance and beauty. The air and light had a different quality as well, the whole place felt like a living harmony, energy manifesting as joy or bliss. I knew that both these dreams were connected to the Vedic lore of the entrapment and release of the light and the waters of truth-consciousness from their cave or mountain. I also knew the dreams were good omens, connected to what I was writing. I did not know, however, that they foreshadowed what I was about to learn next regarding the recovery and release of the light and the waters of truth from their mountain or cave.

Before I travelled to India I had been working on the Kalki chapter. Returning to this point in the book was a challenge. Clearly something was missing in my understanding and I dove into research mode which helped me better understand the symbolism of the divine Purusha, especially in the forms of the Lion and the Horse. By the last week of September 2016, the Kalki chapter had still not come together. Nonetheless, I was feeling expansive and happy with what I was learning, and I knew it was just a matter of time before that chapter and the end of the book sorted itself out. Everything felt on track and I appreciated the gradual unfolding of the larger picture. The book wasn't pulling itself together as fast as I wanted it to, but still I was delighted as deeper levels of the Vedic symbols continued to make themselves known to me.

On September 27, 2016 news came from India that Thea's health was worsening and that she had been admitted into a small private hospital in Bangalore. The number power of that day, month, and year was 9.9.9. One of my colleagues noted that the ten-day Durga Puja festival was about to commence spanning from October 2nd through October 11th.[1] Another colleague noted that the 45th anniversary of Thea's arrival in India and Pondicherry with her son in 1971 fell on September 28 and 29, 2016. As mentioned in Part One, Chapter 5, in 1971 these dates corresponded to the 9th and 10th days of Durga Puja, which symbolizes the Divine Mother's final battle with and victory over Ignorance. Thea passed on the evening of October 9 with her son and brother by her side. Two days later, on the "10th Day of Victory" of the 2016 Durga festival, Thea was cremated at Skambha, at the entrance of her horse pasture, thus ending the story of her 45-year residence and work in India.

Thea had written in *The New Way, Volumes 1&2* that she would likely "withdraw from the Work" in 2016 at the age of 78,[2] though she later told her students that this did not necessarily mean she would leave her body at that time. As it turns out, her withdrawal from the work did involve her departure. Considering Thea's relationship with Time, I was immediately curious about the significance of the date of her passing. *Why 9.10.2016?*[3] The number value of the day (9) and month (10) immediately stood out as significant in terms of the Vedic birth or victory which Thea had spent 45 years of her life illuminating. She recovered the zodiacal context of the Rig Veda in which the 9th and 10th months of the 12-month year figure prominently in conjunction with the defeat of the forces of Ignorance. Throughout her works, she repeatedly emphasized the importance of reestablishing the

---

[1] The first day of this festival is calculated as the first day after new moon of Virgo. In 2016, this new moon of Virgo was celebrated on October 1 (due to India's Sidereal calculation of the zodiac), thus Durga Puja began on October 2.

[2] Thea, *The New Way, Volumes 1&2*, p. 254.

[3] In India, the format of dates is Day-Month-Year, so October 9th, 2016 would there be written: 9 October 2016 or 9.10.2016.

sacred measure and celebration of Makar Sankranti – the passage between the 9th and the 10th month of the Vedic Year – on the December Solstice. She sounded the wake-up call in India that the sacred twelve-month year of the Rishis and the passage into the fourth and highest realm of this sacred year is only properly observed and opened via the Solar or Tropical Year.

> *[T]he sign Makar does not begin when it should for Hindus. It is 23 days AFTER the onset of the sign. Capricorn in all ancient civilisations, foremost of all the Vedic, begins (the sankranti or gateway) at the exact time of the December Solstice, the shortest day of the year.... There is a very deep purpose in this timing to coincide with the shortest day.... [By] positing this gateway 23 days after it actually occurs, that 'door' has passed us by. The result is that the most important of all Vedic injunctions – the 9 becomes the 10 – cannot be realised. It is as simple as that.*
>
> Thea, "A Calendar that Unifies", 2009

For Thea, this Vedic phrase "the 9 becomes the 10" was not just about the passageway between the 9th and the 10th month of the Vedic Year, it was also about the rebirth of the 9th avatar as discussed in Part One, Chapters 13 through 16.

> *The 10 is the same 9 who once having appeared as the Father Transcendent, returns as the Son-Conqueror, the 10th avatar: Kalki. ...[T]he 9 returns as the One...*
>
> Thea, *The New Way, Volumes 1&2*, p. 123

It reflects both the completion of the full circle of 9 and the culmination of the 9 "months" or stages of gestation in the 12-month year, the womb of the Divine Mother via which the Hidden One or Divine Purusha is born forth, establishing the realm of Truth-Consciousness on Earth (Swar). Through her life and yoga, Thea brought forward the true sense and context of this Vedic birth, illuminating its real impact on our evolutionary journey.

With Thea's passing during the week of the Durga Puja, I came to understand that, in terms of Vedic Gnosis, the victory of the Divine Mother over Ignorance on Vijaya Dashami (the 10th Day of Victory) of the Durga Puja is inseparable from her function as the Mother of the Divine Son of the Vedic yajna. I understood that the 9 (3 x 3) nights of the Durga festival symbolize the three trimesters of the sacred year which bring forth the Hidden One. In other words, the 10th day of this festival (after the 9th night) is equivalent to the victorious birth of the Son, Soul or Immanent Divine Purusha born forth from the womb of our evolutionary journey or Matrix. I understood that naturally the victory of the Divine Mother and the victory of the Divine Son is one and the same victory. I was happy to see that the full number power of the 10th day of the Durga Puja festival of 2016 was 3 within a 9-power year[1], mirroring the sacred geometry and law of the 3 within the circle of 9 as set by the radius – the Hero-Son of the yajna.

In looking at the timing of Thea's passing I was amazed to see that the New Moon of the Durga Puja, October 1, fell *exactly* 270 days after Thea's birthday and that her cremation took place *exactly* 280 days after her birthday.[2] These points in her year are respectively equivalent to 0° Capricorn (the passageway from the 9th to the 10th month) and 10° Capricorn – the 7 Point of the circle.

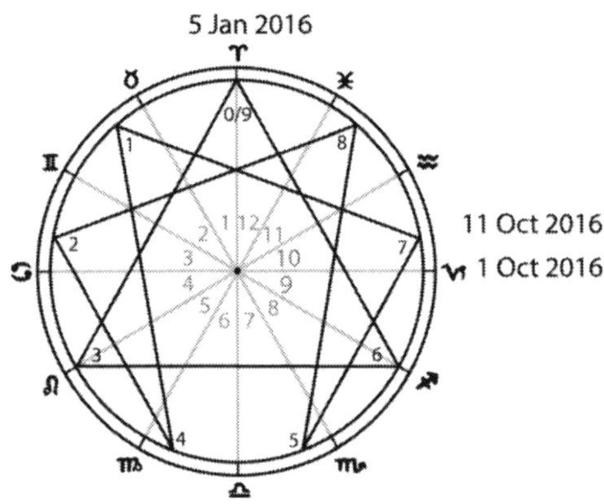

---

[1] 11.10.2016 = **1** + **1** + **1** + 0 + **2** + **0** + **1** + **6** = 12 = 1 + 2 = **3**; and 2016 = **2** + **0** + **1** + **6** = **9**.

[2] January 5 plus 270 days is October 1 in a leap year (such as 2016). January 5 plus 280 days is October 11 in a leap year.

The 7 Point in the circle corresponds to the 280-day gestational period of humans. It also corresponds to the birth of each Gregorian Year on January 1.[1] Thea called the Gregorian Year the "time year" and the Solar (Tropical) Year the "space year".

> *The Mother's inner chamber locates the two 'years' that we must use for time reckoning in an evolved society: the* space year *which begins with the Spring Equinox [in the northern hemisphere] of March, and the* time year *which is situated in the calendar year on January 1st.... That most of the world observes these Vedic dates, except India thanks to the Post-Vedic Astrologers, indicates how much penetration Supermind has made in the evolutionary matrix, though vested interests in India refuse to follow its enlightened lead, just as they refused to accept Sri Aurobindo's superior approach to the Veda.*
>
> Thea, "Supermind and the Calendar – any Connection?", 2011

Thea often noted the immense importance of the fact that the Ganges River descends from its source, *Gaumukh* to its mouth on the Bay of Bengal at 90°E Longitude. In *The New Way, Volumes 1&2* Thea showed the zodiac laid out upon the 360° measure of the Earth's latitude and longitude,[2] and on this map 90°E Longitude corresponds to 0° Capricorn and 10° Capricorn corresponds to 80°E Longitude. The two lines of longitude on the map to the right of undivided India (*Akhand Bharat*) emphasize the 10° span between 90°E-80°E Longitude, equivalent to the 10° span between 0°-10°

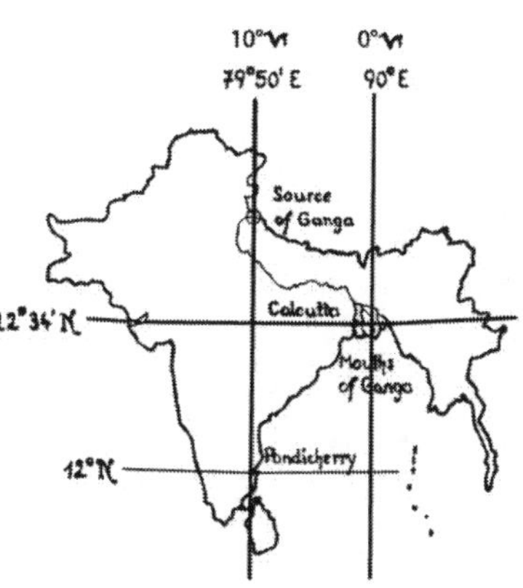

Thea's map of India, The New Way, Vols. 1&2, p. 345, with added 90° E Longitude line & zodiacal degrees.

---

[1] January 1 falls at 10° Capricorn in (280° into) the Tropical Zodiac.

[2] *The New Way, Volumes 1&2*, p. 377.

Capricorn in the Tropical Year. This 10° stretch of the zodiac takes us from the December Solstice to the New Year of the Gregorian calendar. In Thea's 78th year (from the zero point of January 5, 2016) this same span from 0°-10° Capricorn corresponded to October 1 through October 11.

Early in 2016 I drew up a longitudinal ruler to demonstrate that both Gaumukh (79°4′ E) and Pondicherry (79°50′ E) fall in the space of 10° Capricorn on our globe. Upon Thea's passing I added to this picture, demonstrating how the timing of her departure and the Durga festival of 2016, match up with the descent of the Ganges River across the body of India.

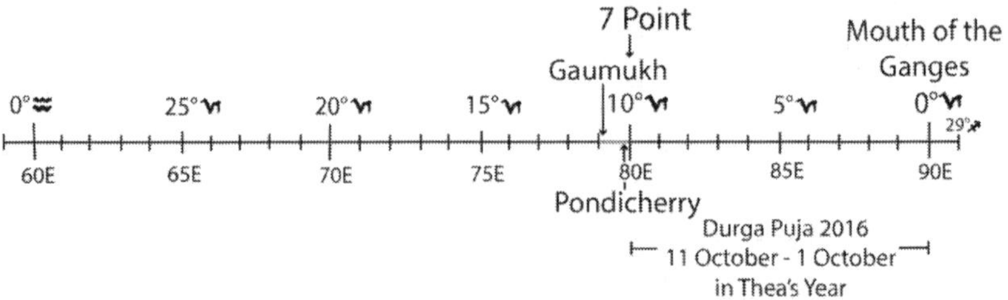

This graphic portrays 32 degrees of longitude, emphasizing the 30° span from 60°E to 90°E Longitude which encompasses much of the body of India. According to Thea's geo-cosmology, this 30° stretch of the Earth's longitude is equivalent to the sign of Capricorn. Via this image and the two preceding it, readers can hopefully appreciate that the timing of Thea's passing highlights some of the central themes of her life's yoga. It is a marvel that the culmination of the 1971 and 2016 Durga Puja festivals served as bookends of her 45 years in India; and it is also a marvel that October 11, 2016 corresponded to 10° Capricorn, the 7 Point of her year. This is the degree of longitude from which the Ganges river is *released* upon the Earth, beginning Her descent through India. Thea's last publication was entitled *Ganga – soul of Indian culture – Her descent to Earth*, wherein she discussed the importance of the geographic measure of the Ganges in conjunction with the reestablishment of the true measure of Makar Sankranti (0° Capricorn) in India.

India has lost the connection with the cosmic harmonies; this is abundantly clear; for as much as Ganga continues to be worshipped, this can no longer be done in ignorance because Ganga does not only embody power – she stands for the highest knowledge of things Earthly: she alone can join the Earth to the heavens and allow the solar realm to reach the planet we inhabit, but which we are mercilessly abusing. With the loss of the higher knowledge she brings by her very own divine Capricorn measure, otherworldliness has become the goal of all spirituality and religions, denying her the potential of saving the planet – the very reason for her sanctity among all the rivers of the Earth. At the Kumbha Mela each year devotees throng to her waters to save their souls – but they forget that she is with us to save the entire planet by providing the Divine Measure to join Heaven and Earth.

...When knowledge is lost, superstition is born. Then we cannot complain when academics insult and demean the beliefs we cherish. For all practical purposes these beliefs are indeed nothing but superstition since the myths have been stripped of their highest science and wisdom....

...India's dharma is to link the world to the heavens. It is done via the correct Makar Sankranti – that is the 0 point of Capricorn at her mouths in the Bay of Bengal.... A mistaken measure is far worse than no measure at all. Pundits and astronomers have brow-beaten Hindus into believing that 'Makar has shifted', *they pontificate. She is* 'no longer there', *they claim. But, pray tell, where is Makar then? Where is the time measure of Ganga's outlet to the world in her temporal body if not at the measurable 0 degree of Capricorn?...*

Ganga has, miraculously, physical dimensions that make her contribution to the Cosmic Truth self-evident....

...The equinoxes and the solstices are the means to attain perfect accuracy for determining the exact moment of entry into Makar/Capricorn. This is 'written' in the position of Ganga herself on the body of Bharat.

Thea, *Ganga – soul of Indian culture*, 2015, pp. 19-20, 25-27

The New Moon of October 1, 2016 marked Thea's passage from the 9th to the 10th sign not only in terms of her yearly cycle, but also in terms of her nine-year cycle (or ennead). Her 9th and final ennead began upon her 72nd birthday, January 5, 2010. This precise timing of her entrance into Makar/Capricorn in her last ennead is demonstrated in the following graphic wherein January 5th, 2010 is placed at the beginning of the cycle, and 6.75 years later (3/4ths of the 9-year cycle), October 1, 2016 falls at 0° Capricorn. Each degree of the 9-year cycle is equivalent to 9 days.

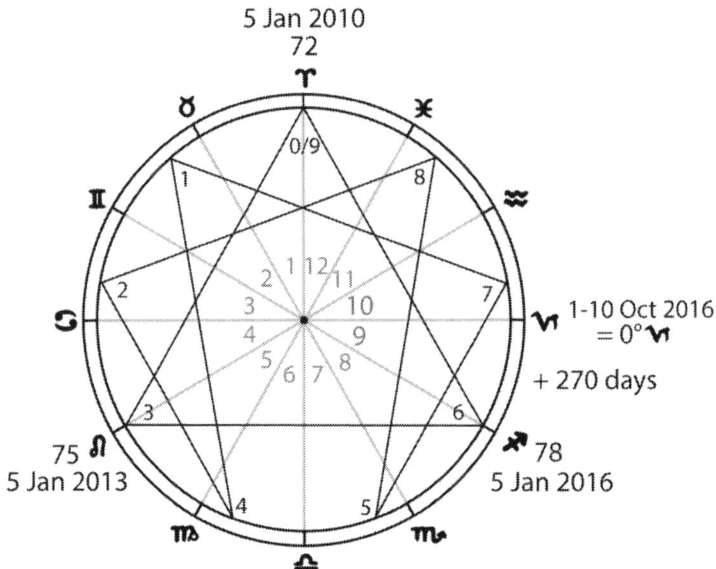

Soon after Thea's passing I stumbled across an email she had written to a colleague on October 15, 2010 indicating the importance of October 10th in her life. She wrote that it was the day in 1986 when she named her center "Skambha", and added, "In a number of other ways 10th October has surfaced, down to the arrival of my first mare in 1984, and the first Collie [at Skambha] was born in Italy on the same date, the mother of all the line to follow. It is also my mother's birthday." She wrote this email highlighting the importance of this date because on October 10, 2010 she experienced the first warning signs of her Cancer, though at the time she did not pursue a diagnosis or treatment. She just let it all play out, not wanting to intervene medically. In May of 2014 (approaching the 4.5 Point of Thea's 9th ennead) a diagnosis and medical intervention became necessary. I was with her in the hospital then and was duly impressed that she recovered enough from that ordeal to forge ahead, continuing her work for two more years. Thea passed a few hours shy of October 10, 2016, six years after the first signs of her illness.

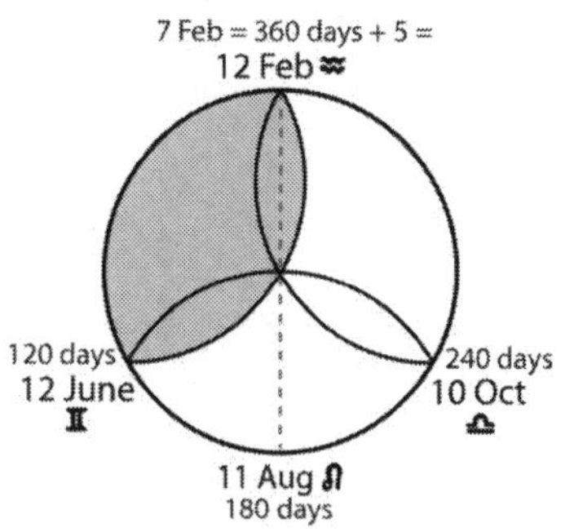

In Part One, Chapter 6, I noted that June 12 falls 120 days into my year, and February 7 falls 360 days into my year. The image I used to portray this geometry also depicts October 10 falling 240 days into my year, marking off the second arc of the vesica piscis in the circle of 360 days. In a leap year such as 2016, this point shifts to October 9, the exact day of Thea's passing. In other words, Thea passed precisely at the 6 Point (0° Sagittarius) of my year. It was clearly not only the end of Thea's life, but also the end of one phase of my life and the beginning of another.

I was happy to see how Thea's passing fit perfectly within her own field of Time and Space, as well as within my own. The descent of gnosis that came down during the week before and the weeks after her departure clearly illuminated the way forward for me. From that point on I saw that the vesica piscis was encoded in the Rig Veda in a multitude of ways and that it was a crucial key of unveiling the veiled gnosis of the Rishis. I knew it was no coincidence that I was given and entrusted with this ancient key – which has been hidden in plain sight for multiple millennia – in conjunction with Thea's passing. I knew I was born to see and recover this key of Vedic gnosis, which began coming forward in my consciousness on February 7, 2016. While writing the first part of this book it was clear enough to me that the Divine Son Agni and his mothers in the Rig Veda are firmly linked to the geometry of the radius, circle and vesica piscis; but up until October 2016, I had no idea that the vesica piscis was the master key of the Rig Veda, unveiling its heavily veiled symbolism and revealing the true context and sense of the Vedic victory.

The visual catalyst for this discovery was an image I had constructed to demonstrate how 3 number units and 4 signs of the Gnostic Circle are contained in the vesica piscis, making 7 (3 + 4) the occult number of the vesica piscis. I was trying to convey how each vesica piscis (and thus each Kali Yuga) marks off one-third of the "thrice-seven" layers or seats of the Rishis' Year.

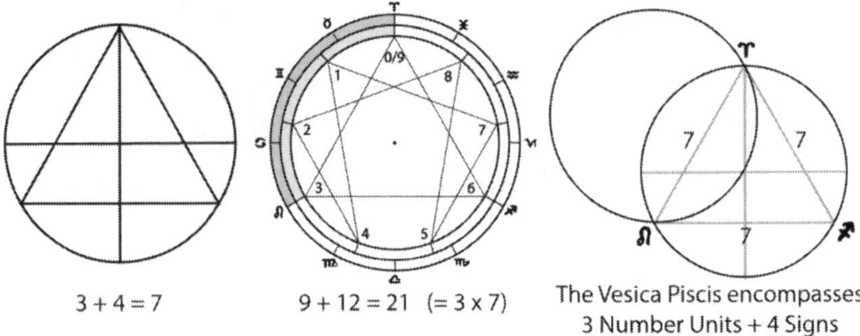

3 + 4 = 7

9 + 12 = 21 (= 3 x 7)

The Vesica Piscis encompasses 3 Number Units + 4 Signs

On October 2, I felt compelled to flip the third image of this triptych around a bit. I flipped it vertically and horizontally and the new view portrayed the descending air trine of the zodiac (Gemini, Libra and Aquarius) as well as the vesica piscis arcing from 0° Libra to 0° Aquarius.

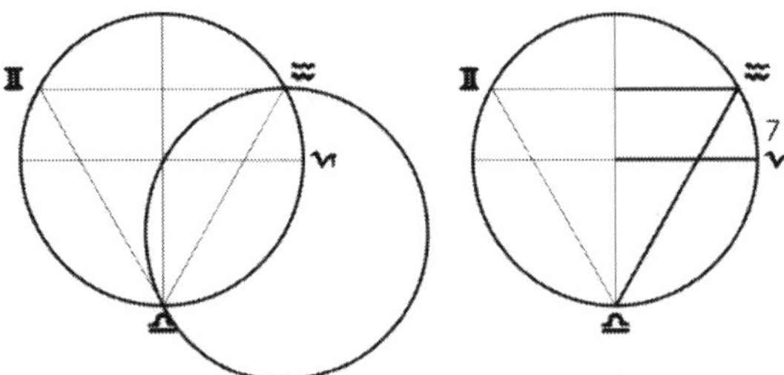

I therein saw the form of the number 7 contained in the air trine. After seeing this, I took off into the hills around my house for a mountain bike ride. As I began riding uphill my knee hurt, so I changed my course to a relatively flat and short ride along a dry creek bed to a dry waterfall. While appreciating the curves and beauty of the creek bed, I spontaneously realized that the symbol of the river in the Rig Veda is code for the vesica piscis of the circle. I thereupon saw that the seventh river of the zodiac arcs from the 7th sign Libra to the 11th sign Aquarius, and that this geometry is the key to understanding the seven rivers of the Rig Veda and their recovery or release "by the stroke" of the Vedic hero, i.e. by the stroke of the radius.

> *[In] the minds of the Rishis [the seven rivers are] released together by the stroke of the God Indra when he smote the Python who coiled across their fountains and sealed up their outflow.*
>
> Sri Aurobindo, *The Secret of the Veda, CWSA, Volume 15*, pp. 93-94

As soon as I got back home, I began to search for evidence in the Rishis' hymns to back up this revelation. The evidence was abundant and sometime past midnight on October 3, I sent Thea an email with a picture of the waterless "waterfall" with some comments about where my trail of yoga and research was leading me. I did not notice at the time that the arc of the trees and the slope of the creek bed together create a subtle vesica piscis.

We call [this] the Waterfall, and hopefully it will start flowing again in the near future. It's probably been 5 months since it rained here last. Today we had a "homeopathic" sprinkle which barely wet the

> *ground. This evening I've been researching the waves and rivers and waters and soma of the [Rishis] in terms of the wave/movement of the vesica piscis through the circle. Saraswati bursts the Hill and slays the Paravatas*[1] *with this wave. Many verses confirm the connection. It's quite a fascinating piece of the Rig Veda puzzle.*

The reference to Saraswati's victorious wave was from Rig Veda 6.61 in which Saraswati's "strong waves" and her flood are said to "burst…the ridges of the hills" and to slay all foes.[2] I understood that her waves are equivalent to the seven rivers and sisters of the Rig Veda. From Sri Aurobindo and Thea's writings on the Vedas, I understood that the breaking open of the "hill" in the Rig Veda is the decisive victory of the Vedic heroes and heroines. It marks the release of the purifying waters of truth and clarity and the recovery of the lost Sun of the Rishis – the Son hidden in the waters. By this victory, the Swar realm of the Rishis is said to be won or attained. I also understood that the act of seeing the vesica piscis as the underlying truth of this symbol, was entirely equivalent to the victory of "bursting open the hill", pen or cave of the world's complete ignorance of this sacred Vedic "river".

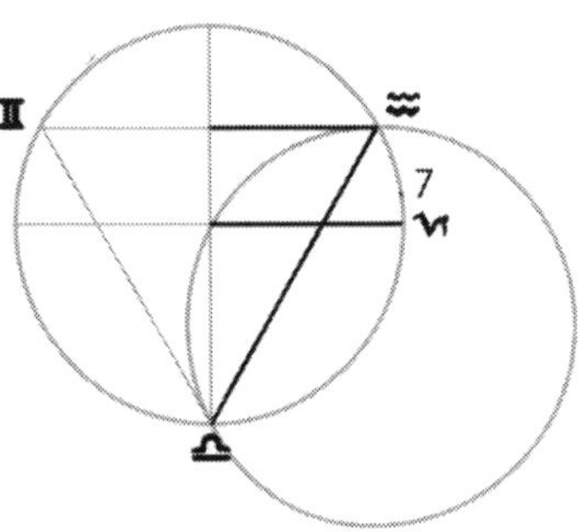

As I contemplated the form of the number seven within the zodiac, it occurred to me as a marvel of gnosis. The top and diagonal lines of the number are born of the inverted triangle and together point upward to the sign of Aquarius (the highest seat of Vishnu) located within the Swar quadrant of the zodiac. I saw that the cross-slash of the 7 is equivalent to the 10th radius or ray of the twelve-month year, which is the gate or

---

[1] *Paravatas* seems to indicate mountains here.

[2] Rig Veda 6.61, tr. R.T.H Griffith.

passage (*sankranti*) into the 10th sign of Capricorn, soon after which follows the 7 Point of the circle of 0/9. I marveled that the diagonal line of the number 7 is equivalent to the chord or spine of the vesica piscis, which stretches across a 120° arc of the circle, from 0° Libra to 0° Aquarius.

Such is the story of how on the first day of the 2016 Durga Puja festival (October 2, 2016[1]), I came to realize that the rivers, waves and waters of the truth of the Rig Veda are all code for the vesica piscis. I understood that the seventh vesica piscis of the zodiac, stretching from 0° Libra to 0° Aquarius, is the seventh river of the Rishis. I understood that the waves of the Aquarian hieroglyph ♒ are symbolic of these rivers or waves of clarity which, according to the Rishis, descend from the realm of truth-consciousness as a result of the Hero's victory. I understood that the wisdom of the river goddess Saraswati is equivalent to gnosis of the vesica piscis and its formative role in the Vedic yajna and the *trayi vidya* of the Rishis. I understood that the goddess Durga rides her *vahana* the Lion to victory in Indian mythology because the Lion is equivalent to the radius – the eternal law, flame, lightning bolt, measure and sword of truth of the field of Time and Space. Soon after that, I became confident that the Divine Daughter of the Rishis (equivalent to the Dawn goddess) is the vesica piscis.

I also understood the cosmological perfection of my birth in the sign of Aquarius in a 7-power year.[2] Essentially the Durga Puja opened a floodgate of new seeing and understanding not only regarding the meaning and importance of the river and the number seven in the Rig Veda, but also regarding the importance of the river and the number seven in my own life. I felt like I was living the mythology in a way, experiencing the descending rivers of truth and clarity that had been long sealed behind thick veils or walls of ignorance. On October 7 (the 6th Day/Night of the Durga Puja) I shared some pictures and notes with Thea trying to give her a better sense of what was coming down the pike regarding

---

[1] A 3-power day (10 + 2 + 2016 = 1 + 0 + 2 + 2 + 0 + 1 + 6 = 12 = 1 + 2 = 3).

[2] 1969 = 1 + 9 + 6 + 9 = 25 = 2 + 5 = 7.

the number seven and the Rishis' rivers of truth, hoping it would make her happy, but she never got them. Her consciousness had begun withdrawing from her body and news came that she passed on October 9, the 8th Day/Night of the Durga Puja.

With Thea's passing naturally came much reflection upon our time together. Our relationship was a bit of a bumpy ride. It was highly charged, often difficult, and at the same time, it was productive and fruitful. Astrologically, her natal Saturn sat at 29° Pisces conjunct my North Node at 0° Aries, which seemed to set the main current of our relationship. This particular synastry is characterized in the following terms:

> *[T]he Saturn person plays the role of teacher in your life in some manner. You have a lot to learn from the Saturn person, who... challenges you to take on your responsibilities.... While there can be a strong tie between the two of you, there can be a sense that you hold each other back.... [You] feel a lot of responsibility towards one another, which can bond you for some time.*

"Synastry: Saturn – North Node Aspects",
Café Astrology (accessed November 2017)

The strong bond was there and the sense of responsibility. From the time I first read *The Gnostic Circle* in March of 2000, I felt responsible for helping Thea with her mission of restoring and reestablishing higher gnosis in the world, and that *never* changed, regardless of the ways we clashed. I would not say that I held her back in any way; but on the reverse side she played an equally expansive and contractive role in my life. She both opened me up and shut me down on a regular basis. The following letter, which I wrote to her on September 28, 2016, gives some picture of our relationship.

> *After reading...of your moving to the hospital suite, I went outside and laid flat on the stone driveway, just wanting to be close to the Earth as I tried to connect with you and what you're going through. Then I went for a slow walk along the trails close to my house letting myself be as open as I could to the love I feel for you ... wishing we could share the beauty I was walking through and*

feeling. I feel sad that I am not there with you in the physical, but I do feel close to you in my heart and that feels timeless and immensely powerful. Protections and obstacles are removed and I think only positive things. I kept thinking "Let's Go!" In the sense of being ready to take on whatever awaits us in the coming days, weeks and months and years, whether you're in a body or not! The walk began to feel like a beautiful waking dream that I was in with you...immersed in the quiet exquisiteness of Earth's immense beauty. The wind and time seemed to suspend itself, or as if everything had gone into slow slow motion.

Sometimes my mind drifted to wishing that things were constructed very differently, i.e. less painful, less distance, less obstacles, but even amidst a certain amount of longing for togetherness, for closer proximity that doesn't seem to be in the cards this go around, I also felt the Divine Matrix of it All, and the upholding Skambha, connecting that which seems far away and distant ... assuring that all is what it needs to be ... regardless of how heartbreaking or uncomfortable. Transforming Heartbreak into Heart-opening it seems is part of the divine program for the time being. In the midst of thinking this ... a song came on my iPhone, whose chorus was "For what it's worth, I was only trying to wake you up". It was hard to tell if the words were "break you up" or "wake you up" ... I had to laugh at that one ... Broken up, woken up ... same difference [or] outcome it seems.

When Thea passed eleven days later I felt great love for her, for her gnosis, for her extraordinary persistence in bringing forth her important work regardless of the many obstacles she faced. I also felt in awe of the forces at hand and in awe of how 2016 was unfolding, what it was bringing and what it was taking away. I searched out and found the letter I had written Thea in February 2016 about my vesica piscis experience.

I woke in the early morning on 7.2.2016 thinking about the connection between the vesica piscis and the Sun's radius and the [Kali] yuga measure. The vesica piscis cuts a 120° (432,000") arc in the circle. I turned on the lights to write/draw out these thoughts and the clock read 4:32. It's pretty amazing to think about this, how the radius of the Sun was set to equal the seconds of degrees of arc cut into the circle by this radius. It's mind boggling ... how this Solar measure has become so well hidden in our world, in India. Connecting the measure to the vesica piscis and to the Yuga seems like it might help people understand the ignorance of considering 432,000 as years, and the importance of understanding it in terms of the Circle (the Sun's Symbol).

Her response was:

Lori, please write a full piece on this for the website and relate it to the Core of the Chamber wherein the Vesica is central to its most profound revelations. You could quote [The Tenth Day of Victory] on this. Bring it all together. The Vesica [Piscis] is ancient and sacred. Show how with the descent of Supermind these ancient truths are 'all made new'. Thea

I responded, "Will do." However, as I began to write it became clear that it was not an article. It quickly took on a larger life and form of its own. Eight months later the article had grown to a 180-page book; and then with Thea's passing came the full descent of the importance of the vesica piscis as a key of Vedic gnosis.

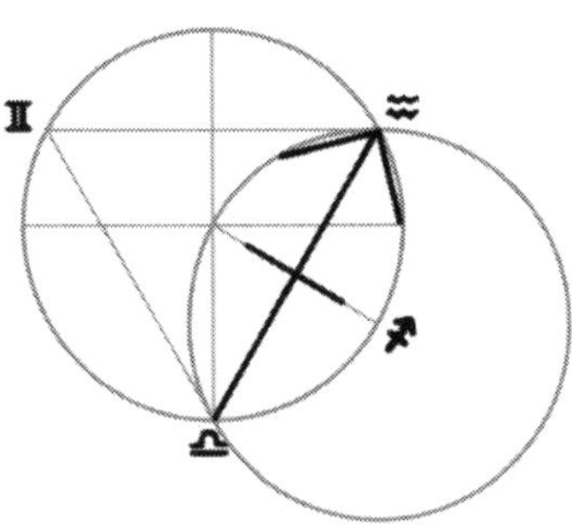

One month later, on November 7, precisely 9 months after my 4:32 am vesica piscis vision and a day shy of passage into the 10th month of my year,[1] I saw that the seventh wave or river of the zodiac (from the 7th sign Libra to the 11th sign Aquarius) was created and propelled by the 9th ray or radius of the zodiac, extending to 0° Sagittarius – the Hero-Horse of the zodiac and of the Vedas. This seeing occurred as both a surprise and a natural culmination of what had been gestating in me for 9 months. It illuminated the occult significance of the Sagittarius hieroglyph as well as the Horse's role (Kalki's role)

[1] February 12 plus 270 days is November 9th (November 8th in a leap year).

in the Vedic victory. It also brought with it an additional downpour of new seeing into the veiled symbolism of the Rishis.

On January 5, 2017,[1] the 79th anniversary of Thea's birth, I went for a walk to our waterfall, imagining Thea was with me and I was showing her what the waterfall looked like when it was flowing. I stood on a rock to take some pictures of the beautiful falls, and after stepping off the rock I saw the number 7 deeply carved into its north face, its grooves glistening with water. In all my years of visiting these falls, I had never noticed this perfectly carved number 7. I went back to the falls nine days later to confirm my suspicion that the 7 on the rock is entirely invisible when the rock is dry. Later, while looking at the picture I took of this large 7 drawn in water and stone, I noticed that the 7 appeared to be part of a thunderbolt symbol, reminding me of the mythology of Indra's thunderbolt which in the Rig Veda cleaves or splits a rock in two, freeing the waters of truth.

> *[Indra] cleft the rock, he let concurrent streams flow forth, and with his skilful art stablished the heavens' wide vault.... [He hurled] down his iron thunderbolt, a joy to Varuṇa's and Mitra's worshipper.*
>
> Rig Veda 10.113.4-5, tr. R.T.H. Griffith

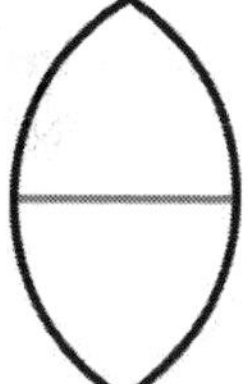

I have paired the vesica piscis and its radius with this verse to demonstrate the true rationale behind the imagery of Indra splitting the rock in two, by which he sets the "rivers" of the zodiac free or releases their eternal truth upon the Earth. In the following chapters I will try to flush out the significance of these waters and the seventh wave or river of the zodiac, and to present

[1] To add to this theme of the 7 on Thea's 79th birth anniversary, the full number power of the date 1.5.2017 was 7 (1 + 5 + 2 + 0 + 1 + 7 = 16 = 1 + 6 = 7).

some of what I learned during and after the week of Thea's passing regarding the veiled symbols of the Rig Veda.

The image below is a fitting symbol of how this information was dropped into my lap so to speak. In the Spring of 2017, I found and placed a stone triangle on my window sill. I centered it directly above the sculpture of Shesha, Vishnu and his consorts, Bhudevi and Sridevi which I had found at a garage sale in 2009. At some point the stone triangle disappeared from the window sill and I could not find it. I later saw that it had fallen into the lap of one of the goddesses. The way the stone landed created the impression of the second goddess reaching out to touch the peak of the triangle with her right hand. I'm not exactly sure which goddess is which in this sculpture; regardless, it is a beautiful symbol of coming to find the triadic key and geometry of Vishnu's avatars and of the Rig Veda.

CHAPTER TWO

The Vesica Piscis in the Rig Veda

> *O Waters, that supreme wave of yours, the drink of Indra [the Bull], which the seekers of the Godhead have made for themselves, that pure, inviolate, clarity-streaming, honeyed* (ghṛtapruṣaṃ madhumantam) *wave of you may we today enjoy. O Waters, may the son of the waters (Agni), he of the swift rushings, foster that most honeyed wave of you.... May the rivers which the sun has formed by his rays, from whom Indra [with his lightning bolt] clove out a moving wave, establish for us the supreme good....*
>
> Rig Veda 4.47, tr. Sri Aurobindo, *The Secret of the Veda, CWSA, Volume 15*, p. 112

After drawing and seeing the relationship between the vesica piscis and the figure 7 on October 2, 2016, it became clear to me that the wave and river of the Rig Veda is code for the vesica piscis which is the basic building block or foundation stone of the zodiac. With this precious key, I immediately understood the mythology of the seven rivers (*saptá síndhūn*) of the Veda and why the number seven (*sapta*) is associated not only with the epic victory in the Rig Veda, but also with the epic victory in St. John's *Revelation.*

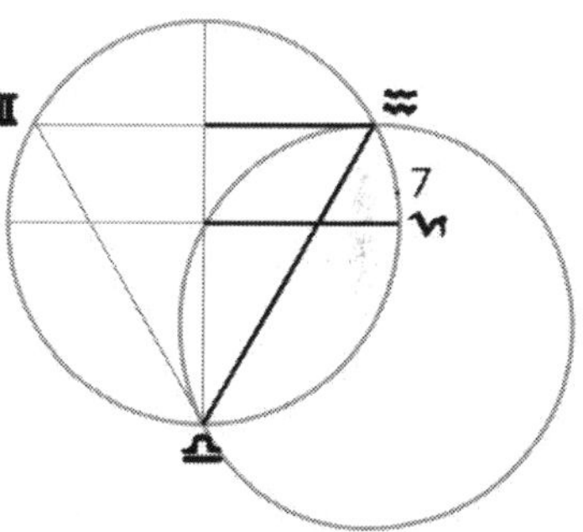

I have constructed the following image to help readers understand how the vesica piscis stretching from 0° Libra to 0° Aquarius can be considered as equivalent to the seventh river of the Rig Veda. The first river issues or *springs* forth from the first sign Aries, the second river from the second sign Taurus and so forth. The seventh river springs forth from the seventh sign Libra, extending up to Aquarius (*Kumbha*), from whence the sacred waters of truth and clarity descend.

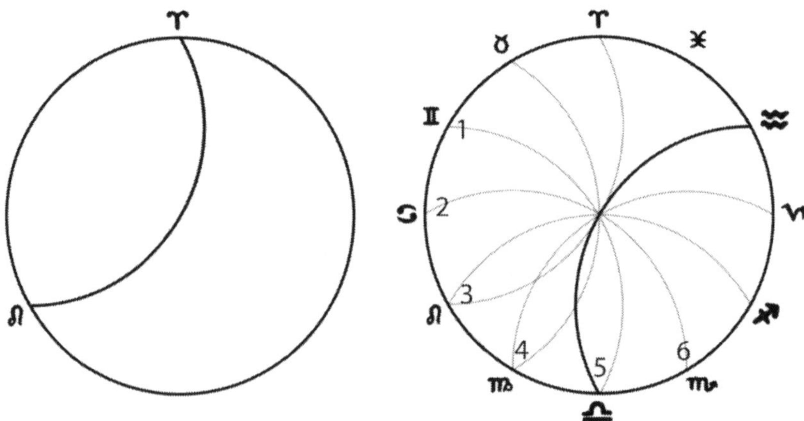

The truth of these Vedic rivers or waters cannot be seen outside the geometry and context of the Earth's sacred year which is measured out and "fixed" by the Earth's Equinoxes and Solstices and by the radius of the circle.

> *[Indra] spread the wide earth out and firmly fixed it, smote with his thunderbolt and loosed the waters....*
>
> Rig Veda 1.103.8, tr. R.T.H. Griffith

After more research, it became entirely apparent that just as there are myriad epitaphs and symbols of the radius in the Rig Veda, there are also myriad epitaphs and symbols of the vesica piscis. In addition to waves and rivers, these symbols include Soma-wine, honey-wine (meath), milk, clarified butter, oil, fat, nectar (*amrita*), mists, rain, clouds, ladles of oil, lakes, streams, springs, fountains and wells. The vesica piscis is also portrayed as pails, bowls, jars or pots (*kumbha*) of water, wine honey, milk, etc. These waters, liquids and their containers are characterized variously as sacred, holy, immortal, golden and glowing. They are also immortalizing, from which comes the mythology of the fountain of eternal youth. In Rig Veda 7.49.1 the "channel" of the waters is said to be dug out by Indra.

> *Forth from the middle of the flood the Waters – their chief the Sea – flow cleansing, never sleeping. Indra, the Bull, the Thunderer, dug their channels: here let those Waters, Goddesses, protect me.*
>
> Rig Veda 7.49.1, tr. R.T.H. Griffith

In other words, the "channel" of the vesica piscis is "dug" out by the radius. While researching this symbolic imagery, I realized that this theme of the vesica piscis in the Rig Veda extended far beyond waters, nectars and other liquids and their containers. It extends into an amazing variety of forms, many but not all of which I will get around to discussing. I found that these were not occasional symbols mentioned sporadically throughout the hymns, but rather sometimes multiple symbols of the same sacred geometry, the same sacred key, densely packed into singular verses or lines of the hymns, as in the following excerpt from Rig Veda 10.101. Symbols of the vesica piscis are in bold.

> *Arrange the **buckets** in their place securely fasten on **the straps**. We will pour forth **the well that hath a copious stream, fair-flowing well** that never fails. I pour **the water from the well** with **pails prepared and goodly straps**, [unfailing], **full, with plenteous stream**. ...Prepare the **cow-stall**, for there drink your heroes: stitch ye the **coats of armour**, wide and many. Make **iron forts**, secure from all assailants **let not your pitcher leak**: stay it securely. Hither, for help, I turn the holy heavenly mind of you the Holy Gods, that longs for sacrifice. **May it pour milk for us**, even as **a stately cow** who, having sought the pasture, yields **a thousand streams. Pour golden juice within the wooden vessel**: with stone-made axes fashion ye and form it.*
>
> Rig Veda 10.101.5-10, tr. R.T.H. Griffith [bold emphasis added]

Seeing the Rishis' pervasive and varied cloaking of the vesica piscis in their language, it became clear that the vesica piscis is a master key to the well-hidden meaning and sense of the Rig Veda.

Due to their eternal relationship, the radius and vesica piscis are consistently paired together throughout the Rig Veda in a multitude of ways. This constant pairing demonstrates that the sacred relationship and sacred geometry between soul and form was the bedrock of the Rishis' gnosis. With this key, the language of the Rishis becomes increasingly transparent.

The Son of the Waters

Before seeing this key, I had never truly understood why Agni is frequently portrayed as the Son or Child of the Waters.

> *We as thy friends have chosen thee, mortals a God, to be our help, [the] Waters' Child, the blessed, the resplendent One, victorious and beyond compare....[Thou] hast gone unto thy mother streams.*
>
> Rig Veda 3.9.1-2, tr. R.T.H. Griffith

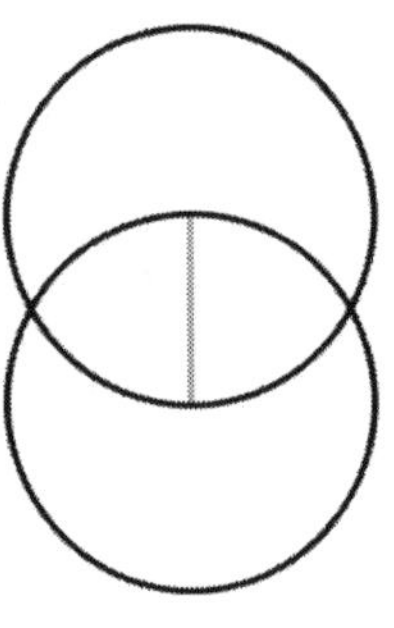

As soon as it became clear that the waters are a symbol of the vesica piscis, this mystery was entirely solved. The vesica piscis is the water and womb which holds in itself the radius, personified or deified as the divine male Child or Son. This Divine Son is portrayed as hidden, seated and growing in the lap of the waters. He is also portrayed as being "enrobed" in the waters, milk, rivers and oil. He is also the "child of mist", enwrapped in mist or in a cloud. This various language is all code for the position of the radius in the "virgin" womb of the vesica piscis, which in Rig Veda 1.65.2 is referred to as "the seat of Law".

> *The Gods approached the ways of holy Law; there was a gathering vast as heaven itself. The waters feed with praise the growing Babe, born nobly in the womb, the seat of Law.*
>
> Rig Veda 1.65.2, tr. R.T.H. Griffith

Indra found meath [in the milch-cow].... That which lay secret, hidden in the waters, he held in his right hand, the rich rewarder.

Rig Veda 3.39.6, R.T.H. Griffith

Large was that covering, and firm of texture, folded wherein [Agni] enteredst the waters....[W]e sought thee hidden in...the waters.

Rig Veda 10.51.1-3, R.T.H. Griffith

Giving birth to the [three luminous worlds of Swar[1]*] giving birth to the Sun in the waters,*[2] *the Brilliant One clothes himself with the waters and the rays.*

Rig Veda 9.42.1, tr. Sri Aurobindo,
The Secret of the Veda, CWSA, Volume 15, p. 566

[Agni] The great Priest of the call has been born; the knower of all heavens...may he take his seat in the lap of the waters: he who upholds us and is held in us.... They worshipped him in the session of the waters, as if the cow of vision lost they followed him by his tracks; where he hid in the secret cavern...the wise thinkers desired and found him. Him greatly desiring Trita.[3]

Rig Veda 10.46.1-3, tr. Sri Aurobindo,
Hymns to the Mystic Fire, CWSA, Volume 16, pp. 412-13

[Agni] breathes in the Waters like a seated swan. Awake in the dawn he has power by the will of his works to give knowledge to the peoples. He is like the god of the nectar-wine and born of Truth and a creator.

Rig Veda 1.65.5, tr. Sri Aurobindo,
The Secret of the Veda, CWSA, Volume 15, p. 577

---

[1] These are the three signs of the fourth quadrant or "world" of the zodiac: Capricorn, Aquarius and Pisces.

[2] Sri Aurobindo's footnote: "Agni, Surya and Soma himself are said to be found in the waters or seven rivers."

[3] Trita, as discussed elsewhere, is an epitaph of triple-born Agni.

> *The friendly Son of Waters [the Floods' Child] by the greatness of Godhead hath produced all things existing.... On every side the bright Floods have encompassed the bright resplendent Offspring of the Waters. The never-sullen waters, youthful Maidens, carefully decking, wait on him the youthful. He with bright rays shines forth in splendid beauty, unfed with wood, in waters, oil-enveloped. To him three Dames are oftering food to feed him, Goddesses to the God whom none may injure....**Here was the horse's birth**; his was the sunlight.... Him, indestructible, dwelling at a distance in forts unwrought lies and ill spirits reach not.... The Son of Waters, gathering strength in waters....He who in waters with his own pure Godhead shines widely, law-abiding, everlasting.... The Waters' Son hath risen, and clothed in lightning ascended up unto the curled cloud's bosom.... Golden in form is he, like gold to look on, his colour is like gold, the Son of Waters.*
>
> Rig Veda 2.35, tr. R.T.H. Griffith [bold emphasis added]

In the Old Testament Bible, this Vedic symbolism came to be expressed as God's appearance as a "pillar of cloud" and a "pillar of fire" to guide the people. These pillars are respectively the vesica piscis and the radius of the circle.

> *[God] went before them in a pillar of cloud by day to lead the way and in a pillar of fire by night to give them light. So they could travel both day and night. The pillar of cloud by day and the pillar of fire by night never departed from the people.*
>
> Exodus 13:21-22, TLV

The Divine Son (and Divine Horse) who is the Child or offspring of the Waters is described in the above hymn as being "oil-enveloped". In other hymns, he springs from holy oil, is "enthroned in oil", is "oil-clad", and is "worshipped with the holy oil".[1] Like the waters and the streams, holy oil, and oil in general is a symbol of the vesica piscis in the Rig Veda. This is made

---

[1] Rig Veda 1.127.2, 5.15.1, 3.17.1, 2.7.4.

abundantly clear in Rig Veda 4.58.5, wherein the Golden Reed or radius is found among or amidst "the streams of oil descending".

> *I look upon the streams of oil descending, and lo! the Golden Reed is there among them.*
>
> Rig Veda 4.58.5, tr. R.T.H. Griffith

This veiled symbolism seems to be the origin of the Judeo-Christian mythology of the "anointed" son of God, and the tradition of anointment as a consecration.

> *O Agni, radiant One, to whom the holy oil is poured, burn up our enemies whom fiends protect.*
>
> Rig Veda 1.12.5, R.T.H. Griffith

Before further discussing the seven rivers and their importance in the Vedic victory, I will present some of the many other symbols of the vesica piscis that I have discovered in the Rig Veda. Knowing these, readers will be in a better position to appreciate subsequent verses, as wells as the previous verses I have shared.

Various Symbols of the Vesica Piscis

In terms of the Earth element or more solid forms, the vesica piscis seems to be depicted alternately as a mountain range, hill, fort, cave, pen, lair, rock, ridge, stone, mouth, dwelling place, bird's nest, robe, veil, plant, imperishable food, woven threads of a garment, a web, braided locks or tresses of hair, a feather, the mound of the breast or udder, a womb, an egg, and as vehicles such as a car or ship. In the verse below the vesica piscis is not only conveyed in the image of rivers and their floods, but also in the image of a pregnant hill.

> *[T]he rivers became rushing floods, floods that cleft (their channel), heaven was made firm like a well-shaped pillar. To this word the contents of the pregnant hill (came forth) for the supreme*

birth of the Great Ones (the rivers or, less probably, the dawns); the hill parted asunder, heaven was perfected (or, accomplished itself....

Rig Veda 5.45.1-3, tr. Sri Aurobindo,
The Secret of the Veda, CWSA, Volume 15, p. 212

The vesica piscis also takes the form of animals, especially female animals such as the cow or mare, as well as female figures, including mother, daughter, wife, maids, sisters, the river goddess Saraswati, the heroine Sarama, water nymphs called Apsaras[1], virgin goddesses, virgin maidens, the Dawn goddess Usha, and Mena the daughter of Vrishan-Aswa (the Bull-Horse).

[Agni] hides himself like a thief with the Cow of vision in the secret cavern of being....He is the close comrade of the Rivers as a brother of his sister. ...Awake in the dawn he has power by the will of his works to give knowledge to the peoples.

Rig Veda 1.65.1-5, tr. Sri Aurobindo,
The Secret of the Veda, CWSA, Volume 15, pp. 576-77

The Gods discovered in the midst of waters beautiful Agni with the Sisters' labour. Him, Blessed One, the Seven strong Floods augmented, him white at birth and red when waxen mighty. As mother mares run to their new-born youngling, so at his birth the Gods wondered at Agni.

Rig Veda 3.1.3-4, tr. R.T.H. Griffith

The Goddesses, the Waters, stayed to meet [the Bull]: they who were wandering separate enclosed him.

Rig Veda 3.56.4, tr. R.T.H. Griffith

---

[1] The Vedic Apsaras appear to be the origin of the Greek Muses, who are sometimes depicted as water nymphs. Like the river goddess Saraswati, the Greek Muses are figures of knowledge, inspiration and wisdom.

The equivalence between the Dawn, the Dawn goddess and the vesica piscis can be found widely throughout the Rig Veda. Dawn is considered by the Rishis to be the Daughter of Heaven.

> *Bright, splendid, like Dawn's lover, [Agni] hath filled the two joined worlds as with the light of heaven. When born, with might thou hast encompassed [Heaven and Earth]: Father of Gods, and yet their Son wast thou.*
>
> Rig Veda 1.69.1, tr. R.T.H. Griffith

> *The radiant Dawns have risen up for glory, in their white splendour like the waves of waters.... Thy ways are easy on the hills: thou passest Invincible! Self-luminous! through waters. So lofty Goddess with thine ample pathway, Daughter of Heaven, bring wealth to give us comfort.*
>
> Rig Veda 6.64.1, 4, tr. R.T.H. Griffith

> *[T]hou, Dawn, hast caused Agni to be kindled, and with the Sun's eye hast revealed creation.*
>
> Rig Veda 1.113.9, tr. R.T.H. Griffith

> *Agni hath looked, benevolently-minded, on the wealth-giving spring of radiant [Dawns].*
>
> Rig Veda 4.13.1, tr. R.T.H. Griffith

> *[Dawns] Daughters of Heaven, bring welfare to the people. The richly-coloured Dawns have mounted eastward, like pillars planted at our sacrifices, [and] flushing far, splendid and purifying, unbarred the portals of the fold of darkness.... With horses harnessed by eternal Order, Goddesses, swiftly round the worlds ye travel, [arousing] from their rest, O Dawns, the sleeping, and all that lives, man, bird, and beast, to motion.... Hither from eastward all at once they travel, from one place spreading in the selfsame manner. Awaking, from the seat of holy Order the Godlike Dawns come nigh like troops of cattle. Thus they go forth with undiminished colours, these*

> *Mornings similar, in selfsame fashion, [concealing] the gigantic might of darkness with radiant bodies bright and pure and shining.*
>
> Rig Veda 4.51, tr. R.T.H. Griffith

> *[Agni], purified with ancient vital vigour, pervading all his Daughter's forms and figures, finding his threefold refuge in the waters, goes singing, as a priest, to the assemblies.*
>
> Rig Veda 9.97.47, tr. R.T.H. Griffith

In the following verses, the seven vesicae piscis that accompany the Sage (i.e. radius) of Sagittarius, are depicted as sisters, virgins and fresh streams.

> *Driving thee in Vivasvān's course, the Seven Sisters with their hymns [made] melody round thee the Sage. The virgins deck thee o'er fresh streams to drive thee to the sieve when thou, a singer, bathest in the wood. The streams of Pavamana, thine, Sage, Mighty One, have poured them forth [like] coursers eager for renown.*
>
> Rig Veda 9.66.8-10, tr. R.T.H. Griffith

One notable misunderstanding of the true significance or identity of these virgins of the Rig Veda is the Islamic myth of the beautiful virgins of paradise or heaven whose vaginas are renowned as ever-ready to accommodate the ever-erect penises of God's elected heroes.[1] I am not suggesting that this is a widely *believed* mythology in the Islamic community, nonetheless, it is a widely *known* mythology as these virgins are reported to be dangled as a reward for martyrs who die in the name of their religious beliefs. I use this as one example of how, once the hidden geometric key of the Rishis was lost, humanity was left to its own distorted imagination to determine what such figures might mean for seekers of the Divine. Readers can hopefully begin to appreciate how human imagination and error has taken

[1] Al-Suyuti, *Al-Itqan fi Ulum al-Qur'an*, p. 351 (*WikiIslam*, accessed May 2017).

us terribly far astray from the ancients' gnosis of the divine. Such distortions might be funny if they weren't so disastrous.

Agni – Awake in the Dawn

The word *Purusha* consists of the roots *pur* and *usha* (or *uṣa*), which can be interpreted as "in front of the dawn" or even "filling the dawn". In the Rig Veda, the Purusha Agni is *uṣarbudham*, "the waker in the dawn". He is sometimes depicted as standing within the Dawn (Usha) and as her lover. He is also called Dawn's "ray of intuition".[1] These are symbolic depictions of the geometry of the radius (Purusha) and the vesica piscis (Usha). The Purusha stands "awake" in the vesica piscis, equivalent to the Dawn of the Rishis' solar gnosis. Agni's awakeness or uprightness within the Dawn is the Vedic essence of the Sanskrit words *bodhi*, *bodha* and *budha*, from which the name *Buddha* arises, meaning "the awakened One". From this same root, *budh,* comes the word *bodhisattva*, which means, in essence, "being awake" or "awake to being". The Vedic and geometric sense of this "awakened One" of the Rishis has been thoroughly lost in the tradition of Buddhism and throughout the world.

> *Agni...has awakened towards the coming Dawn as towards the Sun-cow coming; like the waters spouting up for wide flowing, his flames move towards the heaven.*
>
> *The Priest of the offering awoke for sacrifice to the gods,* ***Agni stood up high in the dawn*** *and perfect-minded; the gathered force of him was seen reddening when he was entirely kindled; a great god has been released out of the darkness.*
>
> Rig Veda 5.1.1-2, tr. Sri Aurobindo, *Hymns to the Mystic Fire, CWSA, Volume 16*, p. 701 [bold emphasis added]

> *The Fire is awake fronting the dawns; one illumined, he becomes aware of the paths of the seers: kindled into a wide might by the*

[1] Rig Veda 7.5.5, tr. Sri Aurobindo, *CWSA, Volume 16*, p. 310.

seekers of godhead, the upbearing flame opens the gates of the Darkness.

Rig Veda 5.3.1, tr. Sri Aurobindo,
Hymns to the Mystic Fire, CWSA, Volume 16, p. 170

The awakeness or awakening (*bodhi*, *bodha* and *budha*) of the Vedic hero, and hence the victory of the Divine Son (or Soul of Mankind) is inseparable from the triadic law and sacred measure of the radius in our field of Time and Space.

Sarama

In the Rig Veda, the goddess Sarama is a mother, a finder of the lost cows, and an envoy of Indra. At some point down the post-Vedic timeline, the goddess Sarama came to be thought of as a dog, referred to as the "hound of heaven". It appears that this goddess is yet another figure of the vesica piscis, indispensable in the accomplishment of the Vedic victory wherein the light (or cows) and waters of truth are found and released from the "hill".

When thou didst tear the waters out of the hill, Sarama became manifest before thee....

Rig Veda 4.16.8, tr. Sri Aurobindo,
The Secret of the Veda, CWSA, Volume 15, p. 218

Saramā went aright and found the cattle.... When at the dawning of this mighty Goddess, Aṅgirases all sang forth with the cattle.... Saramā found the kine by Order's pathway.

Rig Veda 5.45.7-8, R.T.H. Griffith

When [you, Indra, cleft] the water's rock...Saramā showed herself and went before thee. Hymned by Aṅgirases, bursting the cow-stalls, much strength thou foundest for us as our leader.

Rig Veda 4.16.8, tr. R.T.H. Griffith

Sarama brings us to the truth, to the sun-vision which is the way to the bliss....Whether Sarama figures as the fair-footed goddess speeding on the path or the heavenly hound, mother of these wide-ranging guardians of the path, the idea is the same, a power of the Truth that seeks and discovers, that finds by a divine faculty of insight the hidden Light and the denied Immortality.

Sri Aurobindo, *The Secret of the Veda, CWSA, Volume 15*, p. 164

The Veda says, "In the sacrifice" or… "in the seeking of Indra and the Angirases (for the cows) Sarama discovered a foundation for the Son"…. The son is in all probability the son born of the sacrifice, a constant element in the Vedic imagery….

Sri Aurobindo, *The Secret of the Veda, CWSA, Volume 15*, p. 221

*Saramā is able to find the cave where the precious items are hidden by crossing the formidable Rasā, a river that flows around the heavenly sphere (RV 9.41.6), by following the path of cosmic order (*ṛta*). By restoring light to the world and showing Indra the location of the cows, Saramā functions as a savior figure.*

Carl Olson, *The Many Colors of Hinduism*,
Rutgers University Press, 2007, p. 251

Saramā had found the mountain's fissure, that vast and ancient place she plundered thoroughly. In the floods' van she led them forth, light-footed: she who well knew came first unto their lowing. Longing for friendship came the noblest singer: the hill poured forth its treasure for the pious. The Hero with young followers fought and conquered, and straightway Aṅgiras was singing praises….

Rig Veda 3.31.6-7, tr. R.T.H. Griffith

In these last verses from Rig Veda 3.31 "the mountain's fissure" is the radius and the flood and "hill that pours forth its treasure" are symbols of the vesica piscis, as is Sarama herself. She carries in herself (as does Saraswati) the key of the Vedic victory, or in other words, the key of recovering and releasing the Rishis' ancient rivers of gnosis from humanity's caves of Ignorance.

God's Eye

Earlier I discussed the Sun's symbol as equivalent to the Sun's Eye and the Eye of the Gods. In addition to this singular eye, the Rishis also sang of the two eyes of Heaven, which are commonly taken to mean the Sun and Moon. As discussed in Part One, it appears that the second eye refers not only to the Moon, but also to the vesica piscis which is moon-like within the whole circle.

> *When the immortals made the two eyes of Heaven, they set in him the splendour and the beauty. Then there flow as if rivers loosed to their course....*
>
> Rig Veda 1.72.10, tr. Sri Aurobindo, *Hymns to the Mystic Fire, CWSA, Volume 16*, p. 106

> *The heights of heaven were measured into form by the eye of this universal Force [Agni], they were shaped by the intuition of the Immortal. All the worlds are upon his head; the seven far-flowing rivers climbed from him like branches.*
>
> Rig Veda 6.7.6, tr. Sri Aurobindo, *Hymns to the Mystic Fire, CWSA, Volume 16*, p. 67

> *The Child, when blended with the streams, speeding the plan of sacrifice, surpasses all things that are dear, yea, from of old.... With wisdom and with radiant eyes unbar to us the stall of heaven, Speeding...the plan of Holy Law.*
>
> Rig Veda 9.102.1, 8, tr. R.T.H. Griffith

In Rig Veda 7.77 the Dawn Goddess, already discussed as being equivalent to the vesica piscis, is said to bear the Eye of the Gods.

> *[Dawn] hath shone brightly like a youthful woman, stirring to motion every living creature....[S]he hath risen and shone in brightness with white robes about her....Bearing the Gods' own Eye, auspicious Lady, leading her Courser white and fair to look on, distinguished by her beams Dawn shines apparent, come forth to all the world with wondrous treasure.*
>
> Rig Veda 7.77.1-3, tr. R.T.H. Griffith

Soma

When I first began to research Soma, I naturally had to explore the distinction between Soma the god and Soma the wine. It was apparent that the pouring out or release of the waters, rivers or streams of the truth in the Rig Veda is entirely equivalent to the pouring forth and drinking of Soma – the nectar, wine or juice of Immortality (*amrita*). It also became apparent that the word Soma is often used as an abbreviation of Soma wine, in which case it is a symbol of the vesica piscis. The god Soma, however, is an epitaph of the divine Purusha Agni and hence an epitaph of the radius who dwells *within* the wave, waters, nectar, milk or wine of Immortality. In other words, Soma the god dwells *within* the vesica piscis.

> *In the stream's wave wise Soma dwells, distilling rapture, in his seat....*
>
> Rig Veda 9.12.3, tr. R.T.H. Griffith

> *Reposing on the river's wave the Sage [Soma] hath widely flowed around....*
>
> Rig Veda 9.14.1, tr. R.T.H. Griffith

> *It is [Soma] who has revealed the abode of immortality. All worlds have expanded for him who found the Light. Encompassing wisdom on all sides, the Seer, the Hero, moves through all worlds like a chariot, preparing for mortals glory among the Gods.... He, measuring his course, is successful in the encounter.*
>
> Rig Veda 9.94.2-5, tr. by Raimundo Panikkar, *The Vedic Experience*, p. 832

> *[Vamadeva] says that a honeyed wave climbs up from the ocean and by means of this mounting wave which is the Soma (*aṁśu*) one attains entirely to immortality; that wave or that Soma is the secret name of the clarity.... [It] is the tongue of the gods; it is the nodus (*nābhi*) of immortality.*
>
> Sri Aurobindo, *The Secret of the Veda, CWSA, Volume 15*, p. 102

The Soma stalk is another symbol of the radius, described in Rig Veda 9.72.6 as "the stalk that roars, the Sage, the Everlasting One" (tr. R.T.H. Griffith).

> *A far-extended pillar that supports the sky the Soma-stalk, filled full, moves itself every way.*
>
> Rig Veda 9.74.2, tr. R.T.H. Griffith

> *The Soma-stalk hath roared, following with the wave: he swells with sap for man the skin which Gods enjoy.*
>
> Rig Veda 9.74.5, tr. R.T.H. Griffith

The prefix of Soma is thought to be *su*, meaning "to press out", and *ma* which means "to measure" or "mark out". It is an appropriate name for the solar measure, ray or radius which measures and marks out the vesica piscis, establishing the Divine Maya and triple Veda (*trayi vida*) of the Rishis.

> *Cleanse us, God Savitar, with Three, O Soma, with sublimest forms, Agni, with forms of power and might.*
>
> Rig Veda 9.67.26, tr. R.T.H. Griffith

The Cows' Stall and the Sacred Doors

Another prominent variation of the ancient symbol of the vesica piscis, as seen in Rig Veda 9.102.9 recently quoted, is the stall or enclosure of the cow.[1] The release of the cows from their cave, stall or pen and the release of the rivers of truth from the hill or mountain, and the dawning of the light of truth-consciousness is one and the same victory, described in different terms. This victory can be understood as the discovery and release of the true meaning of the Vedic symbols, which naturally conquers or dismantles thousands of years of collective (and toxic) misunderstandings, dogmas and superstitions.

---

[1] It is possible that the lore of baby Jesus being *found* in cow stall (i.e. manger) is an offshoot of this Vedic symbolism.

Creating light for all the world of life, the Dawn hath laid the darkness open as the cows their stall.

Rig Veda 1.92.4, tr. R.T.H. Griffith

[The Dawns] disclosed the stall of cattle: floods streamed for them as in the days aforetime.

Rig Veda 7.90.4, tr. R.T.H. Griffith

[Even] to the wise let that be still a wonder to which the general name of Cow is given. The one hath swelled among mankind for milking.... For sons and progeny, for kine and waters: [Agni] bursts the cow-stall on the day of trial.

Rig Veda 6.66.1, 8, tr. R.T.H. Griffith

Closely related to the image and symbolism of the opening of the stall, is the opening of sacred doors.

[Dawn], as thou with light today hast opened the twin doors of heaven, So grant thou us a dwelling wide and free from foes.

Rig Veda 1.48.15, tr. R.T.H. Griffith

For thee, O Blest Sarasvatī, Vasiṣṭha[1] *hath here unbarred the doors of sacred Order.*

Rig Veda 7.95.6, tr. R.T.H. Griffith

[Agni], rich in food, unbars his wealth like doors....

Rig Veda 1.68.5, tr. R.T.H. Griffith

The sovran all-imperial Doors, wide, good, many and manifold, have poured their streams of holy oil.

Rig Veda 1.188.4, tr. R.T.H. Griffith

---

[1] Vasiṣṭha (Vasishtha) is one of the seven Rishis associated with the seven rivers.

Wide be the Doors, the Goddesses, thrown open, easy to pass, invoked, through adorations, [let] them unfold, expansive, everlasting....

Rig Veda 2.3.5, tr. R.T.H. Griffith

Strong in will this is he [Agni] who has flung wide the doors of the Traffickers purifying for us the illumining ray which gives the many enjoyments.

Rig Veda 7.9.2, tr. Sri Aurobindo,
Hymns to the Mystic Fire, CWSA, Volume 16, p. 316

The Sacred Grass

On our wide grass, Three Goddesses be seated....

Rig Veda 10.70.8, tr. R.T.H. Griffith

Another symbol of the vesica piscis in the Rig Veda is the holy or sacred grass (*barhi*) of the sacrifice, sometimes said to be threefold or to be guarded by three goddesses. This grass could perhaps be understood as multiple radii as well as well as multiple vesicae piscis of the zodiac spread across the 360° sacrificial field or year. Considering how grasses bend, and considering various depictions in the Rig Veda of grasses serving as Agni's hidden seat, I would put the holy grass in the vesica piscis category.

In the depth glowing Pūṣan found the king [Agni-Soma] who was concealed, who was put into a hiding place on his shining sacrificial grass.

Rig Veda 1.23.14, tr. Stella Kramrisch
Exploring India's Sacred Art, Motilal Banarsidass (1994), p. 165

Strew, O ye wise, the sacred grass that drips with oil, in order due, where the Immortal is beheld.

Rig Veda 1.13.5, tr. R.T.H. Griffith

As the knower, bring those who know and sit in the midst on the sacred grass, O lord of sacrifice.

Rig Veda 3.14.2, tr. Sri Aurobindo,
Hymns to the Mystic Fire, CWSA, Volume 16, p. 187

In *Hymns to the Mystic Fire*, Sri Aurobindo likens *barhi* (sacred grass) to *bhrat* and *barhana* meaning "a mass, stream, crest of light or force etc., anything spread wide or streaming out, thus the wide ether, the outstreaming peacock's tail, water flowing in a mass, a stream of flame, the [*barhīmshi*] Agni, radiating light".[1] This imagery of a stream or crest of light would suggest an arc rather than a ray (radius) of light. The following invocation of the sacred grass below, confirms in my mind that the holy grass is indeed a symbol of the vesica piscis which is the eternal wife of the radius,[2] and whose swinging arc can be visualized as the swinging open (or shut) of a door.

Widely expanding may [the sacred grasses] spring apart making themselves beautiful for us as wives for their lords; O divine doors, vast and all-pervading, be easy of approach to the gods.

Rig Veda 1.110, tr. Sri Aurobindo,
Hymns to the Mystic Fire, CWSA, Volume 16, p. 436

Atmospheric Symbols

The vesica piscis also shows up in the air or atmosphere in many ways, including rain clouds, mist, smoke, thunder and the thunderous roar of the Bull or Lion.

Gold-coloured, bannered with the smoke, urged by the wind, aloft to heaven Rise, lightly borne, the flames of fire.

Rig Veda 8.43.4, tr. R.T.H. Griffith

---

[1] Sri Aurobindo, *Hymns to the Mystic Fire, CWSA, Volume 16*, p. 565.

[2] As discussed elsewhere, the radius or Divine Purusha has two eternal wives, the other wife being the circle of the zodiac/yajna.

> *[Guardians of Order], ye whose Laws are ever true... Ye hide [the Sun] in the sky with cloud and flood of rain, and water-drops, Parjanya![1] full of sweetness flow.*
>
> Rig Veda 5.63.1-4, tr. R.T.H. Griffith

> *Far off resounds the roaring of the lion, what time Parjanya fills the sky with rain-cloud.*
>
> Rig Veda 5.83.3, tr. R.T.H. Griffith

> *When from the lightning of thy cloud the rain-floods of the heaven descend.*
>
> Rig Veda 5.84.3, tr. R.T.H. Griffith

> *[Indra] cleft the water-cloud in twain, loosed rivers for their downward flow....*
>
> Rig Veda 8.32.25, tr. R.T.H. Griffith

The god of wind (Vayu) and winds in general appear to be symbols of the radius which drives or compels the movement, arc, cloud or flight of the vesica piscis.

> *[Agni's steeds] are yoked...ploughing blackened lines...urged onward by the wind and rapid in their course.*
>
> Rig Veda 1.140.4, tr. R.T.H. Griffith

> *Like two winds ageing not, two confluent rivers, come with quick vision like two eyes before us.*
>
> Rig Veda 2.39.5, tr. R.T.H. Griffith

In Rig Veda 1.163.11 the radius is depicted as a horse whose "body [is] formed for flight" and whose spirit is "swift as the wind in motion".[2] This theme is repeated in the following verses.

---

[1] Parjanya, the God of Rain is another epitaph of the Purusha/Radius.

[2] Tr. R.T.H. Griffith.

A mighty child in the womb he is called the son of the body; when he is born he becomes one who voices the godhead: when as life who grows in the mother he has been fashioned in the mother he becomes a gallop of wind in his movement.

Rig Veda 3.29.11, tr. Sri Aurobindo,
Hymns to the Mystic Fire, CWSA, Volume 16, p. 211

The moment he is born his might becomes visible when the wind blows behind his flame; he turns his sharp tongue round the trunks and tears his firm food with his jaws of flame.

When quickly he carries his foods on his rapid tongue, this mighty Fire fashions himself into a swift messenger; consuming all he clings to the mad course of the wind, as a driver a swift horse he sets it to gallop for the seeker of the plenitude.

Rig Veda 4.7.10-11, tr. Sri Aurobindo,
Hymns to the Mystic Fire, CWSA, Volume 16, p. 239

The Voice, Word and Song of God

[Agni], Soma Pavamana, like a river, hath stirred the wave of voice, our songs and praises.

Rig Veda 9.96.7, tr. R.T.H. Griffith

At some point in my research it became apparent that the vesica piscis is the word, hymn, song and speech of the Divine Purusha by whatever name, whether it be Agni, the sage, holy singer, or Brihaspati who is the Lord of the Word and "leader of the song" or hymn.

[To] Bṛhaspati, the scatheless...leader of the song, resplendent, worthy of lauds, both Gods and mortals listen. On him wait songs according to the season even as a stream of pious men set moving....His song of praise pervades the earth and heaven: let the wise worshipper draw it, like a courser.

Rig Veda 1.181.1-4, tr. R.T.H. Griffith

Along these same lines, in Rig Veda 9.96 Soma Pavamana (Agni) is characterized not only as the "dweller in the floods" (i.e. in the vesica piscis) but also as "the bearer of the word of men and word of Gods" and as "skilled in holy song".[1] In Sri Aurobindo's translation of Rig Veda 10.8.7 the vesica piscis is portrayed as "the companion-word" of Trita (the triply-born Agni) in his secret cave.

> *By his will Trita in the secret cave desiring by his movements the thinking of the supreme Father, cherished in the lap of the Father and Mother, speaking the companion-word, seeks his weapons.*
>
> Rig Veda.10.8.7, tr. Sri Aurobindo,
> *Hymns to the Mystic Fire, CWSA, Volume 16*, p. 401

As it became apparent that the vesica piscis is the original Holy Word or *Vak*[2] of the Rishis it also became apparent that this "Word of God" has been widely misunderstood and misconstrued throughout the religions of the Age of Pisces and perhaps much further back in time as well. For instance, in Christianity the Word of God is commonly understood to mean either the Divine Son or the holy hymns of the Bible. Humanity must now begin to acknowledge and reconnect with the original Vedic sense and context of the Holy Word and to dismantle all erroneous ideas and distortions that have been heaped upon this symbolic Word for multiple millennia. The meaning of the following Vedic verses becomes more transparent when we know the Word is the vesica piscis. In the first of these verses, multiple vesicae piscis are depicted as demon-slaying "voices of the Fire". In other words, the vesicae piscis are "voices" of the radius which conquer the distortion and mismeasurement of the Rishis' sacrificial year.

---

[1] Rig Veda 9.96.42, 44, 45, tr. R.T.H. Griffith.

[2] *Vak*/*Vac* is translated in *Cologne Digital Sanskrit Lexicon* as "speech, voice, talk, language" and as "speech personified". It is the root of the Latin word "vox", and "vocis", from which arise the English words "voice", "vocal" and "vocabulary".

May the voices of the Fire be sharp weapons to slay the Rakshasa.

Rig Veda 5.2.10, tr. Sri Aurobindo,
Hymns to the Mystic Fire, CWSA, Volume 16, p. 205

Let the path of the Word lead to the godheads, towards the Waters by the working of the Mind....

Rig Veda 10.30.1, tr. Sri Aurobindo,
Hymns to the Mystic Fire, CWSA, Volume 16, p. 210

When a man has firmly established this Fire, he echoes the Words of knowledge and comes to That: for he embraces all seer-wisdoms as the rim surrounds a wheel.

Rig Veda 2.5.3, tr. Sri Aurobindo,
Hymns to the Mystic Fire, CWSA, Volume 16, p. 44

Speak forth three words, the words which light precedeth, which milk this udder that produceth nectar.

Rig Veda 7.101.1, tr. R.T.H. Griffith

True is the crushing word the sage hath uttered....The Footless Maid precedeth footed creatures....The Babe Unborn supporteth this world's burthen, fulfilleth Law and overcometh falsehood.

Rig Veda 1.152.1-3, tr. R.T.H. Griffith

Deep in the ocean lies the bolt with waters compassed round about, and in continuous onward flow the floods their tribute bring to it. When, uttering words which no one comprehended, Vāk, Queen of Gods, the Gladdener, was seated, the heaven's four regions drew forth drink and vigour: now whither hath her noblest portion vanished? The Deities generated Vāk the Goddess, and animals of every figure speak her. May she, the Gladdener, yielding food and vigour, the Milch-cow Vāk, approach us meetly lauded. Step forth with wider stride, my comrade Viṣṇu; make room, Dyaus, for the leaping of the lightning. Let us slay Vṛtra, let us free the rivers let them flow loosed at the command of Indra.

Rig Veda 8.89.9-12, tr. R.T.H. Griffith

> *[Agni] is like* ***a singer of the word*** *and clothes himself with the Rays, he rhapsodises with his flame. This is the shining One...the shining Immortal....*
>
> Rig Veda 6.3.6, tr. Sri Aurobindo, *Hymns to the Mystic Fire, CWSA, Volume 16,* p. 60 [bold emphasis added]

> *The Great Ones seized him in the lap of the waters and the Peoples came to* ***the King with whom is the illumining Word****. Messenger of the luminous Sun, Life that expands in the Mother brought Fire the universal Godhead from the supreme Beyond.*
>
> *Found for those who from age to age speak* ***the word that is new, the word that is a discovery of knowledge****, O Fire, their glorious treasure; but cut him in twain who is a voice of evil, cast him low by thy force of light like a tree with the thunderbolt, imperishable king.*
>
> Rig Veda 6.8.4-5, tr. Sri Aurobindo, *Hymns to the Mystic Fire, CWSA, Volume 16*, p. 68 [bold emphasis added]

> *The fit word have I caught and held as 'twere a courser with the rein.*
>
> Rig Veda 10.18.14, tr. R.T.H. Griffith

> *Never forget this word of thine, O singer, which future generations shall reecho.*
>
> Rig Veda 3.33.8, tr. R.T.H. Griffith

In these verses, the radius and vesica piscis show up as the Fire and his "voices", "the bolt with waters compassed round about", the god and goddess, the horse and its rein, the king and his illuminating word, the singer and his word, the light that "precedeth" the word, the sage and his "crushing word" as well as the "Babe Unborn" and the law that he supports and fulfills. In the following verse, this pair is the arrow and bow, the calf and its mother's udder, as well as the tongue "stirring in the mouth".

> *Laid like an arrow on the bow the hymn hath been loosed like a young calf to the udder of its dam. As one who cometh first with*

full stream she is milked the Soma is impelled to this man's holy rites. The thought is deeply fixed; the savoury juice is shed; the tongue with joyous sound is stirring in the mouth....

Rig Veda 9.69.1-2, tr. R.T.H. Griffith

The Inseparable Pair

Consistently throughout the Rig Veda the symbols of the radius and vesica piscis are intertwined. In the following hymn, this pairing shows up as the speaker and master of the hymn, the tongue who "pours forth the pleasant meath", the Son and "the third secret name of Mother and of Sire" as well as the Son and the jars, the Son and the milky streams of sacrifice, and the Son and the Dawns ("morns") in which he shines.

The Mighty and Far-seeing One hath mounted now the mighty Sūrya's car which moves to every side. The Speaker, unassailable Master of this hymn, the Tongue of sacrifice pours forth the pleasant meath. Within the lustrous region of the heavens the Son makes the third secret name of Mother and of Sire. Sending forth flashes he hath bellowed to the jars, led by the men into the golden reservoir. The milky streams of sacrifice have sung to him: he of the triple height shines brightly through the morns.

Rig Veda 9.75.1-3, tr. R.T.H. Griffith

Another variation of this pairing is the Hero and his bowls or chalices.

The two great meeting Bowls hath [the Hero] united: each of the Pair is laden with his treasure.

Rig Veda 3.55.20, tr. R.T.H. Griffith

With firm support [Indra] parted and stayed the Parents, and, sitting, fixed him there erected, mighty. What time the ample chalice had impelled him, swift waxing, vast, to pierce the earth and heaven, — Him in whom blameless songs are all united: all powers invincible belong to Indra....

Rig Veda 3.31.12-13, tr. R.T.H. Griffith

[Agni Vaisvanara] made the two bowls part asunder like two skins.

Rig Veda 6.8.4, tr. R.T.H. Griffith

There stand the Three Steers, splendid in their brightness, who fill the three world-bowls with genial moisture.

Rig Veda 5.69.2, tr. R.T.H. Griffith

[Wise singers] at sacrifices fix the metres, they measure out twelve chalices of Soma.

Rig Veda 10.114.5, tr. R.T.H. Griffith

The twelve chalices of Soma in this last verse are equivalent to the twelve vesicae piscis of the sacred year.

Arthurian Legend and the Holy Grail

I have long assumed that the Holy Grail or chalice of the Arthurian legend was the bowl of the twelve-month zodiac, equivalent to the round table and its twelve knights. Now it seems more likely that the knights' search for the Holy Grail, a cup bestowing eternal life, is equivalent to the Vedic heroes' quest to find and release the waters (or cows) of truth from their mountain, cave, pen, etc. In other words, the Holy Grail now appears to be the vesica piscis – the pot or vessel (*kumbha*) which holds the waters or nectar of Immortality (*amrita*) drunk by the heroes of the Rig Veda. The twelve knights in Arthurian mythology are symbols of the twelve radii or spokes of the twelve-month year.

Perhaps the most striking Arthurian symbol of the radius and vesica piscis is the undefeatable sword Excalibur lodged in the stone or submerged (hidden) in a lake, only to be won and wielded by the Hero. Whereas the sword in this mythology is the radius, the stone, the lake and the Lady of the Lake are all equivalent to the vesica piscis. The name "Excalibur" appears to have descended from the Vedic roots *aksa* (axis or beam), *kala* (time), and *bhara* (bearing). In other words, it is the axis or skambha which upbears the field of Kala or Time. The Vedic Rishis depicted this upholding axis in many ways, including as the golden sword or weapon of the Hero. In truth, this undefeatable sword is a weapon of gnosis. It lays down the eternal law of Time and Space.

The Lady of the Lake offering Excalibur to King Arthur, by Alfred Kappes (1880), cropped (Wikimedia Commons).

Lightning

I first assumed that lightning in the Rig Veda was always a symbol of the radius. However, in some cases at least, it appears to me that lightning or its flash is also used as a symbol of the vesica piscis. This is also apparent in Rig Veda 2.35 recently quoted wherein Agni is said to be "clothed in lightning" which is equivalent to him being enrobed in waters or oil, i.e. in the vesica piscis. It is also apparent in the following verses wherein Agni is characterized as "the lightning's Child" and lightning is said to be Agni's car or vehicle. In these cases, at least, lightning is a symbol of the vesica piscis.

> *So may Sarasvati, the Hero's Consort, brisk with rare life, the lightning's Child, inspire us, [and] with the Dames accordant, give the singer a refuge unassailable and flawless.*
>
> Rig Veda 6.49.7, tr. R.T.H. Griffith

> *Agni, the Son of Strength, whose car is lightning, whose hair is flame, hath shown on earth his lustre.*
>
> Rig Veda 3.14.1, tr. R.T.H. Griffith

The Heavenly Stone

In Rig Veda 5.56.7 Indra's lightning bolt is referred to as the heavenly stone (*svaryam ásmānam*) which is a symbol of the vesica piscis. This theme is also found in Rig Veda 7.104.

> *Hurl down from heaven thy bolt of stone, O Indra: sharpen it....*
>
> Rig Veda 7.104.19, tr. R.T.H. Griffith

Regarding the Rishis' stone bolt Thea wrote:

> *The tool Indra uses is the Thunderbolt which in the hymns is called the 'heavenly stone'. This is equivalent to the Philosopher's Stone of the alchemists. Its touch effects the magical transmutation of energies. From these waters, released by the Heavenly Stone's touch, Agni emerges. It is therein that Agni is found concealed.*
>
> Thea, *The New Way, Volumes 1&2*, p. 408

Variations of this heavenly stone of the Rishis appear throughout the Bible. It is the Rock of Ages, or the eternal rock from which the nourishing waters of truth are recovered amidst the desert or absence of gnosis.

> *They did not thirst when [the Lord] led them through the deserts. He caused the water to flow out of the rock for them. He split the rock also, and the waters gushed out.*
>
> Isaiah 48:21, TLV

> *[God] brought forth streams also from the rock and caused waters to run down like rivers.*
>
> Psalm 78:16, ISV

> *Take the rod, and gather thou the assembly together, thou, and Aaron thy brother, and speak ye unto the rock before their eyes; and it shall give forth his water, and thou shalt bring forth to them*

water out of the rock: so thou shalt give the congregation and their beasts drink.

Numbers 20:8, KJV

"I [the Lord] will stand there before you by the rock at Horeb. Strike the rock, and water will come out of it for the people to drink." So Moses did this in the sight of the elders of Israel.

Exodus 17:6, NIV

Therefore thus says the Lord GOD, "Behold, I am laying in Zion a stone, a tested stone, a costly cornerstone for the foundation, firmly placed. He who believes in it will not be disturbed."

Isaiah 28:16, NASB

Before further discussing the myriad symbols of the vesica piscis in the Rig Veda and in the Bible as well, it is necessary to hone back in on the symbol of the rivers and to convey the central role the seven rivers play in the culmination of the recovery of the Lost Sun and other treasures of the Rishis.

CHAPTER THREE

The Seven Rivers

[L]oudly roaring Sarasvatī, Mother of Floods, the seventh...full swelling with the volume of their water....

Rig Veda 7.36.6, tr. R.T.H. Griffith

Earlier I shared my October 3, 2016 email to Thea[1] in which I told her I had discovered that the vesica piscis was Saraswati's conquering wave. Below is an excerpt of Rig Veda 6.61 wherein Saraswati is lauded.

> *[Sarasvati] with her might, like one who digs for lotus-stems,[2] hath burst with her strong waves the ridges of the hills. Let us invite with songs and holy hymns for help Sarasvati who slayeth the Paravatas....[She] hast discovered rivers for the tribes of men, and, rich in wealth! made poison flow away from them....[T]his divine Sarasvati, terrible with her golden path, Foe-slayer, claims our eulogy. Whose limitless unbroken flood, swift-moving with a rapid rush, Comes onward with tempestuous roar. She hath spread us beyond all foes, beyond her Sisters, Holy One, [as] Sūrya spreadeth out the days. Yea, she most dear amid dear stream, Seven-sistered, graciously inclined, Sarasvati hath earned our praise.... Seven-sistered, [Sarasvati] sprung from threefold source, the Five Tribes prosperer, she must be Invoked in every deed of might. Marked out by majesty among the Mighty Ones, in glory swifter than the other rapid Streams, created vast for victory like a chariot, Sarasvati must be extolled by every sage.*
>
> Rig Veda 6.61.2-13, tr. R.T.H Griffith

---

[1] An email she never read.

[2] The lotus-stem is a symbol of the radius.

In this hymn Saraswati is said to be seven-sistered. These seven sisters are alternately called the seven rivers and seven mothers or seven mother-rivers (*sindhubhiḥ saptamātṛbhis*[1]) of which Saraswati is considered the seventh (*sáptathī síndhumātā*[2]). Sri Aurobindo also notes that these seven rivers, waters or mothers are equivalent to the seven cows or seven lights of the Rishis.

> *The Seven Rivers of the Veda, the Waters,* āpaḥ, *are usually designated in the figured Vedic language as the seven Mothers or the seven fostering Cows,* sapta dhenavaḥ. ... *The seven Waters are the waters of being; they are the Mothers from whom all forms of existence are born. But we meet also another expression,* sapta gāvaḥ, *the seven Cows or the seven Lights, and the epithet* saptagu, *that which has seven rays.*
>
> Sri Aurobindo, *The Secret of the Veda, CWSA, Volume 15*, p. 123

Saraswati's victory is empowered or enabled by "the ray of intuition" which, as we have already seen, is the radius or Purusha dwelling within the waters.

> *[The Veda speaks] of the great ocean —* maho arṇas, *the upper waters which, as one hymn says, Saraswati makes conscious for us or of which* ***she makes us conscious by the ray of intuition*** *—* pra cetayati ketunā. *The seven rivers seem to be the rivers of Northern India but the Veda speaks of the seven Mighty Ones of Heaven who flow down from Heaven; they are waters that know, knowers of the Truth —* ṛtajña *— and when they are released they discover for us the road to the great Heavens. So too Parashara speaks of Knowledge and universal Life, "in the house of the waters". Indra releases the rain by slaying Vritra, but this rain too is the rain of Heaven and sets the rivers flowing. Thus the legend of the release of the waters which takes so large a place in the Veda puts on the aspect of a symbolic myth. Along with it comes the other symbolic legend of the discovery and rescue, from the dark cave in the mountain, of the Sun, the cows or herds of the*

[1] Rig Veda 1.34.8.

[2] Rig Veda 7.36.6.

> *Sun, or the Sun-world —* svar *— by the Gods and the Angiras Rishis. The symbol of the Sun is constantly associated with the higher Light and the Truth: it is in the Truth concealed by an inferior Truth that are unyoked the horses of the Sun, it is the Sun in its highest light that is called upon in the great Gayatri Mantra to impel our thoughts.*
>
> Sri Aurobindo, *Hymns to the Mystic Fire, CWSA, Volume 16*, p. 16 [bold emphasis added]

I had no idea that Saraswati was specifically identified by the Rishis to be the *seventh* river when I wrote Thea about the victorious wave of this river goddess. When I saw the seventh wave of the vesica piscis moving through the zodiac (from Libra to Aquarius) on October 2, 2016, I simply *knew* that this was *HER* conquering wave or river. It was made apparent to me through the basic geometry of the circle and via all that I had learned from Sri Aurobindo and Thea regarding the forgotten core and essence of the *sanatana dharma* and the 12-month yajna of the Vedic Rishis.

The importance of the theme of the victorious release of the seven rivers is abundantly conveyed throughout the Rig Veda. It is also conveyed in Sri Aurobindo's Lotus of the Avatar symbol wherein his Lotus floats on seven waves. It now appears that the finding and release of the Seven Rivers and the cows of the Vedic sacrifice is entirely equivalent to the finding and release of the truth of their hidden geometry and significance within the context of the Vedic year. Regarding this victory and the connection between the Rivers and Cows of the Veda, Sri Aurobindo wrote:

> *[I have insisted] that there is a close connection between the finding of the Cows and the outflowing of the Rivers (the seven mighty ones of heaven); they are parts of one action, the achievement of the truth and immortality by men,* ṛtaṁ sapanto amṛtam evaiḥ.
>
> Sri Aurobindo, *The Secret of the Veda, CWSA, Volume 15*, pp. 201-02

In *The Secret of the Veda*, Sri Aurobindo wrote a chapter entitled "The Seven Rivers" from which I will share a few hefty passages. Sri Aurobindo's illuminations on this subject take on an entirely new dimension with the added knowledge that the waters, streams and cows are symbols of the vesica piscis which are upheld, discovered and released by the Purusha or hero-gods who are symbols of the radius. Readers may not understand all of the words or concepts which Sri Aurobindo introduces, but still the equivalence between the vesica piscis and the waters becomes increasingly clear. The chapter begins:

> *The Veda speaks constantly of the waters or the rivers, especially of the divine waters,* āpo devīḥ *or* āpo divyāḥ, *and occasionally of the waters which carry in them the light of the luminous solar world or the light of the Sun,* svarvatır āpaḥ. *The passage of the waters effected by the Gods or by man with the aid of the Gods is a constant symbol. The three great conquests to which the human being aspires, which the Gods are in constant battle with the Vritras and Panis to give to man are the herds, the waters and the Sun or the solar world,* gā apaḥ svaḥ.

Sri Aurobindo, *The Secret of the Veda, CWSA, Volume 15*, p. 109

> *"May those divine waters foster me, the eldest (or greatest) of the ocean from the midst of the moving flood that go purifying, not settling down, which Indra of the thunderbolt, the Bull, clove out. The divine waters that flow whether in channels dug or self-born, whose movement is towards the Ocean, — may those divine waters foster me. In the midst of whom King Varuna moves looking down on the truth and the falsehood of creatures, they that stream honey and are pure and purifying,—may those divine waters foster me. In whom Varuna the king, in whom Soma, in whom all the Gods have the intoxication of the energy, into whom Agni Vaishwanara has entered, may those divine waters foster me."*
>
> *It is evident that Vasishtha is speaking here of the same waters, the same streams that Vamadeva hymns, the waters that rise from the ocean and flow into the ocean, the honeyed wave that rises upward from the sea, from the flood that is the heart of things, streams of the clarity,* ghṛtasya dhārāḥ. *They are the floods of the*

supreme and universal conscious existence in which Varuna moves looking down on the truth and the falsehood of mortals, — a phrase that can apply neither to the descending rains nor to the physical ocean.

Rig Veda 7.49, tr. and commentary by Sri Aurobindo,
The Secret of the Veda, CWSA, Volume 15, p. 111

*"**May the rivers which the sun has formed by his rays, from whom Indra clove out a moving wave, establish for us the supreme good.** And do ye, O gods, protect us ever by states of felicity."*

Here we have Vamadeva's madhumān ūrmiḥ, *the sweet intoxicating wave, and it is plainly said that this honey, this sweetness is the Soma, the drink of Indra. That is farther made clear by the epithet* śatapavitrāḥ *which can only refer in the Vedic language to the Soma; and let us note that it is an epithet of the rivers themselves and that the honeyed wave is brought flowing from them by Indra, its passage being cloven out on the mountains by the thunderbolt that slew Vritra. Again it is made clear that these waters are the seven rivers released by Indra from the hold of Vritra, the Besieger, the Coverer and sent flowing down upon the earth.*

What can these rivers be whose wave is full of Soma wine, full of the ghṛta, *full of* ūrj, *the energy? **What are these waters that flow to the goal of the gods' movement, that establish for man the supreme good?** Not the rivers of the Punjab; no wildest assumption of barbarous confusion or insane incoherence in the mentality of the Vedic Rishis can induce us to put such a construction upon such expressions. Obviously these are the waters of the Truth and the Bliss that flow from the supreme ocean. These rivers flow not upon earth, but in heaven; they are prevented by Vritra the Besieger, the Coverer from flowing down upon the earth-consciousness in which we mortals live till **Indra, the god-mind, smites the Coverer with his flashing lightnings and cuts out a passage on the summits of that earth-consciousness down which they can flow.** Such is the only rational, coherent and sensible explanation of the thought and language of the Vedic sages. For the rest, Vasishtha makes it clear enough to us; for he says that these are the waters which Surya has formed by his rays and which, unlike earthly movements, do not limit or diminish the*

> *workings of Indra, the supreme Mind.* ***They are, in other words, the waters of the Vast Truth,* ṛtaṃ bṛhat *and, as we have always seen that this Truth creates the Bliss, so here we find that these waters of the Truth,*** ṛtasya dhārāḥ, *as they are plainly called in other hymns (e.g. V.12.2, "O perceiver of the Truth, perceive the Truth alone, cleave out many streams of the Truth"),* ***establish for men the supreme good and the supreme good is the felicity, the bliss of the divine existence.***
>
> Sri Aurobindo, *The Secret of the Veda, CWSA, Volume 15,* pp. 112-13 [bold emphasis added]

In "The Seven Rivers" Sri Aurobindo presented his translation of and commentary on Rig Veda 3.1, containing abundant and varied references to the radius and vesica piscis which readers should now be better able to recognize. This hymn (below) also demonstrates the extraordinary brilliance of the Rishis who encoded the eternal gnosis (*sanatana dharma*) of the sacred year into words, symbols and languages in a way that has boggled the mind and remained hidden or safeguarded for thousands of years, only to be discovered in the Age of Aquarius, the sign of the Water Bearer, wherein the sacred rivers of truth and clarity are due to be poured out upon humanity.

> *We have made the sacrifice to ascend towards the supreme, let the Word increase. We have made the sacrifice to ascend towards the supreme, let the Word increase. With kindlings of his fire, with obeisance of submission they set Agni to his workings; they have given expression in the heaven to the knowings of the seers and they desire a passage for him in his strength, in his desire of the word.*
>
> *Full of intellect, purified in discernment, the perfect friend (or, perfect builder) from his birth of Heaven and of Earth, establishes the Bliss;* ***the gods discovered Agni visible in the Waters, in the working of the sisters.***

The seven Mighty Ones[1] *increased him who utterly enjoys felicity, white in his birth, ruddy when he has grown. They moved and laboured about him, the Mares around the newborn child; the gods gave body to Agni in his birth.*

With his pure bright limbs he extended and formed the middle world purifying the will-to-action by the help of the pure lords of wisdom; wearing light as a robe about all the life of the Waters he formed in himself glories vast and without any deficiency.

He moved everywhere about the Mighty Ones of Heaven, and they devoured not, neither were overcome, — they were not clothed, neither were they naked. Here ***the eternal and ever young goddesses from one womb held the one Child, they the Seven Words.***

Spread out were the masses of him in universal forms in the womb of the clarity, in the flowings of the sweetnesses; here the fostering Rivers stood nourishing themselves; the two Mothers of the accomplishing god became vast and harmonised.

Borne by them, O child of Force, thou didst blaze out holding thy bright and rapturous embodiments; out flow the streams of the sweetness, the clarity, where the Bull of the abundance has grown by the Wisdom.

He discovered at his birth the source of the abundance of the Father and he loosed forth wide His streams and wide His rivers*. By his helpful comrades and by the Mighty Ones of Heaven he found Him moving in the secret places of existence, yet himself was not lost in their secrecy.*

He bore the child of the Father and of him that begot him; one, he fed upon his many mothers in their increasing. In this pure Male both these powers in man (Earth and Heaven) have their common lord and lover; do thou guard them both.

Great in the unobstructed Vast he increased; yea, many Waters victoriously increased Agni. In the source of the Truth he lay

---

[1] The seven Mighty Ones are the Seven Rivers, also called the Seven Words, "eternal and ever young goddesses" and the "undivided Sisters", all of which are symbols of the seven vesicae piscis that bear the Hero of the sacrifice to his victory.

down; there he made his home, Agni in the working of the undivided Sisters.

As the mover in things and as their sustainer he in the meeting of the Great Ones, seeking vision, straight in his lustres for the presser-out of the Soma wine, he who was the father of the Radiances, gave them now their higher birth, — the child of the Waters, the mighty and most strong Agni.[1]

To the visible Birth of the waters and of the growths of Earth the goddess of Delight now gave birth in many forms, she of the utter felicity. The gods united in him by the mind and they set him to his working who was born full of strength and mighty for the labour.

Those vast shinings clove to Agni straight in his lustre and were like bright lightnings; from him increasing in the secret places of existence in his own seat within the shoreless Vast they milked out Immortality.

Rig Veda 3.1.2-14, tr. Sri Aurobindo, *The Secret of the Veda, CWSA, Volume 15*, pp. 115-16 [bold emphasis added]

Whatever may be the meaning of this passage [from Rig Veda 3.1], — and it is absolutely clear that it has a mystic significance and is no mere sacrificial hymn of ritualistic barbarians, — the seven rivers, the waters, the seven sisters cannot here be the seven rivers of the Punjab. ***The waters in which the gods discovered the visible Agni cannot be terrestrial and material streams****; this Agni who increases by knowledge and makes his home and rest in the source of the Truth, of whom Heaven and Earth are the wives and lovers, who is increased by the divine waters in the unobstructed Vast, his own seat, and dwelling in that shoreless infinity yields to the illumined gods the supreme Immortality, cannot be the god of physical Fire. In this passage as in so many others the mystical, the spiritual, the psychological character of the burden of the Veda reveals itself not under the surface, not behind a veil of mere ritualism, but openly, insistently, —* ***in a disguise indeed, but a disguise that is transparent, so that the secret truth of the Veda appears here, like the rivers of Vishwamitra's hymn, "neither***

[1] This "mighty and most strong" Agni appears to be equivalent to his birth as the Horse of Sagittarius.

veiled nor naked"*. We see that these Waters are the same as those of Vamadeva's hymn, of Vasishtha's, closely connected with the clarity and the honey, —* ghṛtasya yonau sravathe madhūnām, ścotanti dhārā madhuno ghṛtasya*;* ***they lead to the Truth, they are themselves the source of the Truth****, they flow in the unobstructed and shoreless Vast as well as here upon the earth.* ***They are figured as fostering cows*** **(*dhenavaḥ*),** ***mares*** **(aśvāḥ),** ***they are called*** **sapta vāṇīḥ,** ***the seven Words of the creative goddess Vak****, — Speech, the expressive power of Aditi, of the supreme Prakriti who is spoken of as the Cow just as the Deva or Purusha is described in the Veda as Vrishabha or Vrishan, the Bull.*[1] *They are therefore the seven strands of all being, the seven streams or currents or forms of movement of the one conscious existence....*

...Agni is the Deva, the All-Seer, manifested as conscious-force or, as it would be called in modern language, Divine or Cosmic Will, first hidden and building up the eternal worlds, then manifest, "born", building up in man the Truth and the Immortality....

...This divine will carrying in all its workings the secret of the divine knowledge, kavikratuḥ*, befriends or builds up the mental and physical consciousness in man,* divaḥ pṛthivyāḥ*, perfects the intellect, purifies the discernment so that they grow to be capable of the "knowings of the seers" and by the superconscient Truth thus made conscient in us establishes firmly the Beatitude (vs. 2-3)....The rest of the passage describes the ascent of this divine conscious-force, Agni, this Immortal in mortals who in the sacrifice takes the place of the ordinary will and knowledge of man, from the mortal and physical consciousness to the immortality of the Truth and the Beatitude....*

...[O]ur two firmaments [Heaven and Earth] have to be overpassed, for then we find admission to another heaven than that of the pure mind — to the wide, the Vast which is the basis, the foundation (budhna) *of the infinite consciousness, Aditi. This Vast is the Truth which supports the supreme triple world, those highest steps or seats* (padāni, sadāṃsi) *of Agni, of Vishnu, those supreme Names of the Mother, the cow, Aditi. The Vast or Truth is declared to be the own or proper seat or home of Agni,* svaṃ damam, svaṃ

[1] Via this ancient Vedic equivalence between Vak and "cow", "vaca" in Spanish means "cow".

sadaḥ. *Agni is described in this hymn ascending from earth to his own seat.*

This divine Power is found by the gods visible in the Waters, in the working of the Sisters. These are the sevenfold waters of the Truth, the divine waters brought down from the heights of our being by Indra. First it is secret in the earth's growths, oṣadhīḥ, *the things that hold her heats, and has to be brought out by a sort of force, by a pressure of the two* araṇis, *earth and heaven. Therefore it is called the child of the earth's growths and the child of the earth and heaven; this immortal Force is produced by man with pain and difficulty from the workings of the pure mind upon the physical being. But in the divine waters Agni is found visible and easily born in all his strength and in all his knowledge and in all his enjoyment, entirely white and pure, growing ruddy with his action as he increases (v. 3). From his very birth the Gods give him force and splendour and body; the seven mighty Rivers increase him in his joy; they move about this great newborn child and labour over him as the Mares,* aśvāḥ *(v. 4).*

The rivers, usually named dhenavaḥ, *fostering cows, are here described as* aśvāḥ, *Mares, because while the Cow is the symbol of consciousness in the form of knowledge, the Horse is the symbol of consciousness in the form of force. Ashwa, the Horse, is the dynamic force of Life, and the rivers labouring over Agni on the earth become the waters of Life, of the vital dynamis or kinesis, the Prana, which moves and acts and desires and enjoys. Agni himself begins as material heat and power, manifests secondarily as the Horse and then only becomes the heavenly fire.*[1] *His first work is to give as the child of the Waters its full form and extension and purity to the middle world, the vital or dynamic plane,* raja ātatanvān. *He purifies the nervous life in man pervading it with his own pure bright limbs, lifting upward its impulsions and desires, its purifed will in works* (kratum) *by the pure powers of the superconscient Truth and Wisdom,* kavibhiḥ pavitraiḥ. *So he wears his vast glories, no longer the broken and limited activity of desires and instincts, all about the life of the Waters (vs. 4-5). The*

[1] Sri Aurobindo is referring to 3.1.4 in which the Seven Rivers bring forth Agni as the Horse. This symbolic language is explainable through the geometry of the seven vesicae piscis of the zodiac, the seventh of which holds in its "womb" the 9th radius of ray Sagittarius.

sevenfold waters thus rise upward and become the pure mental activity, the Mighty Ones of Heaven. They there reveal themselves as the first eternal ever-young energies, separate streams but of one origin — for they have all flowed from the one womb of the super-conscient Truth — the seven Words or fundamental creative expressions of the divine Mind, sapta vāṇīḥ....

...*The Force rises into the womb or birthplace of this mental clarity* (ghṛtasya) *where the waters flow as streams of the divine sweetness* (sravathe madhūnām)*; there the forms it assumes are universal forms, masses of the vast and infinite consciousness. As a result, the fostering rivers in the lower world are nourished by this descending higher sweetness and the mental and physical consciousness, the two first mothers of the all-effecting Will, become in their entire largeness perfectly equal and harmonised by this light of the Truth, through this nourishing by the infinite Bliss. They bear the full force of Agni, the blaze of his lightnings, the glory and rapture of his universal forms. For where the Lord, the Male, the Bull of the abundance is increased by the wisdom of the superconscient Truth, there always flow the streams of the clarity and the streams of the bliss (vs. 7-8).*

The Father of all things is the Lord and Male; he is hidden in the secret source of things, in the super-conscient; Agni, with his companion gods and with the sevenfold Waters, enters into the super-conscient without therefore disappearing from our conscient existence, finds the source of the honeyed plenty of the Father of things and pours them out on our life. ***He bears and himself becomes the Son, the pure Kumara, the pure Male, the One, the soul in man revealed in its universality****; the mental and physical consciousness in the human being accept him as their lord and lover; but, though one, he still enjoys the manifold movement of the rivers, the multiple cosmic energies (vs. 9-10).*

Then we are told expressly that this infinite into which he has entered and in which he grows, in which the many Waters victoriously reaching their goal (yaśasaḥ) *increase him, is the unobstructed vast where the Truth is born, the shoreless infinite, his own natural seat in which he now takes up his home. There the seven rivers, the sisters, work no longer separated though of one origin as on the earth and in the mortal life, but rather as indivisible companions* (jāmīnām apasi svaṝṇām). *In that entire meeting of these great ones Agni moves in all things and upbears all things; the rays of his vision are perfectly straight, no longer affected by the lower crookedness; he from whom the radiances of knowledge, the brilliant herds, were born, now gives them this high and supreme birth; he turns them into the divine knowledge, the immortal consciousness (vs. 11-12).* ***This also is his own new and last birth.***[1] *He who was born as the Son of Force from the growths of earth, he who was born as the child of the Waters, is now born in many forms to the goddess of bliss, she who has the entire felicity, that is to say to the divine conscious beatitude, in the shoreless infinite. The gods or divine powers in man using the mind as an instrument reach him there, unite around him, set him to the great work of the world in this new, mighty and effective birth. They, the outshinings of that vast consciousness, cleave to this divine Force as its bright lightnings and from him in the superconscient, the shoreless vast, his own home, they draw for man the Immortality. Such then, profound, coherent, luminous behind the veil of figures is the sense of the Vedic symbol of the seven rivers, of the Waters, of the five worlds,*[2] *of the birth and ascent of Agni which is also the upward journey of man and the Gods whose image man forms in himself from level to level of the great hill of being* (sānoḥ sānum). *Once we apply it and seize the true sense of the symbol of the Cow and the symbol of the Soma with a just conception of the psychological functions of the Gods, all the apparent incoherences and obscurities and far-fetched chaotic confusion of these ancient hymns disappears in a moment. Simply, easily, without straining there disengages itself the profound and luminous doctrine of the ancient Mystics, the secret of the Veda.*

Sri Aurobindo, commentary on Rig Veda 3.1, *The Secret of the Veda CWSA, Volume 15*, pp. 116-22 [bold emphasis added]

It is evident in reading *The Secret of the Veda* that Sri Aurobindo had a deep but not full understanding of the symbols of the Veda. He admitted this openly. He illuminated certain essential basics regarding the principle imagery of the Rishis'

---

[1] Agni's "new and last birth" is equivalent to Vishnu's last manifestation as Kalki – the Horse-headed or Horse-riding Hero (the 9 who is the new-born One).

[2] These "five worlds", which are also translated as "five lands" appear to be five signs or rays of the zodiac.

cohesive gnosis, and he understood that much remained to be discovered. Regarding his illuminations, Sri Aurobindo wrote:

> *Such are some of the principal images of the Veda and a very brief and insufficient outline of the teaching of the Forefathers. So understood the Rig Veda ceases to be an obscure, confused and barbarous hymnal; it becomes the high-aspiring Song of Humanity; its chants are episodes of the lyrical epic of the soul in its immortal ascension.…[W]hat more there may be in the Veda of ancient science, lost knowledge, [and] old psycho-physical tradition remains yet to be discovered.*
>
> Sri Aurobindo, *The Secret of the Veda, CWSA, Volume 15*, p. 384

In the following passages from *The Secret of the Veda*, Sri Aurobindo discussed the key words and symbols of the Rishis, which must be properly deciphered in order to understand or further unravel the wholistic sense of Vedic gnosis.

> *Is the winning of Swar simply the recovery of the sun from its shadowing by the storm-cloud*[1] *or its seizure by eclipse or its concealment by the darkness of Night?…[D]oes the conquest of Swar mean simply the winning of heaven by sacrifice?…[W]hat is the sense of this curious collocation of cows, waters and the sun or cows, waters and the sky?*
>
> Sri Aurobindo, *The Secret of the Veda, CWSA, Volume 15*, p. 109

> *Once we have the key to the meaning of the Cows, the Sun, the Honey-Wine, all the circumstances of the Angiras legend and the action of the Fathers, which are such an incongruous patchwork in the ritualistic or naturalistic and so hopelessly impossible in the historical or Arya-Dravidian interpretation of the hymns, become on the contrary perfectly clear and connected and each throws light on the other. We understand each hymn in its entirety and in relation to other hymns; each isolated line, each passage, each*

[1] The storm-cloud here and elsewhere in the Rig Veda is a symbol-figure of the vesica piscis. The vesica piscis "hides" the radius (the golden measure) within itself, and thus can be said to eclipse the Sun or solar ray of the Rishis.

scattered reference in the Vedas falls inevitably and harmoniously into a common whole.

Sri Aurobindo, *The Secret of the Veda, CWSA, Volume 15*, p. 384

We have apparently come to the point in the progressive recovery of Vedic gnosis wherein the crucial geometric key of this "curious collocation" of symbols is found. The Hidden Sun or Divine Son of the Rishis is found in the "waters" of the vesica piscis, which is equivalent to the rivers, the cows, the honey-wine, etc. In case it needs clarifying, the seven rivers or cows which are associated with this victory are the first seven vesicae piscis of the zodiac. The victorious release of these rivers of gnosis from the caves of ignorance decisively establishes and uplifts the zodiac as the singular and unified field of the Rishis' Gnosis, Eternal Truth and triple Veda. The Divine Sun, Son or Hero, who is discovered in these waters and who "releases" these waters, is the radius.

This is a victory for the whole world in the sense that once the geometry and zodiacal gnosis underlying the Vedic lore is reestablished, it exposes and dissolves many thousands of years of profound ignorance and misunderstanding of the world's most ancient sacred text. Once we admit that our world's major religions, diverging spiritual paths and mythologies were born out of pervasive ignorance and misunderstanding of Vedic lore, we can promptly get on with the task of reacquainting ourselves with the Rishis' gnosis which stands as the all-harmonizing nucleus of our world's symbols, mythologies, religions and languages. Many will prefer to hold on to inherited ignorance, but regardless, the Vedic keys have been given by which our long-held distortions can be thoroughly dissolved and the Earth's singular divine play – its sacred Yajna or Yoga – can be understood, enjoyed and fulfilled. The recovery of the lost Sun or Son of the Rishis is ultimately akin to the recovery of the Soul of Creation, whose Divine Maya or sacred measure is the basis of establishing divine order, harmony and unity in human consciousness and in the world.

When coming to terms with the importance of this victory, which amounts to what the Rishis beautifully portrayed as the release of cleansing rivers of truth into the world, it is impossible to ignore that it was accomplished via the collective supramental yoga of Sri Aurobindo, the Mother and Thea. They gestated and birthed this victorious release of the Seven Rivers over the course of 144 years, from Sri Aurobindo's birth in 1872 to Thea's passing in 2016. I began to receive this key on February 7, 2016 but it did not fully descend until the week of Thea's passing, in tandem with the 2016 Durga Puja. The key of the vesica piscis – the river that releases the truth of the Rishis' occult language upon the world – *only* dawned on me and *only* makes full sense via the light Thea shed upon the twelve-month Vedic yajna and upon Indian mythology; and her illuminations were, in turn, born out of the light which Sri Aurobindo and the Mother shed on our world's yajna, yoga, or evolutionary journey.

The 144-year span of their collective yoga by which the truth of the Seven Rivers has been released in this Age of Aquarius is extraordinary for many reasons, including the fact that 144 reduces to the number power of 9 (1 + 4 + 4 = 9) and is also 12 squared (12 x 12 = 144). As noted by some students of Sri Aurobindo and the Mother, twelve-year intervals marked out important milestones in their yoga. In *The Gnostic Circle* Thea explained the importance of 36-year cycles, encompassing four enneads and four quadrants of development (Physical, Vital, Mental and Spiritual). The larger cycle of 144 years is, in turn, comprised of four 36-year quadrants. In this particular womb of Time, each 36-year segment represents one of the four stages or sheaths of the Soul's development in manifestation. 144 also happens to be precisely one-third of 432. 144 is a sacred number in Christian, Jewish and Indian traditions. In India 144 years is precisely the span of the Maha Kumbha Mela cycle which celebrates 12 cycles of Jupiter's 12-year return[1] into the sign of Kumbha (Aquarius),[2] symbolizing the descent of the heavenly

[1] It takes Jupiter approximately 12 years to move through all 12 signs of the zodiac.

[2] As is, this event is miscalculated (i.e., not measured according to the Solar Year).

waters of truth from their kumbha. The regular Kumbha Mela cycle extends itself over the span of 12 years wherein every three years the Mela (gathering) is celebrated in one of four different cities along the sacred Ganges river which descends 12° across the body of India to its mouth at 0° Capricorn.[1]

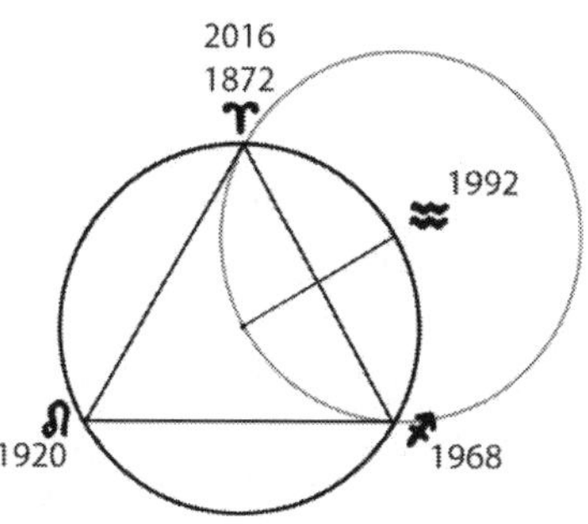

As I mapped out this cycle at the age of 48, I saw that 48 years is precisely one-third (432,000″ or 120°) of the entire 144-year cycle and that I was born half a year after its 6 Point which fell on August 15, 1968. I thereupon remembered that it was circa 1969 that Thea's son had his early morning vision of the vesica piscis, which became a key of Thea's revelations regarding the Mother's Temple and Sri Aurobindo's rebirth, opening up a whole new world of gnosis for Thea. I later remembered that on January 1, 1969, the Mother had a profound experience of the descent of the "superman consciousness" which she described as the "intermediary between man and the supramental being".

> *It was the impression of a personal god...who comes to help. So very strong! And so sweet at the same time, so understanding....It was the start of the year. As if someone on the scale of a god (someone that is) had come to say "Happy new year," with all the power to make it a happy year."*
>
> The Mother, *The Mother's Agenda, Volume 10*, January 4, 1969, p. 4

It is important to note that the radius or upbearer of the last full 120° arc (or river) of the zodiac (as shown above) is the radius of 0° Aquarius. It is the 11th radius of the zodiac, which arcs from the 9th sign (0° Sagittarius) to the 0/9 Point of the circle. The point of 0° Aquarius in this 144-year cycle corresponds to 1992, notably marked by a physical attack on Thea and her companions on her own property at the precipice of Skambha's waterfall as

[1] Ganga first descents westward to 78E Longitude, then flows eastward to 90E.

the result of a water-rights dispute amounting to the illegal hoarding of the river's waters.[1] The placement of this event in the 144-year cycle is astounding considering that the Vedic pillar (skambha) and river are Vedic symbols of the joint radius and vesica piscis, symbols whose truth has been released or borne out 24 years (or 60° of the 144-year cycle) after this violent dispute.

After seeing the 120° arc of the Aquarian radius measuring out the last triad of this cycle from the 9th ray of the zodiac to the 9 of the 0/9 circle, I recalled a vivid dream I had on May 31, 2007 (a 9-power day). In the dream Thea and a few of her collaborators, myself included, were being honored via a trip into space to view the Earth from orbit. In the dream we were being prepared by NASA for the launch, but we did not actually take off before I woke up. A large number 7 was painted onto the surface of the rocket, which I took to be our mission number. A message from Thea accompanied this number on the rocket. The message made it apparent that not all of us would survive the launch, but the sacrifice would be worth it. The message seemed to indicate that the time of the launch was 11:99. Given that this is not a real time of day, this cryptic number has since been a great curiosity to me.

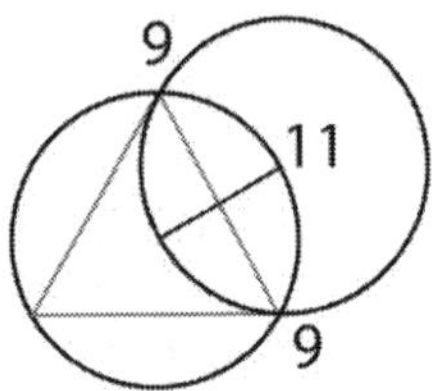

This number or "time" now makes sense to me in terms of the 11th ray and "river" of Aquarius which upholds and brings to conclusion this last arc and third of the sacred year, bridging the two 9's of the Rishis' sacred yajna or "sacrifice" wherein the two circles of 9 and 12 are One. Thea's message indicating that not all would survive the launch now appears as a foreshadowing of her passing precisely the week the number 7 revealed the vesica piscis to me as the key of the Seven Rivers of the Rig Veda.

The synchronicity of Thea's passing with the revelation of the vesica piscis as the sacred river and key of the Rig Veda at the close of the 144-year cycle[2] which began upon Sri Aurobindo's birth in 1872, is a true supramental marvel. Perhaps even more of

---

[1] Notably, the name of this river is Gangavar, thought to mean Ganga's gift.

[2] See the Appendix for a more detailed presentation of this 144-year cycle.

a marvel is the elaborate puzzle or treasure hunt the ancient Rishis or their forbearers composed to preserve and occult their gnosis of the zodiac. They simultaneously hid their treasure within the field or course of the sacred year and celebrated its eventual recovery in the Age of Aquarius. In our modern world such embedded treasures within a program, game or storyline are called "Easter Eggs". The recovery of the Rishis' lost Sun (or Son) from the waters in which it (or he) is hidden can be thought of in terms of an ancient and epic Easter Egg hunt or treasure hunt. It has taken mankind multiple ages just to acquire the keys of entry and to recover the correct entry point into the Rishis' actual field (*kshetra*) of play. This entry point is the zero point of the Vedic Year, which Thea understood to be 0° Aries of the Earth's Solar (Tropical) Year. Without that correct measure, all doorways and passages of the sacred yajna or year are inherently closed or missed, and all treasures therein are inaccessible.

Once the radius, the vesica piscis and the twelve-month Solar Year (i.e. the zodiac) emerge as the main keys of the occulted language of the Rishis, the smoke or mist of fragmentation clears and we can begin to see through the colorful and abundant variation of words and symbols to the singular core and context of the Rig Veda. From this place, we can better see how the symbols, mythologies and religions of our world are coverings which simultaneously eclipse and contain (however distorted) the golden thread of the Rishis' gnosis. The removal of these shadows, veils or coverings of the light is the essence of the words "revelation" and "apocalypse" meaning "to unveil", "uncover" or "uneclipse". This revelation is the task of Vishnu, the Hero-Purusha and Preserver of the Rig Veda. Once he bears his secret truth forward from its covering mists, the Divine Mystery gives way to Divine Gnosis. By this new light, all elaborate superstitions, divisive misinterpretations and dogmas that have naturally amassed around the sealed book of the Divine Mystery can be collectively dissolved, and left behind in the past where they now belong.

CHAPTER FOUR

The Vedic Origin of St. John's Revelation

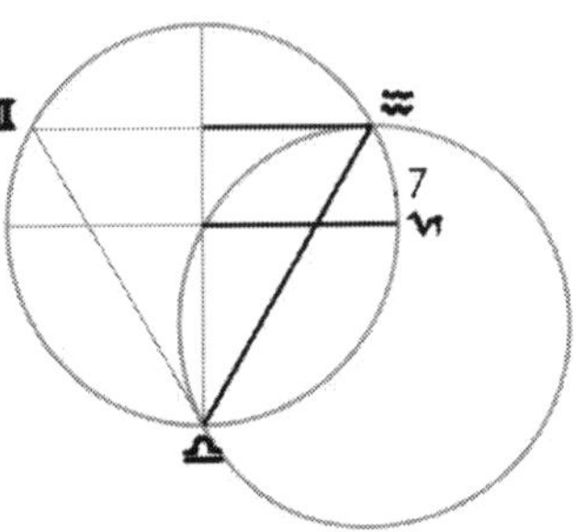

When I first saw the arc of the vesica piscis stretching from the 7th sign of Libra up to the 11th sign of Aquarius as the seventh wave of the zodiac, it became instantly clear that this wave was not only a crucial key to understanding the victorious release of the Seven Rivers in the Rig Veda, but also a crucial key to understanding the pouring out of the seven vials or bowls in St. John's *Revelation.*

> *Then I heard a loud voice from the temple saying to the seven angels, "Go, pour out the seven bowls of God's wrath on the earth."...The seventh angel poured out his bowl into the air, and out of the temple came a loud voice from the throne, saying, "It is done!" Then there came flashes of lightning, rumblings, peals of thunder and a severe earthquake. No earthquake like it has ever occurred since mankind has been on earth, so tremendous was the quake. The great city split into three parts, and the cities of the nations collapsed.*
>
> Revelation 16:1, 17-19, NIV

In *Revelation* we find seven angels who sound seven trumpets and pour out seven vials, bowls, plagues or floods of "God's Wrath" upon the world. This storyline echoes the Vedic portrayal of seven Angiras Rishis (sage-priests) who sing their seven songs and together with the thunder-god Indra, release "the floods of the supreme and universal conscious existence"[1] upon the world, thereby devastating the enemies of Truth and all that is built up upon the foundations of Ignorance in our world.

> *The Ṛṣis' sevenfold quire hath sung aloud to [Agni]. Shared by all Gods, Infallible, the Leader of our holy hymns, Golden-hued Soma, being cleansed, hath reached the bowls.*
>
> Rig Veda 9.103.3-4, tr. R.T.H. Griffith

> *The seven holy voices pour a wave of meath....[P]ouring forth their stream, are the Seven Sisters in the seat of sacrifice.*
>
> Rig Veda 8.103.3-4, tr. R.T.H. Griffith

> *The sages freed [the Dawns] from their firm-built prison: the seven priests drove them forward with their spirit....Indra who shone together with the Heroes...set the waters flowing, all-lucid, widely spread, that move together.*
>
> Rig Veda 3.31.5, 15-16, tr. R.T.H. Griffith

> *May we, seven sages first in rank, engender, from Dawn the Mother, men to be ordainers. May we, Aṅgirases, be sons of Heaven, and, radiant, burst the wealth-containing mountain.*
>
> Rig Veda 4.2.15, tr. R.T.H. Griffith

> *The gold-hued juice, poured out upon the filter.... The Ṛṣis came to [Agni], seven holy singers, when in the bowls he settled as Invoker....[S]even fresh rivers, brighten and adorn thee.*
>
> Rig Veda 9.92.2, tr. R.T.H. Griffith

> *[Indra] measured out the air's wide middle region and gave the heaven support.... [He] slew the Dragon, freed the Seven Rivers,*

[1] Sri Aurobindo, *The Secret of the Veda, CWSA, Volume 15*, p. 111.

> *and drove the kine forth from the cave of Vala.... [W]ith seven guiding reins, Indra, set free the Seven great Floods to flow....*
>
> Rig Veda 2.12.2-3, 12, tr. R.T.H. Griffith

> *I heard a loud voice from the temple saying to the seven angels, "Go, pour out the seven bowls of God's wrath on the earth."*
>
> Revelation 16.1, NIV

In both the Rig Veda and in *Revelation* these floods or waters are associated with the supreme victory over falsehood and an epic purification of the world. It is uplifting (and humorous) to see that the bowls, vials or plagues of God's "wrath" which are poured out by seven angels and depicted as wreaking great havoc on the world in *Revelation 16* are in truth, simply symbols of the vesica piscis. It is worth noting here that the word "angels" hails from the Angiras Rishis of the Veda. The Sanskrit root of *Angiras* (and "angels") is *aṅg*, which Sri Aurobindo described as "only a nasalised form of *ag*, the root of Agni".[1]

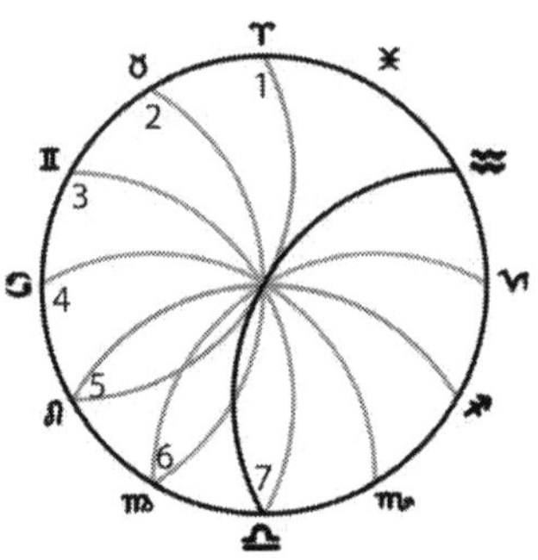

In *Revelation*, the voice (Vak) of the Temple loudly declares, *"It is done!"*, precisely when the seventh angel pours out the seventh bowl *"into the air"*. This is a clear echo of the victorious release of the cleansing and clarifying waters of truth in the Rig Veda. This detail of the water being poured out "into the air" is especially fitting because the seventh wave or bowl of the zodiac is specifically "poured out" between two air signs of the zodiac – Libra and Aquarius.

St. John's *Revelation* is simply a derivative account of the victorious Hero-Son and seven Angiras Rishis (Angirases) of the twelve-month Vedic sacrifice who together release the waters of truth upon the world in the Age of Aquarius. It is impossible to

---

[1] Sri Aurobindo, *The Secret of the Veda, CWSA, Volume 15*, p. 162.

say how much of the Vedic symbolism St. John understood while recording or constructing his revelations; but it is clear enough that the Vedic essence and truth of his vision was entirely lost on the human population throughout the Age of Pisces (234 BCE-1926 CE), and has remained lost on most in these early years of our Age of Aquarius.

As discussed in Part One, Thea revealed the lost zodiacal key and context of St. John's *Revelation* in her 1976 book *The Hidden Manna*. She saw this vision as an accurate prophecy of the world's passage into the Age of Aquarius accompanied by the descent of Supramental Gnosis in our fledgling Age of Unity. She saw the seventh seal as *"the seventh sign after Leo, the sign Aquarius"*.[1] In truth however, Aquarius is the 6th sign after Leo and it has now become apparent that the real logic of the seventh seal and its corresponding seventh bowl is its equivalence to the seventh wave of the vesica piscis, which moves through the "midair" of the zodiac, culminating in the sign of Aquarius (Kumbha). Aquarius is known throughout the world as the Water Bearer, depicted as a Man-Hero pouring out the waters of truth from his jar or *kumbha*. We can now see that this Man and his water jar are symbols of the radius and vesica piscis.

Aquarius the Water Bearer, from William Hone's Everyday Book, 1826 (Wikimedia Commons).

> *Skambha with one half engendered all creation. ...All men behold him with the eye, but with the mind they know not him. Holding aloft the water as a water-bearer in her jar. With the full vase he dwells....*[2]

Atharva Veda 10.8.13-14, tr. R.T.H. Griffith

---

[1] *The Hidden Manna*, p. 205.

[2] Skambha, the radius is the water bearer and is a thoroughly masculine figure. Griffith's translation makes it sound like the water bearer is feminine, but this is not the case. The vessel is feminine and her "bearer" or upholder is masculine.

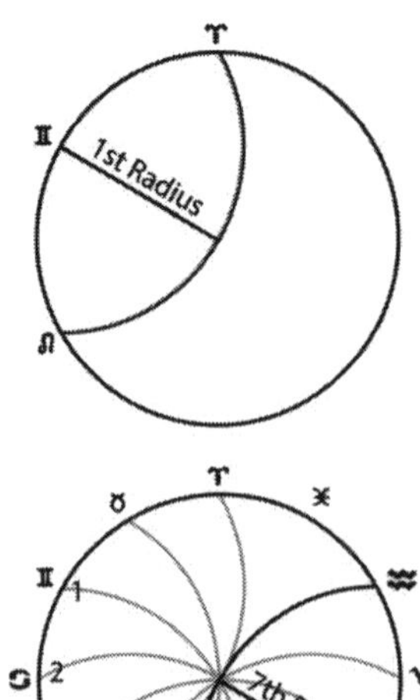

We can also see that this Man or Water Bearer who pours out the water jar from the heights of Aquarius is equivalent to the seventh angel of *Revelation* and to the seventh Rishi or immortal hero of the Rig Veda who upholds, compels and pours out the seventh wave or river of the zodiac. This seventh radius is the radius or ray of the 9th sign (Navagwas) of the zodiac, equivalent to Agni as the heroic Horse or Horse-Man of Sagittarius. I will further discuss this Horse-Hero in the following chapter.

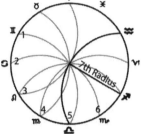

The preponderance of the number seven in St. John's *Revelation* – the seven seals, seven angels, seven stars, seven churches, seven lampstands, seven thunderers, seven trumpets, seven vials or bowls and seven floods – mirrors its preponderance in the Rig Veda where we have the seven rivers, seven words, seven sages, seven singers, seven Angiras Rishis, seven horses, seven delights and the seven-headed thought of the hero.

> *The number seven plays an exceedingly important part in the Vedic system, as in most very ancient schools of thought. We find it recurring constantly,—the seven delights,* sapta ratnāni*; the seven flames, tongues or rays of Agni,* sapta acriṣḥ, sapta jvālāḥ*; the seven forms of the Thought-principle,* sapta dhītayaḥ*; the seven Rays or Cows, forms of the Cow unslayable, Aditi, mother of the gods*, sapta gāvaḥ*; the seven rivers, the seven mothers or fostering cows,* sapta mātaraḥ, sapta dhenavaḥ, *a term applied indifferently to the Rays and to the Rivers."*

Sri Aurobindo, *The Secret of the Veda, CWSA, Volume 15*, p. 97

Each of the seven vesicae piscis leading up to the "pouring out" of the seventh bowl or seventh river from the heights of Aquarius, is the vessel of an accompanying radius. Thus, all these groupings of seven, both in the Rig Veda and in *Revelation* can been seen as either symbols of seven vesicae piscis or as symbols of seven radii. Most are symbols of the vesica piscis. The seven Rishis seers, sages, singers, horses, tongues of Agni, and the seven angels, stars, lampstands, thunderers of *Revelation* are all symbols of the indwelling radius or "Son" of the vesica piscis. In the following verse, the seven radii with their seven vesicae piscis are depicted as seven spear-carrying gods and their seven splendors and glories.

> *The Seven [Gods] carry seven spears; seven are the splendours they possess, [and] seven the glories they assume.*
>
> Rig Veda 8.28.5, tr. R.T.H. Griffith

In Rig Veda 2.12 featured earlier, the hero Indra is said to measure out the "air's wide middle region" in conjunction with freeing the seven rivers and floods. This links Indra's act of measuring and his victory to the victorious seventh wave of the zodiac, which stretches across two air signs, from Libra to Aquarius.

It can now be appreciated that the vesica piscis has equally functioned as a seal, lock or veil of the Rishis' occulted gnosis and as the key, without which the gnosis is for the most part inaccessible or unreadable. It can also be recognized that in lieu of truly understanding the veiled symbols of the Rishis, mankind has inevitably misinterpreted the Vedic lore many times over. These misinterpretations stand as the natural consequence of the denigration, mismeasure and loss of the *only* context in which these symbols truly make sense, which is the context of the Earth's sacred circle, mandala or Book of Life (i.e., the Zodiac).

The story of the long-awaited opening of the seven seals (by the Lamb with seven horns and seven eyes) is told in Chapter 5 of *Revelation*. The sealed scroll or book in this lore is symbolic of the zodiac, and equally symbolic of the Rig Veda which cannot be read by those ignorant of its zodiacal context.

> *Then I saw in the right hand of him who sat on the throne a scroll with writing on both sides and sealed with seven seals. And I saw*

a mighty angel proclaiming in a loud voice, "Who is worthy to break the seals and open the scroll?" But no one in heaven or on earth or under the earth could open the scroll or even look inside it. I wept and wept because no one was found who was worthy to open the scroll or look inside. Then one of the elders said to me, "Do not weep! See, the Lion of the tribe of Judah, the Root of David, has triumphed. He is able to open the scroll and its seven seals." Then I saw a Lamb, looking as if it had been slain, standing in the center of the throne, encircled by the four living creatures[1] *and the elders. He had seven horns and seven eyes, which are the seven spirits of God sent out into all the earth. He came and took the scroll from the right hand of him who sat on the throne. And when he had taken it, the four living creatures and the twenty-four elders*[2] *fell down before the Lamb. Each one had a harp and they were holding golden bowls full of incense, which are the prayers of the saints. And they sang a new song: "You are worthy to take the scroll and to open its seals, because you were slain, and with your blood you purchased men for God from every tribe and language and people and nation.*

Revelation 5:1-9, NIV

This death-conquering Lamb of *Revelation* is equivalent to the immortal calf of the immortal cow in the Rig Veda. The lamb and calf are equally symbols of the radius, and the cow is alternately the zodiac and the vesica piscis. The lamb or calf is Agni, the eternal Purusha borne out in the course of evolution – the Father reborn as the Son. In Chapter 6 of *Revelation*, this newborn Lamb proceeds to open six of the seven seals. Then, in the first verses of Chapter 8, he opens the seventh seal.

When he opened the seventh seal, there was silence in heaven for about half an hour. And I saw the seven angels who stand before God, and to them were given seven trumpets.

Revelation 8:1-2, NIV

---

[1] These four creatures correspond to Vishnu's four preservation signs.

[2] The 24 elders are equivalent to the 24 hours of the day.

Whereas the seven seals, seven eyes, seven trumpets and even the golden bowl of incense of *Revelation* can be understood as symbols of the vesica piscis, the seven angels are symbols of seven radii. The seven horns of the Lamb could be either radii or the "horns" of the vesicae pisces. Other symbols of the radius and vesica piscis in *Revelation*, as featured in the verses below, include an angel robed in a cloud, the seven thunderers and their voices, and the roar of a lion. It is intriguing to see in these verses that St. John is told by the voice (Vak) of heaven to keep sealed or secret what he has learned from the seven angels.

> *Then I saw another mighty angel coming down from heaven. He was robed in a cloud...and he gave a loud shout like the roar of a lion. When he shouted, the voices of the seven thunders spoke. And when the seven thunders spoke, I was about to write; but I heard a voice from heaven say, "Seal up what the seven thunders have said and do not write it down....[I]n the days when the seventh angel is about to sound his trumpet, the mystery of God will be accomplished...".*
>
> Revelation 10:1-4, NIV

These symbols are taken directly from the Rig Veda, wherein the radii are depicted as thundering storm gods, and the vesica piscis as storm clouds.

> *Pourers of floods...clothed in robes of rain, boon-givers of good gifts, roar as the lion's roar.*
>
> Rig Veda 3.26.4-5, tr. R.T.H. Griffith

> *The thunderers roam through regions varied in their hues. Imperial Kings, bedew us with the milk of heaven.*
>
> Rig Veda 5.63.6, tr. R.T.H. Griffith

> *Munificent Heroes, they have cast heaven's treasury down for the worshipper's behoof: They set the storm-cloud free to stream through both the worlds, and rainfloods flow o'er desert spots.*
>
> Rig Veda 5.53.6, tr. R.T.H. Griffith

[T]he clouds that give out their lightnings and their waters of life; the streams of the clarity and the honey ascend out of the subconscient ocean below and seek the superconscient ocean above; and from above that ocean sends downward its rivers of the light and truth and bliss even into our physical being.... The seven sages, the Angirasas, are waiting still and always, ready to chant the word, to rend the cavern, to find the lost herds, to recover the hidden Sun.

Sri Aurobindo, *The Secret of the Veda, CWSA, Volume 15*, p. 383

In *Revelation 21*, St. John describes the victory of the hero, whose bride is said to be the holy city Jerusalem. As discussed earlier in Part One, Chapter 10 of this book, this sacred city/wife is the 12-month zodiac, measured out by the golden rod or reed of the angel. In this same chapter of *Revelation*, the hero Lamb tells John that he will "give water without cost from the spring of the water of life". We can now recognize that this "water without cost" or "water of life" is a veiled symbol of the vesica piscis. I have already quoted some of the verses below, but they are worth rereading now that we have a fuller picture of the geometric keys and zodiacal context of the symbols of this prophecy.

He who was seated on the throne said, "I am making everything new!"...He said to me: "It is done. I am the Alpha and the Omega, the Beginning and the End. ***To the thirsty I will give water without cost from the spring of the water of life****.... One of the seven angels who had the seven bowls full of the seven last plagues came and said to me, "Come, I will show you the bride, the wife of the Lamb." And he carried me away in the Spirit to a mountain great and high, and showed me the Holy City, Jerusalem, coming down out of heaven from God.... It had a great, high wall with twelve gates, and with twelve angels at the gates. On the gates were written the names of the twelve tribes of Israel. There were three gates on the east, three on the north, three on the south and three on the west. The wall of the city had twelve foundations, and on them were the names of the twelve apostles of the Lamb. The angel who talked with me had a measuring rod of gold to measure the city, its gates and its walls.... On no day will* *its gates ever be shut, for there will be no night there.... Nothing impure will ever enter it, nor will anyone who does what is shameful or deceitful, but only those whose names are written in the Lamb's book of life.*

Revelation 21:1-17, NIV [bold emphasis added]

Revelation 22, titled "Eden Restored" in the *New International Version* of the Bible, brings the conclusion of St. John's vision.

The angel showed me the river of the water of life*, as clear as crystal, flowing from the throne of God and of the Lamb down the middle of the great street of the city. On each side of the river stood the tree of life, bearing twelve crops of fruit, yielding its fruit every month. And the leaves of the tree are for the healing of the nations. No longer will there be any curse. The throne of God and of the Lamb will be in the city, and his servants will serve him. They will see his face, and his name will be on their foreheads. There will be no more night. They will not need the light of a lamp or the light of the sun, for the Lord God will give them light. And they will reign for ever and ever.*

Revelation 22:1-5, NIV [bold emphasis added]

It is important to note that the angel's final revelation to John is the revelation of the "river of the water of life" which flows into and sustains the great city and the tree of life with its twelve crops, both of which are clearly symbols of the zodiac. This river is also a key feature of the Garden of Eden in *Genesis*.

A river flowed out of Eden to water the garden, and there it divided and became four rivers.

Genesis 2:10, NIV

This sacred river is once again clearly derivative of Vedic lore.

[Indra] with thunder rent obstructive Vala.... Thou Indra...made four rivers flow full with waves that carry down sweet water.

Rig Veda 1.62.6, tr. R.T.H. Griffith

The four rivers of Indra the Bull and the four rivers of Eden are, in all likelihood, the four vesicae piscis drawn out from the four cardinal points of the circle, forming Vishnu's Flower (or Turtle) and establishing the full twelve signs of the zodiac.

> *O [Agni] thou Home-leader, lead them home, restore them thou who bringest home. Four are the quarters of the earth; from these bring back to us our kine....*
>
> Rig Veda 10.19.8, tr. R.T.H. Griffith

As Sri Aurobindo has noted in *The Secret of the Veda*, the recovery of the cows (kine) and the rivers in the Veda refer to the same victory using interchangeable symbols. As far as I can tell in my research, the word "Eden" hails from the Sanskrit base *uda* meaning "water", and *udan* meaning "a wave" or "water". From these words come *udanya* meaning "watery", *udanyu* meaning "pouring out water, irrigating", and *udanyaja* meaning "born or living in water", which can be said of Agni, or any figure of the Purusha.[1]

In order to understand what exactly St. John's *Revelation* or "Apocalypse" portended, which is the recovery and pouring out of gnosis in the Age of Aquarius, the text must be reconnected to its original Vedic sense. In this sense, the sacred temple or city which the Seer enters is the twelve-month yajna – the temple of our unified field of Time and Space. The Mother's temple vision contained this same gnosis. Outside the context of this twelve-month Vedic Temple or field of Time, the world's mythology of the Immortal Son, conqueror or savior by whatever name, will continue to remain *entirely* divorced from its real basis of truth.

I will close this chapter with an intriguing account of the Vedic revelation and victory wherein the heroine-cow (mother of the calf) strips off her covering, humbling mankind. Upon her disclosure, the herdsman or divine Purusha who never stumbles becomes visible and the streams or waters of the cow descend as

---

[1] All roots and their definitions are from *Cologne Digital Sanskrit Lexicon*.

an imperishable flood. The calf here is called the "shedder [or pourer] of the rain". This imagery makes very little sense, without the key that the cow, dubbed the "lady of all treasure" is the vesica piscis and her rain-bearing (i.e. water-bearing) calf and the hidden herdsman are both figures of the radius – the One who establishes the six regions of the circle. It also makes little sense without the key that the seven horses and cows/sisters are symbols of the seven radii and seven vesicae piscis or rivers of the zodiac whose movement culminates in the pouring out of the purifying waters of gnosis in the sign of Aquarius/Kumbha.

> *[B]earing seven names the single Courser draws [the one-wheeled chariot]. Three-naved the wheel is, sound and undecaying, whereon are resting all these worlds of being. The seven who on the seven-wheeled car are mounted have horses, seven in tale, who draw them onward. Seven Sisters utter songs of praise together, in whom the names of the seven Cows are treasured. Who hath beheld him as he sprang to being, seen how the boneless One supports the bony? ... I ask, unknowing, those who know, the sages, as one all ignorant for sake of knowledge, What was that ONE who in the Unborn's image hath stablished and fixed firm these worlds' six regions.*
>
> *She, lady of all treasure, is come hither yearning in spirit for her calf and lowing....The cow hath lowed after her blinking youngling; she licks his forehead, as she lows, to form it. His mouth she fondly calls to her warm udder, and suckles him with milk while gently lowing. He also snorts, by whom encompassed round the Cow laws as she clings unto the shedder of the rain. She with her shrilling cries hath humbled mortal man, and, turned to lightning, hath stripped off her covering robe. That which hath breath and speed and life and motion lies firmly stablished in the midst of houses. Living, by offerings to the Dead he moveth Immortal One, the brother of the mortal. I saw the Herdsman, him who never stumbles, approaching by his pathways and departing.*
>
> *From [the Cow] descend in streams the seas of water; thereby the world's four regions have their being, Thence flows the imperishable flood and thence the universe hath life.*

Rig Veda 1.164, 2-6, 27-31, 42, tr. R.T.H. Griffith

CHAPTER FIVE

The Stallion's Flood

Send down for us the rain of heaven, ye Maruts,[1] *and let the Stallion's flood descend in torrents. Come hither with this thunder while thou pourest the waters down, our heavenly Lord and Father. Thunder and roar: the germ of life deposit. Fly round us on thy chariot waterladen. Thine opened water-skin draw with thee downward, and let the hollows and the heights be level. Lift up the mighty vessel, pour down water, and let the liberated streams rush forward....*

Rig Veda 5.83.6-8 tr. R.T.H. Griffith

In these verses from Rig Veda 5.83 we can see that the pouring forth of the holy water or wine from its sacred or mighty vessel (or *kumbha*) is connected to the figure of the Horse, which is not only a symbol of the Purusha and radius, but of Sagittarius – the 9th sign of the zodiac, the sign of the Sage. Elsewhere in the Vedas we find that the god Brihaspati also has a roll in liberating the waters from their container or cave, which I will discuss later. In this chapter I will focus on the role of the Horse in releasing the divine waters, equivalent to the flood released by the seventh angel of *Revelation 10:7*. With this liberation and release of the waters, the doors of the higher world of Swar are opened.[2]

---

[1] The Maruts are storm gods (hero-companions of Indra) armed with lightning-spears. They are symbols of the radii of the zodiac.

[2] Rig Veda 2.24, tr. Sri Aurobindo, *The Secret of the Veda, CWSA, Volume 15*, pp. 178-79.

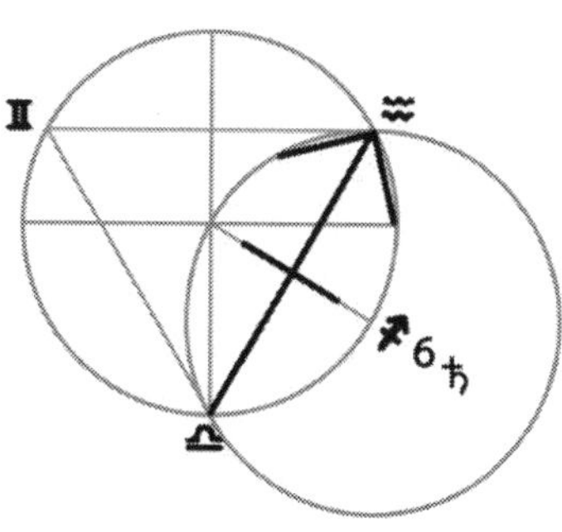

The key to the odd imagery of "the Stallion's flood" is found in the image I first introduced at the tail end of "An Ending and a New Beginning", showing the hieroglyph of Sagittarius within the seventh wave or river of the zodiac. Here I will further flush out this key of the Horse's central role in the victorious release of the sacred waters. In this image[1] we can see that the radius of Sagittarius forms the vesica piscis which extends from 0° Libra to 0° Aquarius wherein the divine waters are released from their *kumbha* or water jar.

> *[He] like a courser in the floods invincible... is resting in the jars.*
>
> Rig Veda 9.20.6, tr. R.T.H. Griffith

0° Sagittarius is the 6 Point of the Circle of 9 and is the seat of the 6th planet Saturn ♄, equivalent to the gods Yama and Shiva, both linked with the destruction or dissolution (*tamas*) flow of the zodiac. This Sagittarius point is the center point (*bindu*) or fulcrum of the seventh wave or river of the zodiac which arcs to 0° Aquarius in the fourth quadrant or Swar realm of the Rishis. Via this basic geometry, we can understand why Saturn is considered the original or ancient ruler of Aquarius. The ray or radius of 0° Sagittarius forms and drives the wave that establishes the zero point of Aquarius. This 9th ray or radius of the zodiac is Agni the Horse, the Immortal Purusha, victorious over death via his self-born Law and self-born path (or yajna) that leads to Vishnu's highest seat in the fourth world of Swar. His "gallop" from Libra into Aquarius is equivalent to the Stallion's Flood of Rig Veda 5.83. It is simultaneously the seventh river of the zodiac and the seventh bowl or vial of St. John's *Revelation*.

[1] I have added the number 6 and the hieroglyph of Saturn to the original image of this Sagittarian arrow.

[Agni] is like a horse in the battle-charge urged to the gallop and like a rushing river, and who then shall hedge in his course?

Rig Veda 1.65.3, tr. Sri Aurobindo,
The Secret of the Veda, CWSA, Volume 15, p. 576

He, the bright Son, when born illumed his Parents who had sprung to life, Great Son great Strengtheners of Law. Urged by the seven devotions he hath stirred the [seven] guileless rivers which have magnified the Single Eye. These [seven] helped to might the Youthful One, high over all, invincible.... The immortal Courser, good to draw, looks down upon the Seven.

Rig Veda 9.9.3-6, tr. R.T.H. Griffith

In Rig Veda 9.71 this Hero-Son (Agni) is called Soma Pavamana, likened to a horse (courser), as well as a steer (bull). He is called the "Winner of the Floods", equivalent to Indra. His covering and his floods are the vesicae piscis.

[T]he Holy One goes like a courser to the Gods. From far away, from heaven, the red-hued noted Sage, Steer of the triple height, hath sung unto the kine. With [a] thousand guidings he, leading this way and that, shines, as a singer, splendidly through many a morn. His covering assumes a radiant hue; where'er he comes into the fight he drives the foe afar. The Winner of the Floods, with food he seeks the host of heaven, he comes to praises glorified with milk. Like a bull roaming round the herds he bellows: he hath assumed the brilliancy of Sūrya.

Rig Veda 9.71.6-9, tr. R.T.H. Griffith

The "triple height" of the steer in this hymn is a reference to the third birth of Agni equivalent to the victorious horse born at the third (*trita*) angle (the 6 Point) of the central trinity or fire trine of the circle. Similar imagery is found in the following verse wherein the hero achieves his "third status", upbears the "vessel" and gallops to the "conquest of riches". The stallion's flood here is described as the "ocean surge of waters".

> *The Lord of Delight conquers the third status; he maintains and governs according to the Soul of universality.*
>
> *Like a hawk, a kite He settles on the Vessel and upbears it; in His stream of movement He discovers the Rays, for He goes bearing his weapons: He cleaves to the ocean surge of the waters; a great King, He declares the fourth status.*
>
> *Like a mortal purifying his body,* ***like a war-horse galloping to the conquest of riches. He pours calling through all the sheath and enters these vessels.***
>
> Rig Veda 9.96.18-20, tr. Sri Aurobindo, *The Life Divine, CWSA, Volume 21-22*, pp. 210, 266 [bold emphasis added]

> *What time, first springing into life, thou neighedst, proceeding from the sea or upper waters, [limbs] of the deer hadst thou, and eagle pinions. O Steed, thy birth is nigh and must be lauded.*
>
> *This Steed which Yama gave hath Trita harnessed, and him, the first of all, hath Indra mounted. His bridle the Gandharva*[1] *grasped. O Vasus, from out [of] the Sun ye fashioned forth the Courser.*
>
> ***Yama art thou, O Horse****; thou art Āditya [the Sun]; Trita art thou by secret operation.... They say thou hast three bonds in heaven that hold thee. Three bonds, they say, thou hast in heaven that bind thee, three in the waters, three within the ocean....*
>
> *Here, Courser, are the places where they groomed thee, here are the traces of thy hoofs as winner. Here have I seen the auspicious reins that guide thee, which those who guard the holy Law keep safely....*
>
> Rig Veda 1.163.1-4, tr. R.T.H. Griffith [bold emphasis added]

Yama, as I have already mentioned, is not simply the Lord of Death as he is commonly depicted, he is also lauded as "the first

---

[1] The Gandharva is the husband of the Apsaras or water nymphs. In other words, he is a figure of the radius. His bridle and his wife are both symbols of the vesica piscis.

immortal, the first [Man] to transcend death".[1] In other words he is the conqueror of Death. In Rig Veda 1.83.5 the Rishi sings of Yama's deathless birth. This is the immortal Purusha Agni born victorious in the course of the Vedic yajna, or in other words, in the course of Earth's evolution. He is Agni's third birth in the fire trine of the zodiac. In the following hymn Yama is described as the first to find the path and pasture of the higher realm of Swar.

> *[He who] travelled to the lofty heights above us, who searches out and shows the path to many. Yama first found for us a place to dwell in: this pasture never can be taken from us.*
>
> Rig Veda 10.14.1-2, tr. R.T.H. Griffith

In our modern world Yama is often associated with both the 9th planet Pluto and the 6th planet Saturn, but in Rig Veda 1.163 and 10.14, Yama appears to be specifically Saturn, positioned in the circle at 0° Sagittarius – the sign of the Horse. Yama's path (equivalent to the Horse's path) into the higher realm can be understood as the path of the vesica piscis extending from 0° Libra to 0° Aquarius. Regarding Yama, Sri Aurobindo wrote:

> *[It] is worth while noting the real character of Yama...in the Rig Veda. In the later ideas Yama is the god of Death and has his own special world; but in the Rig Veda he seems to have been originally a form of the Sun, — even as late as the Isha Upanishad we find the name used as an appellation of the Sun.... He is the guardian of the dharma, the law of the Truth,* satyadharma, *which is a condition of immortality, and therefore himself the guardian of immortality. His world is Swar, the world of immortality,* amṛte loke akṣte, *where, as we are told in IX.113, is the indestructible Light, where Swar is established,* yatra jyotir ajasraṃ, yasmin loke svar hitam.
>
> Sri Aurobindo, *The Secret of the Veda, CWSA, Volume 15*, p. 221

---

[1] Raimundo Panikkar, *The Vedic Experience*, p. 492.

Below I am repeating an excerpt from Hymn 2.35 because it makes more sense now knowing that the flood, the dames, the waters, the food, and the clouds of this hymn are all symbols of the vesica piscis, and knowing that the radius of Sagittarius forms the pillar (skambha) of the seventh wave of the vesica piscis that marks the release of the floods of gnosis from the sacred kumbha.

[The Floods' Child]...the friendly Son of Waters by the greatness of Godhead hath produced all things existing. To him three Dames are offering food to feed him, Goddesses to the God whom none may injure. Within the waters hath he pressed.... ***Here was the horse's birth****; his was the sunlight....Him, indestructible, dwelling at a distance in forts unwrought lies and ill spirits reach not.... The Son of Waters, gathering strength in waters.... He who in waters with his own pure Godhead shines widely, law-abiding, everlasting.... The Waters' Son hath risen, and clothed in lightning ascended up unto the curled cloud's bosom.... Golden in form is he, like gold to look on, his colour is like gold, the Son of Waters.*

Rig Veda 2.35, tr. R.T.H. Griffith [bold emphasis added]

In Rig Veda 1.162 this indestructible or unslayable Hero-Horse is referred to as *vajin devajatasya*,[1] which Griffith translated as "the strong Steed, God-descended". This hero "fill[s] full the channels of the river." This is one-hundred percent a reference not only to the radius and vesica piscis but specifically to the radius of Sagittarius – the 9th radius of the circle which arcs (or gallops) up to Aquarius/Kumbha.

Slight us not Varuṇa, Aryaman, or Mitra, Ṛbhukṣan, Indra, Āyu, or the Maruts, when we declare amid the congregation the virtues of the strong Steed, God-descended. What time they bear before the Courser, covered with trappings and with wealth, the grasped oblation, [the] dappled goat [Agni] goeth straightforward, bleating, to the place dear to Indra and to Pūṣan.

---

[1] *Vajin* is translated as "Stallion", "swiftness", as well as "heroic" and "warlike". *Deva* means "god" and *jatasya* means "born" (*Cologne Digital Sanskrit Lexicon*).

> *...Invoker, ministering priest, atoner, fire-kindler Soma-presser, sage, reciter, with this well ordered sacrifice, well finished, do ye [Agni] fill full the channels of the rivers....*
>
> *The four-and-thirty ribs of the Swift Charger, kin to the Gods, the slayer's hatchet pierces. Cut ye with skill, so that the parts be flawless, and piece by piece declaring [and dissecting] them. Of Tvaṣṭar's Charger there is one dissector, — this is the custom-two there are who guide him. Such of his limbs as I divide in order, these, amid the balls, in fire I offer. Let not thy dear soul burn thee as thou comest, let not the hatchet linger in thy body. Let not a greedy clumsy immolator, missing the joints, mangle thy limbs unduly.* ***No, here thou diest not, thou art not injured****: by easy paths unto the Gods thou goest....May this Steed bring us all-sustaining riches....*
>
> Rig Veda 1.162, tr. R.T.H. Griffith [bold emphasis added]

This is the victorious horse of the Vedic sacrifice. It is important to note that he is allotted "four and thirty ribs" which we can now see as four-times-thirty (120) degrees of the circle, or four months of the twelve-month sacrifice, equivalent to 432,000″. In Griffith's translation of Rig Veda 1.162, the vesica piscis is depicted or disguised as a "flesh-cooking-caldron".[1] Without the geometric key and zodiacal context of this symbolism, the Rishis' "horse sacrifice" (*aswamedha*) has been greatly misunderstood. The epitome, goal or fulfillment of the Rishis' sacrifice (*yajna*) is the *victory* of the immortal Hero-Horse in the course of the year, not a Stallion's death for anyone's benefit. Rig Veda 1.162.21 indicates that despite all divisions or cuts made, the Horse "diest not" nor is he even injured. Rather he travels on to the gods (the Swar realm) by "easy paths". The divisions of the Horse must be seen not in terms of butchery, but in terms of the sacred geometry of the year. The Rishi's prayer for a skillful immolator or sacrificer is a prayer for accurate measurement and observance of the sacrificial year. Otherwise, the body and soul of Time and Space is effectively butchered by incompetent sacrificers. The

[1] Rig Veda 1.162.13.

mismeasured sacrificial year yields no benefit. It only serves to bind the misaligned observers of the sacred year to Ignorance.

In Rig Veda 1.66 Agni is said to strike "like an archer's arrow" and to be "like a steed". The archer, bow and steed are all classic symbols of Sagittarius; and whereas the archer and steed are symbols of the radius, the bow (*dhanvan*) is the arc of the vesica piscis.

> *Like a Seer lauding, famed among the folk; like a steed friendly [Agni, the Conqueror of men] vouchsafes us power....*
>
> *[Agni] strikes with terror like a dart shot forth, e'en like an archer's arrow tipped with flame; Master of present and of future life, the maidens' lover and the matrons' Lord.*
>
> *To him lead all your ways: may we attain the kindled God as cows their home at eve. He drives the flames below as floods their swell: the rays rise up to the fair place of heaven.*

Rig Veda 1.66.2, 4-5, tr. R.T.H. Griffith

The flaming arrow, horse, archer and bow are all symbols of the fire sign Sagittarius, whose flame or radius upholds the swell or wave of the flood which rises into the Swar realm. Sri Aurobindo translated Rig Veda 1.66.5 as:

> *[Agni] is like a river running in its channel and sends in his front the descending Waters: the Ray-Cows move to him in the manifesting of the world of the Sun.*

Sri Aurobindo, *Hymns to the Mystic Fire, CWSA, Volume 16*, p. 95

Agni's river and his driving forth of floods (or cows) is equivalent to the Stallion's flood. As the conquering Horse-Hero (a.k.a. Kalki), he drives forth the seventh vesica piscis which brings us to Aquarius in the final quadrant of the zodiac – the Swar realm of the Rishis wherein the light of the Sun or Soul is no longer hidden by the egoic-mental consciousness. Another version of this same theme is found in Rig Veda 3.1, wherein Agni sets his own streams (and voices) in motion and becomes unhidden.

> *From birth he knew even his Father's bosom, he set his voices and his streams in motion; knew him who moved with blessed Friends in secret, with the young Dames of heaven. He stayed not hidden.*
>
> Rig Veda 3.1.9, tr. R.T.H. Griffith

It is useful to compare Griffith's translation with Sri Aurobindo's translation of this same verse. We can see that the "young Dames", a.k.a. the Virgins of Heaven, are equivalent to the "mighty Rivers of Heaven".

> *At his birth he discovered the teat of abundance of the Father, he loosed forth wide his streams, wide his nourishing rivers;*[1] *he discovered him moving in the secrecy with his helpful comrades, with the mighty Rivers of Heaven, but himself became not secret in the cave.*
>
> Rig Veda 3.1.9, *Hymns to the Mystic Fire, CWSA, Volume 16*, p. 158

This theme of the dames or rivers and the hero born from them is also found in Rig Veda 10.195.

> *While [the hero Purūravas] was born the Dames [sat] down together, the Rivers with free kindness gave him nurture....*
>
> *When, loving these Immortal Ones, the mortal hath converse with the nymphs as they allow him. Like swans they show the beauty of their bodies, like horses in their play they bite and nibble.*
>
> *[Urvasi] flashed brilliant as the falling lightning brought me delicious presents from the waters. Now from the flood be born a strong young hero....*
>
> *I [Purūravas], her best love, call Urvasi to meet me, her who fills air and measures out the region. Let the gift brought by piety approach thee....*
>
> Rig Veda 10.95.7, 9-10, 17, tr. R.T.H. Griffith

---

[1] Sri Aurobindo's note: "Or, he loosed forth the milch-cows."

In Indian mythology, Urvasi[1] is considered the most beautiful of the Apsaras (water nymphs or dames) and is sometimes depicted as having a fish's tail.[2] She is a dawn goddess and a figure of the vesica piscis. The root of her name *uru* means "thigh" and she is said to be born from a Sage's thigh. In astrological lore, the thigh happens to be the part of the body associated with the 9th sign of the zodiac. Hence this lore suggests that Urvasi is equivalent to the seventh river or vesica piscis upheld by the Sage or Horse of Sagittarius. Agni (the Son and Stallion of the floods) in Rig Veda 10.95 is Purūravas whose name amounts to the roaring (*rava*) or thundering Purusha. One of Sri Aurobindo's early poems, titled "Urvasie", is an account of the love between this "water nymph" and Purūravas.

All beauty of earthliness is in thee, all
Luxurious experience of the soul.
O comest thou because I left thy charm
Aiming at purity, O comest thou,
Goddess, to avenge thyself with beauty? Come!
Unveil thyself from light! limit thyself,
O infinite grace, that I may find, may clasp.
For surely in my heart I know thou bearest
A name that naturally weds with mine,[3]
And I perceive our union magically
Inevitable as a perfect verse
Of Veda. Set thy feet upon my heart,
O Goddess! woman, to my bosom move!
I am Pururavus, O Urvasie."

Sri Aurobindo, "Urvasie" (circa 1896), excerpt,
Collected Poems, CWSA, Volume 2, pp. 69-70

The following passage is Sri Aurobindo's description of Agni as the victorious horse, son and warrior. The cattle or cows that Agni restores to youth here are equivalent to the rivers that he releases.

---

[1] Also spelled Urvashi or Urvasie.

[2] Perhaps giving us the origin of Mermaids.

[3] Their names are their true forms – the vesica piscis and the radius.

> *[Agni] is born in the Truth, a master of Truth, a guardian of Truth and Immortality, a getter and keeper of the shining herds, the eternal Youth, and he renews the youth of these mystic cattle. He is triply extended in the Infinite.... He is the horse of battle and the horse of swiftness and again he gives the white horse; he is the Son and he creates for man the Son. He is the Warrior and he brings to man the heroes of his battle. He destroys by his flame... he is a Vritra-slayer.*
>
> Sri Aurobindo, *Hymns to the Mystic Fire, CWSA, Volume 16*, pp. 689-90

The Nine-Rayed Hero

The Hero-Son in the Rig Veda is associated with the War Horse *Dadhikravan*. In Rig Veda 7.41.6 Dadhikravan is said to arrive at "the pure place"[1] – the Swar realm of the yajna, wherein the treasures of the Purusha (Soul) are found. This Horse is a symbol of Vishnu's 9th avatar Kalki who is not only depicted as riding a horse, but also as horse-headed. In Rig Veda 9.108 this hero is the nine-rayed horse-headed Hero-Sage *Navagva Dadhyac*.

> *[Agni] thou hast, splendidest, called all the generations of the Gods to immortality. By whom Dadhyac Navagva opens fastened doors, by whom the sages gained their wish, by whom they won the fame of lovely Amṛta in the felicity of Gods. Effused, he floweth in a stream, best rapture-giver... [supporting] as 'twere the waters' wave. He who from out the rocky cavern took with might the... refulgent watery Cows, Thou masterest the stable full of kine and steeds: burst it, brave Lord, like one in mail. Press ye and pour him, like a steed, laudworthy, speeding through the region and the flood, who swims in water.... Increaser of the water, Steer with thousand streams... Who born in Law hath waxen mighty by the Law, King, God, and lofty Ordinance. Make splendid glory shine on us, thou Lord of strengthening food, God, as the Friend of Gods: Unclose the fount of middle air. Roll onward to the bowls, O Mighty One, effused, as Prince supporter of the tribes. Pour on us rain from heaven, send us the waters' flow: incite our thoughts to win the spoil.... The Mighty One was born Immortal, giving life,*

[1] Tr. R.T.H. Griffith.

lightening darkness with his shine. Well-praised by sages he hath, by his wondrous power assumed the Threefold as his robe.... By whom we bring to us Mitra and Varuṇa and Indra for our great defence.... [Soma enter] the Soma-holder, even Indra's heart, as rivers pass into the sea, acceptable to Mitra, Vāyu, Varuṇa, the noblest Pillar of the heavens.

Rig Veda 9.108.3-16, tr. R.T.H. Griffith

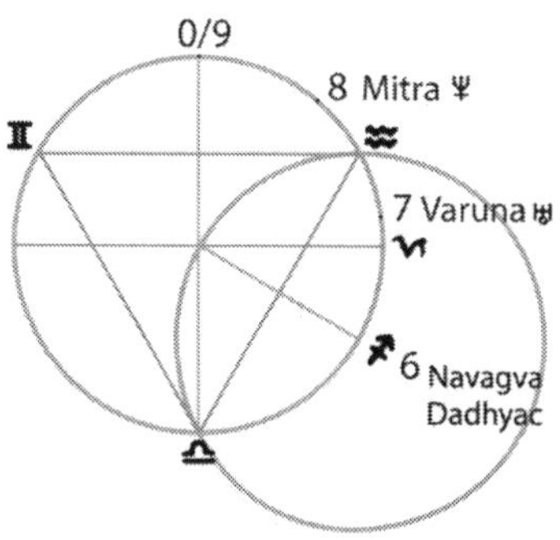

There are perhaps twenty symbols of the vesica piscis in this one passage, including but not limited to the waters' wave, the fountain of midair, the bowls, the rocky cavern, the Soma-holder, the robe and the rivers. *Dadhyac* is another name for Agni, the son of the sacrificial year. *Navagva Dadhyac* is thus the nine-rayed son Agni, the "Mighty One [who] was born Immortal" and who wears "the Threefold as his robe". He is also described as "the noblest Pillar of the heavens". *Navagva Dadhyac's* stream and the wave he supports is equivalent to the Stallion's Flood. According to the Rishis, this nine-rayed hero brings to the Rishis the assistance of Varuna and Mitra who, as Thea discussed in *The New Way, Volumes 1&2* are equivalent to the 7th and 8th planets of our solar system, Uranus and Neptune.

All of this makes perfect sense when we know that the nine-rayed horse is the radius whose stream, wave or "fount of midair" is the wave of the vesica piscis which extends from the air sign Libra to the air sign Aquarius, and thus into the Swar realm of the zodiac guarded by Varuna and Mitra. This same geometry and zodiacal context is conveyed in Sri Aurobindo's discussion of the many names of the one Purusha.

The Deva or Godhead is both the original cause and the final result.... [He] is the Divine Child born into the Worlds who manifests himself in the growth of the creature. He is Rudra and

> *Vishnu, Prajapati and Hiranyagarbha, Surya, Agni, Indra, Vayu, Soma, Brihaspati, — Varuna and Mitra and Bhaga and Aryaman, all the gods. He is the wise, mighty and liberating Son born from our works and our sacrifice, the Hero in our warfare and Seer of our knowledge, the White Steed in the front of our days who gallops towards the upper Ocean.....He is the source and outpourer of the ambrosial Wine of divine delight and we drink it drawn from the sevenfold waters of existence or pressed out from the luminous plant on the hill of being and uplifted by its raptures we become immortal. Such are some of the images of this ancient mystic adoration.*
>
> Sri Aurobindo, *The Secret of the Veda, CWSA, Volume 15*, p. 371

The galloping of the White Steed towards the upper ocean is a symbolic expression of the arc of the Horse or 9th radius of the zodiac "galloping" or swinging into the upper quadrant of the circle. Another example of the Horse's special role in pouring forth the sacred water or wine is found in the following verse wherein he is referred to as a "strong charger".

> *Oh Heroes...Ye poured forth from the hoof of your strong charger a hundred jars of wine as from a strainer.*
>
> Rig Veda 1.116.7, tr. R.T.H. Griffith

The horse's hoof in this scenario appears to be the center-point end of the radius from which "pours forth" the wine of the vesica piscis within the circle.

The Horse's Fountain

As Sri Aurobindo noted in *The Secret of the Veda*, the Vedic theme of the horse and the Vedic victory is closely echoed by the Greek mythology of Pegasus. The white winged horse Pegasus is credited with kicking a rock at the base of a mountain with his moon-shaped hoof, thereby causing the flow of the eternal fountain or spring of wisdom. Sri Aurobindo suggested that this fountain is equivalent to Saraswati, who is both a river and the goddess of wisdom. Clearly, the Pegasus myth is connected to the hero of the Vedic yajna who, with great force, releases the rivers of truth from the mountain, hill, cave or rock.

> *Soon as he sprang to life he forced asunder hosts: forward the Hero looked to manly deed and war. He cleft the rock, he let concurrent streams flow forth, and with his skilful art stablished the heavens' wide vault.*
>
> Rig Veda 10.113.4, tr. R.T.H. Griffith

In Greek mythology, the name of this fountain of wisdom and youth released by Pegasus is "Hippocrene" meaning "Horse's Fountain". It is the wisdom-bearing spring of the Greek Muses. We can now see this Horse-born fountain is equivalent to the "Stallion's flood" of Hymn 5.83. Sometimes Pegasus's four hooves are said to release four sacred streams which can be appreciated as the four arcs of the radius which, when drawn from the four cardinal points of the Earth's year, measure out the full twelve-division of the sacred year or yajna. From this mythology, which is Vedic in origin, comes the figure of the ancient physician Hippocrates.[1] In India this divine physician is known to be Vishnu incarnated as Dhanvantari who in the lore of the Churning of the Milky Ocean (Samudra Manthan) emerges

Parthian era bronze plate depicting Pegasus ("Pegaz" in Persian), excavated in Iran. (Wikimedia Commons). Image altered from black to white background and cropped.

[1] According to *Online Etymology Dictionary*, "The name [Hippocrates] is literally 'one superior in horses;' from hippos 'horse' + kratia 'rule'" ("Hippocratic", Douglas Harper, www.etymonline.com, accessed December 2016). Krati comes from the Greek word *kratos*, indicating supreme strength, authority and rule. This comes from the Sanskrit word *kratu*, which Sri Aurobindo describes as "the sacrificial will", which is equivalent to the supramental consciousness-force of our journey in Time and Space. In the Rig Veda *kratu* is paired with *kavi* (seer) to describe Agni, the seer-will, power and ruler of the Vedic sacrifice. Sri Aurobindo writes that the white horse is "a phrase applied to the god Agni who is the Seer-Will, *kavikratu*" (*The Secret of the Veda, CWSA, Volume 15*, p. 136).

with a pot or kumbha of amrita (the nectar of immortality) in his hands. Dhanvan, which means "bow", is the Sanskrit name for the sign of Sagittarius and Dhanvantari means "moving in a curve". From this iconography, etymology and myth, it appears that the divine physician Dhanvantari is an epitaph of Kalki, the unifier (or healer) of Spirit and Matter, and of mankind.

The Seven-Headed Horse

Another epitaph of this same equine hero is Uchchaihshravas, the seven-headed flying (or celestial) white horse of Indian lore. Uchchaihshravas is the king or prince of horses who emerges from the Churning of the Milky Ocean and is considered to be the vehicle of Indra. In the *Bhagavad Gita* Vishnu declares that "among horses", he is Uchchaihshravas, born from the Amrita (nectar of Immortality).[1] He is equivalent to the single horse with seven names (*saptánāmā*) who draws the "one-wheeled chariot".

> *Seven to the one-wheeled chariot yoke the Courser; bearing seven names the single Courser draws it. Three-naved the wheel is, sound and undecaying, whereon are resting all these worlds of being.*
>
> Rig Veda 1.164.2, tr. R.T.H. Griffith

In Rig Veda 1.121.12, Indra mounts "the well-yoked horses of the wind, best bearers". The wind (*vayu*), here and elsewhere throughout the Veda, is a symbol of the movement of the radius. In Rig Veda 7.60.3 these seven horses are "the Seven gold Coursers who, dropping oil and fatness" carry Sūrya the Sun upwards to the "bright ocean". [2] The drops of oil and fatness in this verse are the vesica piscis. Uchchaihshravas is a figure of the seven horses who become the Swar-conquering Horse of the zodiac – the Horse of Sagittarius – equivalent to the White Horse of Kalki. In addition to Indra, another name for the rider of

---

[1] Bhagavad Gita 10.27, tr. Swami Mukundananda, www.holy-bhagavad-gita.org (accessed December 2016).

[2] Both Rig Veda excerpts in this paragraph are translated by R.T.H. Griffith.

Uchchaihshravas is *Revanta*, the youngest son of Surya. This hero is another epitaph of Agni, the child of the seven mothers, rivers, cows or mares, whose "car" is *rátham amṛtasya dravitnúm* which Sri Aurobindo translated as the "galloping car of the Immortal"[1] and Griffith translated as the "rapid car of Amṛta". This galloping car of Amrita is equivalent to the Stallion's flood – the seventh wave of the vesica piscis in the zodiac.

> *O Fire, O son of Force, the mortal who attains to thy right thinking goes forward and hears the truth beyond; holding the impelling force, borne by the horses of power, luminous and mighty he seeks to possess the heavens.... Hear us, O Fire, in thy house, in the hall of thy session, yoke the galloping car of the Immortal; bring to us heaven and earth, parents of the gods....*
>
> Rig Veda 10.11.7-9, tr. Sri Aurobindo, *Hymns to the Mystic Fire, CWSA, Volume 16*, p. 403

The White Horse of the Rig Veda

The symbol of the victorious White Horse of the Vedic yajna (and of Kalki avatar) is found in various hymns of the Rig Veda. In the fourth verse of Rig Veda 6.6 there is mention of multiple white horses, signifying multiple radii. In other instances, the white horse is singular. The white color of the horse is a symbol of the purification which accompanies the unveiling and restoration of Agni's hidden law (*sanatana dharma*) in the 9th month or stage of his yajna. More specifically white is a symbol of purification accomplished by the all-cleansing waters of truth, equivalent to the Stallion's flood. It is a symbol of the victorious purification, liberation and uplifting of consciousness from the realm of Death (mortal consciousness) into the realm of Immortality (Swar). In Rig Veda 1.118.9 the White Horse is portrayed as "a serpent-slaying steed sent down by Indra, loud-neighing, conquering the foe, high-mettled, firm-limbed and vigorous, winning [a] thousand treasures", and in Rig Veda 1.119.10 as the "conqueror of combatants, invincible in war by arrows, seeking heaven

---

[1] Rig Veda 10.11.9, *Hymns to the Mystic Fire, CWSA, Volume 16*, p. 403.

worthy of fame, like Indra, vanquisher of men". In Rig Veda 10.39.10 this legendary White Horse is attributed with 99 or 9 x 11 "varied gifts of strength",[1] emphasizing the number 9 and perhaps alluding to the connection between the 9th sign of the zodiac and the 11th.

> *On Pedu[2] ye bestowed, Aśvins, a courser white, mighty with nine-and-ninety varied gifts of strength, A horse to be renowned....*
>
> Rig Veda 10.39.10, tr. R.T.H. Griffith

In Rig Veda 7.77 (quoted in the last chapter) this White Horse is led or ridden by the Dawn goddess Usha. This pairing of Usha and the White Horse symbolizes the pairing of the vesica piscis and the radius, and the world's awakening into higher gnosis which naturally includes realizing the geometric keys of this higher gnosis. In the zodiac, this awakening or dawn of higher gnosis is forever linked to the 9th sign of the Horse and the Sage.

The White Horse of St. John's *Revelation*

The Vedic theme of the victorious divine hero on a White Horse is echoed in *Revelation 19*, accompanied by many different symbols of the vesica piscis, which I have highlighted in bold.

> *I saw heaven standing open and there before me was a white horse, whose rider is called Faithful and True. With justice he judges and wages war. His* ***eyes*** *are like blazing fire, and on his head are many* ***crowns****. He has a name written on him that no one knows but he himself. He is dressed in* ***a robe dipped in blood,*** *and his name is* ***the Word of God****. The armies of heaven were following him, riding on white horses and dressed in* ***fine linen, white and clean****. Coming out of* ***his mouth*** *is a sharp sword with which to*

[1] All excerpts of the Rig Veda in this section are translated by R.T.H. Griffith.

[2] Pedu appears to be a name of Kalki who rides a White Horse. The Sanskrit root of Pedu is *pad* meaning foot or step, which is the root of such English words as "pedestal", "pedestrian" and "pedal". It is a fitting name for Vishnu or Agni (a.k.a. the radius) who steps effortlessly and victoriously across the zodiac.

> *strike down the nations. "He will rule them with an iron scepter." He treads* ***the winepress*** *of the fury of the wrath of God Almighty. On his* ***robe*** *and on his* ***thigh*** *he has this name written: king of kings and lord of lords. And I saw an angel standing in the sun, who cried in* ***a loud voice*** *to all the birds flying in midair, "Come, gather together for the great supper of God, o that you may eat* ***the flesh*** *of kings, generals, and the mighty, of horses and their riders, and* ***the flesh*** *of all people, free and slave, great and small." Then I saw the beast and the kings of the earth and their armies gathered together to wage war against the rider on the horse and his army. But the beast was captured, and with it the false prophet who had performed the signs on its behalf. With these signs he had deluded those who had received the mark of the beast and worshiped its image. The two of them were thrown alive into* ***the fiery lake*** *of burning sulfur. The rest were killed with the sword coming out of* ***the mouth of the rider*** *on the horse, and all the birds gorged themselves on their flesh.*
>
> Revelation 19:11-21, NIV

As already mentioned, the thigh is associated with Sagittarius. In this passage the thigh is also a symbol of the vesica piscis, across which is "written" the radius. In the Rig Veda the tongue and mouth are images of the radius and vesica piscis and in *Revelation* this same geometry is portrayed as a sword coming out of the hero's mouth. The "winepress of the fury of God" in *Revelation* is equivalent to the pressing out of Soma-wine or Amrita in the Rig Veda. This wine or nectar of Immortality empowers the hero-god Indra to slay the beast Vritra who is "the Coverer" of the light of truth.

> *These Soma-drops, strong Indra! drink for heroes, poured, pressed out by pressing-stones, are welling forth for thee, for thee the drops are welling forth.*
>
> Rig Veda 1.139.8, tr. R.T.H. Griffith

> *[T]he rivers carry the well-pressed Soma juice to Indra.*
>
> Rig Veda 3.36.7, tr. R.T.H. Griffith

Eating the flesh of kings and people and such can be seen as a crude reference to the vesica piscis given that the vesica piscis is the flesh or body of the radius, and is at the same time the food of the gods. The vesica piscis can also be said to be a "fiery lake" considering that Agni, the god of fire, dwells within its waters. I will discuss the robe as a symbol of the vesica piscis in subsequent chapters. The symbolism of the bird flying in midair in *Revelation* is a frequent symbol in the Rig Veda, which I take to be a symbol of the radius and its flight (arc) through the midair of the circle.

> *[The hero Varuna] knows the path of birds that fly through heaven ...True to his holy law, he knows the twelve moons with their progeny... He knows the pathway of the wind, the spreading, high, and mighty wind....*

Rig Veda 1.25.7-9, tr. R.T.H. Griffith

The Heavenly Warrior and the Beast

The verses of *Revelation 19* featuring the White Horse are dubbed "The Heavenly Warrior Defeats the Beast". In the Rig Veda this Beast is the dragon or serpent Vritra (also known as Ahi) who is conquered by Indra on his horse or horses. As mentioned earlier, this dragon or serpent who "covers" the truth is equivalent to the vesica piscis which in the exquisite minds of the Rishis was simultaneously depicted as the covering veil of the divine light and as the sacred word, wave or thought by which the divine light is recovered and liberated.

> *[Indra] made waters flow together, [slew] Ahi, and sent forth the Seven Rivers, and opened as it were obstructed fountains.... Indra smote down, Agni consumed...[the enemies of the Gods at the height of the conflict]. Of those who gladly sought a hard-won dwelling he cast down many a thousand with his arrow.... Heroes, ye burst the stable of the kine and horses, the stable which the bar or stone obstructed; and piercing through set free the habitations.*

Rig Veda 4.28.1-5, tr. R.T.H. Griffith

Now shall one affirm the goddesses Earth and Heaven with the Dragon of the foundation[1] *by all the things desired that we must obtain; as if to possess that Ocean by their wide ranging they have uncovered the (hidden) rivers that are voiceful with the burning Light.*

Rig Veda 4.55.6, tr. Sri Aurobindo,
The Secret of the Veda, CWSA, Volume 15, p. 499

Your blessing as a boon for suppliants we desire: the Dragon of the Deep, and Aja-Ekapad….

Rig Veda 2.31.6, tr. R.T.H. Griffith

[T]hou [Indra], Impetuous! leagued with Viṣṇu, slewest Vṛtra the Dragon who enclosed the waters.

Rig Veda 6.20.2, tr. R.T.H. Griffith

In Greek mythology, this Beast – who is in truth a guardian or protector of gnosis – is Medusa, a winged-female with snakes for hair. Her name likely hails from the Sanskrit words *medha* and *uṣa*, respectively indicating the Vedic sacrifice and its dawn goddess who, as I have demonstrated, is a figure of the vesica piscis within the yajna or year. As the story goes, Medusa is beheaded by the hero Perseus, and from her decapitated head springs Pegasus and his golden-sworded brother Chrysaor. Medusa's snake-hair can be taken as a symbol of multiple vesicae piscis of the zodiac, and the pairing of the golden-sworded hero and his horse is equivalent to the imagery of Kalki in Indian mythology.

Gorgona (Medusa), 4 c. BCE, Pushkin museum (Wikimedia Commons).

The depiction of Medusa with her outstretched tongue is reminiscent of the goddess Kali, as well as the solar deity of the

[1] Ahibudhnya.

Aztec's Sun Stone (the Eagle's Bowl). The integral truth of these figures and mythologies cannot be properly understood or appreciated outside of the context of the sacred yajna or year of the Rishis. The all-integrating and all-unifying truth or law (*sanatana dharma*) of our existence is solely found *within* the Rishis' unified field of Time and Space, not elsewhere. Via this eternal law, all individual forms, words, symbols, etc., are cohesive extensions of the One Self of all selves (*Ekam Sat*). In higher consciousness, the many expressions, extensions or symbols of the One are experienced and appreciated as such, rather than as disconnected entities, bearing no relation to one another.

CHAPTER SIX

The Crux of Time

> *[The Horse, the white steed] that immaculate Steed which is Agni transmuted, is the vahana [vehicle] of none other than Usha, the divine Earth-Dawn. Agni, as the Horse (9th sign/month), ushers in the Dawn, be it of the Earth day, or the year or twelve months, or the cosmic year of many thousand months.*
>
> Thea, "Culture and Cosmos - 2, Part III"

In the previous chapter I demonstrated the geometric and zodiacal sense of the Stallion's flood and his gallop to victory. In this chapter I am presenting selections from Thea's and Sri Aurobindo's writings, as well as from the Rig Veda which should give readers a fuller perspective of what this victory entails. It is the realization (in the real sense of the word) of the Lost Sun or Divine Soul of one's Being, which is hidden or lost within its own womb and field of Time and Space. This realization is akin to a birth in that one thereupon emerges into an entirely different understanding and experience of Time and Space.

The excerpts from Thea's books discuss the location and the gist of this crux of the Vedic sacrifice at the 6 Point of the circle corresponding to the sixth planet Saturn and the zero point of Sagittarius.

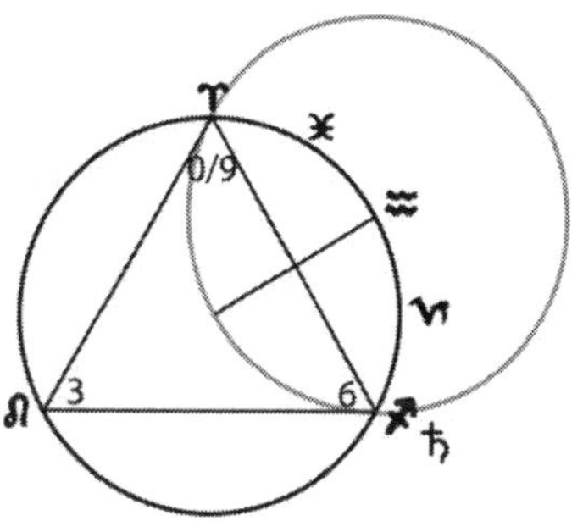

> *[Human beings] never experience the triad beyond Saturn.... [T]he journey ceases at the sixth orbit –*

and in the measure of 12 this is the position that corresponds to the experience of death, as it stands at present.

Thea, *The New Way, Volumes 1&2*, p. 271

The 6 point continually reveals itself to be vitally important, and tremendously dangerous if passage over this point does not serve to open one to the final round of unity and growth on a higher level.

Thea, *The Gnostic Circle*, p. 186

[T]he 6 point can in a sense be termed the point of sacrifice. Some part is given up or transmuted, in order to be utilized in another way. There is an element of sacrifice and at the same time of redemption.... [The sign of Sagittarius] is the sign of the Savior, who, by the process of the transmutation of energy,[1] *brings the movement increasingly back upon itself, even farther into a dimension it has ignored and which must be discovered within its own being, at the centre of itself.*

Thea, *The Gnostic Circle*, p. 188

[O]ur present Aquarian Age falls within the 9th Manifestation – the whole of which is characterized by the ninth zodiacal sign, Sagittarius. Some of the main features of this sign are speed, motion, displacement of mass and the energy generated thereby, the capacity to break through barriers and limits, to establish new boundaries and to escape the pull of inertia.

Thea, *The New Way, Volume 3*, p. 12

[The] completed 9 signs express the new gestation process based on 9. They carry us to 0 Capricorn and the final trinity of the zodiac, the area which at present is merely a void for humanity, a portion of the Whole Time entirely out of the realm of our conscious experience in time.

---

[1] I think of this sacrifice and transmutation of energy as the necessary shedding of old skin, old forms and limitations in order to assume higher forms of expression.

Sagittarius, the ninth sign, is the critical yet glorious bridge joining the nine to the remaining three. The essence of this sign is speed or acceleration of consciousness. Being the ruler of our 9th Manifestation, it stands that this sign must colour our collective experiences over a period of 6,480 years. Humanity as a whole is living the construction of the 9th Manifestation bridge. It is experiencing the process at a speed unknown to previous generations. The full impact of the Sagittarian acceleration is being felt. But is this carrying the species and the planet headlong into the abyss, or is the acceleration a means in itself to construct that Bridge?

...[In traditional astrology, Sagittarius represents elements] which help to carry the individual beyond the borders of his known world, into the new, the unexplored, the vast; all of which has the effect of extending the consciousness to higher dimensions and deeper depths.

Thea, *The New Way, Volume 3*, p. 370

In the solar system [kāla] is Saturn, Kronos, Father Time; and as astrology is linked to the sign Aquarius it must be remembered that the ancient ruler of this sign is Saturn.

Thea, *The Gnostic Circle*, p. 12

Saturn is the planet epitomizing the cosmic manifestation as well as the Time-Spirit, for indeed both are one. What truth can be perceived of the cosmos if one has not perceived the true nature of Time?

Thea, *The New Way, Volumes 1&2*, p. 201

In Medieval etchings of Chronos (Saturn or Kala), the Time-Spirit is often seen carrying a lantern and illuminating the path in front of himself. In this image we are given the understanding of the process: the Time-Spirit is the Light, in Time light is inherent, and this in fact is the key to Earth's evolution.

Thea, *The Gnostic Circle*, p. 112

Of all planets it is Saturn that captures the human being's imagination in terms of his vision of hell, as can be understood from medieval texts such as Dante's Divine Comedy.

Yet in our fuller vision of the Circle...Saturn stands majestically at the portals of this greater experience. The planet therefore becomes a representation of a death and regenerative process. It becomes on the one hand a tomb for all that cannot stand the full rays of the midday Sun, and on the other a womb carrying being into a fuller birth and leading to the experience of Immortality.

...[T]he old ways [of consciousness] fail us, because not offering a vision of the further kingdom – the kingdom of Swar as it is called in the Vedas, which stands beyond Saturn's portals – the evolution of consciousness can only succumb to the patterns it has become accustomed to because of this incomplete perception. At this point the pull of the past, of inertia, overtakes the consciousness and escape from the contractions of Saturn's birth process is secured by means of an undoing of energy, a collapse into a black hole of spiritual/material space. When this greater kingdom is placed outside our cosmic manifestation and in no way related to our planet Earth, it is only logical that the human spirit will devise means to seek this extra-cosmic heaven. Therefore it makes Death, the Dark Lord, the sovereign and ultimate goal of existence. In death it finds the escape and thus fails to bring that kingdom of Swar upon Earth. Yet, precisely beyond Saturn's portals stands the realisation of Immortality by means of a manifestation of the true and full Earth-Soul.

Thea, *The New Way, Volume 3*, pp. 97-98

In astrology the planet Saturn is associated with contraction and crystallization. It can either represent a death or a rebirth. At this critical point of the journey or *yajna* we find ourselves falling back upon the gravity of our past and into old self-defeating patterns, or we find some light of our soul which propels us forward into the higher realms of our evolutionary journey.

Saturn is the power of definition. It is also representative of the power of Time and its aspects of periodicity, in contrast to 'timelessness' which is simply undifferentiated time. Spirituality until the advent of Supermind felt comfortable only with the latter however; it had not been able to find a place in its structure for time in its periods, precisely because spiritualty virtually denies all structure and flees from any system that adequately deals with the precision needed for such an integral vision in which spirit and matter are one....

...[The Mother's Temple is] a reconstruction of Saturn.... Saturn, as embodied in the Mother's Temple, is...the cosmic womb that holds the new creation: out of the chaos the 'death' experience leads to the birth of a cosmos.

Thea, *The New Way, Volume 3*, pp. 167-68

Sri Aurobindo discussed this crucial individual and evolutionary pivot in the following terms:

It is the supramental Truth that is the instrument of this great inner transfiguration. That replaces mentality by luminous vision and the eye of the gods, mortal life by breath and force of the infinite existence, obscure and death-possessed substance by the free and immortal conscious-being.

Sri Aurobindo, *The Secret of the Veda, CWSA, Volume 15*, p. 376

Time Born Anew

In the Rig Veda Agni, the Son of the sacrifice, is essentially the Son of "Father" Time. He is Time (the Sage) reborn or made young again. He is the hero-conqueror of Death, the "Ancient of days, again born newly".[1] This theme is repeated in various ways throughout the Rig Veda.

Ye [Ashwins] gave again the vigour of his youthful life to the sage Kali when old age was coming nigh.

Rig Veda 10.39.8, tr. R.T.H. Griffith

[Indra] filled the heaven and earth and all between them.... The old hath waked the young Moon from his slumber who runs his

[1] Rig Veda 1.92.10, tr. R.T.H. Griffith.

circling course with many round him. Behold the Gods' high wisdom in its greatness: he who died yesterday today is living.

Rig Veda 10.55.3-5, tr. R.T.H. Griffith

The singing-men of ancient time open the doors of sacred songs, – Men, for the mighty to accept. Combined in close society sit the seven priests, the brother-hood, Filling the station of the One. [Agni-Soma] gives us kinship with the Gods, and with the Sun unites our eye: The Sage's offspring hath appeared. The Sun with his dear eye beholds that quarter of the heavens which priests have placed within the sacred cell.[1]

Rig Veda 9.10.6-9, tr. R.T.H. Griffith

The maidens with long, tresses hold [Agni] in embrace; dead, they rise up again to meet the Living One. Releasing them from age with a loud roar he comes, filling them with new spirit, living, unsubdued.

Rig Veda 1.140.8, tr. R.T.H. Griffith

The maidens (virgins) with long tresses who hold Agni in their embrace are multiple vesicae piscis of the zodiac. The Sage in these verses can be thought of as the personification of Time. The "Sage's offspring" is Father Time's offspring or Son. It is important to note here that the base of the word "sage" is "age", a word which indicates the movement of Time or specifice stages of Time. As mentioned before, the 9th sign of Sagittarius is the sign of the Sage or wisened elder. In addition to being a symbol of the 9th sign of the zodiac, this figure of the elder, Father Time or Sage also represents the *completed* cycle or circle of 0/9. In terms of math and geometry, the number 9 is the "eldest" (the

[1] I believe Griffith mistranslated *divás padám* as a "quarter of the heavens". *Padám* indicates a step, as in the full step of the radius through the circle which encompasses *one-third* of the sacrificial year, rather than *one-quarter*. He translated "sacred cell" from *guha*, indicating a hiding place. *Divás padam* and *guha* in this verse both appear to me as symbols the vesica piscis, which is both the step and hiding place of the Vedic Hero-Son (i.e. of the radius).

Father) of the circle of 0/9, and the number 1 is the Child or Son. In the Rig Veda, this elder, Sage or Father becomes the victorious Son, youth or "the Living One", renewing the eternal cycle of life and conquering Death. In the Yajur Veda knowledge of this Hero-Purusha (below called Prajâpati) is described as the key of leaving Death behind.

> *I know this mighty Purusha whose colour is like the Sun, beyond the reach of darkness. He only who knows him leaves Death behind him. There is no path save this alone to travel. In the womb moves Prajâpati: he, never becoming born, is born in sundry figures. The wise discern the womb from which he springeth.*
>
> Yajur Veda 31.18, tr. R.T.H. Griffith

Readers can now count themselves among "the wise" who know the vesica piscis, and simultaneously the circle of the zodiac, is the womb from which this Hero "springeth" forward. In *Revelation*, the Hero-Son declares:

> *I am the Living One; I was dead, and now look, I am alive for ever and ever! And I hold the keys of death and Hades.*
>
> Revelation 1:18, NIV

Sri Aurobindo wrote about this victory over death, which Thea posits at the 6 Point (0° Sagittarius) of the 360° circle, as the central idea of the Vedic Rishis.

> *[T]he central idea of the Vedic Rishis was the transition of the human soul from a state of death to a state of immortality by the exchange of the Falsehood for the Truth, of divided and limited being for integrality and infinity. Death is the mortal state of Matter with Mind and Life involved in it; Immortality is a state of infinite being, consciousness and bliss.... This is the "great passage" discovered by the Ancestors, the ancient Rishis.*
>
> Sri Aurobindo, *The Secret of the Veda, CWSA, Volume 15*, pp. 45-46

This Vedic theme is the subject of Sri Aurobindo's epic poem *Savitri.*

> *[The] victor Light rode on her*[1] *deathless Force;*
> *A centaur's mighty gallop bore the god.*

Savitri, Part 1, Book 2, Canto 3: The Book of the Traveller of the Worlds, CWSA, Volumes 33-34, p. 126

> *A Godhead stands behind the brute machine.*
> *This truth broke in in a triumph of fire;*
> *A victory was won for God in man,*
> *The deity revealed its hidden face.*
> *The great World-Mother now in her arose:*
> *A living choice reversed fate's cold dead turn,*
> *Affirmed the spirit's tread on Circumstance,*
> *Pressed back the senseless dire revolving Wheel*
> *And stopped the mute march of Necessity.*
> *A flaming warrior from the eternal peaks*
> *Empowered to force the door denied and closed*
> *Smote from Death's visage its dumb absolute*
> *And burst the bounds of consciousness and Time.*

Savitri, Book 1, Canto 2: The Issue, CWSA, Volumes 33-34, p. 21

> *The trudge of Time changed to a splendid march;*
> *The divine Dwarf towered to unconquered worlds....*
> *Life now became a sure approach to God,*
> *Existence a divine experiment*
> *And cosmos the soul's opportunity.*
> *The world was a conception and a birth*
> *Of Spirit in Matter into living forms,*
> *And Nature bore the Immortal in her womb,*
> *That she might climb through him to eternal life.*
> *His being lay down in bright immobile peace*
> *And bathed in wells of pure spiritual light;*
> *It wandered in wide fields of wisdom-self*

---

[1] "Her" can be understood here as the Mother, Maya, Prakriti, Shakti, or whatever name of the Divine Feminine. Earlier in this same canto, Sri Aurobindo refers to Her as "Love's Body".

Lit by the rays of an everlasting sun....
All now suppressed in us began to emerge.

Thus came his soul's release from Ignorance,
His mind and body's first spiritual change.
A wide God-knowledge poured down from above,
A new world-knowledge broadened from within:
His daily thoughts looked up to the True and One....

Savitri, Book 1, Canto 3: The Yoga of the Soul's Release, CWSA, Volumes 33-34, pp. 42-44

Cam'st thou not down to open the doors of Fate,
The iron doors that seemed for ever closed,
And lead man to Truth's wide and golden road
That runs through finite things to eternity....

The Voice replied: "Remember why thou cam'st:
Find out thy soul, recover thy hid self,
In silence seek God's meaning in thy depths,
Then mortal nature change to the divine.
Open God's door, enter into his trance....

Thou shalt see the Eternal's body in the world,
Know him in every voice heard by thy soul,
In the world's contacts meet his single touch;
All things shall fold thee into his embrace.
Conquer thy heart's throbs, let thy heart beat in God:
Thy nature shall be the engine of his works,
Thy voice shall house the mightiness of his Word:
Then shalt thou harbour my force and conquer Death."

Savitri, CWSA, Book 7, Canto 2: The Parable of the Search for the Soul, CWSA, Volumes 33-34, p. 476

CHAPTER SEVEN

The Seven Seers Who Are Navagwas

The Rishis portrayed and celebrated the crux and hero of the yajna in various ways, perhaps most concisely in the following verse.

> *Dadhyac Navagva opens fastened doors, by whom the sages gained their wish, [by] whom they won the fame of lovely Amṛta.*
>
> Rig Veda 9.108.4, tr. R.T.H. Griffith

The hero Dadhyac Navagva (or Navagwa) is the nine-rayed horse or horse-headed Sage, who is a symbolic figure of the 9th radius and sign of the zodiac. The Rishi indicates that this nine-rayed horse-hero[1] opens the closed doors of the progressive journey of the yajna. These are the doors of the higher worlds of truth-consciousness which the Rishi of Rig Veda 2.24 has told us are shut or opened "by the months and the years".[2] The exact number of sages who gain their wish and win the immortalizing Amrita (i.e. the immortal vesica piscis) in tandem with the nine-rayed Horse-Sage is not given in Rig Veda 9.108, but from other accounts it is clear that their number is seven.

> *Our sires of old, Navagvas, sages seven, while urging [Indra] to show his might, extolled him, dwelling on heights, swift, smiting down opponents, guileless in word, and in his thoughts most mighty.*
>
> Rig Veda 6.22.2, tr. R.T.H. Griffith

---

[1] Or Kalki in terms of Vishnu's avatars.

[2] Tr. Sri Aurobindo, *The Secret of the Veda, CWSA, Volume 15*, p. 179.

As Sri Aurobindo noted in *The Secret of the Veda*, the Rishis overlapped the imagery of the nine-rays (*navagwas*) and the seven seers.

> *[In] VI.22 we are told of the ancient fathers, the seven seers who were Navagwas,* pūrve pitaro navagvāḥ sapta viprāso.... *[T]he Navagwas are seven or nine....*
>
> Sri Aurobindo, *The Secret of the Veda, CWSA, Volume 15*, pp. 174-75

The Rishis' use of the word *navagwas* to describe the seven seers is resolved via the geometry of the zodiac, in which the seventh radius (seer, sage, rishi, singer, sage, horse, etc.) of the seventh vesica piscis is simultaneously the ninth radius of the zodiac.

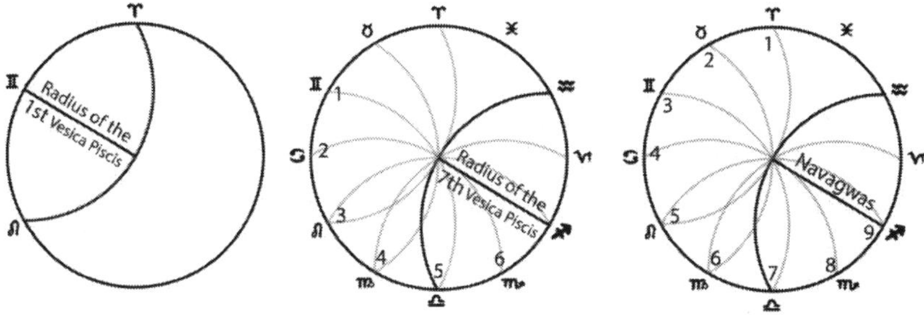

It is for this reason that the Hero-Horse can equally be referred to as nine-rayed Dadhyac and as seven-headed Uchchaihshravas. This is the *one radius* or Hero-Purusha of the zodiac which can be said to recover and liberate the seven sacred rivers (or cows) from the heights of Aquarius (Kumbha).

Throughout the Rig Veda the seven radii of the first seven vesicae piscis of the zodiac are portrayed as seven Angiras Rishis, seven singers, seven seers, seven sages, and seven horses. In *Revelation*, they are the seven angels, seven lamp stands, seven thunderers and such. In Rig Veda 5.45 the seven singers or seven radii are called the "Bards of approaching Dawn" as well as Angirases. They are also the seven coursers or horses of Surya who bring forth the lost Sun, Son or "bright young sage". The Rishi of this hymn celebrates the emergence of the Sun or Son of

Truth and the simultaneous opening of the doors and stables and the freeing of cows, streams and mighty waters, all of which are symbols of the vesica piscis, as is the Dawn itself.

> *Bards of approaching Dawn who know the heavens are come with hymns to throw the mountain open. The Sun hath risen and [opened] the stable portals: the doors of men, too, hath the God thrown open.*
>
> *Sūrya hath spread his light as splendour: hither came the Cows' Mother, conscious, from the stable, to streams that flow with biting waves to deserts; and heaven is stablished like a firm-set pillar.*
>
> *This laud hath won the burden of the mountain. To aid the ancient birth of mighty waters. The mountain parted, Heaven performed his office. The worshippers were worn with constant serving....*
>
> *Come, let us carry out, O friends, the purpose wherewith the Mother threw the Cow's stall open, [that] wherewith Manu conquered Visisipra, wherewith the wandering merchant gained heaven's water.*
>
> *Here, urged by hands, loudly hath rung the press-stone wherewith Navagvas through ten months sang praises. Saramā went aright and found the cattle. Aṅgiras gave effect to all their labours.*
>
> *When at the dawning of this mighty Goddess, [the seven] Aṅgirases all sang forth with the cattle, — Their spring is in the loftiest place of meeting, — Saramā found the kine by Order's pathway.*
>
> *Borne by his Coursers Seven may Sūrya visit the field that spreadeth wide for his long journey. Down on the Soma swooped the rapid Falcon. Bright was the young Sage moving mid his cattle.*
>
> *Sūrya hath mounted to the shining ocean when he hath yoked his fair-backed Tawny Horses. The wise have drawn him like a ship through water: the floods obedient have descended hither.*
>
> ***I lay upon the Floods your hymn, lightwinning, wherewith Navagvas their ten months completed.*** *Through this our hymn*

may we have Gods to guard us: through this our hymn pass safe beyond affliction.

Rig Veda 5.45, tr. R.T.H. Griffith [bold emphasis added]

A central part of this victory is the figure of the Navagwas singing praises "through ten months" or completing ten months of sacrifice. Below I am repeating Sri Aurobindo's commentary on these crucial months from *The Secret of the Veda* which I already included in Part One, because now the key of the vesica piscis has helped to solve this ancient Vedic mystery which Sri Aurobindo admitted he was not in the position to solve.

[W]e find that it is with the help of the [nine] Navagwas that Indra pursues the trace of the lost kine, but it is only with the aid of the ten Dashagwas that he is able to bring the pursuit to a successful issue and find that Truth, satyaṃ tat, *namely, the Sun that was lying in the darkness. In other words, it is* ***when the nine-months' sacrifice is prolonged through the tenth****, it is when the Navagwas become the ten Dashagwas by the seven-headed thought of Ayasya, the tenth Rishi,* ***that the Sun is found and the luminous world of Swar in which we possess the truth of the one universal Deva, is disclosed and conquered****. This conquest of Swar is the aim of the sacrifice and the great work accomplished by the Angiras Rishis.*

Sri Aurobindo, *The Secret of the Veda, CWSA, Volume 15*, p. 177 [bold emphasis added]

[The recovery of the lost Sun] is won in twelve periods of the upward journey, represented by the revolution of the twelve months of the sacrificial year, the periods corresponding to the successive dawns of a wider and wider truth, until the tenth secures the victory. What may be the precise significance of the nine rays and the ten, is a more difficult question which we are not yet in a position to solve; but the light we already have is sufficient to illuminate all the main imagery of the Rig Veda.

Sri Aurobindo, *The Secret of the Veda, CWSA, Volume 15*, pp. 181-82

Thea equated the prolonging of the nine-month sacrifice "through the tenth [month]" with passage into the 10th sign of the zodiac (Capricorn/Makar) and thus passage into the fourth quadrant of Swar. However, the description of the Rishis seems to imply passage not simply *into* the 10th sign but passage *through* the entire 10th sign of the zodiac.

> *I hold for you in the waters (i.e. the seven Rivers) the thought that wins possession of heaven (this is once more the seven-headed thought born from the Truth and found by Ayasya), by which* ***the Navagwas passed through the ten months****; by this thought may we have the gods for protectors, by this thought may we pass through beyond the evil.*[1]
>
> Rig Veda 5.45.11, tr. Sri Aurobindo, *The Secret of the Veda, CWSA, Volume 15*, p. 175 [bold emphasis added]

This prolonging of the sacrifice *through the tenth month* makes fuller sense with the key of the vesica piscis, wherein it becomes apparent that the imagery of Indra tracing the lost kine with the help of the nine-rayed Navagwas depicts the sweep of the 9th ray of the zodiac up *through* the entire 10th month of the zodiac, landing at 0° Aquarius wherein the rivers, waters or floods of gnosis are released from their cave or *kumbha*, and the victory over falsehood is secured.

The seven-headed thought of Ayasya is clearly related to the seven-headed horse of Indra. Both are agents of the Vedic victory, but whereas the horse is a symbol of the radius, the divine thought or Word of the Rishi is a symbol of the vesica piscis. The seven-headed thought could perhaps be a symbol of any vesica piscis of the circle considering it encompasses three units and four signs (3 + 4 = 7) of the yajna; but it seems particularly symbolic of the seventh vesica piscis which rises up to Vishnu's highest seat in the realm of Swar. I will discuss the seven-headed thought of Ayasya further on, but first it is necessary to explore, in more depth, the lore of Brihaspati and his divine Word.

---

[1] Sri Aurobindo writes after this verse, "The statement is explicit."

CHAPTER EIGHT

Brihaspati and the Divine Word

Bṛhaspati the wise, the eager, closely looks upon both, the waters and the vessel.

Rig Veda 1.190.7, tr. R.T.H. Griffith

Thou, O Bṛhaspati, with Indra for ally didst hurl down water-floods which gloom had compassed round.

Rig Veda 2.23.18, tr. R.T.H. Griffith

Striving to win waters and light... Bṛhaspati with lightning smites the foeman.

Rig Veda 6.73.3, tr. R.T.H. Griffith

That secret name borne by the lowing cattle within the cave Bṛhaspati discovered, and drave, himself, the bright kine from the mountain, like a bird's young after the egg's disclosure. He looked around on rock-imprisoned sweetness as one who eyes a fish in scanty water. Bṛhaspati, cleaving through with varied clamour, brought it forth like a bowl from out the timber. He found the light of heaven, and fire, and Morning: with lucid rays he forced apart the darkness.... Bṛhaspati cleft the rock and found the cattle.

Rig Veda 10.68.7-11 tr. R.T.H. Griffith

This Vedic symbolism of the "rock-imprisoned sweetness", honey (*aśnāpinaddhaṃ madhu*) or oil, is found in the Old Testament of the Bible.

> *[The Lord] nourished [Joshua] with honey from the rock, and with oil from the flinty crag....*
>
> Deuteronomy 32:13, NIV

This honey and oil is the concealed divine treasure, food or nourishment of the gods and Rishis, which is found, released and enjoyed by the Vedic heroes.

> *He found the treasure brought from heaven that lay concealed, close-hidden, like the nestling of a bird, in rock, enclosed in never-ending rock. Best Aṅgiras, bolt-armed, he strove to win, as 'twere, the stall of kine; so Indra hath disclosed the food concealed, disclosed the doors, the food that lay concealed.*
>
> Rig Veda 1.130.3, tr. R.T.H. Griffith

Brihaspati is featured in the Vedas as one of the gods who accomplished the breaking open of the cave or rock, releasing the seven rivers, and making Swar visible. He accomplishes this with *Brahmaṇā*, the divine Word. An alternate name of Brihaspati is Brahmanaspati. Both names mean "Master of the Word" which is an honorific title of the Purusha or radius of the yajna.

> *This self-expressive Soul, Brihaspati, is the Purusha, the Father of all things; it is the universal Divinity; it is the Bull of the herds, the Master and fertilizer of all these luminous energies....*
>
> Sri Aurobindo, *The Secret of the Veda, CWSA, Volume 15*, p. 323

> *[In Hymn II.24] Brihaspati is described driving up the cows, breaking Vala*[1] *by the divine word,* brahmaṇā, *concealing the*

[1] "Vala is the concealer, the withholder of the Light and it is the concealed Light that Indra restores to the sacrificer" (Sri Aurobindo, *The Secret of the Veda, CWSA, Volume 15*, p. 125).

> *darkness and making Swar visible. The first result is the breaking open by force of the well which has the rock for its face and whose streams are of the honey,* madhu, *the Soma sweetness,* aśmāsyam avataṃ madhudhāram. *This well of honey covered by the rock must be the Ananda or divine beatitude of the supreme threefold world of bliss...based upon the three supreme principles, Sat, Chit-Tapas and Ananda; their base is Swar of the Veda, Mahar of the Upanishads and Puranas, the world of Truth.* ***This secret well of honey is drunk by all those who are able to see Swar*** *and they pour out its billowing fountain of sweetness in manifold streams together,* tam eva viśve papire svardṛś obahu sākaṃ sisicur utsam udriṇam. *These many streams poured out together are the seven rivers poured down the hill by Indra after slaying Vritra, the rivers or streams of the Truth,* ṛtasya dhārāḥ; *and they represent, according to our theory, the seven principles of conscious being in their divine fufillment in the Truth and Bliss. This is why the seven-headed thought, — that is to say, the knowledge of the divine existence with its seven heads or powers, the seven-rayed knowledge of Brihaspati,* saptagum, *has to be confirmed or held in thought in the waters, the seven rivers, that is to say the seven forms of divine consciousness are to be held in the seven forms or movements of divine being;* dhiyaṃ vo apsu dadhiṣe svarṣām, *I hold the Swar-conquering thought in the waters.*
>
> Sri Aurobindo, *The Secret of the Veda, CWSA, Volume 15*, pp. 178-79 [bold emphasis added]

The following is an excerpt from R.T.H. Griffith's translation of the same hymn.

> *[Bṛhaspati] with might bowed down the things that should be bowed, and in his fury rent the holds of Śambara*[1]*.... [H]e made his way within the mountain stored with wealth. That was a great deed for the Godliest of the Gods: strong things were loosened and the firmly fixed gave way. He drave the kine forth and cleft Vala through by [brahmaṇā], dispelled the darkness and displayed the*

[1] Śambara is a demon (a lord of falsehood) whose fortresses are destroyed by the heroes of the Rig Veda.

> *light of heaven. The well with mouth of stone that poured a flood of meath, which Brahmaṇaspati hath opened with his might —* ***All they who see the light have drunk their fill there****...together they have made the watery fount flow forth.*
>
> Rig Veda 2.24.2-4, tr. R.T.H. Griffith [bold emphasis added]

The "bowing down of the things that should be bowed" can be understood as a reference to the vesica piscis. The imagery of this hymn makes better sense when we realize that symbols of the vesica piscis pervade the whole thing. The vesica piscis is herein and throughout the Rig Veda, simultaneously *that which conceals the light* – such as Vala, the mountain, the cave, the rock, etc., and *that which contains the light* – such as the kine (cows), the well, the Word, the flood, the fount, among many other vessels of the divine flame, ray or radius. In other words, in the fantastic minds of the Rishis, the lock is simultaneously the key and it is only ignorance of the form of the vesica piscis and its formative role in the twelve-month yajna that obstructs, hides or holds back the waters and treasures of the Rishis' divine gnosis.

In Hymn 2.24 Griffith translated *brahmaṇā* as "prayer". Sri Aurobindo's translated it as "the divine word" by which Swar is made visible. Sri Aurobindo discussed *brahmaṇā*, also spelled *brahman*, at length in *The Secret of the Veda*, clarifying the confusion between the original conception of *brahman* as the Word and the later conception of *brahman* as the Priest of the Word. He explained that *brahman* originally implied the sacred Word of the Rishis, and only later came to be equivalent with Brahman – the supreme universal Soul, Purusha or Being. This original essence of *brahman* is important to note because the Word in the Rig Veda is *feminine*. It is the Goddess Vak. The sacred Word is the vessel of the Purusha or Priest and is another symbol of the vesica piscis whose "master" or "lord" is the radius. We see in Rig Veda 2.24 that this sacred Word is described by the Rishi as a weapon akin to Saraswati's wave, by which the Hero-Purusha accomplishes the breaking open of Vala, the cave of Ignorance. Below are various descriptions of this sacred Word from *The Secret of the Veda*, the Vedas and elsewhere.

> *Brahman in the Veda signifies ordinarily the Vedic Word or mantra in its profoundest aspect as the expression of the intuition arising out of the depths of the soul or being. It is a voice of the rhythm which has created the worlds and creates perpetually. All world is expression or manifestation, creation by the Word.*
>
> Sri Aurobindo, *The Secret of the Veda, CWSA, Volume 15*, p. 355

> *[Agni] is the seer, the supreme mover of thought, the mover too of speech and the Word, the power in the heart that works. ... [He is] the impeller of action and movement, the divine guide of man in the act of sacrifice....[H]e is the messenger who knows earth, knows how to ascend the difficult slope of heaven,[1] ...knows the way to the home of the Truth, — he mediates between God and man.*
>
> Sri Aurobindo, *Hymns to the Mystic Fire, CWSA, Volume 16*, p. 689

> *As a power of expression the word is termed* gīḥ *or* vacas*; as a power of affirmation,* stoma. *In either aspect it is named* manma *or* mantra, *expression of thought in mind, and* brahman, *expression of the heart or the soul — for this seems to have been the earlier sense of the word* brahman, *afterwards applied to the Supreme Soul or universal Being....*
>
> *To be the sacred and effective word, it must have come as an inspiration from the supra-mental plane, termed in Veda, Ritam, the Truth, and have been received into the superficial consciousness either through the heart or by the luminous intelligence,* manīṣā.... *This is the "heart" of Veda and Vedanta,* hṛdaya, hṛd, *or* brahman. *There in the present state of mankind the Purusha is supposed to be seated centrally.*
>
> Sri Aurobindo, *The Secret of the Veda, CWSA, Volume 15*, p. 27

[1] The messenger and the difficult slope of heaven are symbols of the radius and vesica piscis.

This sacred Word and heart of the Veda is the vesica piscis, personified as the Goddess Vak and as the Goddess Saraswati who is portrayed as a river goddess as well as the goddess of wisdom. Vak contains in herself and bares forth the Purusha.

> *It is I [Vak] who draw the mighty bow of the God, that an arrow may pierce the hater of the Holy Word. ...At the world's summit I bring forth the Father. My origin is in the Waters, in the ocean.*
>
> Rig Veda 10.125.6-7, tr. by Raimundo Panikkar, *The Vedic Experience*, p. 97

> *May this ancestral Queen [the Sacred Word]...stride forth toward primordial creation!...The wise who knows from birth this world's hidden thread discerns the coming to birth of all the Gods. From the bosom of the Sacred Word [the Seer] brought forth the Word.*
>
> Atharva Veda 4.1.2-3 tr. by Raimundo Panikkar, *The Vedic Experience*, p. 105

> *He who dwells in speech, who is different from and interior to speech, whom speech does not know, whose body is speech, who inspires speech from within, he is the Self, the Inner Inspirer, the Immortal.*
>
> Bṛhadāraṇyaka Upanishad 3.7.17,
> tr. by Raimundo Panikkar, *The Vedic Experience*, p. 111

> *[In the beginning], was only the Lord of the Universe, His Word was with him. This word was second. He contemplated. He said, "I will deliver this Word so that she will produce and bring into being all this world."*
>
> Tāṇḍya Mahā Brāhmaṇa 20.14.2,
> tr. by Raimundo Panikkar, *The Vedic Experience*, p. 107

In the New Testament of the Bible, this Vedic theme is presented in similar terms.

> *In the beginning was the Word, and the Word was with God, and the Word was God.*
>
> John 1:1, NIV

In *Deuteronomy* of the Old Testament, the Divine Word seems to be more closely connected to the Vedic waters.

> *Let my teaching fall like rain and my words descend like dew, like showers on new grass, like abundant rain on tender plants.*
>
> Deuteronomy 32:2, NIV

The speaker in this Biblical verse is Moses, who is perhaps best known for his role in the parting of the waters of the Red Sea. This imagery of Moses parting of the waters is, in my view, a clear symbol of the radius holding apart the two sides (or arcs) of the vesica piscis. In the Rig Veda, the Purusha or Divine Hero is basically enrobed in or "bedewed" by the waters, honey, oil, soma, etc., or in other words, by the vesica piscis. He is the Water Bearer or rain bearer. He is equally enrobed in or bedewed by his companion-word, song or hymn.

> *Drink our libation, Lord of hymns: with streams of meath thou art bedewed.*
>
> Rig Veda 3.40.6, tr. R.T.H. Griffith

> *Acting the Sage, he flows enrobed in waters and song as' twere a stall that kine may prosper.*
>
> Rig Veda 9.94.1, tr. R.T.H. Griffith

> *Mover of speech [and Lord of Holy Law], we robe [the Sage Soma] with our songs....* [1]
>
> Rig Veda 9.35.5, tr. R.T.H. Griffith

> *We will enrobe with sacred song the Lovely One who, as a Steed, is decked with milk for rapturous joy.*
>
> Rig Veda 9.43.1, tr. R.T.H. Griffith

[1] "Lord of Holy Law" here comes from Griffith's translation of the next verse, Rig Veda 9.35.6. In the previous verse (9.35.4) Agni/Soma is depicted as the Sage.

CHAPTER NINE

The Seven-Headed Thought of Brihaspati & Ayasya

> *Brihaspati, coming first into birth from the great Light in the supreme ether, seven-mouthed, multiply born, seven-rayed, dispelled the darknesses; he with his host that possess the stubh and the Rik broke Vala into pieces by his cry. Shouting Brihaspati drove upwards the bright herds that speed the offering and they lowed in reply.*
>
> Rig Veda 4.50.4-5, tr. Sri Aurobindo,
> *The Secret of the Veda, CWSA, Volume 15*, p. 143

Brihaspati is known as the Guru or spiritual guide of the gods. He is commonly associated with Jupiter, the 5th planet of our solar system, and yet is depicted as being seven-rayed, seven-mouthed and seven-faced in the Rig Veda. Sri Aurobindo connects Brihaspati's seven-fold nature to the seven seers who chant the divine Word. This divine Word is, in turn, equivalent to the "seven-headed thought" found by the hero-sage Ayasya. Below is Sri Aurobindo's discussion of these figures, followed by some explanation of how they fit together in the context of the vesica piscis and the Gnostic Circle.

> *Brihaspati is the seven-rayed Thinker,* saptaguḥ, saptaraśmiḥ, *he is the seven-faced or seven-mouthed Angiras, born in many forms,* saptāsyas tuvijātaḥ, *nine-rayed, ten-rayed. The seven mouths are the seven Angirases who repeat the divine word* (brahma) *which comes from the seat of the Truth, Swar, and of which he is the lord* (brahmaṇaspatiḥ). *Each also corresponds to one of the seven rays of Brihaspati; therefore they are the seven seers,* sapta viprāḥ,

sapta ṛṣayaḥ, *who severally personify these seven rays of the knowledge. These rays are, again, the seven brilliant horses of the sun,* sapta haritaḥ, *and their full union constitutes the seven-headed Thought of Ayasya by which the lost sun of Truth is recovered. That thought again is established in the seven rivers, the seven principles of being divine and human, the totality of which founds the perfect spiritual existence.*[1] *The winning of these seven rivers of our being withheld by Vritra and these seven rays withheld by Vala, the possession of our complete divine consciousness delivered from all falsehood by the free descent of the truth, gives us the secure possession of the world of Swar and the enjoyment of mental and physical being lifted into the godhead above darkness, falsehood and death by the in-streaming of our divine elements.*

Sri Aurobindo, *The Secret of the Veda, CWSA, Volume 15*, p. 182

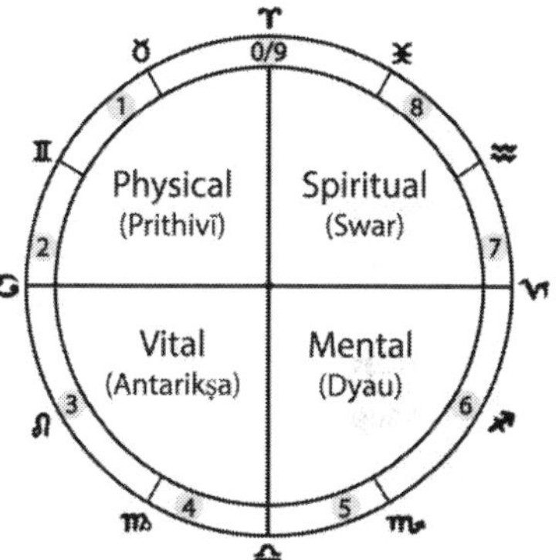

In *The New Way, Volumes 1&2* Thea discussed the significance of Brihaspati's association with both the 5th planet and the number 7. She revealed that the key of this dual identity is found in the Gnostic Circle wherein the Rishis' divisions of the circle by 9 and by 12 are known to be contained in One Circle – the thrice-seven (21 or 9 + 12) seats of the Divine Mother Aditi. I constructed the above depiction of the Gnostic Circle, without the Enneagram, to emphasize how the 9 numbers – which correspond to 9 planets or orbits of our solar system – fit within the 12 months of the sacred year. This image includes Thea's seeing of the four sheaths of the body in conjunction with the four quadrants or

[1] Sri Aurobindo, who did not have access to the geometric (and zodiacal) key of the Rishis' seven rivers, equated these rivers to "the seven principles of being divine and human" which he conceived of as the divine trinity of Sat-Chit-Ananda (Truth-Consciousness-Bliss) connected to the material trinity of Mind, Life and Matter, via the fourth principle of the Supermind.

worlds of the zodiac.[1] In this image, we can see that the 5th planet (Brihaspati or Jupiter) resides in the 7th house of the zodiac, the house of Libra in the mental quadrant of the zodiac. Thea presented this information via the figure below, along with some commentary on the Vedic figures therein.

> *Brihaspati is seven-rayed, and indeed Jupiter (Brihaspati) is found in Libra, the seventh sign. By his intercession the caves of Vala where the Panis have hidden the Sun are shattered....*
>
> Thea, *The New Way, Volumes 1&2*, p. 404

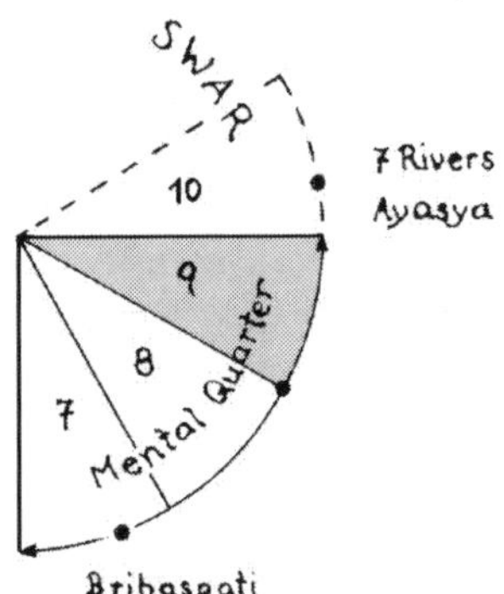

The 7th-10th months of the zodiac, The New Way, Vols. 1&2, p. 413.

> *It is impossible in this short space to take up all these elements and explain their function as seen with the aid of the Gnostic Circle. This task must be undertaken at a later date and then the Rig Veda will be analysed from beginning to end with our key and in light of Sri Aurobindo's revelations. For now it must be said that Ayasya is connected to Brihaspati the seven-rayed one. Brihaspati is Jupiter arisen out of the seventh level of Space, – hence he is seven-rayed. Ayasya conquers by the aid of the seven-headed Thought or Word. The numbers (or months) nine and ten are part of his work because that seventh level of Space becomes the seventh power of Time in the tenth sign, Capricorn. This is the culmination of the sacrifice, for it is when this point is reached that the 'seven rivers' are released. It is also when the walls are shattered between the ninth and tenth levels that the fourth world [of Swar] is manifest.*
>
> Thea, *The New Way, Volumes 1&2*, p. 412

Thea's call for a new analysis of the Rig Veda is even more pressing now in light of the emergence of the dual key of the radius and vesica piscis as principle and multiply disguised figures in the Rig Veda. With this new key, I have found myself

[1] Thea, *The New Way, Volumes 1&2*, p. 413.

revisiting not only the hymns of the Rig Veda, but also Thea's diagram and her thoughts on its cast of characters – Brihaspati, Ayasya, the seven rivers, as well as the seven Angirases, and the nine-rayed and ten-rayed heroes (the Navagwas and Dashagwas).

The first thing I noticed when reviewing Thea's image was that the four-month or 120° slice of the circle that she featured in *The New Way, Volumes 1&2* to make her point, are precisely the four months encompassed by the seventh wave or river of the zodiac, arcing from 0° Libra to 0° Aquarius. I placed this seventh wave on her image and added the hieroglyph of Sagittarius at the fulcrum point of the wave as well as the hieroglyphs of Libra and Aquarius. When I did this I also realized that Thea's conclusion regarding the culmination of the Vedic victory at the 7 Point of the circle, as well as her placement of Ayasya at this same point, needs to be reconsidered in light of new information.

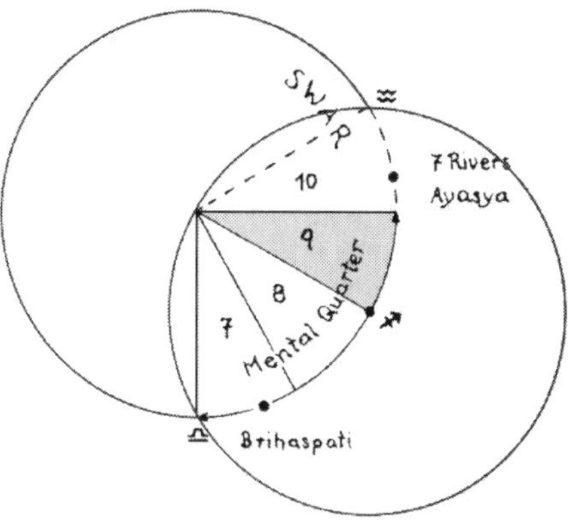

Via the recovery of the truth of the Seven Rivers of the Rig Veda, it now appears that the point of victory and release of these sacred waters is 0° Aquarius. This assessment of the location of the victorious release of the sacred rivers or waters of the Divine Purusha is not only based on the geometry of the vesica piscis within the zodiac, it is also based on the ancient association of Aquarius with the triumphant pouring out or release of the waters of truth from the Kumbha which, we can now clearly see, is the vesica piscis. It appears to me that the realization of the vesica piscis as the underlying truth of the sacred river of the Rig Veda is entirely equivalent to setting this river and its accompanying rivers free from the hold or obstructive powers of Ignorance. These "rivers" instantly eradicate long-reigning confusion and superstition, revealing the real context of the Rishis' symbolism.

Ayasya

In this same light or via this same key and context of the Rig Veda I believe that Sri Aurobindo's supposition of Ayasya as the 8th or 10th Rishi needs to be reconsidered.

> *Ayasya is described as our father who found the vast seven-headed Thought that was born out of the Truth and as singing the hymn to Indra. According as the Navagwas are seven or nine, Ayasya will be the eighth or the tenth Rishi.*
>
> Sri Aurobindo, *The Secret of the Veda, CWSA, Volume 15*, pp. 74-75

It is apparent now that the seven Rishis or singers in the Rig Veda function as the indwelling radii of the first seven vesicae piscis of the zodiac. I have established that the seventh radius of the seventh vesica piscis is the 9th ray (*Navagwas*) of Sagittarius.

> *Mid shout, loud shout, and roar, with the Navagvas, seven singers, hast [Indra], heavenly, rent the mountain....*
>
> Rig Veda 1.62.4, tr. R.T.H. Griffith

I believe that Ayasya is simply another epitaph or depiction of this same much celebrated pillar of the zodiac, and thus another epitaph and depiction of Agni, the victorious Horse or Horse-Man of the zodiac. Ayasya's role as the finder (*vinda*[1]) of the sacred thought or hymn is entirely equivalent to the finder of the trapped cows or rivers in the Vedas. The name of "finder" is simply another epitaph or role of the radius which is the eternal founder, finder and preserver of the light-bearing vesica piscis and zodiac throughout the Ages. The heroes Agni, Indra and Vishnu (all names of the One Deva) are all depicted as finders of this light of truth in the Rig Veda.

The primary root of Ayasya, *ayas*, indicates an iron or metal weapon, and the suffix *ya* suggests movement. Given this

---

[1] Sri Aurobindo's birthname Aravinda meaning "Lotus" is comprised of *ara* meaning a ray or "spoke of a wheel" (i.e. radius) and *vinda* "finder".

etymology, the name Ayasya can itself be taken as indicative of the radius of the circle, which is portrayed by the Rishis as both a weapon and a pillar of gnosis.

> *[Agni] dwells within the revealings of knowledge.... Its form is of golden light, iron is its pillar and shines in heaven as if the swift lightning; in the happy field it is shaped or in the field of the gleaming. May we win possession of the sweet honey which is in that home.*
>
> Rig Veda 5.62.6-7, tr. Sri Aurobindo, *The Secret of the Veda, CWSA, Volume 15*, p. 520

> *Be gracious, Indra, let my days be lengthened: sharpen my thought as' twere a blade of iron. Approve whatever words I speak, dependent on thee, and grant me thy divine protection.*
>
> Rig Veda 6.47.1, tr. R.T.H. Griffith

In addition to the iron weapon of the hero which is sometimes an iron thunderbolt and sometimes an iron blade, the Rishis also sung of iron forts, fortresses, an iron-pillared car, iron tusks and even an iron mouth. These can be taken as symbols of the vesica piscis which is eternally up-pillared and fortified by the radius. In Rig Veda 10.67 Ayasya's seven-headed hymn or thought is said to spring from eternal law, which we now know is the eternal law of the radius as well as the eternal law of the Soul.

> *This holy hymn, sublime and sevenheaded, sprung from eternal Law, our sire discovered. Ayasya, friend of all men, hath engendered the fourth [world][1] as he sang his laud to Indra.*
>
> 10.67.1, tr. R.T.H. Griffith

Ayasya is depicted as giving rise to the fourth world of Swar via his song to Indra. In my mind this song to Indra is equivalent to

[1] Griffith wrote "fourth hymn" here, from *turiyam svid*, which Sri Aurobindo considered to be the "fourth world, Turiyam above the three" (*Hymns to the Mystic Fire, CWSA, Volume 16*, p. 45).

the vesica piscis which arcs to Indra's (i.e. Vishnu's) highest seat, Aquarius. Another indication of this same geometry is the fact that Ayasya's thought is "established in the waters" and enables the Navagwas to pass *through* the ten months, which in the zodiac brings us precisely to 0° Aquarius.

> *The seven-headed thought of Ayasya enables him to become* viśvajanya, *which means probably that he occupies or possesses all the worlds or births of the soul or else that he becomes universal,*[1] *identifying himself with all beings born, — and to manifest or give being to a certain fourth world (Swar),* turīyaṃ svij janayad viśvajanyaḥ (X.67.1)*; and* ***the thought established in the waters which enables the Navagwa Rishis to pass through the ten months, is also* svarṣā, *that which brings about the possession of Swar. The waters are clearly the seven rivers and the two thoughts are evidently the same.***
>
> Sri Aurobindo, *The Secret of the Veda, CWSA, Volume 15*, p. 176

In Rig Veda 6.3, Agni is said to be archer-like with "thighs of swift motion", both of which are descriptors of Sagittarius (*Dhanvan*). In this same hymn, Agni sharpens his iron (*ayasaḥ*) blade or weapon, which Sri Aurobindo translated as an "edge of steel". Given this depiction and other factors already presented, it seems likely that Ayasya, the finder of the seven-headed thought, is simply an epitaph of the radius of the seventh vesica piscis of the zodiac – the radius of 0° Sagittarius.

Ayasya's equivalence to the Hero-Son of the Rig Veda is clear enough in Hymn 1.62, wherein Earth and Heaven (the Rodasi) are symbols of the vesica piscis and the circle – "the two, eternal and in one nest".

> *The Rishi [of Hymn 1.62] proceeds to define the result of the work of Ayasya, which is to reveal the true eternal and unified form of*

[1] The Hero becoming *viśvajanya* or universal in the Rig Veda is another indication of his movement or arc into the sign of Aquarius (in the Swar quadrant of the zodiac) which is specifically associated with Universal Consciousness or Universal Mind, which Sri Aurobindo came to call Supermind.

> *earth and heaven. "...Ayasya uncovered by his hymns the two [Rodasi], eternal and in one nest; perfectly achieving he upheld earth and heaven in the highest ether (of the revealed superconscient,* paramaṃ guhyam*) as the Enjoyer his two wives." The soul's enjoyment of its divinised mental and bodily existence upheld in the eternal joy of the spiritual being could not be more clearly and beautifully imaged.*
>
> Sri Aurobindo, *The Secret of the Veda, CWSA, Volume 15*, p. 181

Ayasya's work "to reveal the true eternal and unified form of earth and heaven"[1] is the goal and promise of the Hero-Son of the Rig Veda, by whatever name attributed to him.

As I was researching the root of Ayasya's name, it became clear that *ayas* or "iron" is a descriptor of both the radius and the vesica piscis throughout the Rig Veda. For instance, references to the iron fortress, iron home, iron mouth or iron jaw are symbols of the vesica piscis, and references to the iron blade, iron shaft, iron thunderbolt, iron column or pillar are symbols of the radius. In Rig Veda 7.95.1, Saraswati's stream is described as an iron fort.

> *This stream Sarasvati with fostering current comes forth, our sure defence, our fort of iron.*
>
> Rig Veda 7.95.1, tr. R.T.H. Griffith

In Rig Veda 10.101.8, the iron fort is specifically associated with a pitcher or kumbha.

> *Make iron forts, secure from all assailants let not your pitcher leak: stay it securely.*
>
> Rig Veda 10.101.8, tr. R.T.H. Griffith

---

[1] I.e., his work to reveal Heaven on Earth, which Sri Aurobindo referred to as the Life Divine or the Supramental Manifestation, equivalent to the Rishis' fourth world of Swar.

CHAPTER TEN

Mitra, Varuna & Their Maya

[Mitra and Varuna] make heaven to rain down by the Maya of the Mighty Lord....

Sri Aurobindo, *The Secret of the Veda, CWSA, Volume 15*, p. 513

Guardians of Order, ye whose Laws are ever true, in the sublimest heaven your chariot ye ascend. O Mitra-Varuṇa whomsoe'er ye: favour, here, to him the rain with sweetness streameth down from heaven.

Rig Veda 5.63.1, tr. R.T.H. Griffith

Mitra, your floods pour water full of sweetness.

Rig Veda 5.69.2, tr. R.T.H. Griffith

The fathers who discovered the Truth, received his creative knowledge, his Maya, and by that ideal and ideative consciousness of the supreme Divinity they formed an image of Him in man, they established Him in the race as a child unborn, a seed of the godhead in man, a Birth that has to be delivered out of the envelope of the human consciousness.

Sri Aurobindo, *The Secret of the Veda, CWSA, Volume 15*, p. 358

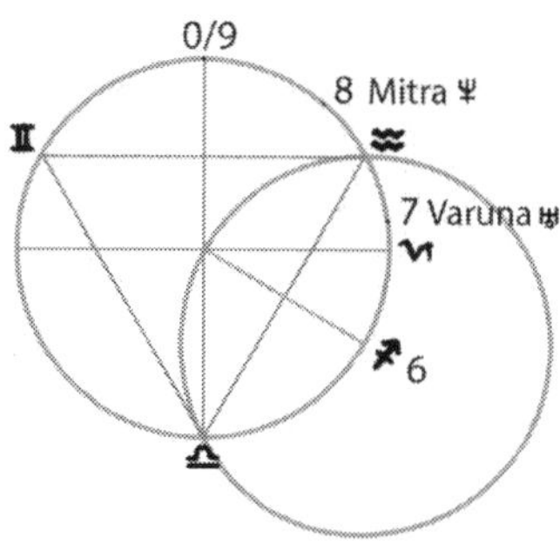

The Vedic gods Mitra and Varuna are described as kings or keepers of eternal law, and as lords of rivers, which are epitaphs or depictions of the radius. They are joint guardians of the Swar realm of the Rishis, equivalent to Neptune and Uranus in the fourth quadrant of the zodiac. The pouring down of their streams, rain or bounty is intimately tied to the Divine Maya which Sri Aurobindo described as "the divine truth-knowledge".[1]

> *Kings, guards of mighty everlasting Order, come hitherward, ye Princes, Lords of Rivers. Send us from heaven, O Varuṇa and Mitra, rain and sweet food, ye who pour down your bounties.*
>
> Rig Veda 7.64.2, tr. R.T.H. Griffith

> *The robes which ye put on abound with fatness: uninterrupted courses are your counsels. All falsehood, Mitra-Varuṇa! ye conquer, and closely cleave unto the Law Eternal. This might of theirs hath no one comprehended....*
>
> Rig Veda 1.152.1-2, tr. R.T.H. Griffith

> *Oceanic Varuna is king of all these waters. "In the uprising of the rivers" it is said "he is a brother of seven sisters, he is in their middle." And another Rishi has sung, "In the rivers Varuna is seated upholding the law of his works....[I]n the midst of [the divine, pure and purifying waters] King Varuna marches looking down on the truth and the falsehood in creatures."*
>
> Sri Aurobindo, *The Secret of the Veda, CWSA, Volume 15*, p. 503

> *Firm is the seat of Varuṇa: over the Seven he rules as King....*
>
> Rig Veda 8.41.9, tr. R.T.H. Griffith

[1] *The Secret of the Veda, CWSA, Volume 15*, p. 522.

Varuna on Makar, unknown author, 1675 (Wikimedia Commons).

As Thea noted in her writing, Varuna's firm seat is the 7 Point of the circle, 10 degrees into the sign of Capricorn or Makar. Thea saw Varuna's seat in Capricorn as the reason why his vehicle (or vahana) is Makar –the water dragon, sea monster or crocodile. In my mind this figure of Capricorn, like the Kumbha or water pot of Aquarius, is another symbol of the vesica piscis, as is the Fish of Pisces, the Virgin of Virgo and probably the Crab of Cancer. In the Rig Veda it appears that the dragon Makar is equivalent to the dragon or serpent Vritra (or Ahi) who must be conquered before the waters of Kumbha (Aquarius) are reached and released. The names of the dragon or serpent may vary but they are simply varying epitaphs of the same "beast".

> *There as [Vṛtra] lies like a bank-bursting river, the waters taking courage flow above him. The Dragon lies beneath the feet of torrents which Vṛtra with his greatness had encompassed.*
>
> Rig Veda 1.32.8, tr. R.T.H. Griffith

In my mind this dragon lying beneath the flow and feet of the torrents of the liberated waters is a symbolic depiction of the 10th sign Capricorn (Makar) lying beneath the 11th sign Aquarius and the 12th sign Pisces which is associated with the feet.

Mitra (Neptune) is seated at the 8 Point of the circle (20° Aquarius). The placement of Mitra (a.k.a. Maitreya) in the sign of Aquarius is supported by the fact that Mitra means "Friend" and Aquarius is known as the Friend of the zodiac. The roots of Mitra are *mi*, meaning to "fix", "found", "build" and "construct", as well as to "mete out" and "measure"; and *trá* (*trai*), meaning "protector" or "defender"[1] (i.e. guardian). In this etymological light, it seems that Mitra is a cognate of our modern word

---

[1] These definitions of *mi* and *trá* (*trai*) are from *Cologne Digital Sanskrit Lexicon. Tra*, the root of *traya*, means "three".

"meter". "Friend" is yet another epitaph or descriptor of the radius which is characterized as the One Purusha called by many names – Agni, Indra, Vishnu, etc. In Rig Veda 1.154 this Friend is associated with Vishnu's highest step and with "the fount of sweetness", both of which are symbols of the vesica piscis. In Rig Veda 3.5 Agni is described as the Friend of the rivers and of the mountains, both of which are symbols of the vesicae pisces.

> *May I attain to and enjoy that goal of his movement, the Delight, where souls that seek the godhead have the rapture; for there in that highest step of the wide-moving Vishnu is that Friend of men who is the fount of the sweetness.*
>
> *Those are the dwelling-places of ye twain which we desire as the goal of our journey where the many-horned herds of Light go travelling; the highest step of wide-moving Vishnu shines down on us here in its manifold vastness.*
>
> Rig Veda 1.154.5-6, tr. Sri Aurobindo,
> *The Secret of the Veda, CWSA, Volume 15*, p. 344

> *The Fire [Agni] when he has been kindled high becomes Mitra, the Friend — Mitra the priest of the call, Varuna, the knower of the births, Mitra, the friend, the priest of the pilgrim sacrifice, one rapid in his impulsions, the dweller in the house, the friend of the Rivers, the friend of the Mountains. He guards from hurt the beloved summit-seat of the being, mighty, he guards the course of the Sun; Fire guards in the navel-centre the seven-headed thought,[1] sublime, he guards the ecstasy of the gods.*
>
> Rig Veda 3.5.4-5, tr. Sri Aurobindo,
> *Hymns to the Mystic Fire, CWSA, Volume 16*, p. 172

In the following excerpts from *The Secret of the Veda*, Mitra and Varuna are portrayed as the supreme Lords of Maya. Maya is described herein as "the comprehending, measuring, forming Knowledge", "part of an infinite, supreme and faultless creative

---

[1] This line describes the radius (the indwelling flame, fire or ray) of the seven-headed thought (i.e. of the vesica piscis).

wisdom", and as Mitra and Varuna's "rich and wonderful weapon by which they make heaven to rain down".

> *The well-accorded happiness of the Truth is Mitra's law of working; for it is upon Truth and divine Knowledge that this harmony and perfect temperament are founded; they are formed, secured and guarded by the Maya of Mitra and Varuna. That well-known word comes from the same root as Mitra. Maya is the comprehending, measuring, forming Knowledge which whether divine or undivine, secure in the undivided being of Aditi or labouring in the divided being of Diti, builds up the whole scene, environment, confines, and defines the whole condition, law and working of our existence.... But Mitra is a Lord of the Light, a Son of Infinity and a Guardian of the Truth and his Maya part of an infinite, supreme and faultless creative wisdom. He builds, he joins together in an illuminated harmony all the numerous planes, all the successive steps, all the graded seats of our being. Whatsoever Aryaman*[1] *aspires to on his path, has to be effected by the 'holdings' or laws of Mitra or by his foundations, statuses, placings,* mitrasya dharmabhiḥ, mitrasya dhāmabhiḥ. *For* dharma, *the law is that which holds things together and to which we hold;* dhāma, *the status is the placing of the law in a founded harmony which creates for us our plane of living and the character of our consciousness, action and thought.*

Sri Aurobindo, *The Secret of the Veda, CWSA, Volume 15*, pp. 511-12

> *Mitra and Varuna have an unwounded vision and are better knowers of the Path than our sight; for in the Knowledge they are seers of Swar.... [I]n their purified judgment they open the eye of consciousness to all wisdom by the perception in men. Thus all-seeing and all-knowing they by the law, by the Maya of the mighty Lord, guard our actions, even as they govern the whole world in the power of the Truth. That Maya is established in the heavens, it ranges there as a Sun of light; it is their rich and wonderful weapon. They are far-hearers, masters of true being, true themselves and increasers of truth in each human creature. They nourish the*

---

[1] Aryaman is another epitaph of the Divine Purusha. Thea indicates that his "seat" is 0° Leo in the zodiac (*The New Way, Volumes 1&2*, p. 387).

> *shining herds and loose forth the abundance of heaven; they make heaven to rain down by the Maya of the Mighty Lord. And* ***that celestial rain is the wealth of the spiritual felicity which the seers desire; it is the immortality****.*
>
> Sri Aurobindo, *The Secret of the Veda, CWSA, Volume 15*, p. 513 [bold emphasis added]

In *The Secret of the Veda*, Sri Aurobindo discussed a hymn to Mitra and Varuna which he entitled "The Givers of the Rain" (Rig Veda 5.63), further illuminating the relationship and geometry of the Lord and his eternal divine companion Maya.

> *Mitra and Varuna are by their united universality and harmony the guardians of the divine Truth and its divine Law eternally perfect in the ether of our supreme being; thence they rain down the abundance of the heavens and its bliss upon the favoured soul. Seers in man of that world of Truth, as they are by their guardianship of its law rulers of all this becoming, they give us its rain of spiritual wealth and immortality. The Life-powers range with the voice of the truth-seeking thought through earth and heaven and the two Kings come to their cry* ***with the brilliant clouds[1] full of the creative waters. It is by the Maya, the divine truth-knowledge of the Lord, that they thus rain down heaven;*** *that divine knowledge is the Sun, the Light, the weapon of Mitra and Varuna ranging abroad to destroy the ignorance.* ***At first the Sun, the body of the Truth, is concealed in the very storm of its outpourings[2]*** *and only the sweetness of their streaming into the life is felt; but the Maruts as Life-Powers and Thought-Powers range abroad seeking in all the worlds of our being for the brilliant rays of the concealed knowledge to be gathered as a shining wealth;* ***the voice of the Rain is full of the flashings of the Light and the movement of the divine Waters; its clouds become robes for the Life-Powers.*** *Through it all by the formative knowledge of the mighty Master of Truth and by the law of the Truth, the two kings maintain the divine workings in us, governing by the Truth*

[1] These clouds and their waters are symbols of the vesica piscis.

[2] This Sun concealed in the cloud is the radius. It is possible that the storm is a symbol of the full zodiac, with its multiple "clouds" (i.e. multiple vesicae piscis).

> *all our being, and finally set in its sky the Sun, now revealed, as a chariot of the richly varied splendours of the knowledge, the chariot of the journey of the spirit to the highest heavens.*
>
> Sri Aurobindo, *The Secret of the Veda, CWSA, Volume 15*, p. 522 [bold emphasis added]

Sri Aurobindo's full translation of Rig Veda 5.63 is as follows:

> *Guardians of the Truth, you ascend your car and the law of the Truth is yours in the supreme ether.*[1] *He whom here you cherish, Masters of the wideness and the harmony, for him increases full of the honey the rain of heaven.*
>
> *Emperors, you rule over this world of our becoming, O Mitra and Varuna, in the getting of knowledge you are seers of the realm of Light; we desire from you the rain, the felicitous wealth, the immortality, and lo! the Thunderers [or builders] range abroad through earth and heaven.*
>
> *Emperors, strong Bulls of the abundance, Masters of earth and heaven, O Mitra and Varuna, universal in your workings, you approach [the Storm Gods'] cry with your clouds of varied light and you rain down Heaven by [Maya] the power of the knowledge of the Mighty One.*
>
> *This is your knowledge, O Mitra and Varuna, that is lodged in heaven; it is the Sun, it is the Light; it ranges abroad as your rich and varied weapon. You hide it in heaven with the cloud and with the raining. O Rain, full of the honey start forth thy streamings.*[2]
>
> *The Life-Powers yoke their happy car for the bliss, even as might a hero for battle, O Mitra and Varuna, in their seekings for the herds of Light; thundering they range the varied worlds, and you pour out on us, rulers imperial, the water of Heaven.*[3]

---

[1] "The infinity of the superconscient being" (Sri Aurobindo's footnote).

[2] This imagery is equivalent to the victorious release of the sacred rivers.

[3] The "pouring out of the water of Heaven" is equivalent to the imagery of Aquarius as the Water Bearer of the zodiac. As I wrote this chapter during the month of Aquarius (2017), heavy and sustained rains from an "Atmospheric River" damaged the Oroville Dam in California, forcing 188,000 people to be evacuated from the

O Mitra and Varuna, the Rain speaks its language rich and varied and full of the light and the movement; the Life Powers have put on your clouds for raiment. Utterly by the knowledge you rain down Heaven ruddy-shining and sinless.

O Mitra and Varuna illumined in consciousness, by the Law, by the knowledge of the Mighty One you guard the workings; by the Truth you govern widely all the world of our becoming; you set the Sun in heaven, a chariot of various splendour.

Rig Veda 5.63, tr. Sri Aurobindo,
The Secret of the Veda, CWSA, Volume 15, pp. 523-25

Maya and the Vesica Piscis

While researching the relationship between Mitra, Varuna and Maya, it quickly became apparent that Maya yet is another important occult symbol-expression of the vesica piscis. Along with all the other symbols of the vesica piscis in the Rig Veda, it has been widely misunderstood and misconstrued throughout much of recorded history and consequently in our modern world as well. As previously noted Maya has come to be equated with illusion in our modern world. Sri Aurobindo defined Maya as "the creative knowledge-will of the Deva"[1] deriving from "its root-significance, to measure, form, build or plan out."[2] He also noted that in the Vedas, "There are two kinds of Maya, the divine and undivine, the formations of the truth and the formations of the falsehood."

I believe now that this dual nature of Maya is entirely attributable to the fact that, on the one hand, the vesica piscis is a veil, cloud, robe or cover eclipsing the light and, on the other hand, it is the water, womb or vessel in which the Hero-Son of the Rishis is born forward to reestablish his own eternal law or dharma within his field of Time and Space. In ignorance, the vesica piscis is a covering, a shut door, a closed pen, a dragon,

area on my 48th birthday. Due to the *controlled release of water*, and a break in the rain, an epic and disastrous uncontrolled release of waters was avoided.

[1] *The Secret of the Veda, CWSA, Volume 15*, p. 523.

[2] Ibid., p. 545.

demon, or beast withholding or entrapping the light and treasures of the Sun and the Rivers (or Cows). In gnosis, the vesica piscis is the divine form, treasure, container, vessel, mother, wife, body, word, voice, song and river of the divine flame, ray or Purusha.

> *By the Names of the Lord and hers they shaped and measured the force of the Mother of Light; wearing might after might of that Force as a robe the lords of Maya shaped out Form in this Being.*
>
> Rig Veda 3.38.7, tr. Sri Aurobindo, *The Life Divine, "The Divine Maya", CWSA, Volumes 21-22*, p. 120

> *God created the world in Himself through Maya; but the Vedic meaning of Maya is not illusion, it is wisdom, knowledge, capacity, wide extension in consciousness. Prajna prasrita purani. Omnipotent Wisdom created the world, it is not the organised blunder of some Infinite Dreamer; omniscient Power manifests or conceals it in Itself or Its own delight, it is not a bondage imposed by His own ignorance on the free and absolute Brahman.*
>
> Sri Aurobindo, *The Hour of God, "The Object of Our Yoga", CWSA, Volume 12*, pp. 96-97

> *The Masters of Maya shaped all by His Maya; the Fathers who have divine vision set Him within [Maya] as a child that is to be born.*
>
> Rig Veda 9.83.3, tr. Sri Aurobindo, *The Life Divine, "The Divine Maya", CWSA, Volumes 21-22*, p. 120

> *[W]hen He the eternal Unborn assumes by his Maya, by the power of the infinite Consciousness to clothe itself apparently in finite forms, the conditions of becoming which we call birth.*
>
> Sri Aurobindo, *Letters on Yoga I, CWSA, Volume 28*, pp. 17-18

In the Atharva Veda, Maya is the unkillable or immortal queen Virāj, whose calf is the Hero-Purusha.

> *[Virāj] mounted up, and, into four divided, she took her station in the air's mid-region.[1] ...Her calf, her well-beloved calf, was Indra: Gāyatri was her rope, the cloud her udder. Waters from Vāmdevya come, from sacrifice [from yajna]....[T]hey[2] killed her. A year went by and she again existed....She rose, approached the [Gods]: they called her: their cry was, Come, O Māyā, come thou hither. Her dear calf was Virochana Prāhrādi: her milking vessel was a pan of iron....She mounted up, she came unto the Fathers. The Fathers called to her, O Food, come hither. King Yama was her calf, her pail was silvern....Earth was her milking-pail, the calf beside her [was] Manu Vaivasvata, Vivasvān's offspring....She rose, she came unto the Seven Rishis. They called her, Come, Rich in Devotion! hither. King Soma was her calf, the Moon her milk-pail. Brihaspati Āngirasa, her milker, drew from her udder Prayer and Holy Fervour. Fervour and Prayer maintain the Seven Rishis. He who knows this becomes a meet supporter, a priest illustrious for his sacred knowledge....The son of [Sūrya], Chitraratha [Agni], was her dear calf, her pail a lotus-petal. Her dear calf was Vaisravana Kubera, a vessel never tempered was her milk-pail.*
>
> Atharva Veda 8.10.8-28, tr. R.T.H. Griffith

Hopefully readers can appreciate that the multiple references to Virāj (Maya) and her calf in this excerpt, are symbols of the vesica piscis and the radius. Viraj's recurring milk pails are symbols of the vesica piscis, as are Gayatri, the rope, the cloud, the udder, the waters of Vamdevya, the cry of the Rishis, the pan of iron, food, the Moon, Brihaspati's prayer and the lotus petal. Maya in this scene rises from death in conjunction with the seven Rishis, which in my mind parallels the victory of the seventh wave of the vesica piscis. The calf or son of this particular wave of the zodiac, as already discussed, is the radius of 0° Sagittarius, the 6 Point of the circle, which is Agni's victorious seat. Agni's multiple epitaphs in this Atharva Veda chapter include, Indra, Virochana, Yama, Manu, Soma, and Kubera. The roots of

---

[1] This division of Virāj into four indicates four months of the year encompassed by the vesica piscis which arcs through the mid-region of the circle.

[2] "They" in this hymn are the gods, the fathers and men, i.e. ... symbols of the Purusha and radius.

Virochana appear to be *vira* "hero" and *channa* "hidden", indicating the hero hidden in the waters or in the womb of Maya.

Kubera is a dwarf king, who is Lord of treasure and wealth. He is lord of the Guhyakas or Hidden Ones who live in mountain caves. In my view, these "Hidden Ones" are the radii who "live" in the "caves" of the vesicae piscis. Kubera is also king of the Kinnaras (Centaurs) who are half human and half horse, a chimera associated with the 9th sign of the zodiac – the sign of the Sage. The connection between the Sage, the radius and the vesica piscis of the circle is abundantly clear in Rig Veda 6.47.

> *This Sage hath measured out the six expanses[1] from which no single creature is excluded....He formed the nectar in three headlong rivers. Soma supports the wide mid-air above us....He found the wavy sea of brilliant colours in forefront of the Dawns who dwell in brightness. This Mighty One...hath propped the heavens up with a mighty pillar. Drink Soma boldly from the beaker, Indra, in war for treasures, Hero, Vṛtra-slayer!.... May helpful Indra as our good Protector, Lord of all treasures, favour us with succor.... In every figure he hath been the mode: this is his only form for us to look on. Indra moves multiform by his [mayabhih].*
>
> Rig Veda 6.47.3-18, tr. R.T.H. Griffith

In this hymn, Griffith translates *mayabhih* – an epitaph of Maya – as "illusions". We can now appreciate that this "only form" of Indra, or the Hero-Purusha by whatever name, is the vesica piscis which is simultaneously his self-extension, his self-expression and his self-knowledge. We can appreciate that Maya, in truth, is not an illusion, but rather the "infinite, supreme and faultless creative wisdom"[2] of the indwelling or hidden Purusha.

---

[1] In Atharva Veda 10.7.35, Skambha is the name given to this "Sage" (i.e. the radius) who measures out the six expanses or regions of the circle or zodiac.

[2] Sri Aurobindo, *The Secret of the Veda, CWSA, Volume 15*, p. 512.

CHAPTER ELEVEN

Hidden Treasure

In this chapter we will continue to look at how the Rishis' keys, treasures and measures of gnosis were simultaneously hidden and laid out in a myriad of ways throughout the Rig Veda. Rig Veda 4.58 (below) is one of many good examples of how the Rishis' words are largely indecipherable or nonsensical without the keys of the vesica piscis and radius within the larger context of the twelve-month Vedic sacrifice. I have highlighted the many symbols of the vesica piscis in this hymn.

> *Forth from the ocean sprang the* ***wave of sweetness****: together with the stalk it turned to* ***Amṛta****, that which is* ***holy oil's*** *mysterious title: but the Gods' tongue is truly* ***Amṛta's*** *centre.*
>
> *Let us declare aloud the name of* ***Ghṛta****, and at this sacrifice hold it up with homage. So let the Brahman hear* ***the praise*** *we utter. This hath the four-horned Buffalo emitted.*
>
> ***Four are his horns, three are the feet*** *that bear him; his heads are two, his hands are seven in number.* ***Bound with a triple bond*** *the Steer* ***roars loudly****: the mighty God hath entered in to mortals.*
>
> *That* ***oil in triple shape*** *the Gods discovered laid down within the Cow, concealed by Paṇis. Indra produced one shape, Sūrya another: by their own power they formed* ***the third*** *from Vena.*
>
> *From inmost* ***reservoir in countless channels flow down these rivers*** *which the foe beholds not. I look upon the* ***streams of oil descending****, and lo! the Golden Reed is there among them.*
>
> ***Like rivers our libations flow together****, cleansing themselves in inmost heart and spirit.* ***The streams of holy oil*** *pour swiftly downward like* ***the wild beasts that fly before the bowman****.*

> *As rushing down the* ***rapids of a river****, flow swifter than the wind* ***the vigorous currents, the streams of oil in swelling fluctuation*** *like a red courser bursting through* ***the fences****....*
>
> *The universe depends upon [Soma's] power and might within* ***the sea****, within* ***the heart****, within all life.*
>
> Rig Veda 4.58.1-7, 11, tr. R.T.H. Griffith

Sri Aurobindo discussed and partially translated this hymn in *The Secret of the Veda.*

> *Certainly, this does not mean that rivers of ghee — or of water, either — rising from the heart-ocean or any ocean were caught on their way by the wicked and unconscionable Dravidians and shut up in a hundred pens so that the Aryans or the Aryan gods could not even catch a glimpse of them.... The Rishi Vamadeva would have stood aghast at such an unforeseen travesty of his ritual images.... For even if the rivers of the Punjab all flow out of one heart-pleasing lake, yet their streams of water cannot even so have been triply placed in a cow and the cow hidden in a cave by the cleverest and most inventive Dravidians.*
>
> *"These [rivers] move" says Vamadeva "from the heart-ocean; penned by the enemy in a hundred enclosures they cannot be seen; I look towards the streams of the clarity, for in their midst is the Golden Reed. Entirely they stream like flowing rivers becoming purified by the heart within and the mind; these move, waves of the clarity, like animals under the mastery of their driver. As if on a path in front of the Ocean (sindhu, the upper ocean) the mighty ones move compact of forceful speed but limited by the vital force (*vāta, vāyu*), the streams of clarity; they are like a straining horse which breaks its limits, as it is nourished by the waves."...*
>
> *...This goal is, again, explained to be that which is all honey,—* ghṛtasya dhārā madhumat pavante*; it is the Ananda, the divine Beatitude. And that this goal is the Sindhu, the superconscient ocean, is made clear in the last rik, where Vamadeva says "May we taste that honeyed wave of thine" — of Agni, the divine Purusha, the four-horned Bull of the worlds — "which is borne in the force of the Waters where they come together."*
>
> Rig Veda 4.58, tr. and commentary by Sri Aurobindo,
> *The Secret of the Veda, CWSA, Volume 15*, pp. 105-06

Symbols of the radius in this hymn include the stalk, the gods' tongue, the Brahman (priest), the buffalo, steer or bull, the mighty god, the shape of Indra, Vena, the Golden Reed and Soma. The form of Surya appears to be the Sun symbol. Via this equivalence, we can see that the "third" form of Surya and Indra (the Sun symbol and the radius) is the vesica piscis.

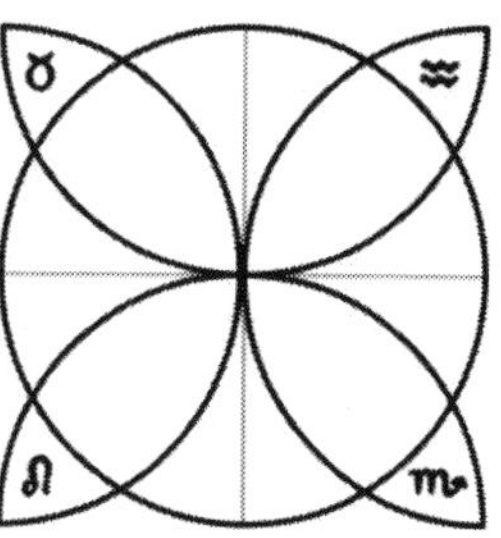

At first I thought the "four-horned" and triply-bound "Bull of the worlds" of this hymn is equivalent to Vishnu's four-legged "tortoise" and that his four horns, three feet and two heads refer to the 4, 3 and 2 divisions of the whole circle. This may be true, but considering that the Bull is the indwelling Purusha of the vesica piscis, I imagine that the 4, 3 and 2 may also indicate the four signs, three number units and the two end points of the vesica piscis. The numbers 4, 3 and 2 are especially notable in relation to the Purusha because, as discussed in the first half of this book, the measure of the Solar Purusha or radius is 432,000 miles and his Maya or measure is 432,000″ of the 360° circle. The Bull's seven hands could be equivalent to the seven-measure of the vesica piscis (3 number units + 4 months). These hands could also be Agni's seven rays, tongues or radii by which he accomplishes his victory over ignorance and darkness from his seat at 0° Sagittarius, the 6 Point of the circle. This point is Agni's third seat or station – the passageway into the last third of the zodiac.

> *Agni, we know thy three powers in three stations, we know thy forms in many a place divided. We know what name supreme thou hast in secret: we know the source from which thou hast proceeded.*[1] *The Manly-souled lit thee in sea and waters, man's Viewer lit thee in the breast of heaven, [there] as thou stoodest in*

[1] "Three powers in three stations" is translated by Griffith from *tredhā trayāṇi*. Sri Aurobindo translated this second verse of 10.45 as "O Fire, we know the triple three of thee, we know thy seats borne widely in many planes, we know thy supreme Name which is in the secrecy, we know that fount of things whence thou camest" (*Hymns to the Mystic Fire, CWSA, Volume 16*, p. 410).

the third high region the Steers increased thee in the water's bosom. Agni roared out...guardian of the Soma, Good Son of Strength, a King amid the waters, in forefront of the Dawns he shines enkindled. Germ of the world, ensign of all creation, he sprang to life and filled the earth and heavens. Even the firm rock he cleft when passing over, when the Five Tribes brought sacrifice to Agni.

Rig Veda 10.45.2-6, tr. R.T.H. Griffith

Once again there are multiple symbols of the radius and the vesica piscis in the small space of these verses. Symbols of the vesica piscis include Agni's forms, the seas and waters, the breast of heaven, the water's bosom, Agni's roar, the Dawns which enkindle Agni, and the rock he cleaves in two. Soma, in this instance, is the vesica piscis as well. It is the nectar of immortality (*amrita*) that the Purusha "guards". Symbols of, or references to the radius include Agni, the "Manly-souled", 'man's Viewer',[1] the steers, the guardian, the king amid the waters, the germ of the world and ensign of all creation. Hopefully by now readers are getting at least some feel for the Rishis' language of unity, wherein all words and language were to them extensions, forms and vehicles of the One, and wherein the One was hidden or cloaked in many variations. Also, hopefully readers are getting some sense of the vast and multi-dimensional intelligence it took to encode and preserve gnosis of the Soul's unified field of Time and Space in this extraordinary manner.

The Five Tribes

On many occasions, the Vedic Rishis' sing of the five tribes, five-fold peoples, five races, five worlds or five lands. We have already seen this pentad in Rig Veda 6.61 (a hymn to Saraswati) and in Rig Veda 10.45 featured in the previous section. The five

---

[1] Sri Aurobindo translated these two references to the Purusha as "He of the god-mind" and "he of the divine vision" (*Hymns to the Mystic Fire, CWSA, Volume 16*, p. 410).

tribes, worlds, lands, etc., in these hymns and elsewhere in the Rig Veda may be explained by the fact that the arc of the vesica piscis, bridges five signs and five radii of the zodiac.

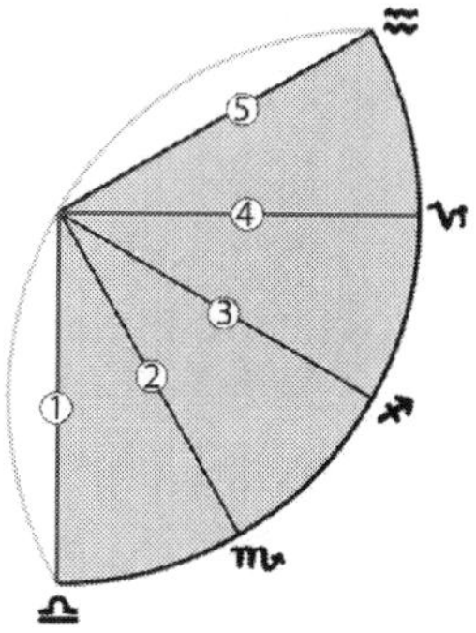

He who with might the Five Lands hath pervaded, like Surya with his lustre, and the waters — His strength wins hundreds, thousands none avert it, as the young maid repelleth not her lover.

Rig Veda 10.178.3, tr. R.T.H. Griffith

I hear that thou [Indra] wast born sole Lord of heroes of the Five Races, famed among the people.

Rig Veda 5.32.11, tr. R.T.H. Griffith

May Brahmanaspati draw nigh, may...the Goddess come, and Gods bring to this rite which gives the five-fold gift of the Hero, lover of mankind.

Rig Veda 1.40.3, tr. R.T.H. Griffith

Dadhikras[1] *hath o' erspread the Fivefold People with vigour, as the Sun lightens the waters.*

Rig Veda 4.38.10, tr. R.T.H. Griffith

In Rig Veda 1.164.12, this same geometry is suggested in the description of Agni as "*the five-footed Sire of twelve forms who is wealthy in his store of water*".[2] The store of water here is the vesica piscis and the five-feet of the sire are five rays of the twelve-month zodiac. In Rig Veda 10.55 the Rishi sings of five tribes that Indra "loveth well", followed by a description of Indra looking all around himself with "four-and-thirty lights".

---

[1] Dadhikras is Dadhikravan the victorious war-horse (radius) of Sagittarius whose arc makes a bridge from Libra to Aquarius, across the four signs Libra, Scorpio, Sagittarius and Capricorn.

[2] Tr. R.T.H. Griffith.

> *Great is that secret name and far-extending, whereby thou madest all that is and shall be. The Five Tribes whom he loveth well have entered the light he loveth that was made aforetime. He filled the heaven and earth and all between them.... With four-and-thirty lights he looks around him, lights of one colour though their ways are diverse.*
>
> Rig Veda 10.55.2-3, tr. R.T.H. Griffith

Considering the geometry of the Purusha or radius of the circle, *"four and thirty lights"* in this verse needs to be understood as *four times thirty (4 x 30)* lights, equivalent to the 120° arc of the vesica piscis which encompasses four 30° signs of the zodiac.

Vena – Another Name of the Purusha

In *The Secret of the Veda* Sri Aurobindo equates Vena to the God Soma,[1] thus adding him to the list of the many names of the divine Purusha or Godhead. Sri Aurobindo describes Soma in the following terms.

> *He is the source and outpourer of the ambrosial Wine of divine delight and we drink it drawn from the sevenfold waters of existence or pressed out from the luminous plant on the hill of being and uplifted by its raptures we become immortal. Such are some of the images of this ancient mystic adoration.*
>
> Sri Aurobindo, *The Secret of the Veda, CWSA, Volume 15*, p. 371

Vena is the name given to the Hero-Purusha of Rig Veda 10.123. His wave is equivalent to the seventh wave of the zodiac and thus to the Stallion's wave or flood by which the immortal rivers are found and released from the Swar realm. I have highlighted some symbols of the vesica piscis in this hymn.

> *See, Vena, born* ***in light****, hath driven hither, on* ***chariot of the air****,*

[1] *The Secret of the Veda, CWSA, Volume 15*, p. 104.

> *the Calves of [the Cow] Pṛśni.*[1] *Singers with* ***hymns*** *caress him as an infant there* ***where the waters and the sunlight mingle****.*
>
> *Vena draws up his* ***wave from out the ocean****,* ***mist****-born,* ***the fair one's back*** *is made apparent, Brightly he shone aloft on Order's summit: the hosts* ***sang glory*** *to* ***their common birthplace****.*
>
> *Full many, lowing to their joint-possession, dwelling together stood* ***the Darling's Mothers****. Ascending to the lofty height of Order, the bands of singers sip* ***the sweets of Amṛta****.*
>
> *Knowing* ***his form****, the sages yearned to meet him: they have come nigh to hear the wild Bull's* ***bellow****. Performing sacrifice they reached* ***the river****: for the Gandharva found* ***the immortal waters****.*
>
> *The* ***Apsaras, the Lady****,* ***sweetly smiling****, supports her Lover in sublimest heaven. In his* ***Friend's dwelling*** *as a Friend he wanders: he, Vena, rests him on* ***his golden pinion****.*
>
> *They gaze on thee with longing in their spirit, as on a strong-****winged*** *bird that mounteth sky-ward; On thee with* ***wings of gold****, Varuṇa's envoy, the Bird that hasteneth to the home of Yama.*
>
> *Erect, to heaven hath the Gandharva mounted, pointing at us* ***his many-coloured weapons****; Clad in* ***sweet raiment beautiful to look on****, for he, as light, produceth* ***forms that please us****.*
>
> Rig Veda 10.123.1-7, tr. R.T.H. Griffith

The Sanskrit word *vena* is a cognate of *venu* meaning “reed”. Another relative of *vena* is *veni*, meaning “weaving” or “braiding”. *Veni* is also the “confluence or meeting of two or more rivers or streams in a common point of union”.[2] The rivers of the zodiac can easily be seen as being woven or braided together. From *venu*, *vena* and *veni* I imagine come the English words “vine” and “vein”, the Latin verb “venire” as well as the goddess and planet “Venus”, considered to be the consort of the hero Mars. Images of the radius or radii in Vena’s hymn include

---

[1] Pṛśni or Prisni is a name of the sacred Cow, who with her many calves or sons (i.e., radii) is a figure of the zodiac, the cosmic mother, bride or wife of the Purusha.

[2] All definitions in this paragraph are from *Cologne Digital Sanskrit Lexicon*.

Vena, the calves, the singers, the hosts, the darling, the sages, the wild bull, the Gandharva (lover of the Apsaras), the Friend, the bird, Varuna, Yama, and the light that produces forms.

Soma and Indu

I have already briefly discussed the equivalence of the god Soma and the radius. This is again apparent in Rig Veda 9.94.

> *Acting the Sage, [Soma] flows enrobed in waters and song as 'twere a stall that kine may prosper. The worlds expand to him who from aforetime found light to spread the law of life eternal.*
>
> Rig Veda 9.94.1-2, tr. R.T.H. Griffith

> *It is [Soma] who has revealed the abode of immortality. All worlds have expanded for him who found the Light. Encompassing wisdom on all sides, the Seer, the Hero, moves through all worlds like a chariot, preparing for mortals glory among the Gods.... He, measuring his course, is successful in the encounter.*
>
> Rig Veda 9.94.2-5, tr. by Raimundo Panikkar, *The Vedic Experience*, p. 832

In this section we will look at other symbols connected to Soma, including the Soma stones and the immortalizing drops of Soma, as well as the equivalence of Soma and Indu. In Rig Veda 9.66 Soma is called *Soma Pavamana*, an epitaph of Agni. *Pavamana* is said to mean something on the order of "flowing clear" or "purified"; but it is important to note that whereas *pava* indicates "purification", this root word is joined with *mana* indicating a "measure" or "measuring cord".[1] This conveys the message that the measure, and thus the law of the Purusha (i.e. of the radius) is *purifying*. It purifies the distorted, disjointed and disharmonious field of the divided Mental consciousness, allowing the knower of this law to become *Kshetrajna* – a knower of the unified field of Time and Space.

---

[1] The definitions and roots of *pavamana* are from *Cologne Digital Sanskrit Lexicon*.

Wise Soma Pavamana, thou encompassest on every side thy stations as the seasons come. Flow onward, generating food, for precious boons of every kind, a Friend for friends, to be our help. Upon the lofty ridge of heaven thy bright rays with their essences, Soma, spread purifying power. O Soma, these Seven Rivers flow, as being thine, to give command: The Streams of milk run forth to thee. Flow onward, Soma in a stream, effused to gladden Indra's heart, bringing imperishable fame. Driving thee in Vivasvān's course,[1] *the Seven Sisters with their hymns made melody round thee the Sage. The virgins deck thee o'er fresh streams to drive thee to the sieve when thou, a singer, bathest in the wood. The streams of Pavamana, thine, Sage, Mighty One, have poured them forth. Like coursers eager for renown. They have been poured upon the fleece towards the meath-distilling vat: The holy songs have sounded forth....*

Agni, thou pourest life; send down upon us food and vigorous strength; drive thou misfortune far away, Agni is Pavamana, Sage, Chief Priest of all the Races Five: To him whose wealth is great we pray. Skilled in thy task, O Agni, pour splendour with hero strength on us, granting me wealth that nourishes. Beyond his enemies away to sweet praise Pavamana flows, like Sūrya visible to all. Adorned by living men, set forth for entertainment, rich in food, far-sighted Indu is a Steed. He, Pavamana, hath produced the lofty Law, the brilliant light, destroying darkness black of hue. From tawny Pavamana, the Destroyer, radiant streams have sprung, quick streams from him whose gleams are swift. Best rider of the chariot, praised with fairest praise mid beauteous ones, gold-gleaming with the Marut host, may Pavamana, best to win the booty, penetrate with rays, Giving the singer hero strength.

Rig Veda 9.66, 3-11, 19-27, tr. R.T.H. Griffith

This hymn describes Agni's victory as the Sage or Horse of Sagittarius. Agni as Soma Pavamana is depicted in this hymn as a Sage and as the Sun of the sacrifice who is visible to all. In other words, at this stage of the sacrifice the Divine Maya (or measure) and Soul of Time and Space is no longer hidden. Soma Pavamana

---

[1] The Sun's course.

is also described as the "best rider of the chariot" and as the "Mighty One" who pours forth the seven rivers. Depicted as a Stallion (Steed), Indu appears to be equivalent Agni-Soma Pavamana in this hymn. Both Soma and Indu are depicted in the Rig Veda as the Purusha (i.e. the radius) of the sacred wave or stream, dwelling in, bearing forth or pouring out the waters of truth and clarity.

> *Indu as, Indra's Friend, on us pour with a stream of sweetness....*
>
> Rig Veda 9.2.9, tr. R.T.H. Griffith

> *Soma, while filtered, with his wave flows through the long wool of the sheep....*
>
> Rig Veda 9.106.10, tr. R.T.H. Griffith

> *Indu, to us for this great rite, bearing as 'twere thy wave to Gods, Unwearied, thou art flowing forth....The Wise One in the Singer's stream.*
>
> Rig Veda 9.44.1-2, tr. R.T.H. Griffith

> *This deathless Indu, like a steed, strong and of full vitality, belongs to thee, the Orderer. Here, by us, for the worshipper, is the wise bolt that works with skill. It brings the bubbling beverage....*
>
> Rig Veda 10.144.1-2, tr. R.T.H. Griffith

> *Soma...takes his seat...while they cleanse him in the bowls. He as it were impregns the cow, and babbles on, the Lord of Song. He is effused and beautified, a God for Gods, by skilful men. He penetrates the mighty floods collecting all he knows therein. Pressed, Indu, guided by the men, thou art led to the cleaning sieve. Thou, yielding Indra highest joy, takest thy seat within the bowls.*
>
> Rig Veda 9.99.6-8, tr. R.T.H. Griffith

In researching Soma, I naturally came upon the prevalent image of the Soma stones or pressing stones in the Rig Veda. At first I thought of the stone as a symbol of the lingam and therefore, of the radius; but many passages I researched seemed to indicate that the stones are symbols of the vesica piscis. The Rishi of Rig Veda 10.92 tells us that through the pressing stones, "the Sage became exceeding vast." The Sage is the radius (also characterized as the dwarf Vamana) which becomes vast as it forms the vesica piscis, arcing or stepping across the Rishis' 360° field of Time and Space. In Rig Veda 2.1.1, Agni is brought to life by the waters and by the stone. This depiction suggests the stone is equivalent to the water of the vesica piscis which hides and eventually births forth or reveals Agni.

> *Thou, Agni, shining in thy glory through the days, art brought to life from out the waters, from the stone....*
>
> Rig Veda 2.1.1, tr. R.T.H. Griffith

> *I desire from the Fire, powerful for the sacrifice the work of the supreme bliss; they speak of [Agni] as the living son of the stone.*
>
> Rig Veda 10.20.7, tr. Sri Aurobindo,
> *Hymns to the Mystic Fire, CWSA, Volume 15*, p. 407

In Rig Veda 2.24.4, the vesica piscis is described as a well of meath (honey-wine) with a "mouth of stone".

> *The well with mouth of stone that poured a flood of meath, which Brahmapaspati hath opened with his might....*
>
> Rig Veda 2.24.4, tr. R.T.H. Griffith

In verse 10.94.8 it appears that the stones are paired with "ten conductors"[1] which in my mind indicates ten vesicae piscis paired with ten radii. In many hymns the pressing stones are plural without identifying quantity, and in others the stones are identified as two in number.

[1] Tr. R.T.H. Griffith.

Thou, Soma, hast a running stream, joyous, most strong at sacrifice: Flow bounteously bestowing wealth. Effused as cheerer of the men, flowing best gladdener, thou art a Prince to Indra with thy juice. Poured forth by pressing-stones, do thou with loud roar send us in a stream most excellent illustrious might.

Rig Veda 9.67.1-3, tr. R.T.H. Griffith

Begat the fire between two stones, the spoiler in warriors' battle, He, O men, is Indra.

Rig Veda 2.12.3, tr. R.T.H. Griffith

At first the imagery of two pressing stones did not entirely make sense to me because I did not see how two vesica piscis could be said to press out Soma together. Then I came upon Atharva Veda 10.6.15 and Rig Veda 1.28 which identified the pressing stones as a mortar and pestle, two stones which can easily be seen as a symbol of the vesica piscis and its radius.

The pestle and mortar are really the stones of the Soma press.

Atharva Veda 10.6.15, tr. R.T.H. Griffith

There where the broad-based stone raised on high to press the juices out, O Indra, drink with eager thirst the droppings which the mortar sheds.

Where, like broad hips, to hold the juice the platters of the press are laid, O Indra, drink with eager thirst the droppings which the mortar sheds.

There where the woman marks and leans the pestle's constant rise and fall, O Indra, drink with eager thirst the droppings which the mortar sheds.

Where, as with reins to guide a horse, they bind the churning-staff with cords, O Indra, drink with eager thirst the droppings which the mortar sheds.

1.28.1-4, tr. R.T.H. Griffith

In this last verse the pestle and mortar (the radius and vesica piscis) are equivalent to the churning staff and its cords, as well as the horse and its reins. In Rig Veda 1.109.3, the two pressing stones are said to be "in the bowl's lap", which seems to indicate the larger bowl of the circle, but given the way the Rishis nested, intertwined and overlapped their symbols, it could also indicate the vesica piscis.

> *[In] the bowl's lap are both the press-stones.*
>
> Rig Veda 1.109.3, tr. R.T.H. Griffith

India's ubiquitous sculptures of the Shiva Lingam resting upright on its Yoni-base appear to be symbols of the pestle and mortar and thus equivalent to the pressing stones of the Rig Veda. In this light it is clear that this symbol-form has a geometric and Vedic basis and is not solely a symbol of the union of the Divine Masculine and Feminine. These two pressing stones, like all other symbols of the Rig Veda, must be understood in the context of the twelve-month Vedic year and its sacred geometry. Otherwise they lose their real truth and power.

Lingam-Yoni (Wikimedia Commons).

Another symbol that at first puzzled me in my research on Soma and Indu was their immortal and immortalizing drop (*drapsa*). At first I was thinking of this drop, which is a common symbol in the Rig Veda, in the context of the small *bindu* (dot or point) of the circle, but later realized it is a *bigger* drop. I realized that it is yet another symbol of the vesica piscis.

> *These Soma-drops, strong Indra! drink for heroes, poured, pressed out by pressing-stones, are welling forth for thee, for thee the drops are welling forth.*
>
> Rig Veda 1.139.6, tr. R.T.H. Griffith

Forth on their way the glorious drops have flowed for maintenance of Law, [knowing] this sacrifice's course. Down in the mighty waters sinks the stream of meath, most excellent, Oblation best of all in worth.

Rig Veda 9.7.1-2, tr. R.T.H. Griffith

Still slowly and in gradual drops, O Indu, unto Indra flow.

Rig Veda 8.80.3, tr. R.T.H. Griffith

Driving the drops at our assemblies, Indu completely traverses the fleecy filter.[1]

Rig Veda 9.97.56, tr. R.T.H. Griffith

In the following verse, the drops of Soma are said to be like cows which are seated in the sacrificial grass. This grass, as already discussed, is another symbol of the vesica piscis, as is the covering robe and streaming milk.

The drops of Soma juice like cows who yield their milk have flowed forth, rich in meath, unto the Shining One, and, seated on the grass, raising their voice, assumed the milk, the covering robe where with the udders stream.

Rig Veda 9.68.1, tr. R.T.H. Griffith

In the verse below, Indra is the indwelling force, generator or Purusha of the wave and its movement which is equivalent to the hymn-song. He is said to be "gladdened" by bright drops.

Indra, thy [hymn-song] moves quickly like a joyous wave of water-floods: Bright shine the drops that gladden thee.

Rig Veda 8.14.10, tr. R.T.H. Griffith

---

[1] The wooly fleece or covering of the sheep or goat is yet another symbol of the vesica piscis in the Rig Veda, as is the cleansing filter.

Indra and the other heroes of the Rig Veda are said to be drinkers of the strengthening, immortalizing and bliss-inducing Soma drops or Soma wine.

> *[To Indra] the Soma-drinker come, for his enjoyment, these pure drops.... Thou, grown at once to perfect strength, wast born to drink the Soma juice, Strong Indra, for preeminence. O Indra, lover of the song, may these quick Somas enter thee: May they bring bliss to thee the Sage.*
>
> Rig Veda 1.5.5-7, tr. R.T.H. Griffith

> *Indra, Bṛhaspati, rainers of treasure, rejoicing at this sacrifice drink the Soma. Let the abundant drops sink deep within you: vouchsafe us riches with full store of heroes.*
>
> Rig Veda 4.50.10, tr. R.T.H. Griffith

> *This poured libation, Indra, drink, immortal, gladdening.... Streams of the bright have flowed to thee here at the seat of holy Law.*
>
> Rig Veda 1.84.4, tr. R.T.H. Griffith

> *We have drunk Soma and become immortal; we have attained the light, the Gods discovered. Now what may foeman's malice do to harm us? What, O Immortal, mortal man's deception?*
>
> Rig Veda 8.48.3, tr. R.T.H. Griffith

From all of this we can now understand that the true essence of the Soma nectar of the Rishis is not merely some mind-altering drug or drink as is often believed. Certainly such intoxicants existed in the time of the Rishis, just as did honey or milk, and all the other symbol-forms of the Rig Veda, but the deeper truth of this drink of the gods is found in the basic geometry of the yajna. It is a symbol of the vesica piscis which, together with the radius is the central key and form of the Rishis' gnosis. It is a symbol of the eternal law and form of the indwelling Soul which bestows Bliss and Immortality upon those who "drink" or know its truth.

Soma, Indu and the Crescent Moon of Shiva

Shiva in Rishikesh (Wikimedia Commons).

Both Soma and Indu are closely associated with the Moon in the Rig Veda. I initially thought that perhaps this association had something to do with the Moon's tidal effect on water; but then during the 2016 Durga festival while gazing upon the thin waxing crescent Moon in the night sky, I realized that just as Shiva's stone lingam is a symbol of the radius and upholding Purusha, the crescent Moon often placed in Shiva's hair is a symbol of the arc of the vesica piscis. Shiva, as mentioned earlier is part of the Trimurti – the triple form (*murti*) of the one God or Deva. He is linked with the guna of destruction or dissolution and is the consort of Durga the lion-riding destroyer of Ignorance. According to Indian lore, the divine river Ganges descends through the locks and tangles of Shiva's hair and carries forth the seed of his son who is said to be born on a bank of Sara reeds and thus is called *Sarabhu* (river-born). *Sara* is the basis of the name of the river goddess Saraswati as well as the name of the river-finding heroine Sarama, and is translated as "liquid", "waterfall" and "cascade", as well as "moving" or "going". It appears that the bank of Sara reeds (river reeds) wherein Shiva is reborn (and river-born) is yet another symbol of the radius and the vesica piscis portrayed by the ancient Rishis as the Child or Son of the Waters. The reeds or grasses of the river bank (*śarāsaḥ kuśarāso*) can be understood as multiple radii of the vesica piscis and zodiac.

In this Shiva mythology and in the Rig Veda we find that even the "freeing" of braided hair is used as a symbol of the freeing of the rivers and waters of divine Truth. In the Rig Veda, the Purusha's golden or braided hair flows over him like a robe and is yet another symbol of the vesica piscis.

Pour on us rain celestial, quickly streaming, refreshing, fraught with health and ready bounty. Flow, Indu, send these Winds... setting them free like locks of hair unbraided.

Rig Veda 9.97.17, tr. R.T.H. Griffith

This Soma flows like gladdening oil for him who wears the braided locks: He shall give us our share of maids.

Rig Veda 9.67.11, tr. R.T.H. Griffith

[The] Trtsus under Indra's careful guidance came speeding like loosed waters rushing downward.

Rig Veda 7.18.15, tr. R.T.H. Griffith

In this last verse it would be reasonable to suppose that the Trtsus (related to Trita) are figures of the river of the vesica piscis; but in Rig Veda 7.83.8 they are described as being "white-robed", having "braided hair", and being "skilled in song" which seems to be a portrayal of the radius or radii of the circle.

Sindhu

While researching Indu's equivalence to the god Soma and the radius, I also researched the river Sindhu.[1] It is clear enough that the river in general is a symbol of the vesica piscis in the Rig Veda, so I remain somewhat perplexed that Sindhu is sometimes depicted as a masculine figure in addition to being depicted as feminine in the translations I have been using.

This river with his lucid flow attracts you, more than all the streams, — Even ***Sindhu with his path of gold****.*

Rig Veda 8.26.18, tr. R.T.H. Griffith [bold emphasis added]

---

[1] The origin of *India* and *Hindu* is thought to be *Sindhu*, linked to *Indu*. The root of these words appears to be *indh* "to kindle, light, set on fire" (*Cologne Digital Sanskrit Lexicon*), typically referring to Agni, the flame-ray in the Rig Veda.

May the great Dragon of the Deep rejoice us: ***as one who nourishes her young comes Sindhu****, with whom we will incite the Child of Waters whom vigorous course swift as thought bring hither.*

Rig Veda 1.186.5, tr. R.T.H. Griffith [bold emphasis added]

The Rivers have come forward triply, seven and seven.[1] ***Sindhu in might surpasses all the streams that flow.*** *Varuṇa cut the channels for thy forward course, O Sindhu, when thou rannest on to win the race. Thou speedest o'er precipitous ridges of the earth, when* ***thou art Lord and Leader of these moving floods****. His roar is lifted up to heaven above the earth: he puts forth endless vigour with a flash of light. Like floods of rain that fall in thunder from the cloud, so Sindhu rushes on bellowing like a bull. Like mothers to their calves, like milch kine with their milk, so, Sindhu, unto thee the roaring rivers run. Thou leadest as a warrior king thine army's wings what time thou comest in the van of these swift streams....Flashing and whitely-gleaming in her mightiness, she moves along her ample volumes through the realms, most active of the active, Sindhu unrestrained, like to a dappled mare, beautiful, fair to see....**Sindhu hath yoked her car**, light-rolling, drawn by steeds, and with that car shall she win booty in this fight. So have I praised its power, mighty and unrestrained, of independent glory, roaring as it runs.*

Rig Veda 10.75.1-9, tr. R.T.H. Griffith [bold emphasis added]

The fact that Sindhu is said to surpass all the other rivers or streams in might in this hymn makes me think that it is a reference to the seventh wave of the vesica piscis in the zodiac. Perhaps the gender issue is akin to the fact that Soma in the Rig Veda sometimes refers to the god Soma (the radius), and sometimes to the Soma-wine (the vesica piscis). Perhaps others with a better understanding of Sanskrit can help to sort out the dual gender of Sindhu.

---

[1] This imagery is to be understood in terms of the "thrice-seven" (21 = 9 + 12) construction of the Vedic year. "Seven and seven" refers to two arcs of the vesica piscis which mark out 2/3rds of the zodiac landing at 0° Sagittarius (the 6 Point).

The Eternal Food or Manna of the Gods

I mentioned in an earlier chapter that food is another symbol of the vesica piscis. Given that food is such an important symbol and component of the Vedic sacrifice, this conclusion warrants a bit more explanation. One indication of this equivalence is that Soma wine itself is considered the food of the gods. Another indication is that just as Agni is said to be seated or dwelling in the waters of the Rig Veda, he also sits or dwells in food that does not spoil. He not only dwells in "everlasting food", he also eats it.

> *Shine forth enkindled, Radiant One [Agni]. Sit in the chamber of the Law, sit in the chamber of the food.*
>
> Rig Veda 5.21.4, tr. R.T.H. Griffith

> *Thou art a Singer, Son! our feast-companion: Agni at birth prepared his food and pathway.*
>
> Rig Veda 6.4.4, tr. R.T.H. Griffith

> *Wonderful, rich in nourishment, [Agni] dwells in food....*
>
> Rig Veda 1.141.2, tr. R.T.H. Griffith

> *In thee, O Food, is set the spirit of great Gods.*
>
> Rig Veda 1.187.6, tr. R.T.H. Griffith

> *Lords of flowing rain, dwell in the place of food.*
>
> Rig Veda 8.25.5, tr. R.T.H. Griffith

> *[Indra is borne] onward by the long-maned Steeds who stretch themselves as' twere for food....*
>
> Rig Veda 10.105.5, tr. R.T.H. Griffith

> *Each time he comes from heaven, the Pure One from of old: from ancient days the Child eats everlasting food.*
>
> Rig Veda 6.15.1, tr. R.T.H. Griffith

I am not sure how Vedic scholars have, to date, explained the odd imagery of these verses depicting Agni residing in "the chamber of food" and horses stretching themselves out as if "for food", but these oddities entirely make sense when the horse is known to be equivalent to the radius, and the food equivalent to the vesica piscis. One of Agni's many titles is "Lord of food". He generates or pours forth abundant food or sustenance.

> *[Agni] art the Sovran Lord of foodful spoil and wealth. Thou shinest brightly forth, thou burnest to bestow: pervading sacrifice, thou lendest us thine help.*
>
> Rig Veda 2.1.10, tr. R.T.H. Griffith

> *With [Surya is Agni]...lord of food that comes from kine, Controller of the gift of unempoisoned food.*
>
> Rig Veda 8.25.20, tr. R.T.H. Griffith

> *Agni, thou pourest life; send down upon us food and vigorous strength....*
>
> Rig Veda 9.66.19, tr. R.T.H. Griffith

> *O Maruts, when the sage*[1] *hath poured the Tṛṣṭup forth as food for you, Ye shine amid the mountain-clouds. When, Bright Ones, fain to show your might ye have determined on your course, the mountain-clouds have bent them down. Loud roaring with the winds the Sons of Pṛśni [the Cow] have upraised themselves: They have poured out the streaming food.*
>
> Rig Veda 8.7.1-3, tr. R.T.H. Griffith

The streaming food of Rig Veda 8.7.13 is further described as "plenteous food, sustaining all". *Trstup* is commonly considered to be a meter or rhythm of a verse, song or hymn. Here it is equivalent to food and to the vesica piscis as "poured forth" by

---

[1] This is Agni as the Sage of Sagittarius, the Water Bearer and pourer forth of the seventh "river" or vesica piscis of the zodiac.

the radius. In these next verses Agni, "who brings forth abundant food", is portrayed as a "vigorous" horse who is "Sovran of the streams", akin to the stallion of the floods in Rig Veda 5.83.6. As discussed earlier, this is Agni seated at 0° Sagittarius, the 6 Point of the circle.

> *[T]his Hero comes with rapid ears, going to Indra's special place ...[where the Immortals have their seat]. Like a good horse is he led out, when on the path that shines with light the mettled steeds exert their strength....He moves, a vigorous Steed, adorned with beauteous rays of shining gold, becoming Sovran of the streams. He, over places rough to pass, bringing rich treasures closely packed...descends into the reservoirs. Men beautify him in the vats, him worthy to be beautified, Him who brings forth abundant food. Him, even him, the fingers ten and the seven songs[1] make beautiful, well-weaponed, best of gladdeners.*
>
> Rig Veda 9.15.1-8, tr. R.T.H. Griffith

In Rig Veda 4.23, Agni's everlasting or unpoisoned food is a symbol of the Rishis' eternal law which we now know is inseparable from the sacred geometry of the Divine Purusha, Soul or radius within its own field of Time and Space.

> *Eternal Law hath varied food that strengthens; thought of eternal Law...removes transgressions. The praise-hymn of eternal Law, arousing, glowing, hath oped the deaf ears of the living. Firm-seated are eternal Law's foundations in its fair form are many splendid beauties. By holy Law long lasting food they bring us; by holy Law have cows come to our worship. Fixing eternal Law [Indra], too, upholds it swift moves the might of Law and wins the booty.*
>
> Rig Veda 4.23.8-10, tr. R.T.H. Griffith

---

[1] "Ten fingers" likely refers to ten radii. The 10th radius of the 12-month yajna establishes 0° Capricorn/Makar, the entrance into Swar, and the seven songs are the first seven vesicae piscis of the zodiac, the seventh arcing up to 0° Aquarius.

In the Bible and in the Quran, the word for this eternal food is *manna*. The root of *manna* is the Sanskrit word *anna* meaning "food". The first syllable of *manna* is *ma* meaning "to measure, mete out, mark off".[1] It now appears that the Biblical lore of manna (bread) falling from the sky or from the heavens to feed the Israelites, and of Jesus feeding thousands with a few loaves of bread and two fish, is a veiled retelling of Vedic lore, wherein the food from heaven and the fish are equivalent to the vesica piscis. It also appears that this same ancient lore is the origin of the Eucharist, wherein the sacred food and wine is thought to be equivalent to the body and blood of Christ. This Christian ritual appears to have arisen long after humanity lost sight of the Vedic gnosis in which the vesica piscis is simultaneously the food and the body of the Divine Son.

Walking on Water

The miraculous instance of Jesus walking on water directly after he feeds the masses with two fish and a few loaves of bread, can also be seen in the light of the Rishis' Divine Son – the radius – who stands upright or erect in the waters of the vesica piscis. The lore of Jesus walking on water is preceded by *Psalm 77* of the Old Testament which refers to God's "path through the sea".

> *The clouds poured down water,*
> *the heavens resounded with thunder;*
> *your arrows flashed back and forth.*
> *Your thunder was heard in the whirlwind,*
> *your lightning lit up the world;*
> *the earth trembled and quaked.*
> *Your path led through the sea,*
> *your way through the mighty waters,*
> *though your footprints were not seen.*
>
> Psalm 77:17-19, NIV

---

[1] *Cologne Sanskrit Digital Lexicon.*

The truth to be seen and acknowledge is that this Christian mythology and imagery has descended from the mythology and imagery of the Vedic Purusha (or radius) by whatever name, who is often depicted as being clothed or "robed in waters".

> *As Savitar's productive Power, as him who sends down bliss, I call Agni who clothes him[self] with the sea.*
>
> Rig Veda 8.91.6, tr. R.T.H. Griffith

> *With strength we follow [Agni-Soma]...him who [enrobed in water] brings might and wins the kin....*
>
> Rig Veda 9.16.2, tr. R.T.H. Griffith

> *Engendering the Sun in floods, engendering heaven's lights... [Agni-Soma robed] in the waters...flows purely on, a God for Gods.... He, thundering, hath produced the Gods.*
>
> Rig Veda 9.42.1-3, tr. R.T.H. Griffith

> *Robed in the flood, the Mighty One hath clad himself with milk and settled in the [Bowls].*
>
> Rig Veda 9.107.18, tr. R.T.H. Griffith

> *Forth from the middle of the flood the Waters...flow cleansing, never sleeping. Indra, the Bull, the Thunderer, dug their channels....*
>
> Rig Veda 7.49.1, tr. R.T.H. Griffith

> *The Bull who hath a thousand horns ... rises up from out the sea....*
>
> Rig Veda 7.55.7, tr. R.T.H. Griffith

> *Agni advances with his lofty banner: the Bull is bellowing to the earth and heavens. He hath attained the sky's supremest limits. The Steer hath waxen [risen] in the lap of waters.*
>
> Rig Veda 10.8.1, tr. R.T.H. Griffith

CHAPTER TWELVE

The Cow and the Horse

Paved with the rock is this our treasure-chamber; filled full of precious things, of kine, and horses.

Rig Veda 10.108.7, tr. R.T.H. Griffith

Rejoicing in the Soma-draughts, Hero [Indra], burst open, like a fort, the stall of horses and of kine.

Rig Veda 8.32.5, tr. R.T.H. Griffith

These sages, have thrown open...the stall of kine and horses.

Rig Veda 10.25.5, tr. R.T.H. Griffith

Perhaps the most pervasive theme in the Rig Veda is the finding and liberation of hidden treasure or wealth. We have seen that this includes the recovery of the lost Sun or Son, the emergence of the light and treasures of Dawn, and the recovery of lost or pent up cows or rivers. It is important to add here that frequently cows and horses are paired together as symbols of imprisoned wealth or treasures which come forward with the Dawn into the Light of Day. Sri Aurobindo understood the Vedic cows and horses to be symbols of the spiritual riches of the supramental world of Swar. It is now apparent that the Rishis' animal treasures are geometric keys and building blocks of the Vedic year. We have seen that the cow is a symbol of the vesica piscis and that the male horse or stallion is a symbol of the radius. It is true that the pairing of radius and vesica piscis is often simply a pairing of male and female, bull and cow, or stallion and mare, but given how often the Horse represents the radius in the Rig Veda, I believe that the Cow-Horse pairing can be taken as a symbol of the eternally conjoined vesica piscis and radius. Regarding the Cow and Horse, Sri Aurobindo wrote:

> *The rivers, usually named dhenavaḥ, fostering cows, are here described as* aśvāḥ, *Mares, because while* ***the Cow is the symbol of consciousness in the form of knowledge, the Horse is the symbol of consciousness in the form of force****. Ashwa, the Horse, is the dynamic force of Life, and the rivers labouring over Agni on the earth become the waters of Life, of the vital dynamis or kinesis, the Prana, which moves and acts and desires and enjoys.*
>
> Sri Aurobindo, *The Secret of the Veda, CWSA, Volume 15*, p. 119

It is easy enough to see that the vesica piscis can be accurately described as a "form of knowledge". Likewise, the radius can be accurately described as a "form of force" which lies within, upholds and compels the "form of knowledge" (the cow, the river, the wave, etc.). Sri Aurobindo's discussion of the pairing of the Cow and Horse continues:

> *[W]e find that in [Rig Veda 6.44.12, the] image of the cavern-pen in the hill, as elsewhere, the Cow and Horse go together....And always the Cow and the Horse represent a concealed and imprisoned wealth which has to be uncovered and released by a divine puissance. With the conquest of the shining herds is also associated the conquest or the birth or illumination of the Dawn and the Sun.... [A]ssociated with the Herds, the Dawn and the Sun are the Waters; for the slaying of Vritra with the release of the waters and the defeat of Vala with the release of the herds are two companion and not unconnected myths.*
>
> Sri Aurobindo, *The Secret of the Veda, CWSA, Volume 15*, p. 146

> *[T]he interpretation of the Angiras myth gives us the key to the whole secret of the Veda. For if the cows and horses lost by the Aryans and recovered for them by the gods, the cows and horses of which Indra is the lord and giver and indeed himself the Cow and Horse, are not physical cattle, if these elements of the wealth*

> *sought by the sacrifice are symbols of a spiritual riches, so also must be its other elements which are always associated with them....*
>
> Sri Aurobindo, *The Secret of the Veda, CWSA, Volume 15*, p. 245

In *The Secret of the Veda* Sri Aurobindo discussed his theory that the hymns of the Rishis are not to be taken literally, but rather, as "the symbolic gospel of the ancient Indian mystics".[1] He understood that their sense was "spiritual and psychological".[2] Discussing the difficulties of recovering the full sense of the Vedic lore and its symbols, he wrote:

> *More we cannot at present attempt; for the Vedic symbolism as worked out in the hymns is too complex in its details, too numerous in its standpoints, presents too many obscurities and difficulties to the interpreter in its shades and side allusions and above all has been too much obscured by ages of oblivion and misunderstanding to be adequately dealt with in a single work. We can only at present seek out the leading clues and lay as securely as may be the right foundations.*
>
> Sri Aurobindo, *The Secret of the Veda, CWSA, Volume 15*, pp. 246-47

It can now be better appreciated that Sri Aurobindo's "leading clues" did in fact establish the right foundation by which the complexities, obscurities and difficulties of the Rishis' symbolic language would be progressively solved. It can also now be appreciated that the Vedic symbolism of finding treasure trapped in the caves of the Rig Veda is equivalent to finding the hidden meaning or the true sense embedded and trapped in the Rishis' symbolic language for thousands of years. The constant pairing of the Cow and Horse as treasures liberated by the Vedic Heroes occurs to me as a very concise symbol of the conjoined vesica piscis and radius – the master key that unlocks and releases much of the trapped or occulted meaning of the Rig Veda.

---

[1] *CWSA, Volume 15*, p. 246.

[2] Ibid.

> *The cow and horse,* go *and* aśva, *are constantly associated. Usha, the Dawn, is described as* gomatīaśvavatī*; Dawn gives to the sacrificer horses and cows. As applied to the physical dawn* gomatī *means accompanied by or bringing the rays of light and is an image of the dawn of illumination in the human mind. Therefore* aśvavatī *also [like the cow] cannot refer merely to the physical steed; it must have a psychological significance as well. A study of the Vedic horse led me to the conclusion that* go *and* aśva *represent the two companion ideas of Light and Energy, Consciousness and Force, which to the Vedic and Vedantic mind were the double or twin aspect of all the activities of existence. It was apparent, therefore, that the two chief fruits of the Vedic sacrifice, wealth of cows and wealth of horses, were symbolic of richness of mental illumination and abundance of vital energy.*
>
> Sri Aurobindo, *The Secret of the Veda, CWSA, Volume 15*, p. 44

The Cow and the Horse in Thea's Yoga

From the early 1980s the Cow and the Horse became central figures in Thea's life and yoga. In 1986, she established the Aeon Centre of Cosmology (Skambha) in the Palani Hills where her yoga with the Cow and Horse evolved into the creation of a dairy, a cheese factory and a horse racing operation. Thea wrote that from the beginning of her interactions with the Cow and Horse, they served to demonstrate the supramental consciousness-force at play in the timing of their conceptions and births. While writing this chapter I found out that Thea's first horse was given to her on January 30, 1982 when the Sun was in the sign of Aquarius. This is fitting given what we have learned about the role the radius (or Horse) of Sagittarius plays in the liberation of the waters (and Cows) in the sign of Aquarius/Kumbha. The following passage is taken from a letter Thea wrote in 1985 explaining her involvement with the Cow and Horse to a student.

> *Because of a particular Yoga I have been doing here in Kodai, truly a Vedic yoga unknown today, the Cow and the Horse have shot into prominence in my life. The latter is the Vedic symbol of*

energy. So Light and force or energy: the Cow, and the Horse: Consciousness-Force.

In 1981 a cow was given to us.... In 1982 a horse was given! I immediately saw the connection with the Veda since the cow arrived on 30 July (in Leo) and the horse exactly six months later on 30 January. ...[This] Horse came in the sign Aquarius, or Chit (of Sat-Chit-Ananda) meaning consciousness/light. The Cow came in Leo or Tapas/force. Their roles were reversed but together they clearly formed this pole, this Consciousness/Force axis in the wheel, the twelve-month year.

I saw the Vedic meaning right away and then began our collective experience with the Horse and the Cow. That was the beginning. Thereafter all conceptions and births from this cow were unbelievably significant and 'timed'.... You realise in no way could I have 'arranged' all this.... Of course this all boggles the mind. Who is controlling it all? How can this possibly be? I explain it as the controlling power of time, based on the harmony of the Seed. But is this really an explanation? You see, there is an Intelligence here; a PURPOSE....I am only a witness engaged in the Act of Seeing. And this is the supreme purpose of the Individual.

A letter from Thea to Dr. Patricia Heidt, November 11, 1985

In 1990 when Thea established her cheese company (*Caroselle – The Gourmand's Cheese*), she wrote an article explaining why its logo featured the head of a horse and not a cow.

[T]hese symbols — Cow and Horse — go hand in hand. They can never really be separated in the language of symbols for the true Knowledge. But in India they have been separated for all practical purposes. The emasculated condition of the ancient Dharma is reflected in the fact that only the Cow is actively worshipped. The Horse (and by consequence the vir energy) is relegated to a secondary position, if at all it is given any consideration.

Thea, "Cow and Horse as Vedic Symbols",
December 23, 1990, www.aeoncentre.com

If seen as symbols of the radius and vesica piscis, the full significance of the sacred link between the Horse and the Cow becomes crystal clear. Together they unlock the occulted sense of the Rig Veda, which constitutes the dawning of the *real* sense or light of the triple Veda.

> *Dawn on us with prosperity, O Uṣas, Daughter of the Sky, Dawn with great glory, Goddess, Lady of the Light, dawn thou with riches, Bounteous One.*[1] *[Dawns], bringing steeds and kine, boon-givers of all wealth, have oft sped forth to lighten us.... Uṣas, as thou with light today hast opened the twin doors of heaven....*
>
> Rig Veda 1.42.1-2, 15, tr. R.T.H. Griffith

> *[The riches Dawn] brings with her are also a figure and certainly do not mean physical wealth. Dawn is described as* gomatī-aśvāvatī*...and since the epithets* gomatī *and* aśvāvatī *applied to her are symbolical and mean not "cowful and horsed", but radiant with illuminations of knowledge and accompanied by the swiftnesses of force.... The Dawn is the inner dawn which brings to man all the varied fullnesses of his widest being, force, consciousness, joy; it is radiant with its illuminations, it is accompanied by all possible powers and energies, it gives man the full force of vitality so that he can enjoy the infinite delight of that vaster existence....*
>
> *Thus the luminous figure of the Dawn liberates us from the material, ritual, ignorant misunderstanding of the Veda which would lead us stumbling from pitfall to pitfall in a very night of chaos and obscurity; it opens to us the closed door and admits to the heart of the Vedic knowledge.*
>
> Sri Aurobindo, *The Secret of the Veda, CWSA, Volume 15*, pp. 136-37

> *Usha is the divine Dawn, for the Sun that arises by her coming is the Sun of the superconscient Truth; the day he brings is the day of the true life in the true knowledge, the night he dispels is the*

---

[1] As already discussed, the Dawn (and the Dawn goddess Usha or Uṣas), is a symbol of the vesica piscis. In Rig Veda 6.64.1 the Dawns are said to be like "waves of water" (tr. R.T.H. Griffith).

night of the ignorance which yet conceals the dawn in its bosom. Usha herself is the Truth, sūnṛtā, *and the mother of Truths. These truths of the divine Dawn are called her cows, her shining herds; while the forces of the Truth that accompany them and occupy the Life are called her horses. Around this symbol of the cows and horses much of the Vedic symbolism turns; for these are the chief elements of the riches sought by man from the gods. The cows of the Dawn have been stolen and concealed by the demons, the lords of darkness in their nether cave of the secret subconscient. They are the illuminations of knowledge, the thoughts of the Truth,* gāvo matayaḥ, *which have to be delivered out of their imprisonment. Their release is the upsurging of the powers of the divine Dawn.*

Sri Aurobindo, *The Secret of the Veda, CWSA, Volume 15*, p. 244

CHAPTER THIRTEEN

Recovering the Divine Hero

[T]he good which Agni…is to create for the human soul, giver of the sacrifice, is that divine Truth now withheld from man, the hidden light, the lost Sun….

Sri Aurobindo, *Hymns to the Mystic Fire, CWSA, Volume 16*, p. 548

[May Agni] found in us the perfect hero-might and the perfect power of the Horse.

Rig Veda 5.6.10, tr. Sri Aurobindo, Ibid., p. 267

[T]he son born to us is clearly an image of some inner birth: Agni himself is our son, the child of our works, the child who as the Universal Fire is the father of his fathers….

Sri Aurobindo, Ibid., p. 15

By truth the divine, immortal and undammed rivers with their streams of honey, O Agni, as a horse that sets its breast against the wind when loosed to its gallopings, so have ever & always [the rivers] grown in mass for the flowing.

Rig Veda 4.3.12, tr. Sri Aurobindo, Ibid., pp. 657-58

The seven rivers, the mighty ones of heaven, the waters that have knowledge, the waters of Swar are also [Agni's] mothers.

Sri Aurobindo, Ibid., p. 690

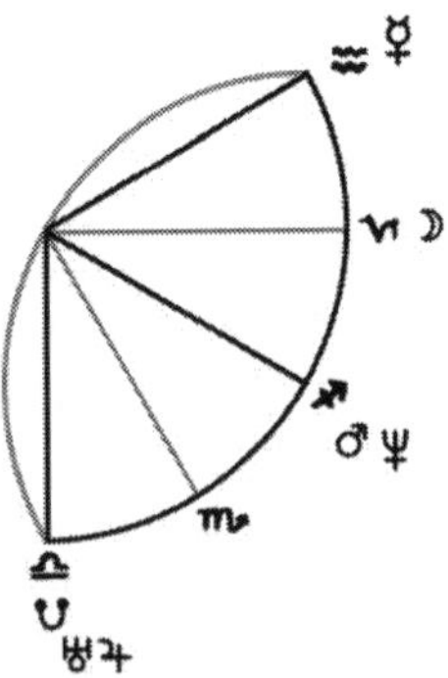

After seeing the geometry of the seventh river of the Rig Veda, it occurred to me that this geometry is embedded in my natal chart. This "river" of the zodiac is anchored by my South Node (Ketu) at 0° Libra (conjunct my natal Uranus and Jupiter) and arcs up to my natal Mercury at 0° Aquarius.[1] My natal Mars and Neptune sit conjunct the 0° Sagittarius fulcrum point of this vesica piscis – the 6 Point of the circle of 9. The planet Mars is named after the Greek war-god or hero, equivalent to Agni. As already discussed this 6 Point at 0° Sagittarius is Agni's victorious birth as the War Horse, Horse-Man or Horse-riding hero of the Vedic yajna. Agni's victory here can be understood as the liberation of the Masculine principle, or the energy of Mars, from the division, destruction, death, delusion and abuse which thrives in the realm of Scorpio. This liberation is the birth of the Soul's truth-consciousness in the last triad of the Hero's journey, yajna or yoga, enabling passage into the higher realm of Swar.[2] Seeing the Sagittarian axis or skambha of the seventh river of the zodiac in conjunction with my natal Mars and Neptune positioned in late Scorpio helped me better appreciate the collapse and loss of my father, the central hero-figure in my young life. Losing him set me on the Vedic path of bringing forth the lost hero, hidden sun, skambha or soul of my own being before I knew such a path existed.

I have already written some about this crucial 6 Point of our evolutionary journey in "The Crux of Time". Essentially it is the point in our development wherein the contractions and pressures on our Being either result in the birth or crystallization of a higher

---

1 The planet Mercury is known as the "Messenger of the Gods" and the South Node (Ketu) as the "Dragon's Tail" which rules the number 7 in Indian numerology. Ketu and Jupiter "the Guru" are both associated with spiritual wisdom and illumination and Uranus "the Sky God" is the 7th planet and a ruler of Aquarius.

2 In my chart, the passage into the Swar realm or 4th quadrant of the zodiac is marked by my natal Moon sitting in the first degrees of Capricorn.

axis or center of being that serves as a base for new growth and exploration of new territory, or in the unfortunate crystallization of our Ignorance, which can only result in collapse, reversion, escape, self-sabotage or death. Regarding the establishment of a stable center, axis or skambha, Thea wrote:

> *There is no way in which a new society can truly be formed while the ego exerts its pull and draws energy from the real Core, the central Sun, the seat of Divine Purpose.*
>
> *At the centre of the gnostic being this Sun must be unveiled. Its power is sufficient to organise all parts of the being around itself even in difficult times of transition such as the present, times of the great Birth....[T]he existence of the unveiled Sun works as a magnet compelling the rebellious parts to ultimately loosen their hold and join their energies for the integration of the Whole.*

Thea, *The New Way, Volume 3*, p. 374

> *In the Rig Veda the axis that is formed [via simultaneous Expansion and Contraction] is known as Skambha, the cosmic Pillar, support of the worlds and the fulcrum of creation. Panikkar defines it in the Glossary to his book, The Vedic Experience, as 'The cosmic pillar, understood to be the stable center of the universe (axis mundi) and its hidden support.'*
>
> *Being creation's 'centre' this axis or skambha supports movement, essential to all consolidated bodies in this universe whose essence is perforce movement. In point of fact, it would be the first stirrings within that original 'something' that ultimately creates an axis which in turn becomes the binding energy of that particular body. The ancients on the subcontinent called that first stirring OM – the primordial sound at the Origin and which reverberates endlessly in the great diversity that is the universal manifestation.*

Thea, 'The Great Divide - Part II,
Puranic Cosmology Updated, November 17, 2009

> *[T]he ancients in the subcontinent focussed on the method to bring the human being to the point where he or she could join the cosmic*

symphony in full awareness of its overall Harmony embracing both the vast and the small in a sublime experience of Oneness....

...[That point] is attained through centering of the consciousness on the axis of being that comes through a perfect balance in time and space. In that innermost dimension the truths of the cosmos are unveiled through the lived experience, as the Rig Vedic Hymn of Origins reveals.

Thea, 'The Great Divide - Part II, *Puranic Cosmology Updated*, November 17, 2009

A forging of an axis of this sort, balancing change and stability, is the means by which an integrated new creation, expressing itself individually and collectively, can come about and hasten the establishment on Earth of the life divine.

Thea, "Change and Stability — the heart of the 'New World'", *The Vishaal Newsletter, Volume 1.4*, October 1986

Vishnu as Kurma supporting Mount Mandara and sitting in lotus position. 17th century (Wikimedia Commons, via www.BritishMuseum.com).

The reestablishment of this axis and the finding of the lost or hidden Sun, Son or flame of Agni is one and the same victory. In the mythology of the Samudra Manthan, this is the emergence and victory of Vishnu as the flying seven-headed divine white horse Uchchaihshravas or as the divine physician Dhanvantari from the waters in which he was hidden.[1] It is simultaneously the realization of the skambha or pillar of creation that is the heart and binding force of the myth. It is the realization of the Eternal Law and Divine Maya of our Soul which opens the divine doors and propels us into to the supramental

[1] Like the seven-headed horse, Dhanvantari the Divine Physician is a symbol-figure of Sagittarius. He emerges from the waters with a pot (kumbha) of amrita (the nectar of immortality) in his hands. The seven heads of the horse correspond to the seven radii of the seven vesicae piscis (seven rivers).

realms and heights of our evolutionary journey. This axis or center is born from the womb of Time and Space via the painful contractions (generated by our own Ignorance) which precede or accompany the 6 Point of the yajna. Once one passes through this death-birth experience, Time is henceforth experienced as an extension of the Soul's consciousness-force. Thea wrote that the 6 Point of the yajna and its corresponding planet Saturn represent "the forged psychic being on its voyage homeward."[1] In the Rig Veda this return homeward is depicted as the horse or horses galloping to the gods and to the divine goal, or in other words, into the fourth quadrant of the zodiac (Swar).

> *Increasing by his strengths, rejoicing in his illuminations [Agni] goes a swift galloper towards the gods....*
>
> *Thou in whom all the Riches meet together in the plenitude like horses by their gallopings in their speed towards the goal*
>
> Rig Veda 10.6.4, 6 tr. Sri Aurobindo, *Hymns to the Mystic Fire, CWSA, Volume 16*, p. 397

Without forging this axis or realizing the divine law of our soul we remain uncentered and thus unable to hold our seat on the galloping horse of Time. We are unable to fully understand, integrate and let go of the dead weight, obsolete structures and baggage of our past which prevent us from completing the voyage "homeward" towards our divine self-knowledge and self-expression. Along these lines, Thea wrote:

> *[P]assage through the sign of Scorpio would ideally bring about the death of that which served as a pedestal to the growth but which has no place in the higher evolution of man. In a word, when there is ego during the passage through Scorpio, the individual must become liberated from some of the 'excess baggage', otherwise it is not possible to advance further. In that case the being remains caught in the wheel of eternal rebirth in ignorance, stoping in his development in Scorpio, much as we have described*

[1] Thea, *The Gnostic Circle*, p. 222.

in the case of Tibet and its painful efforts to go beyond and meet the orbit of Saturn [the 6 Point] in a cleansed condition. To experience the higher sphere it is impossible to carry the seeds of the old consciousness into that realm. The gnostic being who has the realisation of immortality has experienced the true meaning of Scorpio, which is to have died to a certain sheath of ourselves, to have become rid of the protective sack of the Mother and to have the psyche come forward and become the beacon of light during the further process. For this individual the symbol of Scorpio has become the Eagle, a transmutation[1] *which merely means that he has realized his immortality and become rid of that which is death, the illusion of his ego.*

In Scorpio all that which is no longer of use falls away, the truth alone remains [in Sagittarius]. Scorpio is...the plunge through the void of death into the fire of life of Sagittarius, the very process the entire races of Earth are actually living through in this 9th Manifestation. Most of humanity has never lived through such a birth.

Thea, *The Gnostic Circle*, pp. 224-25

The sign of Sagittarius can never be understood unless one passes through the experience of Death; the Knowledge that is acquired in the ninth stage of one's development, as expressed in the sign of Sagittarius, is precisely a Knowledge which 'comes from the other side' – what is to us the other side, to move into the realm of the Immortals and from there receive the higher light. The eighth sign is the Abyss, the plunge into the darkness, the death. From this state there is the opposite movement that is experienced, the soaring into the light of the spirit, the ninth stage.

Thea, *The Gnostic Circle*, p. 45

Scorpio is the sign of Death in traditional astrology. It was the same in the Vedic Age, ample proof of which is given in the reference to Martanda, the eighth son of Aditi, the 'fallen star', whose very name comes from the root meaning death.

---

[1] This is a "transmutation" of Scorpio (i.e. of Mars energy) from the lower symbol of the Scorpion, a lowly and deadly creature, to the high-flying Eagle with its far-reaching range of movement and vision.

If the energy of Mars is not transmuted or released (the 'release' of the cow/rays), death meant the obliteration of the consciousness and disconnection with the physical plane. It meant that the 'victory' in the 10th month of Capricorn, traditionally known as the exaltation of Mars, could not be achieved on Earth and connected to its evolutionary processes, but only in 'heaven'. The decline of the Dharma saw this drama enacted in full, with spiritual energies posited in that 'heaven' beyond and withheld from a process which alone could unify and conquer on Earth.

On the other hand, when the Mars transmutation occurred and the Sacrifice was 'pleasing', the energy was released which provided fuel for the rise to the mountaintop or the sign/month Capricorn.... Interestingly, at that point Agni became the Horse, the white steed – indeed, horse-power. This was indicated by the 9th sign sandwiched between Scorpio and Capricorn: Sagittarius, precisely the sign of the Horse....

We may...locate this process of transmutation, of conquering, in the third segment of the Circle.... [I]t may be recalled that an aspect of Agni is the Hindu War God Kartikeya. His birthday is celebrated...[in] late November, or with the correct 0 point, in the sign/month Sagittarius. In Sanskrit the month is known as Kartik.

Thea, "Culture and Cosmos", *The Vishaal Newsletter, Volume 6.4*, October 1991

The Rishi of Rig Veda 6.2 portrayed the Purusha of Sagittarius as "the all-seeing Horse that crosses the mid-world", enabling Man at this 6 Point in the journey to move "beyond the foe and the sin and the stumbling".

Men who see aspire to thee [Agni] with the word and the sacrifice. To thee comes the all-seeing Horse that crosses the mid-world,[1] the Horse that no wolf tears....

Now art thou here in men, one to be aspired to and a beloved guest; for thou art like one delightful and adorable in the city and as if our son and a traveller of the triple world.[2]

---

[1] Griffith, translated this as the Courser who "comes speeding through the air".

[2] I.e., the Swar realm of Capricorn, Aquarius and Pisces. Sri Aurobindo described this triple world as "those highest steps or seats (*padāni*, *sadāṃsi*) of Agni, of

O Fire, thou art driven by the will in our gated house like a horse apt for our work; thou art by thy nature like a farspreading mansion and like a galloper of winding ways and a little child....

O Fire, O friendly Light, O Godhead, turn to the Godheads, mayst thou speak for us the true thought of Earth and Heaven; move to the peace and the happy abode and the men of Heaven. Let us pass beyond the foe and the sin and the stumbling; let us pass beyond these things, pass in thy keeping through them safe.

Rig Veda 6.2.2-11, tr. Sri Aurobindo, *Hymns to the Mystic Fire*, *CWSA, Volume 16*, pp. 56-58

The realization of this pillar or the War Horse of one's Being is a victory over and a passage beyond the narrow limits of one's mortal, mental consciousness. It is the establishment of a consciousness of Immortality in one's being. It is the victory of Agni "born Immortal" or "Yama's deathless birth"[1].

Unveiling of the fourth element [Agni-the divine son][2] carries the experience of harmony to its fullest heights because it alone has the power to clearly define and set each part of creation in its true place within the whole. Indeed, this act is precisely what engenders the process of crystalisation, making this new creation indestructible and real. More may be said: When the truly Integral is known it is only then that we can speak of actual creation. Until then, all is impermanent and a play in preparation of the great Birth.

Thea, *The New Way, Volume 3*, p. 137

In my life this realization or birth of my soul's truth was catalyzed and crystalized (made impervious) by the download of gnosis I

Vishnu" (*CWSA, Volume 15*, p. 118), and as "the triple world of Sachchidananda which we desire as the goal of this long journey, this great upward movement. It is thither that the many-horned herds of the conscious Thought, the conscious Force are moving—that is the goal, that is their resting-place" (Ibid., p. 350).

[1] From Rig Veda 9.108.12 and 10.83.5, tr. R.T.H. Griffith.

[2] The fourth element is the Son of the Father-Mother-Daughter trinity, or the 1 of the 9-6-3 trinity. It is Agni's birth as the Horse, the triadic and 9-fold One.

received regarding the seventh river of the zodiac. This download and birth was perfectly synchronized with the week of Thea's passing at the 6 Point of my 47th year. From that point on, I felt propelled into an entirely new level of seeing and understanding of the work I had been engaged in for twenty-plus years. Doors of perception that had been tightly closed, simply opened and it was time to find and to see what I was meant to find and see. The final piece of this birth or birth process came on November 7, 2016[1] when I understood that the radius or Horse of Sagittarius upholds the victorious seventh river or wave of the Rishis. From that point on I felt the solidness or realness of the upholding pillar, skambha or Immortal Purusha of my own being.

It was a dramatic and irreversible shift in my consciousness. Thereupon vanished the unconscious and hard to admit desire for *someone else* to show up as the hero and set things right in my being or in the world. This desire was hard to admit because I have faithfully subscribed to a self-reliant, "be your own hero" approach to life. Nonetheless, it was still there due to the fact that I had not been entirely connected to my higher truth. I simply figured it would be *someone else* who came forward with the goods or treasures, winning the proverbial day. In other words, this unconscious desire for a savior was based on an unconscious assumption of self-deficiency. When the geometric and zodiacal key of the Vedic rivers and the "Stallion of the Floods" came forward in my consciousness, this underlying sense of deficiency was simultaneously exposed and dismantled.

This experience of birthing forth my inner War Horse or Stallion of the Floods reminded me of a dream I had had seven years earlier in the month of Sagittarius on November 28th, 2009. In the dream, I was on a hike and came across a black stallion in the woods who was three times the normal size of a horse. I stood still as he approached me. After looking down at me, he lowered his head and lightly nipped my shoulder. I got over my fear and put my arms around his neck and planted my cheek on his face and mane. After this blissful hug, he reared up to his full height,

[1] Nine months after the book began to descend.

upon which I woke out of the dream. I had the impression in the dream that he was the king of Horses or the essential Horse, full of wildness, strength, power, beauty, intuition and sensitivity.

Reaching this point of fortification in my journey in November of 2016, wherein the full truth of this Horse figure became apparent, did feel like finding a hidden Sun, lost pillar, or lost internal support of my being around which the movement of my entire life was perfectly organized and perfectly centered. It reminded of something the Palm Leaf reader in Bangalore had told me in 2000. In addition to saying I would solve a great problem for the world, he also said that my power would come at the age of 45. I had no idea at the time what he meant, or if his seeing into the future would bear true in any way shape or form. As it turns out, he was two years off and my "power" and the problem I was to solve involved recovering the vesica piscis as a master key of the Rig Veda, thereby releasing its many pent up treasures and "rivers of truth" upon the world, including the truth of Agni's (the Son's) hiding place in the waters. I was truly amazed by this unfolding, which was beyond anything my mind could have imagined regarding the great problem I was supposed to solve. I will close this chapter with some passages from Sri Aurobindo and Thea's writings, as well as from the Rig Veda, which underscore the essence of this recovery of the Vedic waters and their Hidden Child. It is the recovery of the sacred geometry or Divine Maya of the Soul.

> *[Agni] is the hidden one Guha, said to be concealed in the Earth*[1] *and the Waters. Time and time again the Vedas speak to us of this sacred Flame Child who is found at the secret core.*
>
> Thea, *The New Way, Volumes 1&2*, pp. 479-80

> *[T]he Veda speaks of the seven Mighty Ones [Rivers] of Heaven who flow down from Heaven; they are waters that know, knowers*

---

[1] In the pairing of Heaven and Earth (the Rodasi), Heaven is the circle and Earth is the vesica piscis (the "daughter" of the circle). Both are depicted as Agni's mothers.

of the Truth — ṛtajña — and when they are released they discover for us the road to the great Heavens.

Sri Aurobindo, *Hymns to the Mystic Fire, CWSA, Volume 16*, p. 16

Mayst thou, O Agni, about our Word for thy pivot bring to light for us Heaven & Earth and the rivers that are self-revealed....

Rig Veda 1.140.13, tr. Sri Aurobindo,
Hymns to the Mystic Fire, CWSA, Volume 16, p. 602

[Agni] in the growths of earth holds up his greatness, both the progeny born and what is in the mothers; he is Knowledge in the house of the Waters, and life universal; the thinkers have measured and constructed him like a mansion.

Rig Veda 1.67.5, tr. Sri Aurobindo,
Hymns to the Mystic Fire, CWSA, Volume 16, pp. 96-97

Agni, the divine force, is able to pour out these liberated rivers of being, these showers of richness & sweetness, because he manifests himself in man with the inborn knowledge of the divine Purusha and the secret hold from which he pours out this sevenfold stream of the workings of Prakriti with all its riches.

Sri Aurobindo, *Hymns to the Mystic Fire,*
CWSA, Volume 16, p. 623

The heights of heaven were measured into form by the eye of this universal Force,[1] *they were shaped by the intuition of the Immortal. All the worlds are upon his head; the seven far-flowing rivers climbed from him like branches.*

Rig Veda 6.7.6, tr. Sri Aurobindo,
Hymns to the Mystic Fire, CWSA, Volume 16, p. 67

Agni was born first and supreme in the Rivers, in the foundation of the vast mid-world....

---

[1] This "eye" that measures or brings the heights of heaven into form is the vesica piscis. The "universal Force" and "the Immortal" are references to Agni – the immortal flame, ray or radius.

He came forth with a vibrancy of light, the first and supreme force, in the native seat of Truth, in the lair of the Bull,[1] *desirable and young and beautiful of body and wide in lustre; the seven Beloved brought [to birth the Bull].*

Rig Veda 4.1.11-12, tr. Sri Aurobindo,
Hymns to the Mystic Fire, CWSA, Volume 16, p. 216

Fire is the sevenfold [Manusha],[2] *he is lodged in all the rivers; to him we have come, the dweller in the triple abode, the Fire of the thinker, slayer of the Destroyers, ancient and supreme in the sacrifices....*

Rig Veda 8.39.8, tr. Sri Aurobindo,
Hymns to the Mystic Fire, CWSA, Volume 16, p. 347

---

[1] Agni in this hymn is the Bull. His lair and his birthplace "in the Rivers" are symbols of the vesica piscis.

[2] Sri Aurobindo's translation of *sapta manusha* in this verse was "sevenfold human". *Manusha* is comprised of the root words or names *Manu* and *Usha*, indicating the Divine Son awake within the Divine Dawn. *Sapta manusha* is a reference or name of Agni, the Hero-Son born out at 0° Sagittarius in the sacred year. He is the seventh radius of the seventh vesica piscis of the zodiac.

CHAPTER FOURTEEN

The River and the Maid of the Mist

As I uncovered the truth of the Seven Rivers and their release from the Kumbha of Aquarius I felt a deeper level of appreciation for many of my life circumstances. I especially felt a deeper appreciation for the presence of the river in my life. My first address was 900 Monongalia Avenue named after the Monongahela River which ran northward along the western edge of Morgantown, West Virginia where I was born. When I was 1.5 years old my family moved to Newport News, Virginia, whose western border was the James River. Our first house there was on River Road, sitting at the confluence of three roads and across the street from the river. In December of 1972 my family moved to a house directly on the James River. The river was four or five miles wide where we lived and was a huge presence, feature and playground of my young life. It was also the foreground of spectacular sunsets and moonsets which deeply affected me growing up. I drew the moonset picture above from memory of the view from my bedroom window.

While contemplating the importance of the river in my life, I recalled a camping trip my father took my brothers and I on to the High Falls of the Cheat River in West Virginia. I happened to be 7 years old at the time. We spent much of this multi-day trip playing in the river which was a natural water park. We repeatedly walked upstream and floated downstream. During one such float I found myself in a fast current about to careen over the edge of the High Falls which to me at the time seemed like certain death. Seconds before plunging over I got sucked into an eddy which safely deposited me onto the river bank. The High Falls of the Cheat River are only 15 feet high and I most likely would have been fine if I had gone over, but the distinct and memorable feeling or impression I took away from that experience was that *something* protected me. Just after it happened I remember thinking for the first time that perhaps God was real. I also remember that the bathing suit I wore on that trip featured a realistic print of a Lion on the front and that our German Shepherd Thor[1] was with us.

As I was writing about the significance of the Seven Rivers and the number 7 in the Fall of 2016 I wondered what the Sun's transit to 10° Capricorn – the 7 Point of the 2016/2017 Solar Year – would bring. Usually this point falls on New Year's Day, but due to the leap year, it fell on New Year's Eve. That evening my mother sent me a video of the massive Iguazu Falls of South America for no other reason than she thought the falls were beautiful. The image reminded me that she conceived me at Niagara Falls which for whatever reason I had not previously included in my contemplations of the importance of the river in my life. I then began to research Niagara Falls which refers to the triple falls of the Niagara River. I found that the etymology of Niagara hails from a Native American tribe known as the Ongiaras. This name is said to mean "straight" as well as "the thunder of the waters". I thereupon realized that the Ongiaras tribe and Niagara River and its Falls, are etymologically linked to the Angiras Rishis of the Rig Veda. [2]

Angiras is a name of Agni[3] and the Angirases (or Angiras Rishis) are the Seven Rishis of the Rig Veda who assist in Indra's victorious release of the sacred rivers or cows. Agni and Indra (two names of the same Hero-Purusha) are both thunder gods

---

[1] For whatever reasons, my parents had named our dog Thor (after the Norse-Thunder God) and our cat Lightning.

[2] I don't believe anyone else has recognized this connection.

[3] Sri Aurobindo, *The Secret of the Veda, CWSA, Volume 15*, p. 161.

armed with the thunderbolt[1] or with strong thunder[2]. This victorious Purusha, sometimes referred to as Indra-Agni (*Indragni*), breaks open the "cave" to release the waters of truth and clarity from their restraints.

> *[Indra-Agni] oped with sideway opening the sea with its foundations seven — Indra all powerful in his might.... By [Indra-Agni's] hest, flowing away, the rivers, run which they released from their restraint.... Inspire him with your holy hymns, the Hero bright and glorious, Him who with might demolisheth even the brood of Śuṣṇa,*[3] *and winneth for us the heavenly streams. Inspire him worshipped with fair rites, the glorious Hero truly brave. He [broke] in pieces Śuṣṇa's brood who still expected not the stroke, and won for us the heavenly streams. Let all the others die away. Thus have we sung anew to Indra-Agni, as sang our sires, Aṅgirases, and Mandhātar. Guard us with triple shelter and preserve us: may we be masters of a store of riches.*
>
> Rig Veda 8.40.5-12, tr. R.T.H. Griffith

This winning of the heavenly streams or rivers which are also known as cows, is inseparable from the recovery of the lost Sun or Son who is hidden in these waters or cows.

> *[The] release [of the cows/rivers] is the upsurging of the powers of the divine Dawn. It is also the recovery of the Sun that was lying in the darkness; for it is said that the Sun, "that Truth", was the thing found by Indra and the Angirases in the cave of the Panis. By the rending of that cave the herds of the divine dawn which are the rays of the Sun of Truth ascend the hill of being and the Sun itself ascends to the luminous upper ocean of the divine existence, led over it by the thinkers like a ship over the waters, till it reaches its farther shore.*
>
> Sri Aurobindo, *The Secret of the Veda, CWSA, Volume 15*, p. 244

---

[1] Rig Veda 6.59.3, tr. R.T.H. Griffith.

[2] Rig Veda 7.93.4, tr. R.T.H. Griffith.

[3] Śuṣṇa (Shushna/Shesha) is a serpent-demon, akin to Vritra and Ahi.

On New Year's Day 2017, I woke up wondering if there was any mythology associated with Niagara Falls, and promptly found "The Maid of the Mist" myth.

> *[The Maid of the Mist] lost her husband and her hope at a young age, and the beautiful girl could not find her way through the sorrow upon sorrow that was her lot in life. So she stepped one day into her canoe, singing a death song softly to herself, and paddled out into the current. Soon the canoe was caught by the rough waves and hurtled toward the falls. But as it pitched over and she fell, Heno, the god of thunder who lived in the falls, caught the maiden gently in his arms and carried her to his home beneath the thundering veil of water.*
>
> *Heno and his sons ministered to the grieving girl, and she stayed with them until her heart healed within her. Then the younger son spoke words of love to the maiden and they married, to the delight of the god of thunder. A young son was born to the couple, and he followed his grandfather everywhere, learning what it meant to be a god of thunder.*
>
> *The only shadow on the happiness of the maiden in the mist was a continual longing to see her people one more time. Her chance came in an unexpected and unwelcome way. A great snake came down the mighty river and poisoned the waters of her people.…Heno heard the voice of the serpent and rose up through the mist of the falls. He threw a great thunderbolt at the creature and killed it in one mighty blast. The giant body of the creature floated downstream and lodged just above the cataract, creating a large semi-circle that deflected huge amounts of water into the falls at the place just above the god's home.…To this day, an echo of the Heno's voice can be heard in the thunder of the mighty waters of Niagara Falls.*
>
> S.E. Schlosser, *Spooky New York*, © 2005, Globe Pequot Press

This Native American myth made my jaw drop because it is basically a version of the Vedic mythology of Indra the Thunder-God who kills the serpent (or dragon) Vritra with his lightning bolt and frees the rivers. It also mirrors the Vedic mythology of Agni – the Divine Son who is hidden in waters which are often described as maids and mists. I had already learned that both the maid and the mists in the Rig Veda are equally symbols of the vesica piscis. The hero and his sons in the Ongiaras' Niagara myth live in the veil or mists of the waters, just as the thunder god Agni lies hidden in the veil and mists of the Vedic waters.

Ceaselessly [the divine Waters] flow from the depths, pure, never sleeping, the Ocean their sponsor, following the channels ordainded by the Thunderer. Now may these waters quicken me! ...In the midst of the Waters is moving the Lord, surveying men's truth and men's lies. How sweet are the Waters, crystal clear and cleansing. How may these great divine Waters quicken me.

Rig Veda 7.49.1- 3, tr. Raimundo Panikkar, *The Vedic Experience*, p. 119

These who delight in flowing juice...Indra and Agni, Gods armed with the thunderbolt, we call this day to come with help.... [T]he Maid [hath] come footless unto those with feet.

Rig Veda 6.59.3-6, tr. R.T.H. Griffith

The never-sullen waters, youthful Maidens, carefully decking, wait on him the youthful. He with bright rays shines forth in splendid beauty, unfed with wood, in waters, oil-enveloped.

Rig Veda 2.35.4, tr. R.T.H. Griffith

The well thou clavest, settest free the fountains, and gavest rest to floods that were obstructed. Thou, Indra, laying the great mountain open, slaying the [Demons], didst loose the torrents. ...Strong Indra, thou by slaying e'en the Dragon that lay extended there hast shown thy vigour....[Agni] child of the mist, strong waxing, couched in darkness, Him the bolt-hurling Thunderer with his lightning smote down and slew [the serpent Shushna].

Rig Veda 5.32.1-4, tr. R.T.H. Griffith

Mortals we have chosen thee, a god, for our comrade to protect us, [Agni] the Child of the Waters, full of happiness and light, victorious, to whom no hurt can come....

When he has passed beyond the forces that make to err, beyond those that cling perpetual, the long-lasting who have no hurt have followed and found him like a lion who has taken refuge in the Waters.

Rig Veda 3.9.1, 4, tr. Sri Aurobindo,
Hymns to the Mystic Fire, CWSA, Volume 16, pp. 178-79

The Maiden's name in the Niagara myth is said to be Lelawala, which could easily be a derivative of the Sanskrit words *lila* (*leela*) indicating the play or Maya of the Divine Purusha, and *vala* indicating a veil or enclosure. In my thirties I read a book by Gene D. Matlock titled *India Once Ruled the Americas!*, which posited the idea that "The Native-Americans Are Indians After All!" Matlock wrote, "The One and Only Reason Why We Don't Know About India's True Role in Human History Is Our Self-Imposed Ignorance of Indian Mythology, History and Traditions!"[1] I have seen evidence for the truth of this statement in my research and studies over the years, but the etymological similarity between Ongiaras and Angiras and the mythological similarity between the "Maid of the Mist" story and the lore of the Rig Veda stand out to me as particularly convincing evidence that Vedic culture was long ago established in at least certain parts of the Americas.

I was amazed to find the equivalence of the Niagara Falls mythology and Vedic mythology some 48 years after I was conceived there; and I was equally amazed that the Maid of the Mist story somewhat mirrored my experience in 1976 when I was narrowly saved from plunging over the High Falls of the Cheat River. The story of the sad maid also reminded me of the heartbreak of losing my father and then being pulled into a higher perspective and experience of life via Sri Aurobindo's influence, and finding my home so to speak, in the realm of his vast consciousness. I could see that the various details of that river trip, including my age at the time, my Lion bathing suit and the presence of our dog Thor, made a seamless tapestry of interwoven

---

[1] Gene D. Matlock, *India Once Ruled the Americas* (2000), p. 170.

symbols that would make their meaning known much later in my life, in the context of the Vedic river and its veiled hero who is depicted both as a roaring lion and as a thunder-god.

After looking up the mythology of the Niagara River, I looked up the mythology of the Monongahela River whereupon I was born. After reading Matlock's book, I began to wonder if the name of the Monongahela River and tribe was taken from Menaka (a.k.a. Mena), the wife of the mountain god Himvat. What I didn't know at the time was that Menaka is a water goddess (*Apsara*) who, as it turns out, is a symbol-figure of the vesica piscis. Oddly enough there is a Meneka Peak in Virginia, nine miles from a town called Seven Fountains. The only mythology I could find associated with the Monongahela River was the lore of two monsters – a Fish-Man (*Monongy*) and a giant Turtle (*Ogua*). Amazingly enough these two monsters happen to be symbols of Vishnu's first and second avatars who save creation from apocalyptic floods, as discussed earlier in this book. The root of Monongahela, Monongy and Menaka could be the Sanskrit word *mana* meaning, among other things, "a measure"[1].

In my experience, all of this converging history, etymology and mythology is yet another demonstration of how the Soul controls its own field of Time and Space, unfolding its multifaceted, multidimensional and Supramental Being with a continuity and coherency of purpose of which the human mind is for the most part unaware.

---

[1] *Cologne Sanskrit Digital Lexicon.*

CHAPTER FIFTEEN

The Passing of the Mantle

Another example of this experience of supramental convergence and coherency in my life involves an intriguing dream I had on June 8, 2014, nearing the one-third mark of my 45th year. In the dream, I was walking northward along a vast beach, hand in hand with a young boy. At first the beach seemed entirely deserted and then we came upon Jesus walking in the opposite direction. Without saying a word, Jesus took off his white robe (in need of a wash), gave it to me and walked away. The boy then asked if this exchange meant I would carry on with Jesus's teachings. I took this to imply carrying on Christian teachings and replied, "No, he gave the robe to ME." I was certain that if he wanted someone to carry on the Christian religion, he would not have given the robe to me, someone who looks forward to the day when the limiting dogma of the Christian religion, together with the limiting dogma of all religions, promptly gives way to real and all-unifying gnosis throughout the world.

This dream came ten days after arriving home from a four-month trip to India. I spent the first month of this trip in Pondicherry where I celebrated my 45th birthday and assisted Thea with an exhibition she put together, entitled *The Future Realisation*. The exhibition honored and displayed the sacred geometry and Vedic gnosis of the Mother's original temple vision which was irrevocably misconstrued in Auroville. Assisting with this exhibition felt like the perfect way to begin the 45th year and 6th ennead of my life (45-54), leaving behind the previous ennead, seven years of which I was ill with Lyme Disease. I felt deeply fortunate to be well enough to travel to India and to collaborate with Thea in Pondicherry fourteen years after my experience in the Sri Aurobindo Ashram visitor center regarding the third level of the Supramental Descent. In March of 2014 I returned to Thea's center (Skambha) near Kodaikanal and assisted with various projects. In late April it became apparent that Thea's untreated cancer needed medical intervention and I became part of her support team at a hospital in Madurai. Due to an expiring Indian visa I had to say goodbye to Thea the day after she had major surgery. Although she had survived the surgery, it was entirely uncertain how well she would recover and how much extra time on planet Earth the surgery would allow her.

In June of 2014 the Jesus dream simply occurred to me as a metaphor for trusting my own being, my own heart, my own wisdom and my own journey. At the time I had absolutely zero inkling of the symbolism or even the presence of the robe in the Rig Veda. Two years later, upon the week of Thea's passing, I came to understand that the waters of the Rig Veda which cloak, veil or *enrobe* the Divine Son Agni are equivalent to the vesica piscis. Throughout the seven-month span between February and September of 2016, I had already seen the radius and the vesica piscis as keys of certain Indian mythologies, including Vishnu's avatars and the yugas. I had also seen Agni and other veiled symbols of the radius in the Rig Veda but the vesica piscis was harder to see. It was more deeply veiled, covered or occulted by the Rishis. Then, after the first week of October 2016, it became abundantly visible.

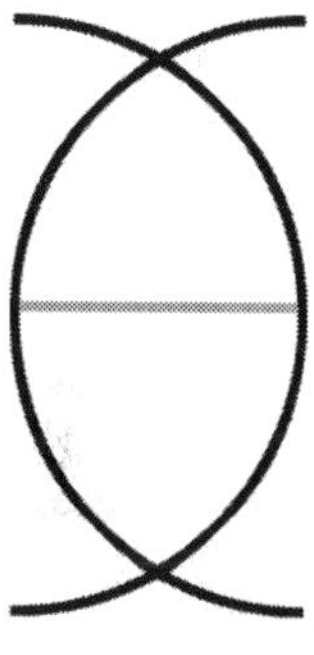

Thus, it came to pass that the week of Thea's passing I came to understand the symbolism of Jesus giving me his robe at the ocean's edge. I had, of course, heard the expression "the passing of the mantle", which I understood as the passing on of a responsibility or work, but I did not know that the word "mantle" actually refers to a robe or cloak, and I had no idea whatsoever that the robe was a Vedic symbol of the vesica piscis. That was a complete and amusing surprise. Researching the subject more, I found that the word "mantle" hails from the Sanskrit word *mand* meaning "to deck", "adorn", "clothe", "glorify" and "mark off"

among other things.[1] I found that the origin of the expression "to pass on the mantle" is attributed to a story in the Old Testament, dubbed "The Call of Elisha" (*2 Kings 2*). In this Biblical episode, Elijah transcends the world and leaves his cloak to Elisha. The amazing part of the story is that this cloak or mantle happens to have the super power of *parting waters*, which in my mind makes it a clear symbol of the vesica piscis whose arcing "rivers" or waters are held apart by the radius.

The "passing of the mantle" is such a charged issue when it comes to carrying on the work of a teacher, leaving room for many internal difficulties and clashes amongst those left behind. Beyond my inherent sense of responsibility for helping the world understand the importance of the collective teachings of Sri Aurobindo's lineage, I did not expect any mantle to be passed on to me upon Thea's departure. Nor did I expect that Jesus passing his robe to me (in the company of a male child) in my dream would amount to understanding that the "robe" of the Divine Son is the vesica piscis "worn" by the radius of the circle. Regardless, it is crystal clear to me now that, in conjunction with Thea's passing, I was given this sacred "robe" or "mantle", which turns out to be a key of Vedic gnosis. Along with this sacred "mantle" came the large responsibility of sharing its truth as a key of the Rishis' *sanatana dharma* with the world.

It is a key which has the power to clear up thousands of years of world-wide distortion of Vedic gnosis, especially distortions regarding the Divine Son, his sacrifice, his sacred city, his sacred word, his holy hymn, his holy waters, his anointment with oil, his walking on water, his victory over death, etc. It also illuminates the role the Divine Mother plays in the victory over the pervasive Ignorance that has rooted itself deeply our world.

---

[1] *Mand* is the root of *mandala* commonly translated as "circle". The ten books of the Rig Veda are called Mandalas. Considering that these 10 Mandalas together portray a victory established in 10 months of the Vedic year, it is possible that the 10 Mandalas of the Veda are a symbol of this 10-month victory. This is plausible knowing that the months of the Vedic Year are measured out by arcs of the radius or vesica piscis through the circle. Each arc of the vesica piscis is itself part of a full circle or mandala. *Mand* is also the root of *Mandir*, meaning "temple".

The Robe in the Rig Veda

The following verses demonstrate how the symbol of the robe was utilized by the Rishis to simultaneously express and veil the geometric key of the vesica piscis.

> *I call the pure Agni who clothes him[self] with the sea.*
>
> Rig Veda 8.91.4 (repeated in verses 5-6), tr. R.T.H. Griffith

> *[The streams] cleanse thee [Agni] for the Gods, gold-coloured, wearing water as thy robe....*
>
> Rig Veda 9.109.11, tr. R.T.H. Griffith

> *King [Soma Pavamana], hath clothed [himself] in the robe of rivers, mounted the straightest-going ship of Order.*
>
> Rig Veda 9.89.2, tr. R.T.H. Griffith

> *[Agni] puts on glory and beauty like a robe; he is our Horse of swiftness full of inspiration to be groomed by us, he is the immortal wide in knowledge.*
>
> Rig Veda 2.10.1, tr. Sri Aurobindo,
> *Hymns to the Mystic Fire, CWSA, Volume 16*, p. 51

> *I clothe [Agni] the bright One with my hymn as with a robe, him with the car of light, bright-hued, dispelling gloom.*
>
> Rig Veda 1.140.1, tr. R.T.H. Griffith

> *O Soma...river-like he hath swelled with surge, with the stalk's juice, exhilarating, resting not, into the vat that drops with meath. Like a dear son who must be decked, the Lovely One hath clad him in a shining robe.*
>
> Rig Veda 9.107.12-13, tr. R.T.H. Griffith

> *With his bright limbs [Agni] has built wide the mid-world purifying the will by his pure seer-powers; wearing light like a robe around the life of the waters he forms his glories vast and*

ample....[H]ere young and eternal in one native home the seven Voices held in their womb the one Child.

Rig Veda 3.5.5-6, tr. Sri Aurobindo,
Hymns to the Mystic Fire, CWSA, Volume 16, p. 157

Laid like an arrow on the bow, the hymn hath been loosed like a young calf to the udder of its dam....The golden-hued, Immortal [Agni-Soma], newly bathed, puts on a brightly shining vesture that is never harmed. He made the ridge of heaven to be his radiant robe, by sprinkling of the bowls from moisture of the sky. Even as the beams of Sūrya...together rush they forth, [these] swift outpourings in long course of holy rites: no form save only Indra shows itself so pure. As down the steep slope of a river to the vale, drawn from the Steer the swift strong draughts have found a way.

Rig Veda 9.69.1-7, tr. R.T.H. Griffith

I also found that sometimes the various female symbols of the vesica piscis are themselves depicted as wearing shining robes or raiment.

We see her there, the Child of Heaven apparent, the young Maid, flushing in her shining raiment.

Rig Veda 1.113.7, tr. R.T.H. Griffith

Here is the place of thy [Agni's] joy we have made for thee as a wife for her lord passionate, beautifully-robed; descended, widely manifest take there thy seat; lo these (thy energies), O perfect worker, move to thy encounter.

Rig Veda 4.3.2, tr. Sri Aurobindo,
Hymns to the Mystic Fire, CWSA, Volume 16, p. 654

[Dawn], like a dancer, puts her broidered garments on as a cow yields her udder so she bares her breast.[1] *Creating light for all the world of life, the Dawn hath laid the darkness open as the cows their stall. We have beheld the brightness of her shining; it spreads*

---

[1] In this sentence Dawn's garments as well as her breast and the cow's udder are symbols of the vesica piscis.

> *and drives away the darksome monster.... Bending her looks on all the world, the Goddess shines, widely spreading with her bright eye westward. Ancient of days, again [and] again born newly, decking her beauty with the self-same raiment....[T]he Lady shines with all her lover's splendour. The bright, the blessed One shines forth extending her rays like kine, as a flood rolls his waters. Never transgressing the divine commandments, she is beheld visible with the sunbeams.*
>
> Rig Veda 1.92.4-12, tr. R.T.H. Griffith

> *[Dawn] hath shone brightly like a youthful woman, stirring to motion every living creature....She hath made light and chased away the darkness. Turned to this All, far-spreading, she hath risen and shone in brightness with white robes about her.... Bearing the Gods' own Eye, auspicious Lady, leading her Courser white and fair to look on, distinguished by her beams Dawn shines apparent, come forth to all the world with wondrous treasure.*
>
> Rig Veda 7.77.1-3, tr. R.T.H. Griffith

Just as the radius and vesica piscis are eternally bound in holy matrimony, so is the masculine Purusha forever united with his feminine consort or Prakriti. Her "robes" of light or "robes" of water are his. Her body is his. She is his skin in a sense, his raiment, adornment, and his glory. They are eternally knit together, as are Matter and Spirit.

> *[L]et thy soul and mine be knit together, and as a loving husband take thy consort.*
>
> Rig Veda 10.10.3, tr. R.T.H. Griffith

As discussed in Part Two, Chapter 8, the Purusha's song or hymn is sometimes depicted as a robe. In *Hymns to the Mystic Fire*, Sri Aurobindo described the Rishis' portrayal of the veiled sacred Word (Vak) as "a beautifully robed wife" who "lays open her body" to her husband.

> *[T]he Vedic Word is described (X.71) as that which is supreme and the topmost height of speech, the best and the most faultless. It is something that is hidden in secrecy and from there comes out and is manifested. It has entered into the truth-seers, the Rishis, and it is found by following the track of their speech. But all cannot enter into its secret meaning. Those who do not know the inner sense are as men who seeing see not, hearing hear not, only to one here and there the Word desiring him like a beautifully robed wife to a husband lays open her body.... This is quite clear and precise; it results from it beyond doubt that even then while the Rig Veda was being written the Riks were regarded as having a secret sense which was not open to all. There was an occult and spiritual knowledge in the sacred hymns and by this knowledge alone, it is said, one can know the truth and rise to a higher existence.*

Sri Aurobindo, *Hymns to the Mystic Fire*, *CWSA*, *Volume 16*, p. 8

The verse Sri Aurobindo is referring to in this passage is as follows:

> *[C]ertain ones, though seeing, may not see her, and other ones, though hearing, may not hear her. But to some the Word reveals herself quite freely, like a fair-robed bride surrendering to her husband.*

Rig Veda 10.71.4, tr. Raimundo Panikkar,
The Vedic Experience, pp. 94-95

In Rig Veda 1.26.1, the Rishi petitions Agni, dubbed the "Lord of prospering powers", to put on or "assume" his robes.[1] In Rig Veda 1.162 the "God-descended" and immortal Horse-Hero (*vajin devajatasya*) is described as clothed in a robe.

> *[T]hey spread upon the Horse [a robe] to clothe him.*

Rig Veda 1.162.16, tr. R.T.H. Griffith

---

[1] Tr. R.T.H. Griffith.

The Robe in the Bible

The Vedic symbol of the robed Purusha (or Lord) pervades the Bible, though how much its authors knew of the veiled symbol and its connection to the sacred year of the Rishis is unclear.

> *The Lord reigns, he is robed in majesty; the Lord is robed in majesty and armed with strength; indeed, the world is established, firm and secure.*
>
> Psalm 93:1, NIV

> *[The heavenly warrior on the white horse] is dressed in a robe dipped in blood, and his name is the Word of God.... On his robe and on his thigh he has this name written: king of kings and lord of lords.*
>
> Revelation 19:13, 16, NIV

> *I saw the Lord, high and exalted, seated on a throne; and the train of his robe filled the temple.* [1]
>
> Isaiah 6:1, NIV

> *Who is this, robed in splendor, striding forward in the greatness of his strength? "It is I, proclaiming victory, mighty to save.... I have trodden the winepress*[2] *alone...".*
>
> Isaiah 63:1, 3, NIV

> *After this I looked, and there before me was a great multitude that no one could count, from every nation, tribe, people and language, standing before the throne and before the Lamb. They were wearing white robes and were holding palm branches in their hands.... [The elder said,] "These are they who have come out of the great tribulation; they have washed their robes and made them white in the blood of the Lamb.... For the Lamb at the center of the*

[1] Like in *Revelation*, this temple is the zodiac. The train of the robe is the arc of the vesica piscis.

[2] The winepress is equivalent to the pressing out of Soma wine in the Rig Veda, and thus to the pressing out of the vesica piscis by the radius.

> *throne will be their shepherd; he will lead them to springs of living water.*[1] *And God will wipe away every tear from their eyes."... "Blessed are those who wash their robes, that they may have the right to the tree of life and may go through the gates into the city."*
>
> Revelation 7:9, 13-14, 17; 22:14, NIV

In these verses from *Revelation* both the robes and the palm branches are symbols of the vesica piscis[2], and the tree of life and city are symbols of the twelve-month Vedic year or sacrifice. The image of washing and whitening robes in the blood of the Lamb makes little sense unless the Lamb is understood to be Agni – the cleansing and purifying Son of the Vedic year or sacrifice. In truth, the Vedic sacrifice (i.e. the Divine Son's sacrifice) has nothing to do with bloodshed. This sacrifice (*yajna*) is simply the Earth's twelve-month year which is a microcosm of "the Lord's" unified field of Time and Space. It is the field and womb via which the Purusha or eternal Soul of creation is born forward out of darkness or unconsciousness, self-disclosing or making visible his eternal law and his divine measure, thus initiating the cleansing of his field, eradicating falsehood and its toxic wastes. This cleansing or purification in the Rig Veda consistently takes place via the waters, wine, streams, bowls, filters or stones of the vesicae piscis. The white robes in *Revelation*, as well as the White Horse, are symbols of this purification.

The multitude in white (or cleansed) robes in *Revelation* indicates a multitude of vesicae piscis-clad radii in the circle, and perhaps eventually a multitude of people on Earth who will establish this victory or birth of the Universal Soul in their own field of Being and Becoming. In Rig Veda 9.86 it is clear that the timing of this purification is tied to the 9th sign of Sagittarius, the

---

[1] These springs of living waters, as already discussed, are the vesicae piscis of the zodiac (the Circle or Book of Life), and the Lamb is the Radius/Divine Purusha.

[2] In the Rig Veda, leaves and branches are symbols of the vesica piscis and thus of Immortality. Examples can be found in Rig Veda 5.43.4, 6.7.6, and 7.43.1. In this light, we can understand why the palm leaf was known in ancient times (in the ancient Near East and Mediterranean regions especially) and as a symbol of eternal life and victory over death.

sign of the Horse and the Sage, whose radius is the Son or indwelling ray of the seventh vesica piscis (cow, sister, river, etc.) of the yajna or sacrificial year. In this hymn, the purified Purusha (Agni as Soma Pavamana) is depicted as a Bull enrobed in milk.

> *Seven Milch-kine glorify the Tawny-coloured One while with his wave in wool he purifies himself. The living men, the mighty, have impelled the Sage into the waters' lap, the place of sacrifice.... He hath assumed the rays of Sūrya for his robe, spinning, as he knows how, the triply-twisted thread. He, guiding to the newest rules of Holy Law, comes as the Women's Consort to the special place.... On flows the King of rivers and the Lord of heaven: he follows with a shout the paths of Holy Law.... The Sisters Seven, the Mothers, stand around the Babe, the noble, new-born Infant, skilled in holy song, Gandharva of the floods, divine, beholding men, Soma, that he may reign as King of all the world.... The wave of flowing meath hath wakened up desires: the Steer enrobed in milk plunges into the streams.... Dweller in floods, King, foremost, he displays his might, set among living things as measurer of days. Distilling oil he flows, fair, billowy, golden-hued, borne on a car of light, sharing one home with wealth. Loosed is the heavens support, the uplifted cheering juice: the triply-mingled draught flows round into the worlds. The holy hymns caress the stalk that claims our praise, when singers have approached his beauteous robe with song. Thy streams that flow forth rapidly collected run over the fine fleece of the sheep as thou art cleansed. When, Indu, thou art balmed with milk within the bowl, thou sinkest in the jars, O Soma, when expressed.*
>
> Rig Veda 9.86.25-47, tr. R.T.H. Griffith

I hope readers can appreciate that most of the imagery in the above hymn is nonsensical without understanding the geometric relationship between the radius and the vesica piscis, and their place and function within the twelve-month year. The images of hymns caressing a stalk and of a bull enrobed in milk make no real sense without understanding that the hymns and robes are symbols of the vesica piscis and the stalk and bull are symbols of the radius. This whole hymn is one of many portrayals of the release of the seven rivers, via the Hero-Sage of Sagittarius. The Sage establishes "the newest rules of Holy Law" and "comes as the Women's Consort to the special place". The special place of this Sage – who is the radius or "consort" of the seventh wave or river of the zodiac – is either his own seat at 0° Sagittarius or his arrival at 0° Aquarius/Kumbha in the Swar realm of the zodiac. I believe it is the latter given that Aquarius is Vishnu's highest step or seat wherein the waters of truth are released and the Holy Law of the Rishis is seen anew, cleansed of all distortion, mismeasure and misdirection.

CHAPTER SIXTEEN

Vishnu's Highest Step

> *An existence, wholly self-aware and therefore entirely master of itself, possesses the phenomenal being in which it is involved, realises itself in form, unfolds itself in the individual.*
>
> *That luminous Emergence is the dawn which the Aryan forefathers worshipped. Its fulfilled perfection is that highest step of the world-pervading Vishnu which they beheld as if an eye of vision extended in the purest heavens of the Mind. For it exists already as an all-revealing and all-guiding Truth of things....*
>
> Sri Aurobindo, *The Life Divine, CWSA, Volume 21-22*, p. 339

This entire book seeded itself in my consciousness in the month of Aquarius via a vision of the 432,000-mile measure of the solar radius marking out the 432,000″ measure of the vesica piscis within the circle. This vision came with the impression that the vesica piscis would not only clear up many misconceptions regarding ancient gnosis, but would also help to shed light on the progress collectively made by Sri Aurobindo, the Mother and Thea towards the restoration of the triadic gnosis of the Vedic Rishis. More specifically, the vesica piscis gave me the impression that its sacred measure would help to uplift Thea's illuminations regarding the Rishis' 12-month *yajna*, and regarding the connection between the yugas, the zodiac and Vishnu. At the time of the vision, I did not know exactly how the vesica piscis would accomplish these things. I had no idea whatsoever that it would lead to uncovering the vesica piscis as the hidden geometric key of Matsya, Kurma and Vishnu's other avatars. I also had no idea that it was the key of releasing the hidden significance of the heavily veiled symbolism of the Rig Veda, including the symbolism of the release of the pent up sacred rivers or cows by the heroes of the Rig Veda.

As these long-buried truths dawned on me, I could better see the reality underlying the mythology of Vishnu's preservation and reestablishment of the *sanatana dharma* on Earth, which is inseparable from the restoration of the true function and measure of the Rishis' sacrificial year as Thea discussed at length in her writings. I could see that the uplifting of the geometry and zodiacal context of Vishnu's avatars along with the geometry and zodiacal context of the Rig Veda was a necessary and inevitable outcome of Vishnu's work in our current Age of Aquarius, exposing and dismantling thousands of years of Ignorance which is now to be left in the past as we move forward and deeper into our new Age. I could see clearly how Sri Aurobindo illuminated and fulfilled the duty of this avataric lineage which many naturally think is purely a myth. Sri Aurobindo initiated the descent of supramental gnosis necessary for the unlocking of this "secret" of the Veda. From 1908 he turned his consciousness and energy toward the restoration of India's and the world's spiritual gnosis; and on November 24, 1926 at the age of 54, in the month of Sagittarius, he experienced the descent of Krishna's (i.e. Vishnu's) consciousness. According to Thea's measure of the Ages, this descent corresponded with the first year of Vishnu's Age of Aquarius. Now 90-91 years into the Age of Aquarius (2016-2017), the golden thread or seed of Sri Aurobindo's supramental yoga has led to the victorious release of the sacred rivers or waters of the Veda from their kumbha or cave. Whereas it is apparently my job, as an Aquarian, to release the true sense of these rivers of Gnosis upon the world at this point in time, it was 100 percent a job given to me by Sri Aurobindo.

Via this unfolding it has become apparent that Vishnu's victory – his highest step into the sign of Aquarius, which is likened to an "eye of vision" – is fully intertwined with the realization and recovery of the vesica piscis as a key of the Rig Veda and of the Vedic victory. In truth, there is no Vedic victory without the realization and recovery of this "eye of vision".

The wise ones see [the supreme step of Vishnu] extended in heaven like a shining eye of vision; it is the highest seat of Vishnu that is the goal of the Vedic journey.

Sri Aurobindo, The Secret of the Veda, CWSA, Volume 15, pp. 346-47

This key element of the Vedic victory is also evident Rig Veda 1.154 wherein Vishnu's steps are equivalent to three vesicae piscis. In his highest step Vishnu is specifically equated with the "fount of sweetness" which is a symbol of the vesica piscis.

[Vishnu's] three steps are full of the honey-wine and they perish not but have ecstasy by the self-harmony of their nature; yea, he being One holds the triple principle and earth and heaven also, even all the worlds....

May I attain to and enjoy that goal of his movement, the Delight, where souls that seek the godhead have the rapture; for there in that highest step of the wide-moving Vishnu is that Friend of men who is the fount of the sweetness.

Rig Veda 1.154.4-5, tr. Sri Aurobindo,
The Secret of the Veda, CWSA, Volume 15, p. 344

Sri Aurobindo translated 1.154.5 in such a way that implies the hero is the fountain (*utsa*) of sweetness (*madhave*). In other translations this sacred fountain of truth, eternal youth and immortality, springs up *within* Vishnu's step. We can now see that this fountain, alternately translated as a well of honey or meath, is the spring or arc of Vishnu's step into the sign of Aquarius.

May I attain to Viṣṇu's glorious mansion where the faithful rejoice, where, close beside the Strider, within his highest footstep springs the well of purest honey!

Rig Veda 1.154.5, tr. Raimundo Panikkar, *The Vedic Experience*, p. 152

May I attain to that his well-loved mansion where men devoted to the Gods are happy. For there springs, close akin to the Wide-Strider, the well of meath in Viṣṇu's highest footstep.

Rig Veda 1.154.5, tr. R.T.H. Griffith

Similar symbolism is found in Rig Veda 10.113 wherein Vishnu is credited with creating the "stalk" that makes this "meath" flow.

> *[Indra] drank of Soma juice and waxed exceeding strong. This majesty of his Viṣṇu extols and lauds, making the stalk that gives the meath flow forth with might.*
>
> Rig Veda 10.113.1-2, tr. R.T.H. Griffith

The Emergent Supramental Purusha

We can now understand that, in the symbolic language of the Rishis, the Hero-Purusha Agni dwells within and forms the well, spring, fountain, wave or womb of the vesica piscis, and that he is equivalent to the radius of the circle or mandala of creation. He sets the Divine Law and its harmonies. He establishes the Divine Maya, manifesting and moving through Her. He is the supramental knower, architect and enjoyer of the forms and the field of Time and Space. He is the Divine Son of the Sacred Year.

The Vedic yajna is the womb of this supramental or divine Purusha or Soul, bearing it forth in the measured stages and course of Time, i.e. in the stages and course of evolution. Regardless of what else appears to be happening on planet Earth, this is the underlying hidden agenda. This agenda is not hidden by some nefarious cabal, but simply by the veils or dark womb of our own unconsciousness. Regardless of our ignorance of the process, the indwelling supramental Purusha bears itself forward though all circumstances, utilizing everything, positive and negative, for its fuel, or in Thea's terminology "the negative and the positive serve the purposes of the One".[1]

Sri Aurobindo's avataric task did not only involve restoring the truth of Vishnu's lineage and uplifting certain keys of Vedic Gnosis, it also involved bringing forward the Supramental Purusha in our world, manifesting and illuminating its presence. Given this task, it is necessary that his victories would unfold in such a way as to demonstrate the supramental control or all-

---

[1] Thea, "September Trilogy – plus One, September 15, 2001 (www.aeongroup.com).

harmonizing, all-organizing consciousness-force of the Purusha within its field of Time and Space. This book is wholly a product of this same supramental control or force, operating behind all circumstances, and behind the veils of my mental consciousness to bring forth the revelations herein. I will close this chapter with a few excerpts from Sri Aurobindo, the Mother and Thea's writings which convey the essence of the supramental consciousness and its capacity to organize its own field of creation or manifestation.

> *The Infinite, we may say, organises by the power of its self-knowledge the law of its own manifestation of being in the universe, not only the material universe present to our senses, but whatever lies behind it on whatever planes of existence. All is organised by it not under any inconscient compulsion, not according to a mental fantasy or caprice, but in its own infinite spiritual freedom according to the self-truth of its being, its infinite potentialities and its will of self-creation out of those potentialities, and the law of this self-truth is the necessity that compels created things to act and evolve each according to its own nature. The Intelligence — to give it an inadequate name — the Logos that thus organises its own manifestation is evidently something infinitely greater, more extended in knowledge, compelling in self-power, large both in the delight of its self-existence and the delight of its active being and works than the mental intelligence which is to us the highest realised degree and expression of consciousness. It is to this intelligence infinite in itself but freely organising and self-determiningly organic in its self-creation and its works that we may give for our present purpose the name of the divine supermind or gnosis.*
>
> *The fundamental nature of this supermind is that all its knowledge is originally a knowledge by identity and oneness and even when it makes numberless apparent divisions and discriminating modifications in itself, still all the knowledge that operates in its workings, even in these divisions, is founded upon and sustained and lit and guided by this perfect knowledge by identity and oneness. The Spirit is one everywhere and it knows all things as itself and in itself, so sees them always and therefore knows them intimately, completely, in their reality as well as their*

appearance, in their truth, their law, the entire spirit and sense and figure of their nature and their workings....

Sri Aurobindo, *The Synthesis of Yoga, CWSA, Volumes 23-24*, p. 786

[W]hen we look close we shall find that it is really the supermind which organises matter, life, mind and reason. And this actually is the knowledge towards which we are now moving.... [W]e shall see that [intuition] is a concealed supramental force with a self-conscient knowledge in it which informs the whole action of material energy. It is that which determines what we call law of nature, maintains the action of each thing according to its own nature and harmonises and evolves the whole.... That principle is the supramental; that is to say, the hidden secret of Nature is the organization of something out of the infinite potentialities of the self-existent truth of the spirit the nature of which is wholly evident only to an original knowledge born of and proceeding by a fundamental identity, the spirit's constant self-perception.

Sri Aurobindo, *The Synthesis of Yoga, CWSA, Volumes 23-24*, pp. 793-94

***

[E]verything, even apparently accidental things, is organized by the same Consciousness for the same ends – it's obvious.

The Mother, *The Mother's Agenda, Volume 1*, October 30, 1960, p. 459

Everything is organized down to the minutest detail, but it's not preplanned as we do with our ordinary consciousness: the Force Simply PRESSES down and produces the required result.

The Mother, *The Mother's Agenda, Volume 13*, June 24, 1972, p. 214

[The Master of the Yoga] does everything, he decides everything, he organizes everything with an almost mathematical precision and in the smallest details – everything.

The Mother, *The Mother's Agenda, Volume 1*, May 1, 1958, p. 154

I live in a constant sense of wonder! Every minute, what comes is what is necessary: circumstances, reactions...everything, everything, there's a constant vision of the wonderful way in which things are organized, the world is organized. And what he says here, the way things are organized to make you advance fast and give you the maximum, the optimum condition of progress – that's marvelous. And always it comes and presses on the very spot (Mother presses her thumb) where there was a weakness, an incomprehension ... always.

The Mother, *The Mother's Agenda, Volume 11*, June 17, 1970, pp. 236-37

[T]hat Will, that Power, is a Power of perfect harmony in which each thing is in its place, and It organizes everything wonderfully: It comes as an absolutely luminous and perfect organization, which you can see when you have the vision....

...But Sri Aurobindo certainly meant that this Power or this Force is what does everything – everything. When you see It or are one with It, at the same time you know, and you know that That is the only thing that really acts and creates; the rest is the result of the field or the world or the matter or the substance in which It acts – it's the result of resistance, but it's not the Action. And to unite with That means that you unite with the Action; to unite with what's below means that you unite with the resistance....

...But right now, it's not by looking for the why that we will be able to bring about the remedy: it's by taking the true position. That's the only thing that matters. Putting a stop to the resistance through complete surrender, complete self-giving, in all the cells if one can do it. They are beginning to have that intense joy of being only through the Lord, for the Lord, in the Lord....

When that is established everywhere, it will be fine.

The Mother, *The Mother's Agenda, Volume 7*, July 9, 1966, pp. 153-55

***

'Supermind organises the conditions for its manifestation.'... [T]he becoming of its eternal being is organised in and through the evolutionary process....The tools Supermind must use to organise its manifestation are time and space; it needs no others.

Thea, *Chronicles of the Inner Chamber*,
Update 8 – April 4th, 2005, www.matacom.com

CHAPTER SEVENTEEN

Up-Up-Up with the Fish

Thoughts leaped down from a superconscient field
Like eagles swooping from a viewless peak,
Thoughts gleamed up from the screened subliminal depths
Like golden fishes from a hidden sea.
This world is a vast unbroken totality....

Sri Aurobindo, *Savitri, CWSA, Volumes 33-34*, p. 541

"Dreaming of Riding Fish", Carla Sonheim.

In April of 2017, I had reached the point where it was finally time to write the conclusion of this book. I was not entirely sure how to wrap it up. Soon after setting an intention for the right ending, I pulled Pablo Neruda's *Memoirs* from my bookshelf, thinking of putting it in a guest room. Out of the book fell a birthday card that had been hidden in the book for perhaps sixteen years. I hadn't read the book and was impressed that the card had survived many moves and regular, thorough purges of stuff, in order to present itself to me as I was finishing up the first draft of this book in the Spring of 2017. The image on the front of the card was a drawing of a girl holding onto and riding a fish (shown above). Inside this card my sister-in-law had written, "Up, Up with the Fish! Every time I see a drawing of a fish I think about your book".

Up, Up with the Fish was the name of my first book, a memoir dealing with the loss of my father, which to date I have not attempted to publish and probably never will. I realized that I needed to write that book while reading *The Cat in the Hat* by Dr. Seuss, wherein the cat initiates a game entitled "up-up-up with a fish" creating a huge mess, terrifying a fish and two children only to later restore order in their house. *Up, Up with the Fish* is an odd title for a memoir, which I often considered changing but never did. As I wrote this present book, it never once occurred to me that the title of *Up, Up with the Fish* foreshadowed and preceded my unknown task of uplifting the vesica piscis as a key of deciphering the figures and symbols of the Rig Veda. Then out fell the card from Pablo Neruda's book, making this connection clear for me. Considering the triadic nature of the supramental descent[1] which bore this "Fish" forward, I see that I need to add the third "up" to the title. I had removed one "up" to make the title less wordy, but clearly all three "ups" are warranted.

Soon after finding the fish-themed birthday card, I pulled out the 22-year-old manuscript of my memoir, flipped through it a bit and then as I was putting it away, I was amazed to see that a vesica piscis had been imprinted onto the black vinyl back cover via two overlapping cup stains. The mark is only visible when the light shines on the black cover in a certain way. I have no idea when this unintentional and perfect vesica piscis got imprinted onto my *Up, Up with the Fish* manuscript. I had never noticed it before. I am sure I could go through all my books and none of them would have dual cup stains in the shape of a perfect vesica piscis on them. It is truly remarkable that a vesica piscis found its way onto the back cover of my memoir whose title foreshadows the uplifting of the vesica piscis as a key of ancient gnosis.

As I wrote *Up, Up with the Fish*, the Fish had a dual meaning to me. On one hand, it was the voice and perspective of fear – the perspective of the myopic mental-egoic ignorance that has no idea that underlying the big mess or apparent chaos is a hidden

---

[1] The triadic descent of supramental gnosis via the maha yoga of Sri Aurobindo, the Mother and Thea.

Divine Will that justifies or rights everything. On the other hand, the Fish was the repressed or hidden truth underlying the mess and the fear that needed to be brought upward and into the light in order to clean up the mess and restore peace.

While contemplating what this "upping" of the Fish has now come to signify, I remembered the Puranic mythology of Vishnu's first avatar Matsya. In this mythology, Vishnu disguises himself as a small fish or minnow and asks Manu to rescue him from a river. Manu first puts Matsya in a pot (kumbha) and then into progressively larger containers and bodies of water including a lake and a river. Ultimately Manu puts Matsya in the ocean wherein the Fish discloses his identity (as Vishnu) and warns Manu of an oncoming flood. Matsya then instructs Manu to build a boat to protect his family along with seven rishis, nine seeds and various animals. Manu is instructed to fasten the ship to Matsya's horn when the flood arrives so that all aboard will survive the deluge and the world can be repopulated.[1] Whereas the Fish is a symbol of the vesica piscis, its horn is a symbol of the radius, the stabilizing skambha or pillar of creation.

Matsya pulls Manu's boat, Ramanarayanadatta Astri, Volume 2 (Wikimedia Commons).

This mythology of a rescued Fish that in turn saves creation reminded me of two dreams I had soon after writing *Up, Up with the Fish.* One featured a whale in need of saving, and the other featured a whale who saved me. In the first dream, I came upon a beached whale whose iridescent skin was like a rainbow. I started thinking about how to rescue this whale and then its female guardian appeared and told me to get lost. She apparently kept the beautiful whale hidden from humans who would capture and abuse it if they knew about it. However, in the story I wrote about the dream soon after having it, the female protagonist convinced

[1] There are various versions of this tale (which seems to be the origin of the lore of Noah's Ark) in the Puranas, including the Matsya Purana, 1.11-34 and 2.1-19.

the guardian she needed help and together with some others they saved the whale by digging out a river in the sand. Via this river, the whale and its guardian disappeared back into the cover of the ocean. In the second dream, I was rescued by a whale from a lost battle I had been fighting in World War III. The creatures of the world had decided to get involved in the war and I rode inside the hero-whale towards some seemingly assured victory.

In retrospect, these memorable dreams appear to be one more way my soul was already engaged in the process of uplifting the Fish (i.e. the vesica piscis) from its hidden waters, whereupon it becomes a vessel and a weapon of eternal truth, conquering falsehood and ignorance.

Matsya pulls Manu's boat after having defeated the demon, Unknown author, c. 1870, V&A Museum (Wikimedia Commons).

Looking for the Fish in the Rig Veda

The Matsya Purana is thought to have been written approximately 2,000 years ago. Knowing that this Puranic mythology is a parable of the preservation of the Vedic sacrifice, I wondered how the fish was represented further back in time, in the Rig Veda. I found that the fish is not a common symbol in the Rig Veda, unless it goes by another name that has not yet been recognized as a fish. In Griffith's translation of the Rig Veda the fish only appears twice. In his translation of Rig Veda 10.68, the fish does appear to be a symbol of the vesica piscis, mentioned in conjunction with many other symbolic references to the vesica piscis, including the prison of the cows, the secret name, the cave, the kine, the mountain, the egg, the rock-imprisoned honey, the bowl and morning (dawn).

> *[Brihaspati] threw the prisons of the red cows open. That secret name borne by the lowing cattle within the cave Bṛhaspati discovered, and drave, himself, the bright kine from the mountain, like a bird's young after the egg's disclosure. He looked around on rock-imprisoned [honey] as one who* ***eyes a fish in scanty water****. Bṛhaspati, cleaving through with varied clamour,* ***brought it forth like a bowl from out the timber****. He found the light of heaven, and fire, and Morning: with lucid rays he forced apart the darkness.*
>
> Rig Veda 10.68.6-9, tr. R.T.H. Griffith [bold emphasis added]

The only other verse in which a fish (*matsya*) is mentioned, as far as I can tell, is Rig Veda 7.18.6.

> *Eager for spoil was Turvaśa Purodas,*[1] *glad to win wealth, like fishes urged by hunger....*
>
> Tr. R.T.H. Griffith

Surprised that I could not find more references to fish in the Rig Veda, I dug deeper and found that the Sanskrit word for fish, *matsya,* is closely related to the Sanskrit word *matsara* which does occur frequently in the Rig Veda. *Matsara* is equivalent to the bliss inducing soma-wine which is in turn equivalent to the nectar of immortality (*amrita*), and to honey (*madhu*) which are

---

[1] Turvaśa in Rig Veda 7.18.6 is thought to be one of ten kings, associated with ten tribes. Given that the twelve-month yajna is the singular field of the symbols and lore in the Rig Veda, these kings appear to be ten radii of the sacrificial year, the first extending to 0° Aries and the 10th extending to 0° Capricorn. The kings in Rig Veda 7.18 oppose Indra, perhaps for the same reason the vesica piscis is sometimes depicted in the Veda as a cave, pen, covering veil, beast or foe. In vs. 13 and 24, Indra demolishes the seven castles of these foes and dispenses the Seven Rivers.

all symbols of the vesica piscis. Both *matsya*, *matsara* and *madhu* all emerge from the root *mad*, meaning to gladden, inspire, exhilarate, intoxicate, animate and to enjoy heavenly bliss.[1] *Matsara* thus can be translated as "river (*sara*) of bliss". *Matsya* is also translated as "the gay one". The idea of a gay, happy or blissful fish makes no real sense without knowing the connection between the bliss-inducing soma (*matsara*), honey (*madhu*) and the fish (*matsya*). The connection is that they are all symbols of the vesica piscis. They are symbols of the bliss, river or rapture of the hero (radius). In Rig Veda 1.140.1 Agni's abode is said to be bliss. Given what we now know about Agni's seat, womb and home, we can take this as an indication that the vesica piscis is the hero's bliss just as it is his robe or mantle.

> *Offer like a secure seat that womb to Agni the utterly bright who sits upon the altar and his abode is bliss; clothe with thought as with a robe the slayer of the darkness who is pure and charioted in light and pure-bright of hue.*
>
> *He...bends down and goes to [the tawny ones] bellowing as the male to its mates, — putting out his force he gives joy to their bodies (or he makes blissful the forms of things)....*
>
> Rig Veda 1.140.1, 6, tr. Sri Aurobindo,
> *Hymns to the Mystic Fire, CWSA, Volume 16*, pp. 152-53

Agni is known in the Rig Veda as a bliss-giver or bliss winner. The symbolism of finding and winning the cows, the rivers and the bliss all boils down to the victorious recovery of the vesica piscis as a key of the triple Veda.

> *[M]ay that Agni lead us on in his knowledge to that bliss of his which is enjoyed by the gods, which all the Immortals made by Thought and father Dyaus begot it increasing Truth.*

---

[1] Somehow *matsara,* from the Sanskrit root (*mad*) connoting bliss or exhilaration, eventually devolved to mean "selfishness", "envy", "jealousy", "hostility", "wrath" and "anger" (*Cologne Digital Sanskrit Lexicon*), or in other words "madness".

> *He was born the first in the waters in the foundation of the kingdom of the vastness, in the womb of the Truth (asya); without head or feet, concealing his ends, setting himself to his works in the lair of the Bull of Heaven (vṙishabhasya).*
>
> Rig Veda 4.1.10-11, tr. Sri Aurobindo, *Hymns to the Mystic Fire, CWSA, Volume 16*, pp. 638-39

> *The Son of Energy, the Fire, happy and radiant and most glorious in his light; may he win for us by sacrifice the bliss in heaven of Mitra and Varuna and the bliss of the waters.*
>
> Rig Veda 8.19.4, tr. Sri Aurobindo, *Hymns to the Mystic Fire, CWSA, Volume 16*, p. 331

> *[Agni] is enjoyable like a hill and bliss-giving like fast-running water. He is like a charger in the battle rushing to the gallop and like a flowing river, who shall hedge in his course?*
>
> Rig Veda 1.65.3, tr. Sri Aurobindo, *Hymns to the Mystic Fire, CWSA, Volume 16*, p. 93

The winning of this truth-borne bliss is the goal of the twelve-stage Vedic sacrifice.

> *Ananda is the goal of our journey; the manifestation in our lower members of the divine bliss reposing on the divine force & being is the law of our perfection.*
>
> Sri Aurobindo, *Hymns to the Mystic Fire, CWSA, Volume 16*, p. 711

> *[I]n the coming of the supramental Light, the Dawn and the Sun and the shining Mother of the herds...so comes to us the possession of the Truth, by the Truth the admirable surge of the Bliss, in the Bliss infinite Consciousness of absolute being.*
>
> Sri Aurobindo, *Hymns to the Mystic Fire, CWSA, Volume 16*, pp. 28-29

> *The first result [of Brihaspati's victory via the divine word] is the breaking open by force of the well which has the rock for its face and whose streams are of the honey,* madhu, *the Soma sweetness,* aśmāsyam avataṁ madhudhāram. ***This well of honey covered by***

> ***the rock must be the Ananda or divine beatitude of the supreme threefold world of bliss****, the Satya, Tapas and Jana worlds of the Puranic system based upon the three supreme principles, Sat, Chit-Tapas and Ananda; their base is Swar of the Veda, Mahar of the Upanishads and Puranas, the world of Truth.*
>
> Sri Aurobindo, *The Secret of the Veda, CWSA, Volume 15*, p. 178 [bold emphasis added]

Thea knew this triple world of Swar to be the final quadrant of the Vedic year, wherein the last sign of Pisces is equivalent to *Ananda* – the divine Bliss, rapture or pure love that accompanies the Truth (*Sat*) of one's divine Consciousness (*Chit*).[1] The name for Pisces in Sanskrit is either Matsya or Mina. All three of these names of the last sign of the zodiac mean Fish. So, in a sense "Up-Up-Up with the Fish" could be a symbolic name for the entire Vedic journey (or year) whose tail end is the sign of Pisces. In the sacrificial or developmental journey of the zodiac, the Ananda or Bliss of Pisces is attained only via the reestablishment of Truth-Consciousness (Sat-Chit) in the signs of Capricorn[2] and Aquarius. In Rig Veda 3.31 this Bliss is described as "the other shore" of the purifying waters which may be understood as Pisces, the "other shore" of the sign of Aquarius.

> *The Ancient-born I make new that I may conquer. Do thou remove our many undivine hurters and set Swar for our possessing. The purifying rains are extended before us (in the shape of the waters); take us over to* **the state of bliss that is the other shore of them***. Warring in thy chariot protect us from the foe; soon, soon make us conquerors of the Cows. The Vritra-slayer, the Master of the Cows, showed (to men) the cows; he has entered with his shining laws (or lustres) within those who are black (void of light, like the*

[1] Thea, *The Gnostic Circle*, p. 47; *The Magical Carousel, Commentaries*, p. 144.

[2] One of the symbols of Capricorn is a mountain goat with the tail of a fish. The goat is symbolic of the radius/Purusha (Agni) and the mountain he climbs or lives on is the vesica piscis, hence his association with the fish.

Panis); showing the truths (the cows of truth) by the Truth he has opened all his own doors....

Rig Veda 3.31.20- 21, tr. Sri Aurobindo, *The Secret of the Veda, CWSA, Volume 15*, p. 217 [bold emphasis added]

In Thea's luminous book *The Magical Carousel*, two children journey through the twelve signs of the zodiac encountering various characters and challenges along the way. The fish card that fell out of Pablo Neruda's *Memoirs* reminded me that the final Pisces chapter of Thea's fairytale features an illustration of two children riding fish. Upon reaching this ending and new beginning in their journey, the children must break through the veil or bubble that keeps them separate or estranged from the totality of their circumstances. They are told:

Illustration by Brigitta Lange from The Magical Carousel, p. 122.

It is the present that contains everything, all that is past and all that will be.... Now, help me to take away the veils that separate you from the rest.

Thea, *The Magical Carousel*, pp. 126-27

I did a bit of etymological digging and found that the Sanskrit root of Pisces is likely *peś* related *to piś,* pronounced "pesh" and "pish", similar to fish. *Peśa,* sometimes spelled out *peśaḥ* or *pezas,* in the Rig Veda typically refers to a form, shape or an ornament or an embroidered garment. Regarding the root *piś*, Sri Aurobindo wrote:

[Piś means] to form, shape, organise, be reduced to the constituent parts, — all these senses betraying the original idea of separation, division, cutting apart....

Sri Aurobindo, *The Secret of the Veda, CWSA, Volume 15*, p. 73

This cutting apart or division can be understood in terms of the way the radius and vesica piscis carve out divisions within the whole. These divisions or "constituent parts" are never actually separate or divided from the whole. *Pezas* appears to be the root of the English word "pieces", and is likely the root of the Spanish word for fish "pez" (the plural of which is "peces"), as well as "piscina" meaning "fish pond" or "pool". Whereas there may not be a recognized connection between the Sanskrit word *peśas* and *pisces* the fish, I believe this connection exists considering that the primary form, shape or "garment" (*peśas*) the Rishis presented throughout the Rig Veda in myriad ways is the vesica piscis. We have seen that the robe, form or *peśas* the Vedic hero puts on as his robe *is* the vesica piscis.

> *Putting on robes, putting on forms, Fire in the navel-centre of the earth is born a ruddy flame, in the seat of Revelation.*
>
> Rig Veda 10.1.6, tr. Sri Aurobindo,
> *Hymns to the Mystic Fire, CWSA, Volume 16*, p. 389

The hero of the Rig Veda, by whatever name, is sometimes described as wearing all shapes or forms.[1] In terms of simple geometry and the geometry of the Vedic yajna, these are the forms drawn out by the radius and in terms of our existence, these are the individual material forms created, enjoyed and inhabited by the Divine. The Rishis fully understood that the basic, eternal and sacred geometry underlying material creation is the key of experiencing the Soul as the supramental architect and knower of its own unified field of Time and Space. The importance of these geometric keys or forms of the yajna is well spelled out in the Sri Aurobindo's commentary on Rig Veda 7.42.

> *[The opening verse of Rig Veda 7.42] is a prayer for the necessary conditions of the journey, the things that are said here to constitute the form of the pilgrim sacrifice,* adhvarasya peśaḥ, *and among these comes first the forward movement of the Angirases;*

---

[1] Rig Veda 1.13.10, 3. 53.8, 3.56.3, 3.062.6, 7.55.1, 8.22.12, tr. R.T.H. Griffith.

> *"Forward let the Angirases travel, priests of the Word, forward go the cry of heaven (or, of the heavenly thing, cloud or lightning), forward move the fostering Cows that diffuse their waters, and let the two pressing-stones be yoked (to their work)—the form of the pilgrim sacrifice"....*
>
> Sri Aurobindo, *The Secret of the Veda, CWSA, Volume 15*, p. 189

All of the symbolic figures in this verse are describing the occulted pairing and form (*peśaḥ*) of the radii and vesicae piscis in the Rishis' sacrificial year (*adhvarasya*). At this point it seems clear enough that the Sanskrit word *peśaḥ (or pezas*) is the Vedic origin of Pisces the Fish, and that it does, in truth, refer to the form of the vesica piscis in the Rig Veda.

The fact that the sign of Pisces or Matsya/Mina the Fish is the *last* sign of the Rishis' sacred year or journey is a case of the key of the vesica piscis being hidden in plain sight, lying in wait across multiple ages to be recovered in the course of Time from the symbolic waters in which it was hidden. This form or "vessel of the fish" is the Divine Maya, divine form or vessel of the indwelling Soul (the Hidden One, Sun or Son). Its eternal form (together with the radius) is the basis of the Rishis' *sanatana dharma*, measuring out the twelve-month yajna from the Earth's four cardinal points.[1] Its victorious recovery, along with the recovery of the divine Sun or Son hidden in the waters is the central theme of the entire Rig Veda. And although this victory

---

[1] To reemphasize Thea's seeing of this matter, the 12-month Vedic Year (i.e. the zodiac) is not measured out from four *imaginary* (or man-determined) cardinal points in the uneven and *imaginary* (man-configured) constellations scattered along our ecliptic plane. The zodiac is the Earth's sacred Mandala of Life, as clearly marked out and determined by the four cardinal points of the Earth's Solar (Tropical) Year. The four cardinal points of this Mandala of Life are determined by the Earth's axis and her relationship with the Sun. It must be now understood that the Vedic Year or Sacred Year of the Rishis is not at all subtle, subjective or hard to collectively and correctly measure. It is lived and experienced by Earth and by all her creations. Its seasons and impacts on Life and on Earth are obvious. The man-configured and uneven constellations have nothing to do with this sacred, living Matrix, Divine Mother or Mandala of Life, other than as a natural and useful backdrop for tracking the Precession of the Earth's Equinoxes.

has been accomplished via the collective yoga of Sri Aurobindo and his collaborators, now remains the world-yoga of utilizing this key to not only deconstruct our distorted ideas about the Divine Play and about spirituality that have naturally sprung from the heavily veiled truth of the Vedic Sacrifice, but also to increase our own direct experience of the Divine Soul manifesting in our lives and in our world.

As is, our civilization is very much stuck between a rock and a hard place in the evolutionary play. The rock, in this case, is our profound ignorance or unconsciousness of the Soul's unified field. The hard place is in turn a debilitating misunderstanding and misinterpretation of the ancient texts and symbols which hold the keys to becoming a conscious Soul or an awakened One (*Buddha*) within the field of the Soul's expression, awake within the divine Oneness, aware of its exquisite and all-integrating harmonies. These well-established blind spots are naturally codependent upon each other and they are simultaneously dismantled by the restoration of the same eternal truth (*sanatana dharma*) and thus by the same golden reed (the radius or ray of God) which firmly and eternally establishes or lays down "the law of our perfection".

> *[Agni] is the son and becomes the father of the Gods....*
>
> *This is the Fire that has perfect knowledge and is a creator whom none can rend asunder....*
>
> *He is as if our rapturous son born to us in the house and he is like a courser pleased and glad that carries to safety the peoples....*
>
> *Very bright and lustrous is [Agni] like the paramour of Dawn. Let his form be known and his knowledge awake for this human being, let all bear him in themselves, swing wide the gates and walk in the vision of the world of the Sun.*

Rig Veda 1.69.5, tr. Sri Aurobindo,
The Secret of the Veda, CWSA, Volume 15, p. 582

CHAPTER EIGHTEEN

Moving Forward

I will forever remain stunned by the way the key of the vesica piscis was brought forth in my consciousness. It was organized and accomplished despite my ignorance of what was being accomplished. In my mind it is now entirely self-evident that the eternal form of the vesica piscis is a crucial key of deciphering, reestablishing and utilizing the *trayi vidya* and *sanatana dharma* of the Rishis in our modern world. It is thus a crucial key of India's rise as Vishwa Guru in the world. In addition to clearing up long-held misunderstandings regarding Vishnu's avatars, the yuga measure, the twelve-month yajna and the triadic eternal law and gnosis of the Rishis, discovering the hidden key of the vesica piscis in the Rig Veda exposes the fact that most of the world's ideas and stories about God and the divine Hero-Son have been entirely and disastrously separated from their original context, sense and gnosis. In this state of separation, no true light emerges, only the shadowy figures of our imagination, superstition and dogma. Via the realization that the vesica piscis is a measure and form of the zodiac which lies at the heart of the Rig Veda and at the heart of St. John's *Revelation*, it will be increasingly difficult for spiritual seekers to continue to denigrate and ignore the Divine Maya (the Divine Feminine) and to continue pursuing the goal of transcending God's Matrix. It will also be increasingly difficult for spiritual seekers or modern-day yogis to remain ignorant of the Vedic yajna or sacred year of the Rishis, which is the true origin and essence of yoga.

The bulk of our modern-day accumulated assumptions and conclusions about the world's sacred texts, religions, mythologies and symbols need to be deconstructed and upgraded in light of this realization. I look forward to all that this Vedic river of truth will continue to clarify, purify, dismantle, illuminate, integrate and yoke together in our world. Its emergence marks an end of thousands of years of widespread ignorance and disregard of the Vedic lore and symbols that underlie our world's languages, myths and religions. It simultaneously marks the beginning of the time when we have this key to help us to see through all variation and distortion of Vedic truth to the Oneness and singular context from which most of the world's languages, myths and religions have emerged and diverged.

This final chapter named itself "Moving Forward". The title came before the content and reflects the pressing global necessity for humans to move beyond our limited conceptions of our world play and into the greater sense and higher reality of the Oneness which we now only know from the unreliable viewpoint of our disastrously fragmented and myopic consciousness. As I wrote this book, I realized many things did not mean at all what I thought they meant. I began to see through symbols, words, myths and teachings that I had only partially understood at best. Not only that, even though what I was seeing was entirely the result or fruit born of the collective yoga and revelations of Sri Aurobindo, the Mother and Thea, it also opened a doorway or portal into new territory or terrain of the Vedic yajna or hero's journey where they had not yet traveled. I discovered and therein became responsible for revealing or releasing the Vedic rivers, keys and treasures that they had not seen or known. And given the way this door or portal opened and released its floods of descending Vedic, Integral and Supramental Gnosis, no part of me whatsoever is interested in perpetuating or clinging to my previous misconceptions, or anyone else's for that matter.

Sri Aurobindo wrote that the steps of the Supermind are from "truth to greater truth, from right perception to deeper perception, from intuition to intuition, from illumination to utter and boundless luminousness, from growing widenesses to the utter vasts and to very infinitude".[1] It is clear that in order to continuously move forward into greater truth, it is necessary to continually

[1] Sri Aurobindo, *Essays in Philosophy and Yoga, CWSA, Volume 13*, p. 559.

sacrifice or let go of limited or wrong ideas and set positions, otherwise the forward momentum is arrested at a particular stage of development and at a partial perspective or grasp of reality. Yoga is by its nature a *progressive* evolutionary adventure, an "Adventure of Consciousness"[1] wherein partial knowledge of the Self progressively leads to more complete knowledge of the Self. In its highest sense, yoga is not a path of transcendence, it is a path of manifesting our inherent divinity. Sri Aurobindo expressed this higher manifestation in the following terms.

> *The Divine is already there immanent within us, [we] ourselves are that in our inmost reality and it is this reality that we have to manifest; it is that which constitutes the urge towards the divine living and makes necessary the creation of the life divine even in this material existence.*
>
> *A manifestation of the Supermind and its truth-consciousness is then inevitable; it must happen in this world sooner or later....*
>
> *The divine life will give to those who enter into it and possess it an increasing and finally a complete possession of the truth-consciousness and all that it carries in it; it will bring with it the realisation of the Divine in self and the Divine in Nature. All that is sought by the God-seeker will be fulfilled in his spirit and in his life as he moves towards spiritual perfection. He will become aware of the transcendent reality, possess in the self-experience the supreme existence, consciousness, bliss, be one with Sachchidananda. He will become one with cosmic being and universal Nature: he will contain the world in himself, in his own cosmic consciousness and feel himself one with all beings; he will see himself in all and all in himself, become united and identified with the Self which has become all existences. He will perceive the beauty of the All-Beautiful and the miracle of the All-Wonderful; he will enter in the end into the bliss of the Brahman and live abidingly in it and for all this he will not need to shun existence or plunge into the annihilation of the spiritual Person in some self-extinguishing Nirvana. As in the Self, so in Nature, he can realise the Divine. The nature of the Divine is Light and Power and Bliss; he can feel*

[1] *The Adventure of Consciousness* by Satprem is one of the first books I read about Sri Aurobindo's yoga and his teachings on the evolution of consciousness.

> *the divine Light and Power and Bliss above him and descending into him, filling every strand of his nature, every cell and atom of his being, flooding his soul and mind and life and body, surrounding him like an illimitable sea and filling the world, suffusing all his feeling and sense and experience, making all his life truly and utterly divine. This and all else that the spiritual consciousness can bring to him the divine life will give him when it reaches its utmost completeness and perfection and the supramental truth-consciousness is fulfilled in all himself; but even before that he can attain to something of it all, grow in it, live in it, once the Supermind has descended upon him and has the direction of his existence.*
>
> Sri Aurobindo, *Essays in Philosophy and Yoga, CWSA, Volume 13*, pp. 560-64

I believe the title "Moving Forward" inserted itself here at the end of this book because, whereas much of humanity remains stuck in a myopic consciousness that refuses to reconsider or move beyond inherited belief systems and misperceptions which continue to generate and perpetuate great fragmentation, disharmony, toxicity and suffering in our world, the supramental consciousness simply and unwaveringly *moves forward.* The supramental consciousness is the all-consuming and dynamic Oneness of our higher Self which is *entirely unstuck and unencumbered* by the severe limitations of our mental-egoic consciousness and unencumbered by the limitations of our physical and vital layers of being as well. It *moves forward* towards its full manifestation in Time and Space, regardless of our ignorance of its unfolding design, regardless of our static, puny, distorted and often ridiculous ideas about the Divine. The potential lies before individuals and before humanity to cultivate a *direct experience* of the Divine Self, but as with any real adventure or journey, in order to progress one must be capable of recognizing and advancing into new territory when it presents itself. Thea's books *The Magical Caroselle* and *The Gnostic Circle* help to illuminate the pathway or yajna by which the Rishis cultivated and transmitted this direct experience of the Divine. From what I have learned along this sacred journey, approaching the higher or supramental consciousness is wholly a process of defragmentation, returning from one's state of dispersion and disharmony to the all-unifying and all-harmonizing truth of the Soul. This naturally remains an impossibility for those who are, for whatever reasons, unable to move forward beyond their fragmented perspective or belief system.

During my first trip to India I began to understand that Sat-Chit-Ananda (Truth-Consciousness-Bliss) was the Soul's *real* reality, and that so long as I was experiencing a painful reality or suffering, I was seeing things through a fragmented and distorted perspective rather than seeing the bigger picture. From that time on I have always been relieved to remember and to sometimes clearly see that beyond the distortions of my egoic mind, all is a vast perfection. Even if we are temporarily unable to see beyond our own distortions and attachments to our own ignorance, simply admitting that they exist and pollute our environment is a powerful step towards dissolving them and moving beyond them. For me progress has mostly been a matter of choosing to NOT be aligned with, attached to or disheartened by my ignorance or anyone else's for that matter, so that I could be free to move forward towards higher vistas as they presented themselves. In retrospect, it wasn't so much a choice as simply a persistent necessity to come into greater alignment with my Soul, bringing its Truth forward from its many veils of Ignorance.

With Thea's passing and with the descent of the key of the vesica piscis, I do feel like my Soul's intention and design has come forward in a tangible way. I see how everything in my life was arranged so that I would find this key of gnosis. In a way, it was like giving birth to something I didn't even know I had been gestating for 47 years. This unexpected birth reminds me of a dream I had in July of 2011 in which a doctor told me after an examination that I had not really been sick with Lyme Disease, I was just unknowingly pregnant with quadruplets. This shocking surprise presented a drastic change my life's course.

This dream, together with the subsequent surprise birth of crucial keys of Vedic Gnosis, reminds me of the Mother's 1964 comments about *EVERYTHING* leading towards progress and towards a surprise shift or birth which she likened to a chick popping out of an egg.

> *[All conceptions and oppositions] disappeared instantly in a perception of THE WHOLE, in which EVERYTHING — everything — was the result of the same Pressure (downward gesture) towards progress....*
>
> *...[In the march forward] EVERYTHING goes together...it is only the vision of the details that blots out the vision of the whole.*
>
> *Voilà.*
>
> *It will be like the chick popping out of the egg all at once; as long as it's inside, to the superficial vision there's no chick; and all at once, pop! Out it comes.*
>
> *Let's hope so!*
>
> The Mother, *The Mother's Agenda, Volume 5*, October 10, 1964, pp. 229-30

My own version of this surprise birth has put my past, present and future in an entirely new light and has opened up vast new terrain to be traveled into and explored. It is the end of the long journey of finding this key or weapon of gnosis and the beginning of sharing it with the world. It makes me optimistic because I imagine many other people are unknowingly gestating world-uplifting gifts (gifts of their Soul) that they will one day, surprisingly, give birth to and share with the world.

Just as I know that the vesica piscis is an important key of gnosis and its discovery is an important victory, I also know that it will naturally lead to higher keys, higher understandings and higher vistas that remain to be discovered and lived into. I know in the grand scheme of things I know very little and am delighted to be on a real adventure of consciousness wherein one key or stage of discovery and growth naturally leads to or evolves into the next. Given the extraordinary manner of how things have unfolded thus far, I absolutely trust the upward trajectory of the evolution of consciousness and trust whatever must be let go of or integrated in order to move forward into new territory.

As I was writing this chapter I searched *The Mother's Agenda* for her thoughts on the imperative to move forward past old conceptions and found the following passage.

> *The best one can do is not to have any prejudices or preconceived ideas or principles – oh, moral principles, fixed codes of conduct, "what must be done" and "what must not be done," and preconceived ideas with regard to morals, with regard to progress, and then all the social and mental conventions – there's no obstacle worse than that. I know people who wasted dozens of years trying to overcome one of those mental constructions!*
>
> *If one can be like this, open – truly open in a simplicity ... you know, the simplicity of ignorance that knows it's ignorant ... like this (gesture, hands open), ready to receive all that comes ... then, perhaps, something will happen.*
>
> *Naturally, the thirst for progress, the thirst to know, the thirst to transform yourself, and above all the thirst for Love and Truth – if you can keep that, then you go faster. Really a thirst, a need, you know, a need.... All the rest doesn't matter, what you need is THAT.*
>
> *To cling to what you think you know, to cling to what you feel, to cling to what you like, to cling to your habits, to cling to your so-called needs, to cling to the world as it is, that's what binds you hand and foot. You must undo all that, one thing after the other. Undo all the bonds.*
>
> *This has been said thousands of times, but people go on doing the same thing.... Even those who are, you know, very eloquent, who preach this to others, they CLING – they cling to their own way of seeing, their own way of feeling, their own habit of progress, which to them is the only possible one.*
>
> *No more bonds – free, free, free, free! Always ready to change everything, except ONE thing: to aspire. That thirst.*

The Mother, *The Mother's Agenda, Volume 5*, October 7, 1964, pp. 225-26

In a subsequent entry, the Mother discussed the principle of Inertia and how evolutionary shifts occur as catastrophes for that which came before it. Thus, to the unillumined mind stuck in the

Inertia of the Mental consciousness, the advent or descent of the Supramental consciousness occurs as a catastrophe.

> *[A]nything that disturbs the Inertia is, for Inertia, a catastrophe. In the world, the earthly world (it's the only one I can speak of with competence; of the others, I have only overall visions), in the earthly world, for Inertia (which is the basis of the creation and is necessary to fix, to concretize things), anything that disturbs it is a catastrophe. That is to say, the advent of Life was a monstrous catastrophe, and the advent of intelligence in Life another monstrous catastrophe, and now the advent of Supermind is the final catastrophe! That's how it is. And for the unenlightened mind, it really is a catastrophe!*
>
> The Mother, *The Mother's Agenda, Volume 5*, November 28, 1964, pp. 295-96

This passage puts the current state of our world in proper perspective; and it brings into view the inherent choice we have ahead of us – the choice to remain aligned with the toxic and disastrous perspective of our mental-egoic consciousness or to align with the Higher Truth of the Soul currently being born in our world. The Mother described this as a "choice between serving the truth or being destroyed".

> *Before dying, falsehood rises in full swing. Still people understand only the lesson of Catastrophe. Will it have to come before they open their eyes to the truth? I ask an effort from all so that it has not to be. It is only the truth that can save us; truth in words, truth in action, truth in will, truth in feelings. It is a choice between serving the truth or being destroyed.*
>
> The Mother, *The Mother's Agenda, Volume 13*, November 26, 1972, p. 316

I look forward to all the ways our higher truth will continue to establish itself in our world and set us free from the ongoing catastrophes of our fragmented view of Self and World. It is clear enough that the initial descent of the supramental consciousness and certain keys of supramental gnosis have come through Sri

Aurobindo's lineage, but it is also clear through their collective writings, that the supramental consciousness-force will continue to accomplish its self-fulfillment though EVERYTHING and EVERYONE in the natural course of evolution, whether we are conscious of its all-pervasive divine force or not.

> *There can be…an evolution in the light and no longer in the darkness, in which the evolving being is a conscious participant and cooperator, and this is precisely what must take place here. Even in the effort and progress from the Ignorance to Knowledge this must be in part if not wholly the endeavour to be made on the heights of the nature, and it must be wholly that in the final movement towards the spiritual change, realisation, transformation. It must be still more so when there is a transition across the dividing line between the Ignorance and the Knowledge and the evolution is from knowledge to greater knowledge, from consciousness to greater consciousness, from being to greater being. There is then no longer any necessity for the slow pace of the ordinary evolution; there can be rapid conversion, quick transformation after transformation, what would seem to our normal present mind a succession of miracles. An evolution on the supramental levels could well be of that nature; it could be equally, if the being so chose, a more leisurely passage of one supramental state or condition of things to something beyond but still supramental, from level to divine level, a building up of divine gradations, a free growth to the supreme Supermind or beyond it to yet undreamed levels of being, consciousness and Ananda.*
>
> Sri Aurobindo, *Essays in Philosophy and Yoga, CWSA, Volume 13*, pp. 561-62

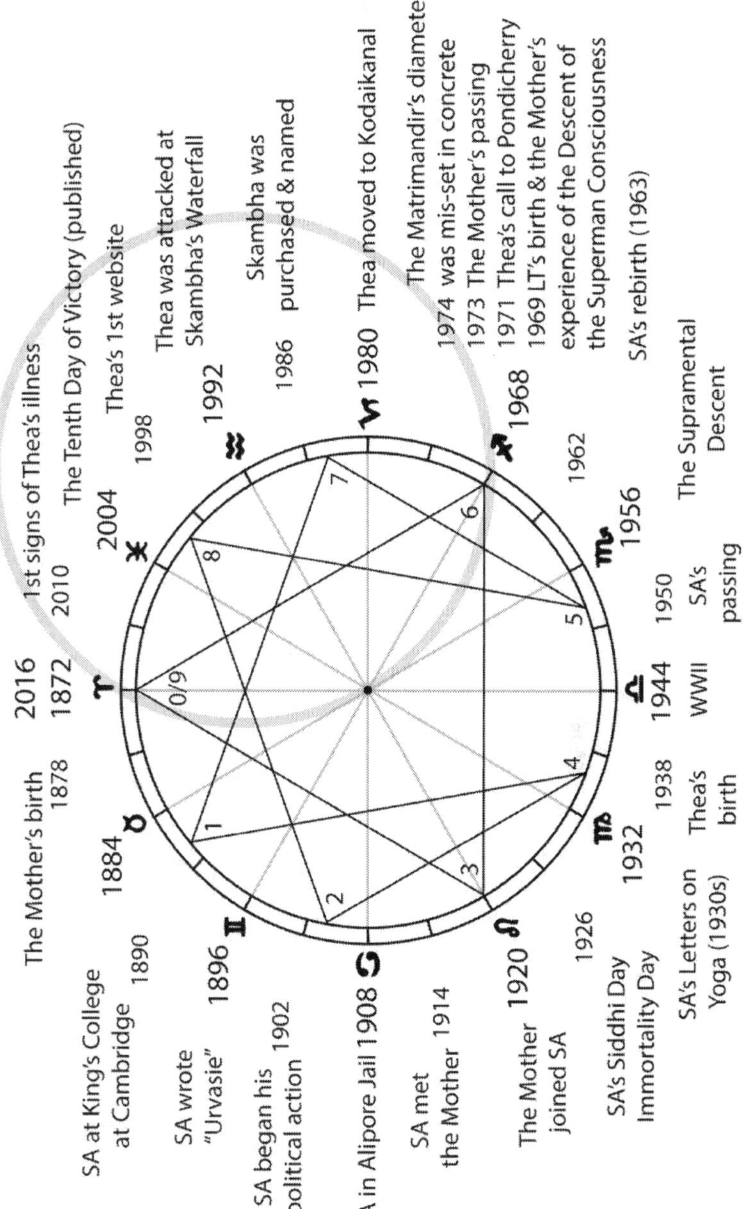
Appendix: 144-Year Span from Sri Aurobindo's Birth (1872) to Thea's Passing (2016)
2016
1872
The Mother's birth
1878
1884
SA at King's College
at Cambridge
1890
1896
SA wrote
"Urvasie"
SA began his
political action
1902
SA in Alipore Jail 1908
SA met
the Mother
1914
The Mother
joined SA
1920
1926
SA's Siddhi Day
Immortality Day
SA's Letters on
Yoga (1930s)
1932
Thea's
birth
1938
1944
WWII
1950
SA's
passing
1956
The Supramental
Descent
1962
1968
SA's rebirth (1963)
1969 LT's birth & the Mother's
experience of the Descent of
the Superman Consciousness
1971 Thea's call to Pondicherry
1973 The Mother's passing
1974 was mis-set in concrete
The Matrimandir's diameter
1980
Thea moved to Kodaikanal
1986
Skambha was
purchased & named
1992
Thea was attacked at
Skambha's Waterfall
1998
Thea's 1st website
The Tenth Day of Victory (published)
2004
2010
1st signs of Thea's illness
0/9
1
2
3
4
5
6
7
8

INDEX

Made in the USA
San Bernardino, CA
16 January 2018